An Augustine sy

An Augustine Synthesis

Arranged Erich Przywara

Sheed and Ward
London

INTRODUCTION

Young Catholic philosophers are often told that they must be Aquinas-minded. St Paul said: 'Let this mind be in you which was also in Christ Jesus' (Phil. ii, 5). Modern States try very hard to make you Government-minded, though the Government will always tell you that what you are becoming is just National-minded: Race-minded. The thing is, that you are wanted to have the same way of thinking, of looking at things, of valuing, as somebody else has, or had. It is hoped that readers of this book may become Augustine-minded.

If we say that Augustine was the greatest man of his time, you may possibly answer: 'Well, but *I* am *not* of his time, so I need not trouble about him'. And if I reply: 'Yes; but he was so great that he practically controlled the western mind for seven centuries or so', I may be answered: 'Oh, *then*, I who am no intellectualist cannot possibly catch up with him, and I may as well give up before starting!'

To this we answer at once: 'This book is not written for intellectualists. The name of Fr Przywara—quite apart from its somewhat alarming spelling—has become synonymous with deep thought and difficult diction—we remember that his German was once said to be so difficult that not even Germans could understand it! Anyway the translation of St Augustine's Latin, which you will read here, is lucid, and you are not going to be asked to read the author's German. He has but collected certain passages from the Saint, *and arranged them in an order*. The very titles of his sections and their chapters are thrilling: "Head and Body—Unity; Multiplicity; Flesh and Blood; Virgin and Mother; Heaven and Earth; Catholic". "Man to God—Man-Untruth to God-Truth; Man-Beggar to God-Goodness; Man straightway to God". "Man in God—Man-Abyss; Night of the Heart; Night in Love; Night of Life; Night between Nights; Old and a Child"—to me, these titles are absolutely challenging: it is difficult to rest till one shall have seen what this is all about.'

INTRODUCTION

Certainly we do not suggest that the book contains only what is as simple as a spelling-book. But there are reasons why whatsoever St Augustine says must be fairly soon intelligible.

The first is, that he was so personally experienced in all that is in man. The 'humanity' of the *Confessions* is such that because that book has been more widely read, out of all religious literature, than anything save the Psalms, the Gospels, and perhaps the *Imitation*, readers have tended to forget that Augustine ever wrote anything else. (Yet write so much he did, that we would deduce even did we not know that he constantly used shorthand secretaries.) That volcanic unmitigated humanity that first drove him into revolt and sin, and, second, kept him loving his mother beyond anything on earth, was never extinguished in him, and one can feel it pulsing and glowing within even his most philosophic utterances. He infused philosophy with passion; and learned to put wise order into his emotions even when he lost none of them. His sermons range from the sublimest mysticism to the proper heating of churches. Whatever Augustine says, sooner or later you will realise it is your fellow-man who is saying it.

The second is, that he had handed himself wholly over to what man's life really aches for—the supernatural love of God. Certain great conflicts are endemic in God-created, God-summoned humanity. One is, the State *versus* Conscience. Another is, Self-Sufficiency *versus* a total self-subordination to God. The exaltation of the human will to the injury of Divine Omnipotence and Paramountcy. The Paramountcy of God!

Now a whole element in modern humanism, or any humanism, consists in the assumption that man can, and must, achieve everything for himself, including his salvation. Poets, even, are applauded when they say that they are the captain of their souls and master of their lives. They are nothing of the sort. In their most strenuous acts of free will they are wholly dependent upon the action of God—an action, of course, which altogether respects what it is acting upon, and which therefore never coerces, nor could coerce, the will that God has created free or at least free-able.

If we contemplate most of our fellow-men, we have to agree that they seldom if ever take into account the direct action of God upon them, let alone that action as raising them to an altogether super-human plane. Even Catholics are apt to see themselves just as beings who are taught what to do and what not to do, though no doubt helped by God to do the former.

INTRODUCTION

But how very few attach a conscious habitual meaning to a phrase like: 'incorporation into Christ': 'inhabitation of the Holy Spirit'! On this elevation of the human creature into a super-human world, Augustine without cease insists.

But the second great theme which preoccupied Augustine was the City or State or Realm of God, for *Civitas* means very much more than any one vast town. We know that both God and Cæsar have their claims, not as equals side by side, for theirs are different *sorts* of reality, yet none the less each of them is 'real', God with His underived and infinite Reality, Cæsar or the State with his derived and limited one. Yet, as things are, and in this our human earthly life, we are real men living in a real Society, and there should be a perfect harmony between the Divine and the earthly lawgivers and their laws. To-day we are witnessing, as history has often witnessed, and as the interval between our Lord's earthly life and St Augustine had often witnessed, the tendency of the State to set itself up on an equality with God, or even to eliminate God, or at least to relegate God and divine things to 'the next world', leaving Cæsar sole autocrat in this one. That is bad enough.

But what Augustine apprehended was the complete collapse of the State and the apparition of a human chaos which could not be harmonised with anything. The Roman Empire had been vowed 'Aeternitati'—to eternity—it was to last for ever. Impossible to exaggerate the influence of this idea upon men's imagination. But Augustine, as his life drew towards its close, had to watch the progressive crumbling of that empire, and he died with the Vandals at his very gates. This enabled him to construct with ever firmer contours his vision of *God's* Realm. It is not for nothing that the Holy Father has, in our own time, caused us to concentrate more and more upon 'Christ the King' They used to say that Christianity had played a real part in the fall of the Roman Empire, by its uncivic qualities. Christianity is not anti-civic; but it certainly renders it impossible to credit any human institution such as all kingdoms, empires, or republics are, with final, universal, or everlasting powers. God alone is paramount; Christ alone is our ultimate King, and would that we observed their claims far more obediently than we do. For we have, clearly set before us, the possibility of State-Absoluteness, or of Chaos. I could have wished that Fr Przywara had quoted more from the *Civitas Dei*. Yet I expect that his selection could not have been bettered. All that precedes his Chapter x leads truly up to it; and what

INTRODUCTION

follows is concerned with the eternal issues into which even the Christian Triumph on this earth advances.

Of course those who are in no way prepared to *think* will not relish this book nor use it. But we beg, at the outset, no one (who is ready to take a little trouble) to fancy that it will be beyond him. On the whole, we are apt to imagine that things are far more difficult than they are. Anything looks hopelessly beyond our powers till we begin to try to do it. I recommend readers to take one chapter, or even one section, at a time; to read it, not worrying much whether or no they 'see' much 'in it'; to lay it aside for a week, and then re-read it. In examinations, when 'unseen' passages of some classical author were set, we were always well-advised to read them straight through hardly troubling to decipher the sense: then we read them a second time, and whole sections fell into sense, leaving only a line or two, here and there, obscure. Finally we tackled those lines and gave them no rest until the general sense forced us to see what they *must* mean. Treat the sections of this book like that, and then re-read the whole of it at a stretch! Your mind will have been enormously enriched: unfathomably deepened.

You may even see why we claim that Augustine, single-handed, shifted the intellectual centre of gravity of our world from East to West; some of you will even desire to read Augustine in his own Latin, grand as any organ-music: I perceive, actually as I write this, that it is of Augustine that the best of César Franck has made me think. And I would ask readers to supplement this book by reading anything that Fr Hugh Pope, O.P., writes upon Augustine, for it is he, maybe, who more than others is undertaking to familiarise our people with that tremendous man.

C. C. MARTINDALE, S.J.

CONTENTS

CONTENTS

CONTENTS

LIST OF ABBREVIATIONS

xiii

LIST OF ABBREVIATIONS

De mendacio.

De mor. Eccl., *De moribus Ecclesiae catholicae et de moribus Manichaeorum libri duo.*

De nat. et gratia, *De natura et gratia, ad Timasium et Jacobum, contra Pelagium, liber unus.*

De ord., *De ordine.*

De pecc. meritis, *De peccatorum meritis et remissione et de baptismo parvulorum, ad Marcellinum, libri tres.*

De perf. just. hominis, *Ad Episcopos Eutropium et Paulum epistola sive liber de perfectione iustitiae hominis.*

De praed. sanct., *De praedestinatione sanctorum liber ad Prosperum et Hilarium primus.*

De quant. an., *De quantitate animae.*

De scta. virg., *De sancta virginitate.*

De spir. et litt., *De spiritu et littera, ad Marcellinum, liber unus.*

De Trin., *De Trinitate libri quindecim.*

De util. cred., *De utilitate credendi.*

De vera relig., *De vera religione liber unus.*

En., *Enarratio.*

Enchiridion, *Enchiridion ad Laurentium sive de fide, spe et caritate liber unus.*

Ep., *Epistolae.*

Ep. ad Cath., *Ad Catholicos epistola contra Donatistas, vulgo de unitate Ecclesiae liber unus.*

Expos. Ep. ad Gal., *Epistolae ad Galatas expositio.*

Expos. quarundam prop. ex epist. ad Rom., *Expositio quarundam propositionum ex epistola ad Romanos.*

In Epistolam Joannis ad Parthos tractatus.

In Joan. Evang., *In Joannis Evangelium tractatus.*

In Ps., *Enarrationes in Psalmos.*

Retract., *Retractiones.*

Serm. (de Script. N.T.), *Sermones (de Scripturio Novi Testamenti)*

Solil., *Soliloquia.*

STANDARD TRANSLATIONS

USED IN THE PREPARATION OF THIS WORK

M. Sir Toby Matthew's trl. (1620), ed. by Dom Roger Hudleston, O.S.B.

S. Nicene and Post-Nicene Letters, ed. by Philip Schaff.

P. Library of N. Letters, ed. by E. B. Pusey.

H. John Healey's trl. (1610).

XL. *De diversis quaestionibus liber i.*
De diversis quaestionibus ad Simplicianum libri ii.
De fide rerum quae non videnter liber i (P).
Enchiridion de fide, spe, et charitate liber i (P).
De agone christiano liber i (P).
De sancta Virginitate liber i (P).
De bono viduitatis liber i (P).
De meadacio liber i (P).
Contra mendacium ad Consentium (P).

XLI. *Di civitate Dei contra Paganos libri xxii* (H).

XLII. *De utilitate credendi ad Honoratum liber i* (P).
*Contra epistolam Manichaei quam vocunt fundamenti
liber i* (s).
*Ad Orosium contra Priscillianistas et Origenistas
liber i.*
De Trinitate libri xv (s).

XLIII. *Contra litteras Petiliani libri iii* (s).
*Epistola ad Catholicos contra Donatistas, vulgo de
unitate ecclesiae liber i.*

XLIV. *De peccatorum meritis et remissione libri iii* (s).
De spiritu et littera liber i (s).
De natura et gratia liber i (s).
De perfectione iustitiae hominis liber i (s).
De gestis Pelagii liber i (s).
De gratia Christi et de peccato originali libri ii (s).
De anima et ejus origine libri iv (s).
*Contra duas Epistolas Pelagianorum ad Bonifacium
libri iv* (s).
Contra Julianum libri iv.
De gratia et libero arbitrio (s).
De correptione et gratia liber i (s).
De praedestinatione Sanctorum (s).

I. TRUTH

1. SENSIBLE WORLD AND INTELLIGIBLE WORLD

1

There is but one thing which I can teach thee; I know nothing more. These things of the senses are to be utterly shunned and the utmost care must be used lest while we bear this body our wings be impeded by their snare; seeing that we need them whole and perfect if we would fly from this darkness to that light, which deigns not even to show itself to those shut up in the cage of the body unless they have been such that whether it were broken through or dissolved they would escape into air which was theirs.

Solil. I, xiv, 24.

2

Let us not seek in this (earthly) beauty that which it has not received, for because it has not received that which we seek it is on that account in the lowest place. But for that which it has received let us praise God, since even to this that is lowest He has given also the great good of outward fairness. Yet let us not cling to it as lovers of it, but let us pass beyond it as praisers of God, that, set above it, we may judge of it, not cleaving to it be judged in it. And let us press onward to that good which is without motion in place, without revolution in time, and from whence all natural things receive in place and time their form and appearance.

Cont. Ep. Fund. XLII, 48.

3

Our body too might be said to be a prison, not because it is a prison which God hath made, but because it is under punishment and liable to death. For there are two things to be considered in our body, God's handicraft and the punishment it has deserved. All this form, stature, gait, well-ordered members, all the disposition of the senses, sight, hearing, smell, taste, touch, all this framework and intricacy of workmanship, could not have been made, save by God, Who made all things in heaven and earth, the highest, and the lowest, visible and invisible. What is there in this that is a punishment to us? That the flesh is corruptible, is frail, is mortal, is needy, will not be so in our reward. For the body will not cease to be a body when it rises from the dead. But what will there not be then? Corruption. 'For this corruptible shall put on incorruption' (1 Cor. xv, 53). If then the flesh is a prison to thee, it is not the body that is thy prison, but the corruption of thy body. For God made the body good, since He is good. Corruption He introduced in His justice, for He is Judge. The former thou hast as a benefaction, the latter by way of punishment.

In Ps. CXLI, 18.

4

When writing on the visible body, I said: 'Hence to love this is to estrange' (*De Trin.* XI, v, 9). This was said of the love whereby something is so loved that he who loves thinks that by the enjoyment of it he is blessed. But there is no estrangement if one love a bodily form to the praise of the Creator, so that enjoying the Creator himself he may be truly blessed.

Retract. II, xv, 2.

5

It is best that the soul of man being weak, and clogged with earthly effects and desires of those things that are so frail and contemptible in respect of the blessings celestial (though necessary for this present life), should desire them at the hand of the one only God, and not depart from His service to obtain them elsewhere, when they may soonest attain his love by neglect of such trifles, and with that love all necessaries both for this life, and the other.

De. Civ. Dei X, xiv.

6

Neither does any man hate his own body. For the Apostle says truly, 'No man ever hated his own flesh' (Eph. v, 29). And when some say that they would rather be without a body altogether, they entirely deceive themselves. For it is not their body, but its heaviness and corruption, that they hate. And so it is not no body, but an uncorrupted and very light body that they want. But they think a body of that kind would be no body at all, because they think such a thing would be a spirit. As to those who seem to persecute their own bodies by restraining their natural desires and by toil, they do it in the right spirit who thus punish it not in order to get rid of their body but in order to have it in subjection and ready for every needful work. For they strive by severely disciplining the body to root out those lusts which are hurtful to the body, that is to say, those habits and affections of the soul that lead to the enjoyment of inferior objects. They are not destroying themselves but are taking care of their health.

De doct. christ. I, xxiv, 24.

7

Owing to that very order of our nature whereby we are made mortal and carnal, we handle visible things more easily and more familiarly than things intelligible; since the former are perceived by bodily senses; the latter are understood by the mind. And we ourselves, namely, our minds are not sensible things, that is, bodies, but intelligible things, since we are life. And yet, as I have said, our familiarity with bodies is so great, and our thought has projected itself outwardly with so wonderful a proclivity towards them, that, when it has been withdrawn from the uncertainty of bodily things, that it may be fixed with a much more certain and stable cognition on that which is spirit, it flies back to those bodies, and seeks rest in the place whence it has drawn weakness. And to this its feebleness we must adapt ourselves; so that if at any time we would endeavour to distinguish more aptly and intimate more readily the inward spiritual things, we must take examples of similitudes from outward things pertaining to the body.

De Trin. XI, i, 1.

8

For to pass by those things which come to the mind from the bodily senses, among which so many are otherwise than they seem to be, that he who is overborne by their resemblance to truth, seems sane to himself, but really is not sane; . . . passing by then those things which come into the mind by the bodily senses, how large a proportion is left of things which we know in such manner as we know that we live? In regard to this, indeed, we are absolutely without any fear lest perchance we are being deceived by some resemblance to the truth; since it is certain that even he who is deceived, yet lives. And this again is not reckoned among those objects of sight which are presented from without, so that the eye may be deceived in it, in such a way as it is when an oar in the water looks bent, and towers seem to move as we sail past them, and hundreds of other things which are otherwise than they seem to be; for this is not a thing that is discerned by the eye of the flesh. The knowledge by which we know that we live is the most inward of all knowledge, of which even the Academic cannot make the insinuation: Perhaps you are asleep, and do not know it, and you see things in your sleep. For who does not know that what people see in dreams is precisely like what they see when awake? But he who is certain of the knowledge of his own life, does not therein say, I know I am awake, but, I know I am alive. Therefore, whether he be asleep or awake, he lives. Nor can he be deceived in that knowledge by dreams, since it is the property of a living person both to sleep and to see in sleep. Nor again can the Academic say in confutation of this knowledge: Perhaps you are mad, and do not know it; for what madmen see is precisely like what they who are sane also see; but he who is mad is alive. Nor does he answer the Academic by saying, I know that I am not mad, but I know that I am alive. Therefore he who says he knows that he is alive, can neither be deceived nor lie. Let then a thousand kinds of deceitful objects of sight be presented to him who says, I know that I am alive; yet he will fear none of them, for even if he is deceived, he is yet alive. But if such things alone pertain to human knowledge, they are very few indeed; unless they can be so multiplied in each kind as not only not to be few, but to reach in the result to an infinite number. For he who says, I know I am alive, says that he knows one single thing. Further, if he says, I know that I know I am alive, there are now two; but that he knows these two is a third thing to know. And similarly he can add a fourth and a fifth, and innumerable others, if he holds out. But since he cannot either comprehend an innumerable number by the addition of units, or say a thing innumerable times, he comprehends this at least, and with perfect certainty, namely, that this is both true and so innumerable that he cannot truly comprehend and say its infinite number. This same thing can be noticed in the case of a will that is certain. For it would be an impudent answer to make to one who should say, I will to be happy, that perhaps he is deceived. And if he should say, I know that I will this, and I know that I know it, he can add yet a third to these two, namely, that he knows these two; and a fourth, that he knows that he knows these two, and so on *ad infinitum*. Likewise, if anyone were to say, I will not to be mistaken; will it not be true, whether he is mistaken or whether he is not, that nevertheless he does will not to be mistaken? Would it not be most impudent to say to him, Perhaps you are deceived? When beyond any doubt, whereinsoever he may be deceived, he is nevertheless not deceived in thinking that he wills not to be deceived. And if he says he knows this, he adds any number he pleases of things known, and perceives that number to be infinite. For he who says, I will not be deceived, and I know that I will not to be so, and I know that I know it, is able to set forth an infinite number here also, however awkward may be the expression of it. And other things too are to be found capable of refuting the Academics, who contend that man can know nothing. . . . For whereas there are two kinds of knowable things—one, of those things which the mind perceives by the bodily senses, the other, of those which it perceives by itself—these philosophers have babbled much against the bodily senses, but have never been able to throw doubt upon those most certain perceptions of things true, which the mind knows by itself, such as is that which I have mentioned, 'I know that I am alive.' But far be it from us to doubt the truth of what we have learned by the bodily senses; since by them we have learned to know the heaven and the earth, and those things in them which are known to us, so far as He who created both us and them has willed them to be within our knowledge. Far be it from us too to deny that we know what we have learned by the testimony of others; otherwise we know not that there is an ocean; we know not that the lands and cities exist which abundant reports commend to us; we know not that those men are, and their works, which we have learned by reading history; we know not the news that is daily brought to us from this quarter or that, and is confirmed by accordant and supporting evidence; lastly we know not at what place or of whom we were born; since on all these things we have accepted the testimony of others. And if it is most absurd to say this, then we must confess, that not only our own senses, but those of other persons also, have added very much indeed to our knowledge.

De Trin. XV, xii, 21.

9

Who doubts that he lives, and remembers, and understands, and wills, and thinks, and knows, and judges? For indeed even if he doubts, he lives; if he doubts, he remembers why he doubts; if he doubts, he understands that he doubts; if he doubts, he wishes to be certain; if he doubts, he thinks; if he doubts, he knows that he does not know; if he doubts, he judges that he ought not to give his consent rashly. Whosoever therefore doubts about anything else, ought not to doubt about all these things; for if they were not, he would not be able to doubt about anything.

De Trin. X, x, 14.

10

Everyone who knows that he is in doubt about something, knows a truth, and in regard to this that he knows he is certain. Therefore he is certain about a truth. Consequently everyone who doubts if there be a truth, has in himself a true thing on which he does not doubt; nor is there any true thing which

is not true by truth. Consequently whoever for whatever
reason can doubt, ought not to doubt that there is truth.

De vera relig. xxxix, 73.

II

The mind knows what it is to know, and whilst it loves this
that it knows, it desires also to know itself. Whereby then
does it know its own knowing, if it does not know itself? For
it knows that it knows other things, but that it does not know
itself; for it is from hence that it knows also what knowing is.
Whence then does that which does not know itself, know itself
as knowing anything? For it does not know that some other
mind knows, but that itself does so. Therefore it knows itself.
Further, when it seeks to know itself, it already knows itself as
seeking. Therefore again it knows itself. And hence it cannot
altogether not know itself, when certainly it does so far know
itself as to know itself as not knowing itself. And therefore, in
the very fact that it seeks itself, it is clearly convicted of being
more known to itself than unknown. For it knows itself as seeking
and not knowing itself, in that it seeks to know itself.
Why therefore is it enjoined upon the mind that it should
know itself? I suppose, in order that it may ponder on itself,
and live according to its own nature: that is, seek to be regulated
according to its own nature, namely, under Him to whom it
ought to be subject, and above those things to which it is to be
preferred; under Him by whom it ought to be ruled, above
those things which it ought to rule. For it does many things
through vicious desire, as though in forgetfulness of itself. For
it sees certain things intrinsically excellent in the still more
excellent nature which is God. And whereas it ought to remain
steadfast that it may enjoy them, it is turned away from Him
by wishing to appropriate those things to itself, and not to be
like to Him by His gift, but to be what He is by its own; and
it moves and slips down into what is less and less, which it thinks
to be more and more; for it is neither sufficient for itself, nor is
anything at all sufficient for it, if it withdraw from Him who
alone is sufficient. And so through want and distress it becomes
too intent upon its own actions and upon the unquiet delights
which it obtains through them; and thus, by the desire of

acquiring knowledge from those things that are without, the nature of which it knows and loves, and which it feels may be lost unless held fast with anxious care, it loses its security, and ponders on itself so much the less in proportion as it feels the more secure that it cannot lose itself. . . .

What is so much in the mind as the mind itself? But because it is in those things which it thinks of lovingly, and is lovingly habituated to sensible, that is corporeal things, it is unable to be in itself without the images of those corporeal things. Hence shameful error arises to block the way, whilst it has not the power to separate itself from the images of sensible things, so as to see itself alone. For they have marvellously cohered with it by the strong bond of love. And herein consists its uncleanness; since, while it strives to think of itself alone, it fancies itself to be that, without which it cannot think of itself. When therefore it is bidden to get to know itself, let it not seek itself as though it were withdrawn from itself, but let it withdraw that which it has added to itself. For itself lies more deeply within, not only than those sensible things which are clearly without, but also than the images of them, which indeed are in some part of the soul, namely, that which beasts also have, although these want understanding, which is the property of the mind. Since therefore the mind is within, it goes forth in some sort from itself, when it exerts the affection of love towards these, as it were, footprints of many intentions. And these footprints are as it were impressed on the memory, at the time when these corporeal things which are without are so perceived, that even when corporeal things are absent, yet the images of them are at hand to those who think of them. Therefore let the mind get to know itself, and not seek itself as if it were absent; but let it fix upon itself the attention of the will, by which it was wandering among other things, and let it think of itself. Thus it will see that at no time did it ever not love itself, at no time did it ever not know itself; but by loving another thing together with itself, it has confounded itself with it and in some sense has grown one with it. And so, while it embraces divers things, as though they were one, it has come to think those things to be one which are diverse. . . .

Let it not then seek to discern itself as though absent, but

take pains to discern itself as present. Nor let it acquire knowledge of itself as if it did not know itself, but let it distinguish
itself from that which it knows to be something other. For how
will it take pains to obey the precept, 'know thyself,' if it knows
neither what 'know' means nor what 'thyself' means? But
if it knows both, then it knows itself also; since 'know thyself'
is not said to the mind in the same way as is 'know the Cherubim
and Seraphim,' for they are absent and we believe in them
according to what is declared to us about certain celestial
powers. Nor again is it as if it were said, 'know the will of that
man,' for this is not within our means to perceive at all whether
by sense or understanding, except by corporeal signs actually
exhibited, and this in such a way that we rather believe than
understand. Nor again is it as if said to a man, Behold thy
own face; which he can only do in a looking glass. For even
our own face is out of the reach of our seeing it; because it is
not there where our look can be directed. But when it is said to
the mind, know thyself; it then knows itself by the very act
by which it understands the word 'thyself'; and this for no
other reason than that it is present to itself.

De Trin. X, iii, 5; v, 7; viii, 11–ix, 12.

12

We say indeed, not unfitly, that we know what a mind is for
the reason that we too have a mind. For neither did we ever
see it with our eyes, and gather a special or general notion from
the resemblance of several minds which we have seen, but
rather, as I have said, because we too have one. For what is
known so intimately, and so perceives itself to be itself, as that
by which all other things also are perceived, that is, the mind
itself? For we recognize the movements of bodies also, by which
we perceive that others live besides ourselves, from the resemblance of ourselves; since in living we also so move our body
as we observe those bodies to be moved, yet when a living
body is moved, there is no way opened to our eyes to see the
mind, a thing which cannot be seen by the eyes; but we perceive
something to be present in that bulk, such as is present in ourselves, so as to move in like manner our own bulk; and this is

9

the life and the soul. Nor is this, as it were, the property of human prudence and reason, since brute beasts also perceive that not only they themselves live but also others, and this reciprocally, and that we ourselves do so. Neither do they see our souls, save from the movements of the body, and that immediately and most easily by some natural agreement. Therefore we both know the mind of any other person from our own, and believe from our own also of him whom we do not know. For not only do we perceive that there is a mind, but we can also know what a mind is by a consideration of our own, for we have a mind.

De Trin. VIII, vi, 9.

13

Whence does a mind know another mind, if it does not know itself? For the mind does not know other minds and not know itself, as the eye of the body sees other eyes and does not see itself. For we see bodies through the eyes of the body, because, unless we are looking into a mirror we cannot refract and reflect into themselves the rays which emerge through those eyes and touch whatever we discern. And clearly to demonstrate whether the fact be so or not demands a most subtle and abstruse discussion. But whatever is the nature of the power by which we discern through the eyes, certainly, whether it be rays or anything else, we cannot discern with the eyes that power itself; but we inquire into it with the mind, and if possible, understand this too with the mind. As the mind, therefore, gathers the knowledge of corporeal things through the senses of the body, so does it that of incorporeal things through itself. Therefore it knows itself through itself, since it is incorporeal.

De Trin. IX, iii, 3.

14

By what is the mind removed, except by itself? And when is it so placed as to be in its own sight, except before itself? Therefore it will not be where it was, when it was not in its own sight; since it has been put down in one place, after being taken away from another. But if it migrated in order to be beheld, where will it remain in order to behold? Is it as it were doubled, so as to be in this and in that place at the same time, viz. both where it can behold and where it can be beheld, that in itself it may be beholding, and before itself beheld? If we ask the truth, it will tell us nothing of the sort, since it is but feigned images of bodily objects of which we conceive when we conceive thus; and that the mind is not such, is very certain to the few minds by which the truth on such a subject can be investigated. It appears, therefore, that the beholding of the mind is something pertaining to its nature, and is recalled to that nature when it conceives of itself, not as if by a move. ment through space, but by an incorporeal conversion. But when it is not conceiving of itself, it appears that it is not in its own sight, nor is its own perception formed from it, but yet that it knows itself as if it were to itself a remembrance of itself.

De Trin. XIV, vi, 8.

15

But nothing is at all rightly said to be known while its substance is not known. Wherefore, when the mind knows itself, it knows its own substance; and when it is certain about itself, it is certain about its own substance. But it is certain about itself; . . . although it is not at all certain whether it is air, or fire, or some body, or a function of some body. Therefore it is not any of these. And of that whole which is bidden to know itself, this is a property, that it is certain that it is that only, which only it is certain that it is. For it thinks thus of fire, or air, and whatever else of the body it thinks of. Nor can it in any way be brought to pass that it should so think that which itself is, as it thinks that which itself is not. It thinks, indeed, all these things through an imaginary phantasy, whether fire, or air, or this or that body, or that part or combination and tempering together of the body; nor assuredly is it said to be all those things, but some one of them. But if it were any one of these things, it would think this one in a different manner from the rest, viz. not through an imaginary phantasy, as absent things are thought of, which either themselves or some of like kind have been touched by the bodily sense; but by some inward, not feigned, but true presence (for nothing is more present to it than itself); just as it thinks that itself lives, and remembers, and understands, and wills. For it knows these things in itself, and does not imagine them as though it had touched them by a sense outside itself, as corporeal things are touched. And if it attaches nothing to itself from the thought of these things, so as to think itself to be something of the kind, then whatsoever remains to it from itself, that alone is itself.

De Trin. X, x, 16.

16

When the human mind knows and loves itself, it does not know and love anything immutable; and each individual man declares his own particular mind by one form of speech when he considers what is taking place within himself; but defines the human mind abstractly by special or general knowledge. And so, when he speaks to me of his own particular mind, as to whether he understands this or that, or does not understand it, or whether he wishes or does not wish this or that, I believe; but when he says something generally or specially true of the human mind, I recognize and give my assent. Whence it is manifest, that each sees a thing in himself in such a way that another person may believe what he says of it, yet may not see it; but another sees a thing in the truth itself, in such a way that another person can also gaze upon it. And of these the former undergoes changes at successive times, the latter consists in an immutable eternity. For we do not gather a generic or specific knowledge of the human mind by similitude, by seeing many minds with the eyes of the body; but we gaze upon indestructible truth, from which to define perfectly, as far as we may, not of what sort is the mind of any one particular man, but of what sort it ought to be upon the eternal plan.

Whence also, even in the case of the images of things corporeal which are drawn in through a bodily sense, and in some way infused into the memory, from which even those things which have not been seen are pictured under a fancied image, whether otherwise than they really are, or even perhaps as they are;

—even here, too, it is demonstrable that where we accept or reject anything rightly, we accept or reject within ourselves by other rules which remain altogether immutable in our minds. For both when I recall the walls of Carthage which I have seen, and imagine to myself the walls of Alexandria which I have not seen, and, in preferring this to that among forms which in both cases are imaginary, make that preference upon grounds of reason, the judgment of truth from above is still strong and clear, and rests firmly upon the utterly indestructible rules of its own law; and if it is covered as it were by the cloudiness of corporeal images, is nevertheless not wrapt up and confounded in them.

But it makes a difference whether, under that or in that darkness, I am shut off from the clear heaven, or whether, as usually happens on very lofty mountains, enjoying the free air between both, I may both look up above to the serenest light and down below upon the densest clouds. For whence is the ardour of brotherly love kindled in me, when I hear that a man suffered grievous torture for the excellence and steadfastness of faith? and if that man is pointed out to me, I am eager to join myself to him, to become acquainted with him, to bind him to myself in friendship. And accordingly, if opportunity offers, I draw near, I address him, I enter into conversation with him, I express my good will towards him in what words I can, and wish that in him too in turn should be brought about and expressed goodwill towards me; and I make the attempt after a spiritual embrace in the way of belief, since I cannot search out so quickly and discern altogether his innermost heart. But if in the course of conversation he were to confess or were through unguardedness to show in any way, that either he believes something unseemly of God, and desires also something carnal in Him, and that he bore these tortures in behalf of such an error, or out of greediness for money which he hoped to get, or from vain desire for human praise, it at once follows that the love with which I was borne towards him, offended, and as it were repelled, and taken away from an unworthy man, remains in that form, after which, believing him such as I did, I had loved him; unless perhaps I am come to love him to this end that he may become such, though I have forced him to be not such in fact. And in that man, too, nothing is changed, though it can be changed, so that he may become that which I had first believed him to be. But in my mind there certainly is something changed, namely, the estimate I had formed of him, which before was of one sort, and now is of another; and the same love, at the bidding from above of immutable justice, is deflected from the purpose of enjoying to the purpose of taking counsel. But the form itself of unshaken and stable truth, wherein I should have enjoyed the man, believing him to be good, and wherein likewise I take counsel that he may be good, sheds in an immovable eternity the same light of incorruptible and most sound reason, both upon the sight of my mind, and upon that cloud of images, which I discern from above, when I think of the same man whom I had seen. Again when I call to mind some arch of beautiful and symmetrical lines which I saw, let us say, at Carthage, a certain reality that had been made known to the mind through the eyes, and transferred to the memory, creates the imaginary picture. But I behold in my mind yet another thing, according to which that work of art pleases me, and by which also, if it displeased me, I should correct it. We judge therefore of those particular things according to that form of eternal truth, and discern that form by the intuition of the rational mind. But those things themselves we often touch if present by a bodily sense, or if absent remember their images as fixed in our memory, or picture, in the way of likeness to them, such things as we ourselves also, if we wished to and were able, would laboriously build up: figuring in the mind after one fashion the images of bodies, or seeing bodies through the body, and after another, grasping by simple intelligence what is above the vision of the mind, namely the reasons and the unspeakable beautiful art of such forms.

De Trin. IX, vi, 9–11.

17

Hence thou must in no manner deny that there is an immutable truth, embracing all such things as are immutably true; a truth which thou canst not call thine, or mine, or any man's, but which is present to all and gives itself to all alike who discern the things that are immutably true, as a light which in some miraculous way is both secret and yet open to all. . . .

Dost thou think then that this truth . . . is superior to that which our mind is, or that it is equal to our minds, or even inferior to them? But if it were inferior, we should judge not according to it, but of it, as we judge of bodies, because they are beneath us, and we commonly say of them not only that they are thus or not thus, but that they ought to be thus or not thus; and similarly in respect to our minds also we know not only that the mind is thus and so, but also, most commonly, that it ought to be thus and so. . . . And we judge these things according to those interior laws of truth which we all alike discern; but of these laws themselves no man judges in any way. For when any one says that eternal things are to be preferred to temporal, or that seven and three are ten, no one says that they must have been so, but, knowing them to be so, does not think of amending them as a critic, but rejoices in them as a discoverer. Again, if this truth were equal to our minds, it also would be mutable. For our minds see this truth, now more, now less, and by this very fact confess themselves to be mutable; whereas truth, abiding within itself, neither increases when it is seen by us in greater, nor decreases when it is seen in lesser measure, but in its purity and incorruptibility it gladdens with light those that turn to it, and punishes with blindness those that turn from it. What, do not we judge of our very minds by it, but of it we can in no way judge. For we say, such a one understands less than he ought, or again, he understands to the extent that he ought. Now the mind ought to understand in the measure that it is able to approach more closely and adhere to the immutable truth. Hence if truth is neither inferior nor equal to our minds, nothing remains but that it should be superior and more excellent. . . .

Behold, Truth itself is before thee, embrace it if thou canst and have thy joy in it, and 'delight in the Lord, and He will give thee the requests of thy heart' (Ps. xxxvi, 4). . . . For if there is anything more excellent, that is God. Whether then such a thing is, or is not, that God is thou canst not deny. . . . For God is, and truly and supremely is. And this, so

I think, we not only hold to by faith as a fact beyond doubt, but by a sure, though as yet slender, form of cognition, we attain to it.

De lib. arb. II, xii, 33, 34; xiii, 35; xv, 39.

18

When we are diligent to be wise, what other course do we take but to focus as it were our whole soul with all the alacrity we are capable of, on that to which we attain by the mind, and set it therein, and fix it there firmly; so that it may no longer take joy in that part of itself which it has entangled in transitory things, but divested of all affections of time and place it may apprehend that which is for ever one and the same? . . . For whithersoever thou turnest, He speaks to thee by the marks which He has impressed upon His works, and when thou art slipping back to exterior things, He recalls thee by the very forms of these things to what is interior; so that thou mayest see that whatsoever delights thee in the body, and allures thee through the senses of the body, is rhythmically ordered; so that you may ask whence is this rhythm, and return within thyself, and learn that thou wouldst be incapable of approving or condemning that which thou reachest through the senses of the body, if thou hadst not within thyself certain laws of beauty to which to refer all the beautiful things of which thou art sensible outside thee.

Gaze at the sky, the earth, the sea, and all the things which shine in them or above them, or creep or fly or swim beneath them. They have forms because they have rhythm; take this away, and they will no longer be. From whom then are they, save from Him, from whom rhythm is; since they have being only in so far as they are rhythmically ordered. . . . Go now to that art whence rhythm proceeds, seek for time and place in it; there will be no 'when,' there will be no 'where'; yet rhythm lives within it; its bounds are not of space, nor is its age that of days. And yet when those who would become artists set themselves to learn their art, they move their bodies in time and place, but their minds in time, since by the passage of time they become more skilled. Pass, therefore, beyond the mind of the artist, so that thou mayest see the everlasting rhythm; then will wisdom shine upon thee from her inmost abode, from the very sanctuary of truth. . . .

If therefore thou art unable to apprehend either by the senses of the body or by meditation in the mind whatever mutable thing thou seest, unless it be held in some rhythmic form, which if it lost, it would fall back into nothingness, doubt not that, in order that these mutable things may not be checked in their course, but by measured motions and by distinctive variety of forms bring time to a close as a poem's ending, there must be some eternal and immutable Form, which is neither contained nor, as it were, diffused in place, neither extended nor varied in time, and through which all mutable things can receive a form and according to their kind fulfil and accomplish their ordered rhythms in space and time.

De lib. arb. II, xvi, 41–42, 44.

III. SOUL AND GOD

19

Man must first be restored to himself, that, making in himself as it were a stepping-stone, he may rise thence and be borne up to God.

Retract. I, viii, 3.

20

As it must be confessed that the human soul is not that which God is, so it must be presumed that among all the things which He created nothing is nearer to God than it. . . . This our God, therefore, must be worshipped by the soul, and that neither in a divided nor in a confused manner.

De quant. animae xxxiv, 77.

21

As the body is naturally raised erect to those bodily things which are most elevated, that is, to things celestial; so the mind, which is a spiritual substance, must be raised erect to those things which are most elevated in spiritual things, not by the elation of pride, but by the loyalty of justice.

De Trin. XII, i, 1.

22

The true honour of man is the image and likeness of God, which is not preserved save in relation to Him by whom it is impressed. The less therefore he loves what is his own, the more he adheres to God. But through the desire to make trial of his own power, man at his own bidding falls down to himself as to a sort of intermediate grade. And so, as he wishes to be under no one as God is, he is thrust on from this same middle state of his, by way of punishment, to that which is lowest, that is, to those things in which the beasts delight. And thus, while his honour is the likeness of God, his dishonour is the likeness of the beast. 'Man when he was in honour did not understand: he is compared to senseless beasts, and is become like to them' (Ps. xlviii, 13). But what way, then, could he pass so great a distance from the highest to the lowest, except through his own intermediate state? For when neglecting the love of wisdom, which remains ever after the same fashion, he lusts after knowledge derived from experiment upon things temporal and mutable, that knowledge puffeth up, it doth not edify (1 Cor. viii, 1). And so the mind is overweighted and thrust out by its own weight, as it were, from blessedness, and learns by its own punishment, through trial of its own intermediate state, what is the difference between the good it has abandoned and the bad to which it has committed itself; and having dissipated and destroyed its strength, it cannot return, save by the grace of its Creator calling it to repentance, and remitting its sins.

De Trin. XII, xi, 16.

23

Recognize in thyself something within, within thyself. Leave thou abroad both thy clothing and thy flesh; descend into thyself; go to thy secret chamber, thy mind. If thou be far from thine own self, how canst thou draw near unto God? For not in the body but in the mind was man made in the image of God. In his own similitude let us seek God: in his own image recognize the Creator.

In Joan. Evang. XXIII, 10.

24

Do not go outside thyself, but return to within thyself; for truth resides in the inmost part of man. And if thou dost find that thy nature is mutable, rise above thyself. But when thou transcendest thyself, remember that thou raisest thyself above the rational soul; strive therefore to reach the place where the very light of reason is lit. For whither does every good reasoner arrive, if it be not to the truth? Since truth certainly does not attain to itself, but is that which reasoners strive to reach, recognize in it a harmony than which nothing can be superior, and bring thyself into accord with it. Confess that thou art not that which it is, since it does not seek itself, and thou hast come towards it by seeking for it, not by advancing in space but by an affection of the mind, to the end that the interior man may come into accord with that which dwells within him, in a joy that is not carnal and of a low order, but spiritual and of the highest.

De vera relig. xxxix, 72.

25

Do thou all within. And if perchance thou seekest some high place, some holy place, make thee a temple for God within. For the temple of God is holy: which you are (1 Cor. iii, 17). In a temple wouldest thou pray? Pray within thyself. Only first be thou a temple of God, because he in his temple will hear him that prayeth.

In Joan. Evang. XV, 25.

26

Return to thyself; but when, again facing upwards, thou hast returned to thyself, stay not in thyself. First return to thyself from the things that are without, and then give thyself back to Him who made thee.

Serm. CCCXXX, 3.

27

Our Father, who has exhorted us to pray, who also bringest about what Thou hast asked of us; since we live better when we pray to Thee and are better: hear me as I tremble in this darkness and reach out Thy right hand to me. Hold Thy light before me and recall me from my strayings, that with Thee as my guide I may return to myself and to Thee. Amen.

Solil. II, vi, 9.

28

O God who art ever the same, let me know myself, let me know Thee.

Solil. II, i, 1.

29

In every place, O Truth, thou givest audience to such as consult thee, and at the same time dost thou answer all their demands, be they never so diverse. Thou givest them clear answers, but everyone doth not clearly understand thee. For all men consult thee about what they will, but they do not always hear what they will by way of answer. He is thy best servant who endeavoureth not to hear that from thee which he desireth, but rather desireth that which he heareth from thee.

Conf. X, xxvi, 37.

30

More happy are they that hear than they that speak. For he that learneth is humble, but he that teacheth laboureth that he be not proud, lest the inclination to please men to their hurt steal over him, lest he displease God that would please men. There is a great dread in teaching, my brethren, great is our trembling over these our words. Believe our heart which you cannot see. May He be merciful to us, may He be favourable to us, who knoweth with what great trembling we speak to you. But when we hear Him suggesting anything and teaching us within our hearts, we are without concern, and without concern we rejoice; for we are under the Master; His glory we seek, His teaching we praise; His truth delighteth us within, where no one maketh or heareth a sound.

In Ps. L, 13.

31

For see, brethren, what there is in a human soul. Of itself it hath no light, nor of itself powers; but all that is fair in a soul is virtue and wisdom; but it neither is wise for itself, nor strong for itself, nor is itself light to itself, nor is itself virtue to itself. There is a certain fountain and origin of virtue, there is a certain root of wisdom, there is a certain, so to speak, if this also is to be said, region of immutable truth; from which if the soul withdraws it is made dark and if it draws near it is made light.

In Ps. LVIII, *Serm.* i, 18.

32

For a lamp is a creature, not a creator; and it is lit by participation of an immutable light. This was John, of whom God the Word saith, 'He was a burning and a shining lamp' (John v, 35). But he is both light and lamp; nevertheless compared with the Word, of Whom it is said, 'the Word was God,' 'he was not the light,' but was sent 'to give testimony of the light.' For 'that was the true light,' which was not lit as a man, but 'which enlighteneth every man' (John i, 1-9). But unless a lantern also were a light, He would not say to His apostles, 'You are the light of the world' (Matt. v, 14), when they had heard that they might not think themselves to be that which He was, who said this. For in a certain passage He saith of Himself, 'I am the light of the world' (John viii, 12), and of themselves He saith to them, 'A city seated on a mountain cannot be hid. Neither do men light a candle and put it under a bushel, but upon a candlestick, that it may shine to all that are in the house. So let your light shine before men' (Matt. v, 14 *sqq.*); that they might know that they were, as it were, lanterns lit by that light which shineth immutably. For no creature, howsoever rational and intellectual, is lighted of itself, but is lighted by participation of eternal Truth.

In Ps. CXIX, *Serm.* xxiii, 1.

33

God therefore, of Himself, because He is the light (John i, 4, 9), enlighteneth pious minds, that they may understand the divine truths which are declared or exhibited. . . . God hath created man's mind rational and intellectual, whereby he may take in His Light; . . . and He so enlighteneth it of Himself, that not only those things which are displayed by the truth, but even truth itself may be perceived by the mind's eye.

In Ps. CXVIII, *Serm.* xviii, 4.

34

Let religion bind us fast to the one omnipotent God; for no creature is interposed between our mind, by which we know Him, the Father, and the truth, that is, the interior light by which we understand Him. Wherefore, let us adore in Him and with Him that very Truth, which is in no part dissimilar to Him, and is the form of all things, which were created by Him alone, and which strive to attain to Him alone.

De vera relig. liii, 113.

35

As the mind to the body, so must also truth be preferred to the mind itself; so that the mind may desire it not only more than the body, but even more than its own self. Thus will the mind be more complete and chaste, when it shall enjoy the immutability of truth rather than its own mutability.

De mendacio vii, 10.

36

For the flesh is not life to itself, but the soul is the life of the flesh. The soul is not life to itself, but God is the life of the soul. . . . And if the soul live after God, then doth the flesh live rightly after the soul.

Serm. (*de Script. Nov. Test.*) CLVI, vi, 6.

37

Be thou subject to God, thy flesh to thee. What can be more just, more beautiful? Thou subject to Him that is greater, it that is less to thee. Obey thou Him that made thee, that that which was made for thee may obey thee. For we know not nor do we commend this order: 'My flesh to thee, and thou to God,' but rather, 'thou to God, and thy flesh to thee.' For if thou despisests 'thou to God,' thou wilt never bring about 'thy flesh to thee.' Thou that obeyest not God shalt be tormented by a slave.

In Ps. CXLIII, 6.

38

The soul obeyeth God enthroned in it, and itself commandeth the members. For thy soul commandeth thy members that so the foot, the hand, the eye, the ear may move. It ordereth the members as its servants, but itself nevertheless serveth its God enthroned within. It cannot rule its inferior well unless it has not disdained to serve its superior.

In Ps. XLVI, 10.

39

In so far as concerns the nature of man, there is in him nothing better than the mind and reason. But he who would live blessedly ought not to live according to them; for then he would live according to man, whereas he ought to live according to God, so that he may attain to blessedness. And to accomplish this, our mind must not be content with itself, but must be subjected to God.

Retract. I, i, 2.

40

'But it is good for me to adhere to my God' (Ps. lxxii, 28); so that our bodies will live on us by adhering to us, but we draw life from God, because it is good for us to adhere to God.

In Ps. CXVIII, *Serm.* x, 2.

41

Remain not in thyself, transcend thyself also; put thyself in Him who made thee.

Serm. (de Script. Nov. Test.) CLIII, vii, 9.

42

That the soul in the contemplation of the supreme wisdom (which is certainly not the soul itself, since it is immutable), can behold itself also, though it is mutable, comes to pass by reason of that distinction whereby the soul is not that which God is, and is yet something, after God, capable of pleasing. But the soul is a better thing when it forgets itself for love of the immutable God, or by comparison with Him utterly despises itself.

De lib. arb. III, xxv, 76.

43

When first I knew Thee Thou didst raise me up, that I might see there was somewhat for me to see, though as yet I was not fit to see it.

Conf. VII, x, 16.

44

O for some most wise and eloquent man who by speech and argument might explain the power of the soul in the body, its power in itself, its power before God, to whom it is the most near when it is the most pure, and in whom it has its whole and its sovereign good! But now though others fail me in this matter, I nevertheless venture not to fail thee. But I have this reward, that while I expound in unlearned fashion what the power of the soul is, I safely put to the test what I myself am capable of. But first I would remove any too broad and boundless a hope you may have, so that you may not imagine that I am going to speak on every manner of soul; for I shall speak only of the human soul, for which alone we must take thought, if we take thought of ourselves. First then, as any one can easily see, the soul quickens by its presence this earthly and mortal body, it gathers it into one and holds it in one, it does not allow it to fall apart and decay; it causes food to be distributed equally among the members of the body, allotting to each what is proper to it; it preserves its harmony and measure, not only in beauty of form, but also in growth and reproduction. But these things may seem to be shared by men even with plants; for we say that the latter also live, and we see and acknowledge that each of them after its kind is taken care of and nourished, grows and begets. Let us therefore ascend a second step, and see what are the powers of the soul in the senses, wherein a more evident and more manifest life is to be perceived. . . .

TRUTH

Consider the power of the soul in the senses, and in that motion which more clearly displays the living creature, wherein we can have nothing in common with things that are rooted to the ground. The soul directs its attention to the sense of touch and feels and distinguishes things hot and cold, rough and smooth, hard and soft, light and heavy. Then, by taste, smell, hearing, and sight it determines innumerable differences in flavours, odours, sounds, and shapes. And among all these things it appropriates to itself and seeks out those which are in accord with its own body, and rejects and shuns those which are contrary to it. At certain intervals of time it removes itself from these senses, and, refreshing their motions by a kind of rest period, revolves in itself the medley of images of things which it has received through the senses; and this all is sleep and dreams. Often as it joyously ranges, it delights in the ease of motion, and without effort orders the concord of the members. In the union of the sexes it plays its part, and by companionship and love makes of two natures one. It conspires not only to the begetting of offspring, but also to the cherishing, protection, and nurture thereof. It attaches itself by long habit to the things among which it guides the body and by which it sustains the body; and as though they were its members it can hardly be parted from them; and this power of habit, which even by a separation from the things themselves, and by lapse of time, is not severed, is called memory. But again, no one denies that the soul, i.e. the vital principle can do all these things even in beasts.

Rise therefore to the third step, which is already peculiar to man, and consider the memory of the innumerable things not made familiar by custom, but committed to the mind and retained by observation and signs: the many works of artists, the tilling of the fields, the building up of cities, the manifold wonders of building and other undertakings, the invention of the many symbols in letters and words, in gesture, in all manner of sounds, in pictures and statues; the many tongues of men, so many things set in hand, newly begun or restored; the vast number of books and all manner of memorials to keep a record of things done, the much thought given to posterity, the many grades of offices, powers, honours, and dignities, whether in families, or in the state at home or on military service, or in sacred or profane displays; the power of reasoning and thought, the stream of eloquence, the various kinds of verse, the thousand simulations for the sake of play or jest, the skill of players and singers, the subtlety of mensuration, the art of calculation, the conjectures about the past and the future from the present;— such things are great and are wholly man's property; yet all this rich store is held in common, some of it by the learned and unlearned, some of it by the just and unjust.

Look upward, therefore, and leap onto the fourth step, whereon begin goodness and all true praise. For here the soul ventures to set itself not only above its own body, whatever part of the universe it is, but also above the whole universe of bodily things, and to think that the good things of the latter are not its own good things, and, having compared them to its own power and beauty, to lay them aside and despise them. And the more it delights in its own gifts, the more it removes itself from base things, and makes itself altogether spotless and clean and adorned with beauty. It strengthens itself against all such things as strive to move it from its intent and purpose. It sets great store on human fellowship, and is unwilling to do anything to another which it would not have done to itself. It follows the authority and the counsels of the wise, and believes that through these God speaks to it. In this admirable action of the soul there yet remain toil and conflict great and most bitter with the pains and the blandishments of this world. For in the very business of cleansing itself there is an underlying fear of death, often not great, but often also most vehement. This fear is not great when the soul has the robust faith (for until it is perfectly cleansed it cannot *see* whether this be true or no) that all things are ordered by God with such providence and justice, that death cannot fall unfairly on any man, even though perhaps an unjust man inflict it upon him. But even on this step death is vehemently feared, since God's justice is the less firmly believed for the reason that it is the more anxiously sought; and it is seen the less clearly in so far as fear lessens that tranquillity which is essential in the investigation of obscure matters. Furthermore, as the soul by its very progress feels more and more how great the difference is between the clean soul and the unclean, it fears the more lest, when its body has been laid aside, God even less than itself will be unable to endure its pollution. And there is no harder thing than both to fear death and to refrain (as the danger itself bids) from the snares of this world. But so strong is the soul that it may accomplish even this, with the help, of course, of the justice of sovereign and true God, whereby this whole universe is sustained and ordered, and whereby it is brought about not only that all things are, but also that they are in such wise that they could not be better. To this justice the soul piously and safely commits itself, to be aided and perfected in the difficult work of its cleansing. . . .

And when this has been accomplished, that is to say, when the soul has been freed from all corruption and washed from every stain, then at length it holds itself in utmost joy within itself; it has no manner of fear for itself, and suffers no anxiety concerning itself at all. This, then, is the fifth step; for it is one thing to achieve purity, another to hold it; and the action whereby the soul restores itself after defilement is other than that whereby it does not suffer itself to be defiled again. On this step the soul in every way forms a conception of how great it is, and having conceived this, it proceeds with incredibly powerful confidence towards God, that is, to the real contemplation of truth, and to that most high and secret reward which was the goal of all its pains.

But this action, that is, the striving to understand those things which truly and supremely are, is the highest form of vision of the soul, than which it has nothing more perfect and good and right. This therefore will be the sixth step of the soul's action; for it is one thing for the eye of the soul to be cleansed, so that it may not look in vain or without purpose, and not see amiss; another to preserve and strengthen that healthy state, and yet another to direct a serene and unswerving gaze upon that which it would see. And those who would do this before they are cleansed and made whole, are so stricken back by that light of truth, that they think there to be in it not only no good, but even much evil; and they take away from it the name of truth, and take refuge with a kind of miserable lust and delight in their own darkness. And therefore most fittingly does the Prophet, inspired by God, say: 'Create a clean heart in me, O God: and renew a right spirit within my bowels' (Ps. l, 12).

For that spirit, I hold, is right, whereby in the search for truth the soul cannot turn from the right path and stray. And this spirit is assuredly not renewed in the soul unless the heart has first been made clean, that is, unless the very thought has set itself free from all desire of mortal things, and strained itself clear from the dregs thereof.

And now in the very vision and contemplation of truth, which is the seventh and last step of the soul, though this is not now a step but an abiding place reached by the other steps, how shall I tell of the joys which are there, of the enjoyment of the true and supreme good, of the spirit of peace and eternity breathing there?

For those therefore who are ascending upwards the first action may be called, for the sake of instruction, quickening; the second, sensation; the third, art; the fourth, virtue; the fifth, tranquillity; the sixth, entry; the seventh, contemplation. They may also be thus named: of the body, through the body, about the body, the soul towards itself, the soul in itself, towards God, with God. And again thus: beauty from another thing, beauty through another thing, beauty about another thing, beauty towards the beautiful, beauty in the beautiful, beauty towards Beauty, beauty in Beauty.

De quant. animae xxxiii, 70-76; xxxv, 79.

45

For God wisheth us to be so suckled with milk, that we abide not therein; but, by growing through milk, that we may arrive at solid food. Man therefore ought not to raise his soul unto pride, but to raise it unto the teaching of the Word of God. For if the soul were not to be lifted up, it would not be said in another psalm, 'To thee, O Lord, have I lifted up my soul' (Ps. xxiv, 1). And except the soul overflow herself, she reacheth not unto the vision of God and unto the knowledge of that immutable substance. For while it is still in the flesh, it is thus addressed: Where is thy God? But the soul's God is within, and is within spiritually, and is lofty spiritually; not as it were by intervals of places, as places are higher through intervals. For if altitude of this kind is to be sought, the birds surpass us in approaching God. God is therefore lofty within, and spiritually lofty, nor doth the soul reach Him, except it transcend itself. For whatever thou thinkest concerning God according to the body, thou errest much. Thou art indeed an infant, if thou thinkest concerning God even according to the human soul, that God may either forget, or be wise in such manner that He may be unwise, or do anything and yet repent of it. For all these things are set out in the Scriptures, that, while we are yet unweaned, God may be commended to us; not that we may take those expressions about Him literally, and understand them as if God repented, and were now learning something that He knew not, and understanding what He understood not, and remembering what he had forgotten. Such things belong to the soul, not to God. Except therefore a man hath passed the measure of his own soul, he will not see that God is what He is, God Who said 'I AM WHO AM' (Exod. iii, 14). . . . Therefore it is not said to thee to be humble with a view that thou mayest not be wise. Be humble, in respect of pride; be exalted, in respect of wisdom. Hear a plain sentence in this matter. 'Do not become children in sense. But in malice be children: and in sense be perfect' (1 Cor. xiv, 20). It has been clearly explained, my brethren, where God would have us be humble and where exalted. Humble, in order to provide against pride; exalted to take in wisdom.

In Ps. CXXX, 12.

IV. BLESSED TRUTH

46

Whereas knowledge and action make a man happy, as in knowledge error must be guarded against, so must wickedness be avoided in action. Now whosoever supposes that he can know truth while he is still living iniquitously, is in error. And it is wickedness to love this world, and those things that come into being and pass away, and to lust after these things, and to labour for them in order to acquire them, and to rejoice when they are abundant, and to fear lest they perish, and to be saddened when they perish. Such a life cannot see that pure, and undefiled, and immutable Truth, and cleave to it, to be for evermore unmoved.

De ag. chr. xiii, 14.

47

Thus also many learn the justifications of God, and yet learn them not. For they know them in a certain way; and again from a kind of ignorance do not know them, since they perform them not. In this sense then the Psalmist is to be understood to have said, 'that I may learn Thy justifications' (Ps. cxviii, 71), meaning that kind of knowledge by which they are performed.

In Ps. CXVIII, *Serm.* xvii, 9.

48

For the sweeter the commandments of Him Who aideth us are, the more doth he who loveth Him search after them, that he may perform them when known, and learn them by doing them; since they are more perfectly understood when they are performed.

In Ps. CXVIII, *Serm.* xvii, 7.

49

Eternal life is the actual knowledge of the truth. See then how perverse and preposterous are those who imagine that their teaching of the knowledge of God will make us perfect, when this is the reward of those already perfect. What else, then, I ask, have we to do but first to love with complete charity Him whom we desire to know?

De mor. Eccl. I, xxv, 47.

50

Since the knowledge of the creature compared to that of the Creator is but a twilight, this day has a morning and an evening: and day breaks when he draws near the love and praise of the Creator. Nor is the creature ever benighted save when love for the Creator forsakes him.

De Civ. Dei XI, vii.

TRUTH

51

We ought so much the more eagerly to seek a most open and clear knowledge of the truth, the more we find ourselves progressing in charity, and in its simplicity to have our heart cleansed, for it is with the interior eye that truth is seen; for, 'Blessed are the clean of heart: for they shall see God' (Matt. v, 8). 'That being rooted and founded in charity, you may be able to comprehend, with all the saints, what is the breadth and length and height and depth. To know also the charity of Christ, which surpasseth all knowledge: that we may be filled unto all the fullness of God (Eph. iii, 17 *sqq.*).

De ag. chr. xxxiii, 35.

52

Let the Christian remember that the very gospel of St. John which urges us so pre-eminently to the contemplation of truth, gives a no less remarkable prominence to the inculcation of the sweet grace of charity. Let him also consider that most true and wholesome precept, 'The greater thou art, the more humble thyself in all things' (Ecclus. iii, 20). For the evangelist who presents Christ to us in a far loftier strain than all the others, is also the one in whose narration the Lord washes the disciples' feet (cf. John xii, 5).

De cons. Evang. IV, X, 20.

53

If in its magnitude knowledge surpasses the magnitude of charity, it doth not edify but puffeth up (1 Cor. viii, 1). When, however, charity shall be so strong in the sweetness of goodness that it cannot be extinguished by the tribulations which discipline useth, then will knowledge be useful, whereby a man gets to know what he has himself deserved and what has been given him by God, through which he discovers that he can do what he knew not that he could do, and what of himself he could not do by any means.

In Ps. CXVIII, *Serm.* xvii, 2.

54

Let knowledge be applied as a kind of scaffolding by which there may mount up the edifice of charity, which shall endure for ever even when knowledge shall be destroyed (cf. 1 Cor. xiii, 8).

Ep. LV, xxi, 39.

55

Since no one can love at all a thing of which he is wholly ignorant, we must carefully consider of what sort is the love of students, that is, of those who do not already know, but are still desiring to know some branch of learning. . . . Thus, if anyone hear an unknown distinguishing symbol, such as, for instance, the sound of some word of which he does not know the meaning, he desires to know what this is; that is to say, he desires to know what thing it is which it is agreed shall be brought to mind by that sound. . . . What then does he love? For certainly nothing can be loved unless it is known. For that man does not love those syllables which he knows already. But if he loves this in them, that he knows them to signify something, this is not our present concern, for it is not this that he seeks to know. For we are now asking what it is in that which he is desirous to know, but which certainly he does not know yet; and we therefore are wondering why he loves, since we know most assuredly that nothing can be loved unless it is known. What then does he love, except that he knows and perceives in the reason of things what excellence there is in learning, in which the knowledge of all signs is contained, and what benefit there is in being skilled in these, since by them human society mutually communicates its perceptions, and if men assembled together were not to interchange their thoughts by conversing, they would be worse than in utter solitude. The soul then discerns this fitting and useful species of knowledge, and knows it and loves it; and he who seeks the meaning of any words of which he is ignorant, studies to render that species perfect in himself, so far as he can; for it is one thing to behold it in the light of truth, another to desire it as within his capacity. For he beholds in the light of truth how great and how good a thing it is to understand and to speak all tongues, and to hear and be heard in them as if he were not a foreigner. The beauty of this knowledge is therefore already discerned by thought, and the thing being known is loved. And that thing is so regarded, and so stimulates the zeal of students, that they are moved with respect to it, and desire it eagerly in all the labour they expend upon the attainment of such a faculty; in order that they may embrace in practice that which they know beforehand by reason. And thus everyone, the nearer he approaches that faculty in hope, the more fervently does he desire it with love. . . . For that species of knowledge touches the mind, and the mind knows and ponders it; and in it the beauty is clearly visible which comes from the association of minds with one another. And it kindles with zeal him who seeks what indeed he knows not, but who gazes upon and loves the known form to which it pertains.

De Trin. X, i, 1, 2.

56

Does the knowledge of life seem better to thee than life itself? Or dost thou conceive knowledge to be some kind of higher and purer life, which no man can know save him who has understanding? And what is understanding except by the light of the mind itself to live a more enlightened and perfect life?

De lib. arb. I, vii, 17.

57

Dost thou hold wisdom to be anything other than truth, wherein we behold and embrace the supreme good?

De lib. arb. II, ix, 26.

58

Since it is in truth that we learn to know and to embrace the supreme good, and since that truth is wisdom, let us discern the supreme good in truth and embrace it and enjoy it to the full. For blessed is he who enjoys the supreme good. And this truth shows forth all good things that are truly good; and men understanding these choose, each according to his capacity, some one or more of these, for their enjoyment. But just as in the case of those who in the sunlight pick out some thing at which they

33

may look with pleasure, and rejoice in the sight of it, there will be some among them perhaps endowed with keener, healthier, stronger eyes, who find nothing to look at with more pleasure than the sun itself, which lights up all the other things in which weaker eyes find their delight; so too the sight of the mind if it be strong and keen, after looking at many true and immutable things in the sure light of reason, directs itself on truth itself, whereby all things are manifested, and cleaving thereto forgets, as it were, the rest, and in it enjoys all things at one time. For whatever in other true things is a cause of delight, must certainly give delight in the Truth itself. This is our freedom, to subject ourselves to that Truth, and He is our God who liberates us from death, that is from the state of sin. . . . For the soul enjoys nothing in freedom except what it enjoys in peace.

De lib. arb. II, xiii, 36–37.

59

When therefore the will which is the intermediate good cleaves to the immutable good, not as a personal possession but as one held in common (as in the case of that of which we have spoken much but have not said anything worthy of it, namely truth), man finds therein the blessed life. And this the blessed life, that is to say, the affection of the mind cleaving to the immutable good, is man's chief personal good. . . . For by truth and wisdom, which are common to all, all are made wise and blessed by adhering to that good. But one man does not become blessed by the blessedness of another; for even when he imitates him, in order to be blessed, he is striving to become blessed by that by which he sees the other so made, namely, by that immutable truth which is common to all. So too no one is made prudent by the prudence of any other man, nor brave by his bravery, nor temperate by his temperance, nor just by his justice; but only by adjusting his soul to those immutable rules and beacons of the virtues, which reside incorruptibly in that truth and that wisdom, which are common to all, to which that other, whom because of his possession of these virtues he had set before himself as a model, had adjusted and attached his soul.

De lib. arb. II, xix, 52.

60

If however you ask what wisdom is . . . it is nothing other than a measure of the mind, that is, one by which the mind holds itself in equilibrium, so that it neither goes to excess, nor limits itself to what is below its capacity. . . . What then is to be called wisdom, save that which is the Wisdom of God? . . . But what do you hold to be wisdom except truth? . . . But truth, in order that it may be, comes into being through some supreme measure, whence it proceeds and whither it returns when perfected. But on this supreme measure no other measure is imposed, for if the supreme measure is the measure according to the supreme measure, it is the measure according to itself. Moreover the supreme measure must necessarily also be the true measure, so true measure is recognized by truth. For there was never truth without true measure, nor true measure without truth. . . . Whoever therefore attains to the true measure through truth, is blessed. This it is to have God in the mind. This it is to enjoy God.

De beata vita iv, 33, 34.

61

From this is every true word we speak, even when with eyes hardly sound or scarcely opened we tremble rashly to turn to it and to see the whole; and this too appears to be no other thing than God. . . . This therefore is the full satisfaction of the mind, this the blessed life, to recognise piously and perfectly by what you were led to the truth, what the truth is which you are enjoying to the full, and by what means you are linked to the supreme measure.

De beata vita iv, 35.

62

For he who inquires how he may attain to a blessed life is truly seeking nothing else but this: where is the highest degree of good? that is to say, where is the highest good of man set, not according to the perverted and hasty opinions of men but according to the sure and unshakable truth? And this is not found by anyone except in the body, or in the mind, or in God. . . .

Not that there be no other goods, but that good is called supreme to which all others are related. For everyone is blessed in the enjoyment of that for the sake of which he desires to have the other things, seeing that it is loved for its own sake and not on account of something else. And therefore the supreme good is said to be there because here nothing is found towards which it can issue forth or to which it is related. There is the place of rest, of desire; there is security of enjoyment; there is the calmest delight of a will wholly virtuous.

Give me a man who sees at once that the body is not the good of the mind, but that the mind is rather the good of the body. Of such an one we should of course refrain from asking whether that highest good or any part of it is in the body. For it were the height of foolishness to deny that the mind is better than the body. Equally foolish would it be to deny that that which gives a happy life or any part of a happy life is better than that which receives it. The mind, therefore, does not receive from the body either the highest good or any part of the highest good. Those who do not see this have been blinded by the sweetness of carnal pleasures, which they do not see to have proceeded from want of health. But perfect health of body shall be the ultimate immortality of the whole man. For God has endowed the soul with a nature so powerful that from that utter fulness of joy which is promised to the saints in the end of time, there overflows also over the lower part of our nature, which is the body, not the beatitude which is proper to the part which enjoys and understands, but the plenitude of health, that is to say the vigour of incorruption. . . .

Give me likewise a man who also sees at once that when the mind is happy, it is not happy by good belonging to itself, else it would never be unhappy; and of such a man we would forbear from inquiring whether that highest and, so to speak, beatific good, or any part of it, is in the mind. For when the mind rejoices in itself as if in good belonging to itself, it is proud. But when it perceives itself to be mutable (as is clear from the one fact that from being foolish it may be made wise), and perceives that wisdom is immutable, the mind must at the same time perceive that wisdom is superior to its own nature and that there is more abundant and certain joy in the participation and the illumination of wisdom than in itself. Thus from causing to subside and desisting from boasting and self-conceit, it strives to cling to God and to be remade and reformed by Him who is immutable, by Him who it now understands is not only every species of all things with which it comes in contact, whether by the bodily senses or by the faculties of the mind, but also the very capacity of taking form before there is a form, since the formless is defined to be that which can be given a form. Accordingly it feels itself to be less stable in proportion as it clings to God who in the highest degree is: and that He in the highest degree is because He neither gains nor loses by any mutability. In itself, however, the mind perceives that that change by which it gains capacity for perfect clinging to God is advantage, that change by which it loses such capacity is pernicious; further that all loss tends towards destruction. And although it is not apparent whether anything reaches that state, it is manifest to every one that loss brings destruction in so far as the thing is not what it was. Whence the mind infers that the one reason why things suffer loss, or are able to suffer loss, is that they were created out of nothing; so that their property of being and of permanence and that by which even for their defects they are ranged in their due place in the complex whole of the universe, is all due to the goodness and omnipotence of Him who supremely is and who is the Author able to create from nothing not only something but also something great; and that the first sin, that is to say the first voluntary loss is the rejoicing in its own power. For it rejoices in something less than it would if it rejoiced in the power of God, which is indubitably greater.

To Him I would that thou submit thyself with all thy piety, and that thou prepare for thyself no other way of seizing and preserving the truth than that which has been prepared by Him who as God has seen the infirmity of our courses. But that way is firstly humility, secondly humility, and thirdly humility. And this I would continue to repeat, however many times the question is asked. Not that there are no other precepts which may be given, yet unless humility both precede and accompany and follow every good action that we perform, being at once the object which we keep before us, the support to which we cling, and the monitor by which we are restrained, pride wrests wholly from our hand any good work in which we are rejoicing. All other vices are to be feared in sins, but pride is to be feared even when we act rightly, lest those things which are done in a praiseworthy manner be lost owing to the desire for praise itself.

Ep. CXVIII, iii, 13-15, 22

63

The rational creature, whether in the form of an angelic spirit or of a human soul, has been so made that it cannot itself be the good by which it is made happy; but it is made happy if its mutability is changed into an immutable good, and if it turn away from this it is miserable. This turning away is its vice; its virtue is the turning towards this good. Our nature therefore is not evil of itself, since the creature is rational by the life of the spirit, even when deprived of that good the participation of which makes it happy, that is to say even when vicious it is better than that body which holds chief place among bodies, namely than this light which is perceived by the eyes of our flesh, since it too is itself a body. But incorporeal nature is superior to every body whatever it may be, and this not by its mass; for mass is a property of bodies alone, but by a certain force by which it rises to heights inaccessible to any and every notion drawn by the mind from the senses of the body. But just as among bodies those which are inferior such as earth and water and the air itself become better by participating in a superior body, that is when illumined by light and quickened by heat, so do incorporeal, rational creatures become better by participating in their Creator, when they unite themselves to Him by pure and holy charity. But if they are completely lacking in this they grow dark and in some fashion harden.

Ep. CXL, xxiii, 56.

64

There is nothing in man that appertains to his substance and nature, besides body and soul. . . . The Epicurean who places man's supreme good in the body, places his hope in himself. . . . It is not the virtue of thy soul that maketh thee happy, but He who hath given thee the virtue, who hath inspired thee to will, and hath given thee the power to do.

Serm. (*de script. Nov. Test.*) CL, iv, 5; vii, 8; viii, 9.

65

The striving after God is therefore the desire of beatitude, the attainment of God is beatitude itself. We seek to attain God by loving Him; we attain to Him, not by becoming entirely what He is, but in nearness to Him, and in wonderful and sensible contact with Him, and in being inwardly illuminated and occupied by His truth and holiness. He is light itself; it is given to us to be illuminated by that light.

De Mor. Eccl. I, xi, 18.

66

For if God is man's supreme good . . . it clearly follows, since to seek the supreme good is to live well, that to live well is nothing else but to love God with all the heart, with all the soul, with all the mind; and, as arising from this, that this love be kept entire and incorrupt, which is the part of temperance; that it give way before no troubles, which is the part of fortitude; that it serve no other, which is the part of justice; that it be watchful in its discernment of things lest deception or fraud steal in, which is the part of prudence. This is man's one perfection, by which alone he can succeed in attaining to the purity of truth.

De Mor. Eccl. I, xxv, 46.

67

Let therefore the rational soul in its mutable nature take the warning that without participation in the immutable good it is impossible for it to attain to justice, salvation, beatitude, and that of its own volition it will find not the good but the evil. Indeed left to itself it is turned away from the immutable good, and by that turning away it is corrupted. Nor can it of itself be made whole but only by the gratuitous mercy of its Creator, which makes it live by faith in this life and stablishes it in the hope of eternal salvation.

Ep. CXL, xxi, 14.

68

There is a nature which is mutable with regard to both space and time, such is the body. There is another nature which is in no way mutable with regard to space but only with regard to time, such is the soul. And there is a nature which is mutable with regard neither to space nor to time; this is God. . . . This highest is blessedness itself; the lowest is that which can be neither blessed nor wretched; the intermediate nature on the other hand lives in wretchedness when it inclines towards the lowest, in blessedness when it turns to the highest. He who believes in Christ does not set his affections on the lowest, nor does he take pride in the intermediate nature, and thus he is meet for union with the highest. And this is the sum of what we are commanded, admonished, and kindled to do.

Ep. XVIII, 2.

69

'Thou shalt love the Lord thy God with thy whole heart, and with thy whole soul, and with thy whole mind'; and 'thou shalt love thy neighbour as thyself' (Matt. xxii, 37, 39). Natural philosophy is here, since all the causes of all natural things are in God the Creator. Ethics are here, since a good and honest life is not formed otherwise than by loving as they should be loved those things which we ought to love, namely, God and our neighbour. Logic is here, since God alone is the truth and the light of the rational soul. Here too is laudable security for the commonwealth; for a state is neither founded nor preserved perfectly save in the foundation and by the bond of faith and of firm concord, when the highest common good is loved by all, and this highest and truest thing is God; when, too, men love one another in Him with absolute sincerity; since they love one another for His sake from whom they cannot hide the real character of their love.

Ep. CXXXVII, v. 17.

II. FAITH—UNDERSTANDING—VISION

I. FROM UNDERSTANDING TO FAITH

70

'Hearken, O daughter, and see' (Ps. xliv, 11). If thou
wilt not hearken, thou shalt not see. Hearken that thou mayest
purify thy heart by faith, as the Apostle says in the Acts of
the Apostles: 'purifying their hearts by faith' (Acts xv, 9).
For it is to this end we hearken to that which we are to believe,
before we see it, that by believing we may purify the heart,
whereby we may be able to see.

In Ps. XLIV, 25.

71

I wish to believe; teach me a reason why thou biddest me
believe. To such an one I answer and say, 'Man, how is it
that thou doest not wish me to bid thee believe? Thou art
full of evil desires. If I tell of those good things of Jerusalem,
thou takest them not in. Thou must be emptied of that wherewith thou art full, that thou mayest be filled with that whereof
thou art empty.' . . . But he will say, 'Tell me, sing to
me, give me the reason. Dost thou not wish me to learn?'
Thou hearest not with good intent; thou knockest not so as
to deserve that it be opened to thee. . . . Babylon beareth
thee; Babylon containeth thee; Babylon nourisheth thee;
Babylon speaks by thy mouth; thou canst take in nothing
save what glitters in time; thou knowest not how to meditate
on eternal things; thou takest not in what thou askest.

In Ps. CXXXVI, 10–11.

72

Therefore let us subject the soul to God, if we would subject
our body to obedience. . . . It is faith which first subdues

41

the soul to God; next, precepts concerning life, by observing which our hope is strengthened, and our charity nourished, and that begins to be visible, which before was only believed.

De ag. chr. xiii, 14.

73

It is no small part of knowledge to join thyself to Him who is knowledge. He hath the eyes of knowledge; have thou the eyes of a believing mind. That which God sees, be thou ready to believe.

In Ps. XXXVI, *Serm.* ii, 2.

74

He that believeth on me goeth into me; and he that goeth into me hath me.

In Joan. Evang. XXVI, 10.

75

And they shall be all taught of God. John vi, 45, 46. . . . All the men of that Kingdom shall be taught of God, not hear from men. Yea, even if they hear from men, within is it revealed, within doth it lighten. What is done by men who from without bring tidings? What am I doing at this moment while I speak? I do but pour into your ears a rumble of words. So unless He that is within reveal it, what is it that I say, or what do I speak? He that tendeth the tree is without, its creator is within. He that planteth and he that watereth worketh from without. This is what we do. 'Neither he that planteth is anything, nor he that watereth; but God that giveth the increase' (1 Cor. iii, 7). This is to say, 'they shall all be taught of God.' All? who? 'Everyone that hath heard of the Father, and hath learned, cometh to me.' See in what way the father draweth: He delights to do this by teaching, not by imposing a necessity upon men.

In Joan. Evang. XXVI, 7.

76

All these beautiful things which you see, which you love, He made. If these are beautiful, what is He Himself? If these are great, how great must He be? Therefore from those things which we love here, let us the more long for Him: that by that very love we may purify our hearts by faith, and His vision, when it comes, may find our hearts purified.

In Ps. LXXXIV, 9.

77

For since the divine power governs the whole of creation, spiritual and corporeal, the waters of the sea are summoned and poured out upon the face of the earth on certain days of every year. But when this was done at the prayer of the holy Elias, the divine power was manifest in the great showers of rain which so rapidly followed, and by which that miracle was granted and dispensed; because so long and so continuous a course of fine weather had gone before, and because in the very hour in which the servant of God prayed, the air itself had not by any aspect of moisture shown signs of the coming of rain (3 Kings xviii, 45). Thus, too, God works ordinarily in the case of storms of thunder and lightning; but because these were wrought in an unusual manner on Mount Sinai, and then sounds were not uttered with a confused noise, but so that it appeared by most sure proofs that certain signs were given by them, they were miracles (Exod. xix, 16). Who but God draws up the sap through the root of the vine to the bunch of grapes, and makes the vine? God, who while man plants and waters, Himself giveth the increase (1 Cor. iii, 7). But when at the command of the Lord water was turned into wine with extraordinary quickness, the divine power was made manifest by the confession even of the foolish (John ii, 9). Who but God ordinarily clothes the trees with leaves and flowers? But when the rod of Aaron the priest blossomed, the Godhead in some way conversed with doubting humanity (Num. xvii, 8). Again earthly matter certainly serves in common to the production and formation of wood of all kinds and of the flesh of animals; and who makes them but He who said, Let the earth bring forth these things (Gen. i, 24), and who governs and directs, by the same word of His, those things which He has created? But when He changed the same matter from the rod of Moses to the flesh of a serpent, immediately and quickly (Exod. iv, 3), that change, which was unusual, although of a thing that was changeable, was a miracle. But who is it that gives life to every living thing at its birth, save He who also gave life to that serpent at the moment at which there was need of it?

And who is it that restored their proper souls to the dry bones when the dead rose again (Ezech. xxxvii, 15 *sqq.*), but He who gives life to the flesh in the mother's womb, that those may come into being who yet must some time die? But when such things happen in as it were a continuous stream of ever-flowing succession, passing from the hidden to the visible, and from the visible to the hidden, by a regular and beaten track, then they are called natural; but when for the admonition of men they are intruded by an unusual form of change, they are called miracles.

De Trin. III, v–vi; 11.

78

Who would not be moved to faith by so remarkable an order of events from the beginning and by this concatenation of the ages, which makes the past credible by means of the present and in which the earlier things are confirmed by the later, the recent by the ancient? A man was chosen from the nation of the Chaldaeans, one endowed with great piety and faith, that to him might be given divine promises to be fulfilled after long centuries in the last days, and it is foretold to him that in his seed all nations shall be blessed (cf. Gen. xii, 2 *sq.*) This man, worshipping the one true God, the Creator of the universe, begets in his old age a son of a wife who through sterility and old age had wholly given up hope of bringing forth a child. From him there proceeded a very numerous people, which multiplied in Egypt whither it had been led from out of the East by divine disposition, continuing to increase according to the promises made and fulfilled. It was as a powerful nation that it was led out of Egypt with terrible signs and wonders, and the wicked peoples having been driven out before them, it was brought to the land of promise and established there and exalted to be a kingdom. Thereafter frequently offending the true God who had bestowed upon them so many benefits, by sin which had become rife among them and by sacrilegious enterprises, they were scourged by various disasters, and consoled by restored prosperity and their history is brought down to the incarnation and manifestation of Christ. And all the promises of this nation, its prophecies, its priesthood, its sacrifices, its temple, all its sacraments announced that this Christ, the Word of God, the Son of God, God himself, was to come in the flesh, was to die and to rise again and to ascend into heaven, that by the power of His name He would have multitudes in every nation consecrate to Him, and that those who believed in Him would have in Him remission of their sins and eternal salvation.

And Christ comes. All that the prophets had foretold is fulfilled in His birth, life, words, actions, sufferings, death, resurrection, and ascension (cf. Matt. i, 22). He sends the Holy Ghost and fills the faithful gathered together in one house (Acts ii, 2 *sqq.*) and waiting with prayers and ardent desire for this promised gift. Filled with the Holy Ghost they immediately speak with the tongues of all nations, they boldly refute errors, they preach the truths of salvation, they exhort men to penance for their past sinful lives, they promise indulgence by the divine grace. Apt signs and miracles follow their preaching of piety and of the true religion. Cruel unbelief is stirred up against them; they suffer the trials foretold to them; they look in trust for the blessings promised them; they teach what was appointed them to teach. Few in number they are scattered as seed throughout the world; they convert the peoples with marvellous ease; in the midst of enemies they grow in number: by persecution they increase in strength; faced with hardships and distress they spread their influence to the ends of the earth. From being very ignorant, despised, and few in number, they become enlightened, distinguished, and numerous, men of illustrious talents and of polished eloquence; they bring under the yoke of Christ the marvellous attainments of men remarkable for their intelligence, eloquence, and learning, and convert them to the work of preaching the way of holiness and salvation. Whether in adversity or prosperity they watchfully observe patience and self-control, and when the days of the world are reaching their close, their consummation testified by the calamities which attend them, these men, since these things also were foretold, wait only the more trustfully for the eternal beatitude of the celestial city. And throughout all this the unbelief of the heathen nations continues to rage against the Church of Christ, but she gains the victory by patient endurance and by the maintenance of unshaken faith in the face of the cruelty of his adversaries. The sacrifice of Him who is revealed truth, which long had been veiled under mystic promises, having taken place, those sacrifices by which it was prefigured are finally abolished by the destruction of the temple itself. The Jewish nation, condemned for unbelief, is rooted out of its own land and dispersed through every region of the world, that it might carry everywhere the Sacred Scriptures and that the testimony of the prophecies by which Christ and the Church were foretold, might be furnished by our adversaries, so that it could not be thought that these predictions had been forged by us to suit the time, in which prophecies too, the unbelief of these very Jews is foretold. The temples, idols, and impious rites of the heathen are gradually and in succession overthrown as had been foretold by the prophets. Heresies bud forth against the name of Christ though under the veil of His name, as had also been foretold, by which the doctrine of our holy religion is disturbed. All these things are now seen to be fulfilled in accordance with the predictions which we read; and these fulfilments are now so many and so great that they lead us to await with confidence fulfilment of the rest. What mind, then, thirsting for eternity, and troubled by the shortness of this present life, can resist the crowning light of this divine corroboration of our faith?

Ep. CXXXVII, iv, 15–16.

79

He restored to the blind those eyes which death was sure some time to close; He raised Lazarus from the dead, who was to die again. And whatever He did for the health of bodies, He did it not to the end that they should exist for evermore; whereas at the last He will give eternal health even to the body itself. But because those things which were not seen were not believed, by means of those temporal things which were seen He built up faith in those things which were not seen. Let no one therefore say that our Lord Jesus Christ doeth not those things

46

now, and on this account prefer the former to the present ages of the Church. . . .

The Lord did those things to invite us to the faith. This faith is now fervent in the Church which is spread throughout the whole world. And now He worketh greater cures, on account of which He disdained not then to exhibit those lesser ones. For as the soul is better than the body, so is the health of the soul a better thing than the health of the body. The blind body doth not now open its eyes by a miracle of the Lord, but the blinded heart openeth its eyes to the word of the Lord. The mortal corpse doth not now rise from the dead, but the soul which lay dead in a living body doth rise again. The deaf ears of the body are not now opened, but how many have the ears of their heart closed, which yet fly open at the penetrating word of God, so that they believe who did not believe, and they live well who lived evilly, and they obey who obeyed not, and we say, 'Such a man is become a believer'; and we wonder when we hear of them whom we had known as hardened. Why then dost thou marvel at one who now believes, and is living innocently, and serving God, but that thou dost behold him seeing, whom thou hadst known to be blind; dost behold him living, whom thou hadst known to be dead; dost behold him hearing, whom thou hadst known to be deaf?

Serm. (de Scrip. N.T.) LXXXVIII, i, 1 – iii, 3.

80

Even if there were no preceding testimonies concerning Christ and the Church, who is there whom the sudden shining of the divine brightness on the human race ought not to move to belief; when we see the false gods abandoned, their images everywhere shattered, their temples overthrown or converted to other uses, the many vain rites plucked out by the roots from the most inveterate usage of men, and the one true God invoked by all? And this has been brought about by one Man, who by men was mocked, seized, bound, scourged, smitten with the palm of the hand, reviled, crucified, and put to death. The disciples whom He picked out to set forth His teaching were of the common people, unlearned, fishermen, publicans, and it was they who, proclaiming His Resurrection and His Ascension, which they asserted that they had seen, and being filled with the Holy Ghost, sounded forth this Gospel in all tongues which they had not learned. And of those who heard them, part believed, part, believing not, fiercely withstood the preachers. And so by their fidelity even unto death for the truth; by their striving, not by returning evil but by steadfast endurance; by their victories, gained not by killing but by dying; the world was converted to this religion; and to this Gospel were converted the hearts of mortals, of men and women, of great and small, of learned and unlearned, of wise and foolish, of mighty and weak, of noble and ignoble, of high degree and low. And the Church, spread abroad throughout all nations, so increased, that even against the Catholic faith itself there arises no perverse sect nor any kind of error, which is found so to oppose itself to Christian truth, as that it affect not and go about to glory in the name of Christ. And such very error would not be suffered to spring up over the earth, were it not that its refutation exercises a wholesome discipline.

De fide rerum q. n. vid., vii, 10.

81

Give heed unto me, the Church says to you, give heed unto me, whom you see, although you be unwilling to see. For the faithful who were in those days in the land of Judæa, were present at, and learnt by being present, Christ's miraculous birth of a Virgin, His passion, resurrection, and ascension, and all His divine words and acts. These things you have not seen, and therefore you refuse to believe. Therefore regard these things, fix your minds on these things, ponder these things which you see, things which are not told you as things past, nor foretold as things future, but are shewn to you as things present. What? doth it seem to you a vain or a light thing, dost thou think it no divine miracle, or but a little one, that in the name of One Crucified the whole human race runs its course?

De fide rerum q. n. vid., iv, 7.

82

In the first place I wish you to understand that the Christian teaching does not hold that the Godhead was so absorbed by the flesh in which He was born of the Virgin, that He either relinquished or lost the governance of the universe. . . . The nature of the soul is far different from that of the body; how much more different must be the nature of God, who is the Creator of both soul and body? God is not said to fill the world in the sense that water, air, and even light fill space, so that with a greater or lesser part of himself He fills a greater or smaller part of the world. He is able to be everywhere present in entirety; He cannot be confined in any place; He can come without leaving the place where He was; He can depart without forsaking the place to which He had come.

The mind of man wonders at this, and because it cannot comprehend it, refuses, perhaps, to believe it. Let it not however go on wondering incredulously at the divine attributes without first wondering at the mysteries within itself. Let it, if it can, raise itself for a little above the body and above those things which it is wont to perceive through the bodily senses and let it contemplate what that is which uses the body as its instrument. . . . How does the soul, which lives nowhere but in a man's body, perceive things which are outside the limits of that body? . . . For it is not anywhere save in its own body, and yet it perceives things beyond the body. For wherever the soul sees anything, there it is exercising the faculty of perception, because seeing is an act of perception; and wherever it hears anything, there it is exercising the faculty of perception, because hearing is an act of perception. Hence the soul is either living in that place where it sees and hears, and consequently is itself in that place, or it exercises perception in a place where it is not living, or it is living in a place and yet at the same moment is not there. All these things are astonishing; not one of them can be stated without seeming absurdity; and we are speaking only of senses which are mortal. What, then, is the soul itself, which is beyond the bodily senses, that is to say, which resides in the intelligence whereby it considers these mysteries? For it is not by means of the senses that it forms a judgment concerning the senses themselves, and are we to suppose that something incredible is told us regarding the omnipotence of God, when it is affirmed that the Word of God, by whom all things were created, did so assume a body from the Virgin and manifest Himself with mortal senses, as neither to destroy His own immortality, nor to change His eternity, nor to diminish His power, nor to relinquish the governance of the world, nor to withdraw from the bosom of the Father, that is from the secret place where He is with Him and in Him?

There is, therefore, no reason to fear lest in the tiny body of His infancy God should seem to have suffered any deficiencies. For it is not in vast size but in power that God is great. In His providence He has given to ants and to bees senses superior to those given to asses and camels; He creates the huge proportions of the fig-tree from one of the minutest of seeds, although many smaller plants spring from much larger seeds; He has endowed the small pupil of the eye with a power which by one glance sweeps almost half the sky in a moment; from one central point in the brain He diffuses the whole fivefold system of nerves over the body; He dispenses vital motion throughout the whole body from the heart, a member comparatively small; and by these and other little things, He, who in small things is great, contrives that which is great from things which are exceedingly little. Such is the greatness of His power that he is conscious of no restraint in that which is restricted. It was this power which made fruitful the Virgin's womb, which associated with Himself a rational soul, and through it also a human body, in short, the whole human nature to be elevated by its union with Him, without His being thereby lowered in any degree; not disdaining to take from it the name of humanity while abundantly giving to it the name of divine. The body of the infant Child was brought from the womb of His mother ever virgin, by the same power which later introduced His man's body through the closed doors into the Upper Room (John xx, 26). Here, if the reason is sought, it will no longer be a miracle; if an example of a similar event is demanded, it will no longer be unique. Let us grant that to God some things are possible which we have to confess are beyond our comprehension. In such things the whole explanation of the work is the power of Him by whom it is wrought.

But in all the varied movements of the creature what work of God's is not wonderful? And yet these daily wonders have by familiarity become small in our esteem. Nay, how many common objects are trodden underfoot which, if carefully examined, amaze us! Take for example the property of seeds: who can either comprehend or declare the variety of species, the vitality, vigour, and latent power by which from small compass they set in motion great things? Now the human nature which He took upon Himself was created without seed by Him who in the realm of nature created seeds also from no pre-existing seeds. In the body which thus became His, He who, without any liability to change in Himself, united the order of all the centuries, was subject to the succession of the seasons and the ordinary stages of the life of man. For His body, as it began to exist at a point in time so it developed with the lapse of time. But the Word of God which was in the beginning and through which the ages of time were created, did not yield to time as bringing about the event of His incarnation, but chose the point of time at which He chose to take our nature upon Him. Human nature was brought into union with the divine; God did not withdraw from Himself.

There are some who insist on an explanation of the manner in which the Godhead was so commingled with man's nature as to constitute the one person of Christ, since this had to be done once, as if they themselves could explain how the soul is so united to the body as to constitute the one person of a man, an event which occurs every day. For just as the soul is united to the body in one person so as to constitute man, so God is united to man in one person so as to constitute Christ. . . . The former event takes place daily in the procreation of the human race; the latter took place once for the salvation of mankind. And yet of the two events, the combination of two immaterial substances ought to be more easily believed than a combination in which the one is immaterial the other material . . . and consequently the combination of the Word of God with the human soul is one which ought to be much more credible than that of soul with body. The latter is realized by us in ourselves, the former we are commanded to believe was realized in Christ. But if both of them were alike foreign to our experience, and we were enjoined to believe that both had taken place, which of the two would we men more readily believe?

Ep. CXXXVII, ii, 4 – iii, 11.

83

Whatever things were wrought in time with a view to producing faith, whereby we might be cleansed so as to contemplate truth, in things that have a beginning, which have been put forth from eternity and are referred back to eternity; these were either testimonies to the mission of the Son of God or they were this mission itself. But some of those testimonies announced Him beforehand as to come, some testified that He had already come. For that He by whom all creation was made was made a creature, must needs find a witness in the whole creation. For unless that one were preached by the apostolate of many, that one would not be accepted when the many were disbanded. And unless the testimonies were such as to appear great to the lowly, it would not be believed that He, being great, should make men great, who as lowly was sent to the lowly. For the heaven and the earth and all that is therein are incomparably greater works of the Son of God, since all things were made by Him, than the signs and portents which broke forth in testimony of Him. But yet men, that in their lowliness might believe these great things to have been wrought by Him, trembled at those lowly things, as if they had been great.

De Trin. IV, xix, 25.

84

The mysteries and secrets of the Kingdom of God first seek out believing men, that they may make them understand. For faith is understanding's step, and understanding is faith's reward. . . . To be sure thou dost see somewhat that thou mayest believe somewhat, and from that thou seest mayest believe what thou seest not. . . . God hath given thee eyes in the body, reason in the heart. Arouse the reason of the heart, awaken the interior inhabitant of thy interior eyes, let it take to its windows, let it examine God's Creation. . . . Believe on Him whom thou seest not because of those things which thou seest.

Serm. (de Script. Nov. Test.) CXXVI, i, 1; ii, 3.

85

Now a man begins to perceive grace from the time when, moved to faith by some interior or exterior admonition, he

begins to believe in God. . . . We see how men are moved to
believe, some one way some another by the selfsame proofs or
signs. For example, Simeon believed in Our Lord Jesus Christ
when still a babe (Luke ii, 25 *sqq.*), recognizing Him through
the revelation of the Holy Spirit. Nathaniel, to the one sentence
which he heard of His: 'Before that Philip called thee, when
thou wast under the fig tree, I saw thee,' answered 'Rabbi:
Thou art the Son of God. Thou art the King of Israel' (John i,
48 *sq.*). And it was but long afterwards that Peter confessed
this, and merited to hear that he was blessed, and that the keys of
the kingdom of heaven were to be given to him (Matt. xvi,
16 *sqq.*). By the miracle wrought in Cana of Galilee, when the
water was turned into wine, which is recorded by John the
Evangelist as the beginning of the signs which Jesus showed,
his disciples believed in Him (John ii, 11). Many He roused to
belief by His words, but many, on the other hand, did not
believe though the dead had been raised to life. Faced with
His cross and death His terrified disciples faltered, yet the
thief believed at a moment when he saw Him not pre-eminent
in His works and his superior, but his equal by the fellowship
of the cross (Luke xxiii, 40 *sqq.*). One even of the disciples
after His resurrection believed not so much the living members
of His body as the open wounds (John xx, 27). Many of the
number of those who crucified Him and had despised Him when
they saw Him working miracles, believed the disciples when they
preached Him and wrought the like miracles in His name
(Acts ii–iv). Since, therefore, one is moved to faith in one
way and another in another, and since the same thing told in
one way moves the hearer to faith, and in another does not, or
may move one but not another, who will dare to declare that
God is wanting in means of calling whom He will?

De diversis quaestionibus ad Simplicianum libri II.

86

If a man says to me, I would understand in order that I may
believe, I answer, Believe, that you may understand. . . .
'I would understand in order that I may believe.' Certainly,
what I am now saying, I say with the object that those may
believe who do not yet believe. Nevertheless unless they under-

stand what I am saying, they cannot believe. Hence what he says is in some part true, 'I would understand in order that I may believe.' And I, too, am right when I say, as does the Prophet (Is. vii, 9, *sec.* LXX), Nay, believe that thou mayest understand. . . . Understand, in order that thou mayest believe my words; believe, in order that thou mayest understand the word of God.

Serm. XLIII, iii, 4; vii, 9.

87

For though God teach inwardly, yet 'faith cometh by hearing: and how shall they hear without a preacher?' (Rom. x, 17, 14). For the fact that it is 'God that giveth the increase' (1 Cor. iii, 7) is no reason why we need not plant and water.

In Ps. CXVIII, *Serm.* xxxii, 4.

88

We are guided in a twofold way, by authority and by reason. In time, authority has the prior place; in matter, reason. . . . Thus it follows that to those desiring to learn the great and hidden good it is authority which opens the door. And whoever enters by it and, leaving doubt behind, follows the precepts for a truly good life, and has been made receptive to teaching by them, will at length learn how pre-eminently possessed of reason those things are which he pursued before he saw their reason, and what that reason itself is, which, now that he is made steadfast and equal to his task in the cradle of authority, he now follows and comprehends, and he learns what that intelligence is in which are all things, or rather what He is who is all things, and what beyond and above all things is their prime cause. But to this knowledge few attain in this life; and beyond it even after this life no one can progress.

Now the authority . . . which is true, firm, supreme is that which is called divine. . . . That authority is to be called divine which not only transcends all human capability, but, taking on the actual form of man, shows man to what depth It has condescended for man's sake; and enjoins him not to be bound by the senses, through which those miracles are seen, but to ascend from them to the intellect, at the same time demon-strating how great the things are of which it is here capable, why it does them, and how little store it sets on them. For its office is to teach its power by works, its clemency by humility, and its nature by the commandments it gives. And all these things by the holy rites in which we are initiated, are bestowed on us the more secretly and enduringly. And in these the life of good men is cleansed, not by vague disputations, but by the authority of the holy mysteries.

De ord. II, ix, 26, 27.

89

In the order of nature it holds that when we learn anything, authority precedes reasoning. For a reason may seem weak when, after it is given, it claims authority to support it. But because the minds of men are obscured by familiarity with darkness, which covers them in a night of sins and evil habits, and cannot perceive in a way proper to the clarity and purity of reason, there is most wholesome provision for bringing the faltering eye into the light of truth under the kindly shade of authority. But since we have to do with those who are unordered in all their thoughts and words and actions, and who are bent on nothing more than on beginning with argument, I will, as a concession to them, take what I think to be a wrong method in disputation. For it delights me to imitate, as far as I can, the gentleness of my Lord Jesus Christ, who took on Himself the evil of death itself, wishing to free us from it.

De mor. Eccl. I, ii, 3.

90

The medicine for the soul, too, which is effected by the divine providence and ineffable beneficence, is perfectly beautiful in degree and distinction. For it is divided between Authority and Reason. Authority demands of us faith, and prepares man for reason. Reason leads to perception and cognition, although authority also does not leave reason wholly out of sight, when the question of who may be believed is being considered. And certainly the supreme form of Authority is that of Truth already known and manifest. But because we are set here below among temporal things, and are kept away from eternal things by our love of them, there is a certain temporal medicine which calls to salvation not those who know but those who believe; and this is the first in order, not of nature and excellence but of time. For on whatever place one has fallen, on that place he must find support that he may rise again. Hence the effort must be made by means of those same carnal forms by which we are kept back, to arrive at an understanding of those forms of which the flesh tells us nothing.

De vera relig. xxiv, 45.

91

For what is believing but consenting to the truth of what is said? And this consent is certainly voluntary. . . . [But] the very will by which we believe is attributed to a gift of God, because it arises out of the free will which we received at our creation, . . . but also beca se God acts upon us by the suasion of our perceptions, so that we may will and believe, either externally, . . . or internally where no man can control what shall enter his mind, although it appertains to his own will whether to consent or to dissent. . . . It surely follows that it is God who both works in man the will to believe and in all things prevents us with His mercy. To yield our consent, however, to God's summons is . . . the function of our own will. . . . For the soul cannot receive and possess these gifts . . . except by yielding its consent. And thus whatever it possesses, and whatever it receives, is from God; and yet the act of receiving and possessing belongs, of course, to the receiver and possessor.

De spir. et litt. xxi, 54; xxxiv, 60.

92

This revealing is itself the drawing. Thou holdest out a green bough to a sheep and drawest it to thee. Nuts are shewn to a child and it is drawn. Even what the child runs to, he is drawn to: drawn by love for it, drawn without hurt to the body, drawn by the bond of the heart. If then, these things, which among earthly delights and pleasures are shewn to those that love them, draw them, . . . doth not Christ, revealed by the

Father, draw? What doth the soul more strongly desire than truth? For what ought it to have an avid appetite, with which to wish that within there may be a healthy palate to judge the things which are true, unless it be to eat and drink wisdom, righteousness, truth, eternity?

In Joan. Evang. XXVI, 5.

93

'No man can come to me, except the Father, who hath sent him, draw him.' (John vi, 44). . . . What is it we are saying here, brethren? If we are 'drawn' to Christ, then we believe against our will. But though it is possible for a man to come to church against his will, to approach the altar against his will, to receive the Sacrament against his will, yet it is impossible for him to believe, unless he is willing. . . . Hear the apostle: 'With the heart we believe unto justice' (Rom. x, 10). . . . Since then man believeth on Christ with the heart, which no man assuredly does against his will, and since he that is drawn seems to be as if forced against his will, how are we to solve the question? . . . Do not think that thou art drawn agains thy will; thy mind is drawn also by love. . . . If it was right for the poet to say, *Trahit sua quemque voluptas* (Virgil, Eclog. 2), 'each has his dear delight which draws him on'—not necessity but pleasure, not obligation but delight; how much more strongly we ought to say that a man is 'drawn' to Christ, if he delights in truth, delights in blessedness, delights in justice, delights in eternal life, all which Christ is. . . . Give me one that longs, give me one that hungers, give me one that is wandering in this wilderness and thirsting and panting for the fountain of his eternal home; give me such an one, and he will know what I would say.

In Joan. Evang. XXVI, 2., 4

94

It remains therefore that this faith is the source of all justice. . . . It is not to free will, so exalted by these gentry, nor to antecedent good works, since faith is the principle and origin of all merit, but to the gratuitous gift of God that we must attribute this faith. Faith, that is to say, is a true grace without any merit of ours; as the Apostle says: 'God hath divided to everyone the measure of faith' (Rom. xii, 3). Good works certainly are done by men, but faith is formed in man, without which those good works can be done by no man; 'for all that is not of faith is sin' (Rom. xiv, 23).

Ep. CXCIV, iii, 9.

II. FROM FAITH TO UNDERSTANDING

95

Understanding is the reward of faith. Therefore seek not to understand that thou mayest believe, but believe that thou mayest understand.

In Joan. Evang. XXIX, 6

96

We believed that we might know; for if we wished first to know and then to believe, we should not be able either to know or to believe.

In Joan. Evang. XXVII, 9.

97

If to believe were not one thing and to understand another, and unless we had first to believe the great and divine thing which we desire to understand, the Prophet would have spoken idly when he said, 'Unless you believe, you shall not understand' (Is. vii, 9, *sec.* LXX). Our Lord himself, too, by His words and deeds exhorted those whom He called to salvation, that they first believe. But afterwards, when He was talking of the gift which He would give to believers, did not say, 'this is eternal life, that they may believe,' but, 'this is eternal life: that they may know Thee, the only true God, and Jesus Christ whom Thou hast sent' (John xvii, 3). Furthermore He said to those who were already believers, 'Seek and you shall find' (Matt. vii, 7). For what is believed to be unknown cannot be called found, nor is any one capable of finding God, unless he first believe that he will eventually find Him. . . . That which we seek on His exhortation, we shall find by His showing it to us, so far as it is possible to such as us to find this in this life . . . and we must surely believe that after this life this will be perceived and attained more clearly and more perfectly.

De lib. arb. II, ii, 6.

98

And you shall know the truth (John viii, 32). . . . They did not believe because they knew, but they believed in order that they might know. For we believe in order to know, we do not know in order to believe. The thing we are to know 'eye hath not seen, nor ear heard, neither hath it entered into the heart of man' (1 Cor. ii, 9; Is. lxiv, 4). For what is faith but to believe what thou seest not? . . . It is truth; but as yet it is believed, not seen. If we continue in that which is believed we shall attain to that which may be seen.

In Joan. Evang. XL, 9.

99

It is for the sake of the interior eyes whose blindness consists in not understanding, that hearts are purified by faith (Acts xv, 9), that they may be opened and may be made more and more clear of vision. For although, unless he understand somewhat, no man can believe in God, nevertheless by the very faith whereby he believes, he is helped to the understanding of greater things. For there are some things which we do not believe unless we understand them, and there are other things which we do not understand unless we believe them. For since 'faith cometh by hearing; and hearing by the word of Christ' (Rom. x, 17), how can anyone believe him who preaches the faith if he (to say nothing of other points) does not understand the very tongue which he speaks? But unless, on the other hand, there were some things which we cannot understand unless we first believe them, the prophet would not say, 'If you will not believe, you shall not understand' (Is. vii, 9. *sec.* LXX). Our understanding therefore contributes to the comprehension of that which it believes, and faith contributes to the belief of that which it comprehends. And the mind itself, in proportion as these things are more and more understood, profits in the very comprehension of them.

In Ps. CXVIII, *Serm.* xviii, 3.

100

For faith has its eyes by which it in some way perceives to be true that which it does not yet see, and by which it very surely perceives that it does not yet see what it believes. Moreover, he who by true reason arrives at an understanding of what he had only believed is in a better state of advancement than he who still only desires to understand what he believes. If, however, he has not this desire and thinks that it is sufficient to hold fast to the faith without aspiring to an understanding, he ignores the true end and utility of faith. For as pious faith has no desire to exist without hope and without charity, it is needful that the faithful should believe what he does not yet see in such a way that he may hope for and love a vision of it.

Ep. CXX, ii, 8.

101

In that day you shall know that I am in my Father, and you in me, and I in you (John xiv, 20). What day shall this be but that of which He saith *and you shall live* (xiv, 19)? For then it shall be that we have power to see that which we believe. For even now He is in us and we in Him. Only, now we believe this, but then we shall also know Although even now we know by faith, but then we shall know by beholding. . . . At that day, therefore, when we shall live by that life whereby death shall be swallowed up, we shall know that He is in the Father, and we in Him, and He in us. For then shall be consummated that same thing which is already begun by Him, that He should be in us and we in Him. . . . 'I will love him and will manifest,' i.e. will love so that I may manifest. For now, He hath loved us to the end that we should believe and keep the commandment of faith; but then, He will love us to the end that we may see, and in seeing receive the reward of our faith. For even now we love by believing in that which we shall hereafter see; but then we shall love by seeing that which we now believe.

In Joan. Evang. LXXV, 4, 5.

102

It is by love that we must stand firm to that [good which is God] and adhere to it, in order that we may enjoy the presence

of that by which we are, and in the absence of which we could
not be at all. For since as yet 'we walk by faith and not by
sight' (2 Cor. v, 7), we certainly do not yet see God . . .
'face to face' (1 Cor. xiii, 12), whom, however, we shall
never see, unless we already love Him now. But who loves
what he does not know? It is of course possible for something
to be known and not loved; but I ask whether it be possible
for what is not known to be loved; since if it cannot, then no
one loves God before he knows Him. And what is it to know
God except to conceive Him and steadfastly perceive Him with
the mind? For He is not a body to be searched out by the
eyes of the flesh. Again, before we have the power to conceive
and perceive God, as he can be conceived and perceived—
for this is permitted to the clean of heart, since, 'Blessed are
the clean of heart: for they shall see God' (Matt. v, 8)—unless
He be loved by faith, it will not be possible for the heart to be
cleansed so that it may be apt and meet to see Him. For where
are those three things, for the building up of which in the mind
the whole apparatus of the divine Scriptures has been erected,
namely faith, hope, and charity (1 Cor. xiii, 13), except in
a mind believing what it does not yet see, and hoping and loving
what it believes? He therefore who is not known, but yet is
believed, can be loved. . . . Faith, therefore, avails to the
knowledge and to the love of God, not as though of one wholly
unknown or not loved at all, but to the end that He may be
known more clearly and loved more steadfastly.

De Trin. VIII, iv, 6; ix, 13.

103

'Not that we are sufficient to think anything of ourselves,
as of ourselves: but our sufficiency is of God' (2 Cor. iii, 5).
. . . No one indeed believes anything, unless he has first
thought that it is to be believed. For however suddenly, however
rapidly, some thoughts fly before the will to believe—and this
soon follows in such wise as to attend them, as it were, in closest
conjunction—it is yet necessary that everything which is believed
should be believed after thought has led the way; although
belief itself is nothing other than to think with assent. . . .
Every one who believes, thinks—both thinks in believing, and

believes in thinking. Therefore as to what pertains to religion and piety, . . . we are certainly not capable of believing anything of ourselves, since we cannot do this without thinking; but our sufficiency, by which we begin to believe, is of God. . . . Since if faith is not a matter of thought, it is of no account, and we are not sufficient to think anything of ourselves, but our sufficiency is of God.

De praed. sanct. II, 5.

104

God forbid that we should think that He hates in us that in which He has created us superior to the other animals. God forbid, I say, that we should believe there to be no need to accept or to seek a reason for what we believe, since it would not even be possible to believe if we had not rational souls. In certain matters pertaining to the doctrine of salvation, which we cannot yet understand but which some day we shall be able to do, it is right that faith should precede reason. Faith thus purifies the heart, rendering it capable of receiving and enduring the great light of reason. Thus it is reason itself speaking by the mouth of the prophet when he says: 'If you will not believe, you shall not understand' (Is. vii, 9. *sec.* LXX). By this the prophet has distinguished these two things and has counselled us to believe that we may at last attain to an understanding of what we believe. Thus it is seen to be reasonable that faith should precede reason. For if this precept is not reasonable, then it is unreasonable; which God forbid us from thinking. If, then, it is reasonable that faith precede reason to attain to certain great truths which cannot yet be understood, it is without doubt true that it is reason, in however small degree, that persuades us to it, so that reason itself precedes faith.

It is on this account that the Apostle St. Peter admonishes us to be 'ready always to satisfy every one that asketh you for a reason of that hope which is in you' (1 Pet. iii, 15). Thus if an unbeliever asks of me the reason of my faith and hope, and if I see that he is not capable of understanding before believing, I will give him this reason by which he may possibly understand, namely, how preposterous it is to demand before

believing the reason of those things which he cannot understand. But if a believer asks a reason, that he may understand
what he believes, his measure of intelligence must be considered
and a reason given within the limits of his comprehension,
so that he may add to his faith as much understanding as he
is capable of, seeing to it however that in attaining to the
plenitude and completion of knowledge he does not depart
from the way of the faith.

Ep. CXX, i, 3, 4.

105

There are three classes of credible things. Some there are
which are always believed, and never understood; such is all
history, ranging over the temporal doings of man. Others
are understood as soon as they are believed; such are all human
reasonings, whether on numbers or on any branch of science
,you please. Thirdly, there are those which are believed and
afterwards understood; such are those dealing with divine
things, which cannot be understood except by those who are
clean of heart; and this is brought about by the keeping of
the commandments, which are accepted as rules for right
living.

De div. quaest. XLVIII.

106

'Forgetting the things that are behind and stretched forth
towards those that are before' (Phil. iii, 13). . . . Perfection
in this life, he tells us, is nothing else than to forget those things
that are behind and of set purpose to stretch forth to those that
are before. For he has the safest purpose who seeks until that
is seized whither we are tending and to which we are stretching
forth. But that is the right intention which starts from faith.
For a sure faith is in some way the starting point of knowledge;
but a sure knowledge will not be perfected except after this
life, when we shall see 'face to face' (1 Cor. xiii, 12). Let
us therefore be thus minded, so as to know that the disposition
to seek the truth is more safe than that which presumes things
unknown to be known. Let us then so seek as if we were about
to find, and so find as if we were about to seek. For 'when a

man hath done, then beginneth he' (Ecclus. xviii, 6). Let us doubt without unbelief of things to be believed; let us affirm without rashness of things to be understood. Authority must be held fast to in the former, truth sought out in the latter. .

De Trin. IX, i, 1.

107

For such is the profundity of the Christian Scriptures, that even if I were to attempt to study them and nothing else from early boyhood to decrepit old age, with the utmost leisure, the most unwearying zeal, and greater talents than I have, I should still daily find something new in them. Not that there is any great difficulty in arriving at the things necessary to salvation from them, but when anyone has accepted these truths with the faith indisputable to a life of piety and uprightness, so many things which are obscured under manifold veils of mystery remain to be apprehended by those who are progressing in the study, and so great is the depth of wisdom not only in the words in which these have been expressed but also in the things themselves which are to be understood, that the experience of the oldest, the ablest, and the most eager students of Scripture illustrates what Scripture itself has said, namely, 'when a man hath done, then shall he begin' (Ecclus. xviii, 6).

Ep. CXXXVII, i, 3.

108

The depth of the word of God engages to the full the study thereof; it doth not refuse understanding. For if all things were closed, there would be nothing whereby what is obscure might be revealed. Again, if all things were hidden, there would be nothing whereby the soul could gather nourishment and get strength to enable it to knock at what was closed.

Serm. (*de Script. Nov. Test.*) CLVI, i, 1.

109

This rule must be observed, that what has not yet been made clear to our intellect, be nevertheless not loosened from the steadfastness of our faith.

De Trin. VIII, i. (Procemium).

110

Faith gives the understanding access to these things, unbelief closes the door on them.

Ep. CXXXVII, iv.

111

A right faith is the beginning of a good life, and to this also eternal life is due. Now it is faith to believe that which you do not yet see; and the reward of this faith is to see that which you believe. In the time of faith, therefore, as in a seeding time, let us not weaken. To the very end let us not weaken, but let us persevere until we gather that which we have sown.

Serm. XLIII, i, 1.

112

The pious believer is not yet fit to behold the light of Wisdom, and though he cannot be where Christ is not, yet he is not with Christ, at least not by sight. . . . *That they may see my glory* (John xvii, 24). . . . 'That they may see,' He is saying, that they may believe. For this is the reward of faith, not faith itself.

In Joan. Evang. CXI, 2, 3.

113

On account of those good things which God will only bestow upon the good, and because of those ills which will only be inflicted on the evil; since both will only be made manifest at the last end, God wishes us to believe in Him. For where is the reward of faith, where indeed the very name of faith, if thou now wishest to see, that thou mayest hold it? Thou shouldst not therefore see in order that thou mayest believe, but believe in order that thou mayest see: believe so long as thou dost not see, lest thou blush with shame when thou dost see. Let us therefore believe while the time of faith lasts, until the time of seeing comes. . . . We walk by faith, so long as we believe that which we do not see, but sight will be ours, when we see Him face to face, as He really is.

Serm. XXXVIII, ii. 3.

For what reward would there be for faith, if what we believed were not hid? But the reward of faith is to see that which we believed before we saw it; as the Scripture proclaims: 'the just man liveth by faith' (Rom. i, 17; Heb. ii, 4). There would then be no justice of faith unless that which we should believe when preached were hidden, and unless we reached the sight of it by believing. . . . Beloved, hear with attention what I am about to say. Since our justice is from faith, and our hearts are cleansed by faith, so that we may see that which we have believed—for both these things are set forth in Scripture: 'Blessed are the clean of heart, for they shall see God,' and 'Purifying their hearts by faith' (Matt. v, 8; Acts xv, 9). Since then this is the justice of faith, to believe what thou seest not, and by the very merit of faith to reach in its time unto sight, Our Lord in the Gospel, when He was promising the Holy Ghost, said this: 'He will convince the world of sin and of justice and of judgment'. . . . 'Of sin: because they believed not in me. And of justice: because I go to the Father: and you shall see me no longer' (John xvi, 8–10). This is justice, because Thou goest to the Father, and they shall no longer see Thee: For this is the justice of faith. For 'the just man liveth by faith'; and he liveth by faith when he seeth not that which he believeth. Since therefore it is the part of justice to live by faith, and no man liveth by faith, save by not seeing what he believeth, that He might create justice itself among men, that is, that they might believe what they do not see, He saith: 'Of justice: because I go to the Father: and you shall see me no longer.' This, He saith, shall be your justice, that you believe in Him whom you do not see, and, cleansed by faith, that you may hereafter, on the day of resurrection, see Him in whom you have believed.

In Ps. CIX, 8.

115

We shall see Him face to face, if we now see Him by faith. Let our faith have eyes, and its truth shall be displayed. Let us believe in Him whom we see not, and rejoicing we shall see, and we shall enjoy Him seen. . . . Prepare your hearts for this vision, prepare your souls for this joy; just as if God willed to shew the sun, He would warn us to make ready the eyes of the flesh. But because He deigneth to shew you the aspect of His Wisdom, prepare the eyes of the heart. 'Blessed are the clean of heart: for they shall see God.'

In Ps. XCVII, 3.

III. WISDOM AND KNOWLEDGE

116

Beasts are able to perceive things corporeal from without through the bodily senses and to fix them in the memory, and remember them, and in them to seek after things advantageous and to shun things which are unsuitable. But to note those things, and to retain them, not only as seized upon naturally but also as deliberately committed to memory, and, when they are actually slipping away into oblivion, to recreate their impress by recollection and thought; in order that as the conception is formed from that which the memory exhibits, so also this very thing which the memory retains may be made lasting by thought; to combine again imaginary objects of vision by taking this or that of what is kept in the memory, and as it were by tacking them on to one another, to examine how it is that in this class similitudes of the true are to be distinguished from the true, and this not in spiritual things but in actual bodily things;—these acts, and the like, although performed in reference to things sensible, and those which the mind has deduced through the bodily senses, yet, as they are not uncombined with reason, are not common to men and beasts. But it is the part of the higher reason to judge of these corporeal things according to incorporeal and eternal considerations, which, if they were not above the human mind, would certainly not be immutable. And yet, unless something of our own were subjoined to them, we should not be able to employ them as standards by which to judge of corporeal things. But we judge of corporeal things from the rule of dimensions and figures, which the mind knows to persist immutably. But that faculty of our own which is thus concerned with the treatment of corporeal and temporal things, is indeed rational, in that it is not common to us with the beasts, but is drawn, as it were, out of that rational substance of our mind, by which we depend upon and adhere to the intelligible and immutable truth, and which is deputed to handle and direct the inferior things. . . . It is clear, that when we live according to God, our mind, which is intent on the invisible things pertaining to Him, ought to be progressively informed by His eternity, truth, charity, but that something of our own rational purpose, that is, of the same mind, must be directed to the using of mutable and corporeal things, without which this life does not go on; but that we be 'conformed to this world' (Rom. xii, 2), by setting such good things as our goal, and by divesting the desire for the blessed state to them, but that whatever in the using of temporal things, we may do it with the contemplation of attaining eternal things, passing lightly over the former, but cleaving to the latter.

De Trin. XII, ii, 2 – iii, 3; xiii, 21.

117

The action by which we make good use of temporal things differs from the contemplation of eternal things, and the former is classed as knowledge, the latter as wisdom. . . . 'Behold piety is wisdom; but to abstain from evil things is knowledge' (Job xxviii, 28). In this distinction it must be understood that wisdom pertains to contemplation, knowledge to action. For in this place he meant by piety the worship of God, which in Greek is called θεοσέβεια . . . . And what is there in eternal things more excellent than God, of whom alone the nature is immutable? And what is the worship of Him but the love of Him, by which we now desire to see Him, and believe and hope that we shall see Him; whom, in proportion as we progress, 'we see now through a glass in a dark manner; but then' in a manifestation. For this is what the Apostle Paul means by 'face to face' (1 Cor. xiii, 12). This is also what John says: 'Dearly beloved, we are now the sons of God: and it hath not yet appeared what we shall be. We know that when He shall appear we shall be like to Him: Because we shall see Him as He is' (1 John iii, 2). Discourse on these and like subjects seem to me to be the very discourse of wisdom. But to abstain from evil things, which Job says is knowledge, is without doubt of temporal things,

since it is in time that we are among the evil things from which
we ought to abstain, in order that we may come to those good
things which are eternal. And therefore, whatsoever we do
prudently, steadfastly, temperately, and justly, pertains to that
knowledge or discipline whereon our action depends in avoiding
evil and desiring good, as does also whatever we gather by the
cognition resulting from research in the way of examples to
be guarded against or imitated, and in the way of necessary
proofs respecting any object appropriate to our use.

When a discourse then relates to these things, I hold it to be
related to knowledge and one to be distinguished from a discourse relating to wisdom, to which those things pertain which
neither have been, nor shall be, but are; and on account of that
eternity in which they are, are said to have been, and to be, and
to be about to be, without any mutability of times. For neither
have they been of such kind as that they should cease to be, nor
will they in the future be of such kind as if now they were not;
but they always have had and always will have the same absolute
being. And they abide, not as if fixed in space as bodily substances
are; but as intelligible things in incorporeal nature they are as
much present to the eye of the mind as things visible or tangible
in space are to the senses of the body. And there are not only
intelligible and incorporeal reasons of sensible things posited in
space which persist, quite apart from their actual locality in
space, but there are also like reasons, themselves certainly intelligible and not sensible, of motions transient in time which
hold, quite apart from any transit of time. To attain to these
with the eye of the mind is given to few; and when they are
attained so far as is possible, he who attains to them does not
abide in them, but is as it were held off by the recoil of the
mind's eye, and thus the act of thought relating to an object not
transitory becomes transitory. And yet this transient thought
is committed to the memory through the discipline by which the
mind is trained; so that the mind which is compelled to leave the
subject may be able to return to it again; although if it should
not return to the memory and find there what it had committed
to it, it would be led thereto like an uninstructed person, as it
had been led before, and would find it where it had first found
it, that is to say, in that incorporeal truth, whence it may once

more be as it were written down and fixed in the memory. For man's thought does not remain on, for example, the incorporeal and immutable property of a square body in the same way as that property itself persists in it; if indeed the mind could arrive at it without the notion of enclosed space. Again, if one were to apprehend the ordered rhythm of certain transient artistic and musical sounds extending over a period of time, that tune, though now resting without time in some secret and profound silence, can still be thought as long as it can be heard by the mind. Yet what the glance of the mind, transient though it was, caught from it and stored in the memory, after so to speak gulping it down, this it will be able to ponder in some measure by recollection, and transfer what it has thus learned into a systematic shape. But if this has been blotted out by absolute forgetfulness, yet once again under the guidance of discipline, one will always come to that which had altogether dropped away, and it will be found such as it was. . . .

If therefore this is the right distinction between wisdom and knowledge, that the intellectual cognition of eternal things pertains to wisdom, but the rational cognition of temporal things to knowledge, it is not difficult to judge which is to be esteemed more and which less. But if another method of discrimination should be employed by which to know these two apart which the Apostle teaches are indubitably different, saying, 'To one indeed, by the Spirit, is given the word of wisdom; and to another, the word of knowledge according to the same spirit' (1 Cor. xii, 8); still the difference between the two which we have laid down is a most evident one, in that the intellectual cognition of eternal things is one thing, the rational cognition of temporal things another; and no one doubts that the former is to be preferred to the latter.

De Trin. XII, xiv, 22–23; xv, 25.

118

John the Evangelist thus began his gospel: 'In the beginning was the word: . . . and the word was made flesh.' This whole passage . . . contains in its earlier portions what is immutable and eternal, the contemplation of which makes us blessed; but in those that follow, eternal things are mentioned in conjunction with temporal things. And hence some things there pertain to knowledge, some to wisdom. . . . Now the words, 'In the beginning was the word: and the word was with God: and the Word was God. The same was in the beginning with God. All things were made by him: and without him was made nothing that was made. In him was life: and the life was the light of men. And the light shineth in the darkness: and the darkness did not comprehend it,' require a contemplative life and must be discerned by the intellectual mind, and the more anyone shall have progressed in this life, the wiser without doubt he will become. But because of the words, 'the light shineth in the darkness: and the darkness did not comprehend it,' faith certainly was needed, whereby that that which was not seen might be believed. For by 'darkness' he intended us to understand the hearts of mortals turned away from light of this kind, and hardly able to behold it. And for this reason he adds, 'There was a man sent from God, whose name was John. This man came for a witness, to give testimony of the light, that all men might believe through him.' But have we come to a thing that was done in time, and this pertains to knowledge, which is limited by the cognition of facts. Now we think of the man John under that image which is impressed on our memory from our general notion of human nature. And whether men believe or not, they think this in the same manner. For both alike know what man is, the outer part of whom that is, his body, they have learned through the eyes of the body; while of the inner, that is, the soul, they possess the knowledge within themselves, since they also are men, and through intercourse with men; so that they are able to picture what is said, 'there was a man, whose name was John,' because they know the ideas conveyed both from hearing them and from speaking of them. But as to what is also in the same sentence, 'sent by God,' this those who accept it at all, accept it by faith. And those who do not accept it by faith, either hesitate through doubt or deride it through unbelief. Yet both, if they are not of the number of those utter fools, who say in their hearts, 'there is no God' (Ps. xiii, 1), when they hear these words, picture both things, namely, what 'God' is, and what 'sent by God' is. And if they do not do this as the things themselves really are, they do it at any rate as far as their ability allows.

Furthermore, we know from other sources the faith which a man sees to be in his own heart if he believes, or not to be there if he does not believe. But we do not know it as we know corporeal things, which we see with our bodily eyes, and picture to ourselves even when they are absent through the images of them which we retain in the memory; nor yet as things which we have not seen, and which in some way or other we give shape to in thought from those which we have seen, and commit them to memory, so that we may recur to them when we will, in order that similarly we may discern them there by recollection, or rather discern their images, whatever these be, that we have fixed there; not again as a living man, whose soul we do not, it is true, see, but conjecture from our own, and from movements of the body contemplate also in thought the living man, in the form that we have learnt him by seeing him. Faith is not thus seen in the heart in which it is by him whose property it is, but most certain knowledge holds it secure, and conscience proclaims it. Although we are bidden to believe for the reason that we cannot see what we are bidden to believe, nevertheless we see that faith in ourselves when it is in us, because faith even in absent things is present, and faith in things which are without us is within us, and faith in things which are not seen is itself seen, and itself none the less is created in the hearts of men in time.

De Trin. XIII, i, 2–3.

119

. . . So that the knowledge of things divine is perfectly called wisdom, and that of things human is properly given the name of knowledge; . . . not indeed so as to attribute to this knowledge everything that can be known by man about human things, wherein there is exceeding much of empty vanity and mischievous curiosity, but only those things by which that most health-giving faith which leads to true blessedness is begotten, nourished, defended, strengthened. But in this knowledge most of the faithful are not strong, however exceeding strong in the faith itself they be. For it is one thing to know only what man ought to believe in order to attain to a blessed life, which must be eternal; but another to know in what way this belief may both help the pious and be maintained against the impious, which last the Apostle seems to call by the special name of knowledge. And when I was speaking of this knowledge before, . . . I showed also that faith respecting things eternal is itself a temporal thing, and dwells in time in the hearts of believers, and yet is necessary in order to attain these same eternal things (Lib. XIII, vii). I argued also that faith respecting the things temporal which He that is eternal did and suffered for us as man, which manhood He bore in time and carried on to things eternal; and that the virtues themselves, whereby in this temporal and mortal life men live prudently, bravely, temperately, and justly, are not true virtues, unless they are referred to that same faith, temporal though it is, which leads on nevertheless to things eternal.

De Trin. XIV, i, 3.

III. ETERNAL SEARCH FOR THE ETERNAL GOD

120

For this name of God by which He is called could not but be known to every creature, even to all nations, before they believed on Christ. For such is the power of true Godhead that it cannot be altogether and utterly hidden from the rational creature, once it makes use of its reason. For, with the exception of a few in whom nature is excessively depraved, the whole human race confesses God to be the author of the world.

In Joan. Evang. CVI, 4.

121

For when that one God of gods is thought of, even by those who suppose that there are other gods whether in heaven or on earth, and call to them and worship them, thought takes the form of an attempt to conceive something than which nothing more excellent or more sublime exists. . . . All concur in believing God to be that which excels in dignity all other objects.

De doct. christ. I, vii, 7.

122

The whole nature of the universe about us, to which we also belong, proclaims that it has a most excellent Creator, Who has given to us a mind and natural reason, whereby to see that things living are to be preferred to things not living, things that have sense to things that are insensible, things that have understanding to things that have not, things immortal to things mortal, things powerful to things impotent, things just to things unjust, things beautiful to things unsightly, things good to things evil, the incorruptible to the corruptible, the immutable to the mutable, the invisible to the visible, the incorporeal to the corporeal, things happy to things miserable. And hence, since without doubt we place the Creator above created things, we must needs confess that He both lives in the highest sense, and perceives and understands all things, and that He cannot die, or suffer corruption, or be changed; and that He is not a body but a spirit; of all the most powerful, the most just, the most beautiful, most good, most blessed.

De Trin. XV, iv, 6.

123

Thou hast created us for Thyself, and our heart knows no rest, until it may repose in Thee.

Conf. I, i, 1.

124

With a hidden goad Thou didst urge me, that I might be restless until such time as the sight of my mind might discern Thee for certain.

Conf. VII, viii, 16.

125

Too late am I come to love Thee, O thou Beauty, so ancient and withal so new; too late am I come to love Thee. And behold, Thou wert within me, and I without; and there made I search for Thee, and in a deformed manner I cast myself upon the things of Thy creation, which yet thou hadst made fair. Thou wert with me indeed, but I remained not with Thee. Those things withheld me from Thee, which yet, if they had not their being in Thee, would not be at all. Thou didst call and cry out, and so didst break through my deafness. Thou didst shine forth and glow refulgent, and so didst chase away my blindness. Thou didst breathe thy fragrance upon me, and I drew in my breath, yet do I pant after Thee. I tasted thee, and still I hunger and thirst for more. Thou didst but touch me, and I do even burn with a desire to enjoy Thee.

Conf. X, xxvii, 38.

126

'Seek ye God, and your soul shall live' (Ps. lxviii, 33). It is because He is hidden that he must be sought in order to be found; and being found He must still be sought because of His immensity. ∴ . . . For He satisfies the seeker in the measure of his capacity and He makes the finder to have greater capacity so that he may again seek to be filled when his ability to receive has grown.

In Joan. Evang. LXIII, 1.

127

What is the meaning of 'Seek His face evermore' (Ps. civ, 4)? I know indeed that 'it is good for me to adhere to my God' (Ps. lxxii, 28); but if He is ever being sought, when is He found? Did the Psalmist mean by 'evermore' the whole of the life we live here, whence we become conscious that we ought thus to seek, since even when found He is still to be sought? True, faith hath already found Him, but hope still seeketh him. But charity hath both found Him through faith, and seeketh to have Him by sight, where He will then be found so as to satisfy us, and no longer to need our search. For unless faith found Him in this life, it would not be said, 'Seek ye the Lord'; and when you have found Him, 'Let the wicked forsake his way and the unjust man his thoughts' (Is. lv, 6 *sq.*). Again, if when found by faith He were not still to be diligently sought, it would not be said: 'But if we hope for that which we see not, we wait for it with patience' (Rom. viii, 25), and that which John saith: 'We know that when He shall appear we shall be like Him: because we shall see Him as He is' (1 John iii, 2). Or when we shall have seen Him face to face as He is, will He still have to be sought, and to be sought for evermore because to be loved for evermore? For we say to any one present, 'I am not looking for you,' meaning, I do not like you. And thus he who is loved is sought even when present, while there is constant charity which busies itself that he never become absent. Besides, he who loveth any one even when he seeth him, without ever being tired of him, wisheth him ever to be present, that is, he always seeketh his presence. And truly this is the sense of the words 'Seek His face evermore,' meaning that finding should not end that seeking by which love is testified, but with the increase of love the seeking of the found One should increase.

In Ps. CIV, 3.

128

'Let the heart of them rejoice that seek the Lord. Seek ye the Lord and be strengthened: seek his face evermore' (Ps. civ,

3 *sq.*). Now that which is evermore being sought seems as though it were never found. How then will the heart of them that seek rejoice, and not rather be saddened, if they cannot find what they seek? For the Psalmist does not say, 'Let the heart of them rejoice' that find, but 'of them that seek the Lord.' And yet the prophet Isaias testifies that the Lord God can be found if He is sought, when he says, 'Seek ye the Lord, and as soon as you have found Him, call upon Him. And when He hath drawn near to you, let the wicked forsake his ways and the unjust man his thoughts' (Is. lv, 6 *sq.*). If then when sought He can be found, why is it said, 'Seek His face evermore'? Is He perhaps to be sought even when found? For incomprehensible things must be investigated in such a way that no one may think he has found nothing, when he has been able to find how incomprehensible is that which he was seeking. Why then does he thus seek; if he comprehends that that which he seeks is incomprehensible, unless it be that he may not cease from seeking so long as he is making progress in his actual inquiry into things incomprehensible, and becomes better and ever better while seeking so great a good, which is both sought in order to be found, and found in order to be sought? For it is both sought that it may be found the more sweetly, and found that it may be sought the more eagerly. What is said in the book of Ecclesiasticus may be taken in this sense, when Wisdom says 'they that eat me shall yet hunger: and they that drink me shall yet thirst' (Ecclus. xxiv, 29). For they eat and drink because they find; and, because they hunger and thirst, they still continue seeking. Faith seeks, understanding finds; whence the prophet saith, 'If you shall not have believed, you shall not understand' (Is. vii, 9 *sec.* LXX). And again, understanding still seeks Him whom it finds; for 'God hath looked down upon the children of men, to see if there be any that understand and seek God' (Ps. xiii, 2). And man, therefore, ought to have understanding to this end, that he may seek God.

De Trin. XV, ii, 2.

129

God by deferring our hope, stretches our desire; by the desiring, stretches the mind; by stretching, makes it more capacious. . . . Let us therefore desire, for we shall be filled. Let us stretch ourselves unto Him, that when He shall come, He may fill us. 'For we shall be like to Him: because we shall see Him as He is' (1 John iii, 2).

In Epist. Joannis ad Parthos, Tr. v, 7.

130

The Psalmist said to God, 'My soul is as without water unto thee' (Ps. cxlii, 6), my soul thirsteth for Thee. It thirsteth, it is parched, it is separated from the waters of the sea. It does not notice that it is not yet separated from the body; desire has already made the separation. . . . But God knows what the parched soul longs for; that is lying hidden in a secret place. Desires for the sea, that is worldly desires, are visibly apparent. . . . But as to him who longs for God, his desire is hidden, since God, whom he longs for, is hidden.

Serm. fragm. P. L. xxxix, 1725.

131

I confess then, that I attempt to be one of those who write because they have made some progress, and who, by means of writing, make further progress. If, therefore, through inadvertence or want of knowledge, anything has been stated by me which may with good reason be condemned, not only by others who are able to discover this, but also by myself—for if I am making progress I ought, at least after it has been pointed out, to see it—such a mistake is not to be regarded with surprise or grief, but rather forgiven and be a cause of congratulation, not because an error was made but because it was renounced. For there is an extravagant perversity in the self-love of a man who desires others to be in error that his error may remain undiscovered.

Ep. CXLIII, 2.

132

When men seek God and strain their minds to the capacity of human weakness to arrive at an understanding, having learnt by experience the wearisome difficulties of the task, whether from the eye itself of the mind striving to gaze upon light unapproachable, or indeed from the manifold and various modes of speech employed in the Sacred Writings, wherein, as it seems to me, the mind is nothing else but exhausted, in order that when glorified by the grace of God it may find sweetness; such men, I say, when, after every ambiguity has been dispelled, they have arrived at something certain, ought of all others most easily to make an allowance for those who go astray in the investigation of so great a mystery. But there are two things most hard to bear with in the case of those who are in error, namely, hasty assumption before the truth has been made plain, and, when it has been made plain, defence of the falsehood thus hastily assumed.

De Trin. II, 1. (Procemium)

133

Let those rage against you who know not what labour is needed to discover the truth, and how difficult it is to avoid errors. Let those rage against you who know not how rare and hard it is to overcome the imaginings of the flesh by the serenity of a pious mind. Let those rage against you who know not the difficulty of giving health to the eye of the inner man that he may be able to gaze upon his Sun, . . . that Sun, of which it is written through the Prophet, 'the Sun of justice hath arisen upon me' (Mal. iv, 2), and of which it is said in the Gospel, 'that was the true light, which enlighteneth every man that cometh into this world' (John i, 9). Let those rage against you who know not with what sighs and groans the least particle of understanding about God can be acquired. And, last of all, let those rage against you who have never been ensnared by such an error as they see you to have been ensnared.

Contra Ep. fund. ii, 2.

134

Thou canst assuredly see how much it would have profited thee if thou hadst only known how to be ignorant in that which thou dost not know, and how this profit is still open to thee. For if understanding pleases thee so much in human nature—and truly, if our nature were without it, we should not differ from brute beasts, so far as our souls are concerned—understand what it is that thou dost not understand, lest thou understand nothing, and do not despise any man who, in order that he may truly understand, understands that he does not understand that which he does not understand.

De anima et eius origine IV, xi, 15.

135

We are speaking of God; is it any wonder if thou dost not understand? For if thou dost comprehend, He is not God. Let there be pious confession of ignorance rather than a rash profession of knowledge. To reach to God by the mind in any measure is a great blessedness; but to comprehend Him is altogether impossible. God is an object for the mind; He is to be understood. A body is an object for the eyes; it is to be seen. But dost thou think to comprehend a body by the eyes? . . . Of whatever thou lookest at thou dost not see the whole. . . . What eye of the heart then comprehendeth God? Enough that it reach to Him if the eye be pure. But if it reach, it reacheth by a sort of incorporeal and spiritual touch, yet it doth not comprehend; and that, only if it be pure. And man is made blessed by touching with the heart that which ever remaineth blessed, and that is this very eternal blessedness and that eternal life, whereby man is made to live; that perfect wisdom, whereby he is made wise; that eternal light, whereby man becomes enlightened. And mark how by this touch thou art made what thou wast not, but thou dost not make what thou touchest to be what it was not before. I repeat, God hath no increase from them that know Him, but they that know Him increase by their knowledge of God.

Serm. (*de Script. N. T.*) CXVII, iii, 5.

136

Whatever man may think, that which is made is not like Him who made it. . . . God is ineffable. We can more easily say what He is not than what He is. Thou thinkest of the earth; this is not God: thou thinkest of the sea; this is not God: of all things which are on the earth, men and beasts; this is not God: of all things which are in the sea, which fly through the air; this is not God: of whatever shines in the sky, the stars, the sun, and the moon; this is not God: of heaven itself; this is not God. Think of the Angels, Virtues, Powers, Archangels, Thrones, Principalities, Dominations; this is not God. What is He then? I could only tell thee what He is not. Dost thou ask what He is? 'Eye hath not seen, nor ear heard: neither hath it entered into the heart of man' (1 Cor. ii, 9; Is. lxiv, 4). Why seekest thou that that which hath not risen up to the heart should rise up to the tongue?

In Ps. LXXXV, 12.

137

What then, brethren, shall we say of God? For if thou hast been able to understand what thou wouldest say, it is not God. If thou hast been able to comprehend it, thou hast comprehended something else instead of God. If thou hast been able to comprehend Him as thou thinkest, by so thinking thou hast deceived thyself. This then is not God, if thou hast comprehended it; but if this be God, thou hast not comprehended it. How therefore wouldest thou speak of that which thou canst not comprehend?

Serm. (de Script. N.T.) LII, vi, 16.

138

In this consideration of creation . . . let the soul ask itself: Who made all these things? Who created them? Who made among them thyself? What are these things which thou art considering? What art thou thyself who art considering them? Who is He who made them to be considered and thee to consider? Who is He? Name Him. That thou mayest name Him, ponder Him. . . . That thou mayest imagine Him, approach Him. For whatever thou dost wish to see clearly, . . . thou dost approach in order to gaze upon it, that thou mayest not be deceived by seeing it afar off. But as those bodies are seen by the eyes, so is He seen by the mind, He is striven for by the heart and is seen. And where is the heart by which He may be seen? 'Blessed,' He saith, 'are the clean of heart: for they shall see God' (Matt. v, 8). . . . But . . . I have observed the whole of creation, as far as I could, I have contemplated the bodily creation in heaven and on earth, and the spiritual in myself who am speaking, who set in motion my limbs, who exert my voice, move the tongue, pronounce words, and distinguish sensations. And when do I understand myself in myself? How then can I comprehend what is above myself? And yet the sight of God is promised to the human heart; . . . and this is the counsel of Scripture: Prepare the means of seeing what thou lovest before thou try to see it. . . . In proportion as charity increaseth in thee, forming and restoring thee to the likeness of God, it extendeth unto thine enemies; that thou mayest be like unto Him who maketh His sun to rise, not only upon the good, but upon the good and upon the evil; and sendeth rain, not only on the just, but on the just and unjust. The nearer thou approachest unto His likeness, the more dost thou advance in charity, and the more thou beginnest to perceive God. . . . All things are as present to the blind as to the seeing. A blind man and one who hath sight, standing on the same spot, are each surrounded by the same forms of things; but one is present to them, the other absent, . . . not because the things themselves approach the one and recede from the other, but on account of the difference of their eyes. . . . Thus also is God everywhere present, everywhere whole. . . . What then dost thou wish to see? What thou dost wish to see is not far from thee. . . . 'In Him we live and move and are' (Acts xvii, 28). . . .

Be therefore like Him in piety, and earnest in meditation; 'for the invisible things of him . . . are clearly seen, being understood by the things that are made' (Rom. i, 20). . . . If thou art unlike, thou wilt turn back; if like, thou wilt exult. And when, being like Him, thou shalt have begun to approach Him, and to feel God, the more charity increaseth in thee, 'for God is charity' (1 John iv, 8), thou wilt perceive somewhat which thou wast trying to say, and yet couldst not say. . . . All other things may be described in some way. He alone is ineffable Who spoke, and all things were made. For He spoke, and we were made (Ps. xxxii, 9); but we cannot describe Him. His Word, by whom we were uttered, is His Son. He was made weak, that He might be spoken by us, however weak.

In Ps. XCIX, 5-6.

139

Have I spoken of God or sounded His praise in any worthy way? Nay, I feel that I have done nothing more than desire to speak, and if I have said anything, it is not what I desired to say. How do I know this, but from the fact that God is ineffable? But what I have said, if it had been ineffable, could not have been spoken. Hence God is not even to be called ineffable, because to say even this is to speak of Him. Thus there arises a curious conflict of words; for if the ineffable is that which cannot be spoken, it is not ineffable if it can be spoken of as ineffable. And this conflict of words is rather to be avoided by silence than to be reconciled by speech. And yet God, although nothing worthy of Him can be spoken, has deigned to accept the worship of men's mouths and has desired us through the medium of our own words to rejoice in His praise. For it is on this principle that He is called *Deus* (God). For the sound of these two syllables in itself conveys no true knowledge of His nature; but yet all who know the Latin tongue are led, when the sound of them reaches their ears, to think of a nature supreme in excellence and eternal.

De doct. christ. I, vi, 6.

140

All things can be said of God, yet is nothing worthily said of God. Nothing is wider than this utter want. Thou seekest a name befitting Him and findest none; thou seekest in what way soever to speak of Him and thou findest Him all things.

In Joan. Evang. XIII, 5.

141

. . . God of whom we ought always to be thinking, and of whom we are not able to think worthily, in praise of whom blessing must at all times be rendered (Ps. xxxiii, 1), and whom no speech is sufficient to declare. . . .

De Trin. V, i, 1.

142

For God is more truly thought than expressed; and He exists more truly than He is thought.

De Trin. VII, iv, 7.

'For I have known that the Lord is great' (Ps. cxxxiv,
5). With mind soaring to the heights, raised above the flesh,
transcending the creature, the Psalmist knew that the Lord
is great. Not all can know by seeing, let them praise what He
hath done. '[the Lord] is sweet; the Lord hath chosen Jacob
unto Himself: Israel for His own possession' (*id.*, 3, 4). Hence
thou also praise Him. For further, 'I have known that the
Lord is great.' The Prophet spoke who entered into the Sanctuary of God, who heard ineffable words which it is not granted
to man to utter (2 Cor. xii, 4), who told what could be said
to man, who kept to himself what could not be told. Let him
then be heard as far as we can, and believed when we cannot.
Let him be heard as far as we can, 'For the Lord hath chosen
Jacob unto Himself: Israel for His own possession.' Let him
be believed as far as we cannot, for he himself knows 'that the
Lord is great.' If we should say to him, explain to us, we pray
thee, His greatness; would not his answer perhaps be: He
whom I see is not so very great if He can be explained by me?
Let him return to His works and tell us. Let him have in his
conscience the greatness of God, which he hath seen, which
he hath commended to our faith, whither he could not direct
our eyes, and enumerate some of the things which the Lord
hath done here; that unto us, who cannot see His greatness
as he can, He may become sweet through those works of His
which we can comprehend.

In Ps. CXXXIV, 9.

144

You have striven perchance to see the Good of all good,
the Good from which all good things come, the Good without
which nothing is good, and the Good which is good without
other things. You have striven to see it, and perhaps in straining
the sight of your minds, you have found yourselves wanting.
This I gather from myself, for such are my feelings. But if there
be anyone, as may be, and well may be, stronger in this mental
sight than I, who fixes the gaze of his heart for long on that
which is, let him praise as he can, let him praise as we can not.
Still, thanks be to Him, Who hath tempered His own praise,

. . . so that both strong and weak may assay it. For in the mission of His servant Moses, when He said, 'I AM WHO AM' and 'Thus shalt thou say to the children of Israel: HE WHO IS hath sent me to you' (Exod. iii, 14); since it is difficult for the human mind to conceive the fact of His special being, and a man was sent to men, though not by man; forthwith God tempered His praise and said this of Himself which could sweetly be apprehended. He would not abide in that praise which the worshipper could not attain to. 'Go,' said He, 'tell the children of Israel: the God of Abraham, the God of Isaac, and the God of Jacob hath sent me to you. This is my name for ever' (ibid., 15). Truly, O Lord, Thou hast that former name, for Thou hast also said, 'I AM: HE WHO IS, hath sent me to you'; why didst Thou forthwith change Thy name so as to say, the God of Abraham, the God of Isaac, and the God of Jacob? Does not the reason of it seem to you to answer and say, that I said, 'I AM WHO AM,' is true, but thou dost not comprehend it; that I said, 'I am the God of Abraham, the God of Isaac, and the God of Jacob,' is true, and thou dost understand it. That I AM WHO AM, belongs to Me; but that I am the God of Abraham, the God of Isaac, and the God of Jacob, belongs to thee. And if thou art unable to see what I am to Myself, understand what I am to thee. . . . In Abraham, Isaac, and Jacob understand His whole Church, understand the whole seed of Israel. . . . 'And if you be Christ's, then are you the seed of Abraham' (Gal. iii, 29).

In Ps. CXXXIV, 6, 7.

145

There are some who attempt to transfer to things incorporeal and spiritual the ideas they have formed from corporeal objects whether through the experience of the bodily senses, or by natural human wit and diligent quickness; so as to seek to measure and conceive of the former by the latter. Others, again, frame whatever sentiments they may have concerning God, according to the nature and affections of the human mind. . . . Yet a third class strive indeed to transcend the whole creation, which assuredly is mutable, in order to raise

85

their thought to the immutable substance, which is God; but encumbered by the burden of mortality, wishing to appear to know what they do not and unable to know what they wish to know, they preclude themselves from entering the very way of understanding by an over bold affirmation of their own presumptuous opinions. . . .

In order, therefore, that the human mind might be purged from falsities of this kind, Holy Scripture, which suits itself to babes, has not avoided words from any class of things actually existing, through which, as by nourishment, our understanding might gradually rise to things divine and transcendent. For, in speaking of God, it has both used words taken from things corporeal, . . . and it has borrowed many things from the spiritual part of creation, whereby to signify that which indeed is not so, but must needs so be said. . . . For divine Scripture is wont to frame, as it were, allurements for children from the things which are found in creation; whereby, according to their measure, and as it were by steps, the affections of the weak may be moved to seek those things which are above, and to abandon those things that are below. But divine Scripture rarely employs those things which are properly said of God, but are not found in any creature, as, for instance, that which was said to Moses; 'I AM WHO AM,' and 'HE WHO IS, hath sent me to you' (Exod. iii, 14). For, since body and soul are also said in some sense to *be*, Holy Scripture certainly would not so express itself unless it meant to understand *be* in some special sense of the term. So too in the case of what the Apostle said: 'Who only hath immortality' (1 Tim. vi, 16); since the soul also is said to be, and is, in a certain manner immortal, it would not say 'only hath,' unless because true immortality is immutability, which no creature can possess, since it belongs to the Creator alone. . . .

Further, it is difficult to contemplate and fully to know the substance of God, who fashions mutable things, yet without any change in Himself, and creates temporal things, yet without any temporal movement in Himself. Hence it is necessary to purge our minds, in order to be able to see ineffably that which is ineffable. And, since we have not yet attained to this, we are nourished by faith, and are led by such ways as are more suitable to our capacity, that we may be rendered apt and able to comprehend it.

De Trin. I, i, 1–3.

146

Although God . . . is ineffable and cannot in any way be spoken of by man to man except by the use of certain terms involving space and time, whereas He antecedes all time and all space; nevertheless He, who created, is nearer to us than many things which were created; 'for in Him we live and move and are' (Acts xvii, 28). Now of these things very many are remote from our mind on account of the dissimilarity of their species; for they are corporeal things. Nor is our mind itself competent to see them in God, in the actual relations in which they were created, so that we may know by this their number and magnitude and degree, even if we do not see them through the bodily senses. For they are remote from our bodily senses, either because they are far off, or because they are inaccessible to our sight or touch owing to the interposition or opposition of alien bodies. Thus it happens that there is greater labour to find them than there is to find Him by whom they were made; for there is incomparably greater happiness for the pious mind in perceiving Him in particles however small, than to grasp them in their entirety.

De Gen. ad litt. V, xvi, 34.

147

For when it is said that God knows us, He gives us a knowledge of Himself so that we may thus understand that we owe this knowledge of Him not to ourselves but to His mercy. And so the Apostle has said in a certain passage: 'But now, after that you have known God,' and corrects this by adding: 'or rather are known by God' (Gal. iv, 9). What can the Apostle wish to be understood by this save that God Himself has given us a knowledge of Himself? But no one knows God except he understand that He is the sovereign and immutable good, by participation in which he is made good. . . . 'He made us, and not we ourselves' (Ps. xcix, 3). But this must not be applied to that nature by which we are men, for God is the creator of this nature, as He is of the heavens and the earth and the stars and of all living things, but rather to that other creation of which the Apostle says: 'For we are His workmanship, created in Christ Jesus in good works, which God hath prepared that we should walk in them.'

Ep. CXL, XXXV, 81.

148

But yet, when I love Thee, what is it that I love? Not the beauty of any body, not the order of time, not the clearness of this light that so gladdens our eyes, not the harmony of sweet songs of every kind, not the fragrancy of flowers, or spices of aromatical odours, not manna, nor honey, nor limbs delightful to the embrace of flesh and blood. Not these things do I love, in loving my God. Yet do I love a kind of light, a kind of voice, a kind of odour, a kind of food, a kind of embracing, when I love my God, who is the light, the voice, the odour, the food, the embracing of my inward man; when-that light shineth into my soul which is not circumscribed by any place, when that voice soundeth which is not snatched away by time, when that odour pours forth which is not scattered by the air, when that food savours the taste which is unconsumed by eating, when that embracement is enjoyed which is not divorced by satiety. This it is which I love, when I love my God.

Conf. X, vi, 8.

149

If to any man the tumult of the flesh be silent, if phantasies of earth and air and sea be silent also, if the poles of heaven be silent, and the very soul of man be silent to itself, and by not-thinking pass beyond itself, if all dreams be silent and all such things as be revealed by the imagination, if every tongue and every sign and everything that hath its existence by passing-on be silent wholly unto any man—since all these things proclaim to him that hath an ear to hear, 'He made us and not we ourselves,' and He endureth for ever (cf. Ps. xcix, 3, 5)—if then, having uttered this, they too be silent, as fastening their attention upon Him that made them; if then He only speak, not by them but by Himself, that we may hear His word, not by tongue of flesh, nor voice of angel nor by the sound of a cloud that is broken by thunder, nor by the dark riddle of a similitude, and we may hear Him, whom in these things we love, Himself apart from them—like as we two did now stretch ourselves up, and in swift thought lay hold a little upon the eternal wisdom, that abideth above all things—if this were to continue and all other visions, in order far inferior, might be withdrawn, and this alone might so transport and swallow up and wrap him who beheld it in those intrinsical joys, so that his life might be for all eternity such as was this moment of understanding, which we did so ardently sigh after; would not this be that whereof is written, 'Enter thou into the joy of thy Lord'? (Matt. xxv, 21).

Conf. IX, x, 25.

150

If anyone supposes that with man, living, as he still does, in this mortal life, it may be possible for him to dispel and clear off every obscurity induced by corporeal and carnal fancies, and to attain to the serenest light of immutable truth, and to cleave constantly and unswervingly to this with a mind wholly estranged from the course of this present life, that man understands neither what he asks, nor who he is that is putting such a supposition. . . . If ever the soul is helped to reach beyond the cloud by which all the earth is covered (cf. Ecclus. xxiv, 6), that is to say, beyond this carnal darkness with which the whole terrestrial life is covered, it is simply as if he were touched with a swift coruscation, only to sink back into his natural infirmity, the desire surviving by which he may again be raised to the heights, but his purity being insufficient to establish him there. The more, however, anyone can do this, the greater is he; while the less he can do so the less is he.

De cons. Evang. IV, X, 20.

IV. WAS—SHALL BE—IS

1. IS

151

May the Lord therefore console thee, that thou mayest 'see the good things of Jerusalem' (Ps. cxxvii, 5). For these good things *are*. Why *are* they? Because they are everlasting. Why *are* they? Because the King is there, I AM WHO AM (Exod. iii, 14). But these good things here are and are not, for they endure not; they slip away, they flow by. Thy children are little; thou dost caress the little ones, the little ones caress thee. Do they abide thus? But thou wishest them to grow, thou wishest their age to increase. But look, when one age is approaching, another is dying. When boyhood cometh, infancy dieth; when old age cometh, manhood dieth; when death cometh, every age dieth. As many successions of ages as thou wishest for, so many deaths of ages dost thou wish for. These things therefore *are* not. Again, are children born to thee to share life with thee on earth, or rather to shut thee out and to succeed thee? Dost thou rejoice in those born to shut thee out? For boys when born speak somewhat in this wise to their parents: 'Now then, begin to think of removing hence, let us too play our part on the stage.' For the whole life of struggle of the human race is a play on a stage; for it is said, 'All things are vanity: every man living' (Ps. xxxviii, 6). Yet, if we rejoice in children who will succeed us, how much must we rejoice in children with whom we shall remain for ever, and in that Father, Who will not die, for Whom we are born, so that we may live with Him for evermore? These are the good things of Jerusalem, for they *are*.

In Ps. CXXVII, 15.

152

For as a torrent is gathered together by the rains, and over-flows, roars, runs, and by running runs down, that is finishes its course; so is all this course of mortal life. Men are born, they live, they die, and when some die others are born, and when these die others again are born, they follow one another, they come, they go, and do not remain. What is permanent here? What is there that doth not run its course? What is there that is not on the way to the abyss as if it had been gathered together from rain? For as a river suddenly drawn together ffrom rain, from the drops of showers, runneth into the sea and is seen no more, nor was it seen before it was collected from the rain; so this human race is collected together from hidden sources, and floweth on, and at death again travelleth to hidden places. This intermediate state soundeth and passeth away.

In Ps. CIX, 20.

153

Which way soever the soul of man turneth, unless towards Thee, it is affixed to pain; yea though it fasten upon delightful creatures, which are .both outside Thee and outside itself. Which . . . by how much the more speedily they grow to be, by just so much the more do they hasten not to be; . . . for they are but parts of things, which exist not all together but, by departing and succeeding, do all constitute one whole, whereof they are the parts. . . . But in those things it cannot repose, for, instead of remaining, they fly away; and who is he that can follow them with his bodily sense? Yea, or who can overtake them, even when they are near at hand?

Conf. IV, x, 15.

154

These days have no true being; they are gone almost before they arrive; and when they come they cannot continue; they press upon one another, they follow the one the other, and cannot check themselves in their course. Of the past nothing is called back again; what is yet to be expected is something which will pass away again; it is not as yet possessed, whilst as yet it is not arrived; it cannot be kept when once it is arrived.

The Psalmist therefore asks, 'what is the number of my days' (Ps. xxxviii, 5), what *is*, not what is *not*; and (for this confounds me by a still greater and more perplexing difficulty) both *is* and *is not*. For we can neither say that that *is*, which does not continue, nor that it *is not* when it is come and is passing. It is that absolute IS, that true IS, that IS in the strict sense of the word, that I long for, that IS which is in the Jerusalem which is the bride of my Lord, where there shall be no death, where there will be no failing, where the day shall not pass away but shall endure, a day which no yesterday precedes nor a morrow ousts. This number of my days, which *is*, I say, make Thou known to me.

In Ps. XXXVIII, 7.

155

Are the years wherein we are eternal, or those wherein our forefathers have been, or those wherein our posterity are to be? . . . Behold we speak and say, 'in this year'; and what have we got of this year, save the one day wherein we are? For the former days of this year are already gone by, and are not to be had; but the future days are not yet come. We are in one day, and we say in this year. Say rather 'to-day,' if thou wouldst speak of anything in the present. For of the whole year what hast thou got that is present? Whatsoever thereof is past, is no longer; and whatsoever is future is not yet. How then, 'this year?' Amend the expression: say, 'to-day.' Thou speakest truth, henceforth I will say 'to-day.' Again, mark this also, how the morning hours are already past, the future hours are not yet come. This, too, therefore, amend, and say, 'in this hour.' And of this hour what hast thou got? Some moments thereof are already gone by, those that are future are not yet come. Say, 'in this moment.' In what moment? While I am uttering syllables, if I shall speak two syllables, the second does not sound until the first is gone by. In fine, in that same one syllable, if it chance to have two letters, the second letter does not sound until the first is gone by. What then have we got of these years? These years are mutable; the eternal years must be in our thoughts, years that stand; years that are not made up of days that come and depart;

years whereof in another place the Scripture saith to God: 'But Thou art always the self-same: and Thy years shall not fail' (Ps. ci, 28).

In Ps. LXXVI, 8.

156

What is *the same*, save that which *is?* What is that which *is?* That which is everlasting. For what is always different at different times, is not, because it abideth not. Not that it altogether is not, but is not in the highest sense. And what is that which *is*, save He who when He sent Moses, said unto him, I AM WHO AM (Exod. iii, 14)? . . . That 'city which is compact together' (Ps. cxxi, 3) partaketh in His stability. Justly therefore he who runneth thither, since he is made a partaker in its stability, saith: 'Our feet were standing in thy courts, O Jerusalem' (Id., 2). For all things stand where nought passeth by. Dost thou too wish to stand there and not to pass by? Run thither. Nobody hath *the same* from himself. Mark this, brethren: the body that he hath is not *the same*, for it standeth not in itself. It is changed with each period of life, it is changed by change of place and time, it is changed through diseases and wastings of the flesh. It standeth not therefore in itself. The celestial bodies stand not in themselves; they have certain changes of their own, though hidden ones; they are certainly changed from place to place; they ascend from the East to the West, and again go round to the East. They therefore stand not, they are not *the same*. Nor doth the human soul itself stand. For with how many changes and imaginations is it altered! By how many pleasures is it changed! By what powerful lusts is it lacerated and torn asunder! Man's mind itself, which is called rational, is mutable, is not *the same*. At one time it wisheth, at another it wisheth not; at one time it knoweth, at another it knoweth not; at one time it remembereth, at another it forgetteth: therefore no one hath *the same* from himself. He who wished to have *the same* from himself, perished; the angel fell and became a devil. The devil pledged the man in a cup of pride; in envy he threw down together with himself him who was standing. These have wished to be *the same* unto themselves; they wished

93

to be princes and lords over themselves, they have been unwilling
to recognize the true Lord, who truly is *the same*, to whom it
was said: 'Thou shalt change them, and they shall be changed.
But thou art always the self-same' (Ps. ci, 27 *sq.*). Let therefore
the humbled soul, after so much weariness, so many ills, difficulties, toils, return unto itself; and let it be in that 'city which
is compact together. . . .'

For in himself man is not, for he is changed and altered if
he participate not in Him Who is *the same*. He *is* when he
seeth God. He is when he seeth Him WHO IS; and by seeing
Him WHO IS, he also according to his measure beginneth
to be. . . . The fulness of delight and the sufficiency of riches
is God Himself, Himself *the same*, Himself in whom the city
is compact together. This will be our abundance also. But
whence? Through charity.

In Ps. CXXI, 5, 6, 8, 12.

157

For every day in this time so comes as to cease to be; every
hour, every month, every year—nothing of these is stationary.
Before it hath come, it is to be; after it hath come, it will not
be . . . [In God] nothing is past, as if it were no longer;
nothing is future, as if it existed not as yet. Whatever is there,
simply *is*.

In Ps. CI, *Serm.* ii, 10.

158

Anything whatsoever, no matter how excellent, if it be
mutable has not true *being;* for true being is not to be
found where there is also *non-being*. Whatever hath in it
the possibility of change, being changed is not what it was.
If that which was is not, a kind of death hath taken place there;
something that was there, and is not, has been destroyed.
. . . Something is changed and is that which was not. I
see there a kind of life in that which is, and death in that which
has been. . . . Examine the mutations of things and thou
wilt everywhere find 'has been' and 'will be.' Think on God
and thou wilt find 'is' where 'has been' and 'will be' cannot
be.

In Joan. Evang. XXXVIII, 10.

159

The more thou lovest *being*, the more wilt thou yearn for eternal life, and wilt long to be so formed that thy affections be not temporal, burnt in and stamped by the love of temporal things; which temporal things before they are, are not; and when they are, pass away; and when they are passed away, will not be. And so when they are future, they not yet are; and when past, they no longer are. How then shall they be held so that they remain, when their beginning, that they may be, is their passing on, that they not be? But he who loves being, approves these things in so far as they are, and loves that which ever is. And if he was inconstant in his love of the former, he will be strengthened in his love of the latter; and if he wasted himself in the love of transitory things, he will be confirmed in the love of what endures; and he will stand fast and attain to that very being, which was the object of his will when he feared the not-being, and, entangled as he was in the love of fugitive things, could not stand firm.

De lib. arb. III, vii, 21.

160

Being is a term for immutability. For all things that are changed cease to be what they were, and begin to be what they were not. True being, pure being, real being has no one save Him who does not change. He has it to whom is said, 'Thou shalt change them, and they shall be changed. But Thou art always the self-same' (Ps. ci, 27 *sq.*). What does 'I AM WHO AM' (Exod. iii, 14) mean but 'I am Eternal?' What does 'I AM WHO AM' mean but 'I cannot be changed?' . . . Since then this is the name of eternity, it is more than that name which He deigned to have, that of Mercy. 'I am the God of Abraham, the God of Isaac and the God of Jacob' (*ibid.*, 15). The first He is in Himself; the second He is turned towards us. For if He willed only to be that which He is in Himself, what should we then be? If Moses understood, nay, because he understood, when it was said to him, 'I AM WHO AM,' . . . he believed how much this concerned man, but he saw how far removed from men this was. For he who has properly understood what that is which truly is, and has in whatsoever way been touched by the light of the supremely true essence, even though but momentarily, as by a flash, sees himself far beneath it, far removed from it, far different from it. . . . As though he were despairing because of his great unlikeness to the excellence of that essence, God, seeing his fear, heartened him in his despair, and it is as though He said: Because I said, 'I AM WHO AM,' . . . thou didst understand what Being is, and thou hast despaired to grasp it. Take hope, 'I am the God of Abraham, the God of Isaac, and the God of Jacob'; thus I am what I am, thus I am Being itself, thus I am with Being itself, so that I may not will to be wanting to men. . . . Let us therefore ineffably praise His essence and love His mercy.

Serm. vii, 7.

161

As wisdom is so called from that quality which is being wise, and knowledge from knowing, so from being (esse) comes that which is called essence. . . . Hence the only immutable substance or essence is He who is God, to whom certainly Being itself (whence comes the term essence) most especially and truly belongs. For that which is changed does not retain its own being, and that which can be changed, though it be not actually changed, is able not to be that which it had been. And therefore that which not only is not change, but also is even incapable of being changed at all, alone falls most truly and indubitably under the category of Being.

De Trin. V, ii, 3.

162

For being in the highest sense of the word is that which ever continues the same, which is throughout like itself, which cannot in any part be corrupted or changed, which is not subject to time, which admits of no variation in its present as compared with its condition at any other time. This is being in its truest sense. For in this significance of the word being there is implied a nature which is self-contained and which endures immutably. This can be said only of God, to whom there is nothing contrary, strictly speaking. For the contrary of being is non-being.

De mor. Eccl. II, i, 1.

163

God always is, nor has He been and is not, nor is but has not been, but as He never will not be; so He never was not.

De Trin. XIV, xv, 21.

164

For what hath any being, save only because Thou art?

Conf. XI, v, 7.

165

For all substance that is not a created thing is God, and all that is not created is God.

De Trin. I. vi, 9.

II. SIMPLE

166

All that is body is certainly composed of parts. . . . For heaven and earth are parts of the whole bulk of the universe; and the earth by itself, and the heaven by itself is composed of innumerable parts. . . . And in each several body size is one thing, colour another, shape another; for the same colour and the same shape may remain with the magnitude diminished; and the same shape and the same size may remain with the colour changed; and the shape may not remain the same, yet the body may be just as large and coloured in the same way. . . . The spiritual creature also, that is, the soul, is indeed if compared with the body the more simple of the two, but if we omit the comparison with the body, it is manifold, and even it is not simple. For it is on this account more simple than the body, that it is not diffused in bulk through extensions in space, but in each body it is both whole in the whole, and whole in each several part of it; and therefore, when anything takes place in any small particle whatever of the body such as the soul can feel, although it does not take place in the whole body, yet the whole soul feels it, since the whole soul is conscious of it. Nevertheless, since in the soul also it is one thing to be skilful, another to be indolent, another to be intelligent, another to be of retentive memory; and since cupidity is one thing, fear another, joy another, sadness another; and since things innumerable and in innumerable ways are to be found in the nature of the soul, some without others, and some more, some less, it is manifest that its nature is not simple but manifold. For nothing simple is mutable; but every creature is mutable.

Now God is truly called in manifold ways great, good, wise, blessed, true, and whatsoever thing seems to be not unworthy to be said of Him; yet his greatness is the same as His wisdom, for He is not great by bulk but by power; and His goodness is the same as His wisdom and greatness, and His truth is the same as all those things; and in Him it is not one thing to be blessed, and another to be great, or wise, or true, or good, or to be wholly Himself.

De Trin. VI, vi, 8; vii, 8.

167

Other things that are called essences or substances admit of accidents, whereby a change, whether great or small, is produced in them. But there can be no accident of this kind in respect of God: and therefore He who is God is the only immutable substance or essence, to whom certainly Being itself, whence is derived the term essence, most especially and most truly belongs.

De Trin, V, ii, 3.

168

That which begins to be spoken of God in time, and which was not spoken of Him before, is manifestly said of Him relatively; yet not according to any accident of God, so that anything should have happened to Him, but clearly according to some accident of that, in respect to which God begins to be called something relatively.

De Trin. V, xvi, 17.

169

There there is primal and absolute life, in which it is not one thing to exist and another to be, but the same thing to be and to exist; and primal and absolute intelligence, in which it is not one thing to be living, another to understand, but to understand is to live, and is to be, and all things are one, like as . . . the knowledge of the omnipotent and wise God, full of all immutable laws of living, and all one in it, as itself it is one with one, with whom it is one. Therein God knew all things which He made by it; and therefore, while ages pass away and succeed one another, nothing passes away or succeeds to the knowledge of God. For things which are created are not known by God for the reason that they have been made; rather is it that they have been made, though they be mutable, because they are known immutably by Him.

De Trin. VI, x, 11.

170

For our mind is mutable; since it takes in by learning what it once knew not, and loses by unlearning what once it knew. And it is deceived by a semblance of truth into approving the false for the true, and by its own dimness, by a kind of darkness as it were, it is hindered from attaining to the true. Hence this is not a substance most truly simple, because here 'to be' is not the same as 'to know,' it can 'be' and yet not 'know.' But to that divine substance this is not possible because what it has it is. Hence it has not knowledge in such sort that the knowledge whereby it knows is one thing and the essence whereby it exists another, but both are one. Nor ought that to be called 'both' which is simply one.

In Joan. Evang. XCIX, 4.

171

In the human mind, assuredly, to be is not the same as to be strong, or prudent, or just, or temperate; for a mind can *be* and yet have none of these virtues. But in God to be is the same as to be strong, or to be just, or to be wise, or whatever you may say of that simple multiplicity or manifold simplicity, whereby His substance may be signified.

De Trin. VI, iv, 6.

172

That which is the knowledge of God is itself also His wisdom, and that which is His wisdom is itself His essence or substance; because, in the marvellous simplicity of that nature, it is not one thing to be wise and another to be, but to be wise is to be.

De Trin. XV, xiii, 22.

173

It is called simple because it is what it has, with the exception of the relation of the Persons to one another, for therein the Father has a Son, yet is not Himself the Son, and the Son a Father, yet is not Himself the Father. But in consideration each of itself, the quality and essence is both one therein, as each lives, that is, has life and is itself life. . . .

According to this, then, they are called simple things that are truly and in principle divine, because their quality and substance do not differ, nor are they divine or wise or blessed by partaking of other things. For the rest the Spirit of understanding is called in Holy Scripture manifold because its powers are many (cf. Wis. vii, 22), but all one with the essence and all included in one.

De civ. Dei XI, x, 1, 3.

174

As the one God is called great, good, eternal, omnipotent, so can He himself be called His own deity, His own greatness, His own goodness, His own eternity, His own omnipotence.

De Trin. V, xi, 12.

175

Man is one thing, in that he is; another, in that he can. For sometimes the man *is*, yet cannot what he wills, sometimes he *is* in such manner that he can what he would. Consequently his 'esse' is one thing, his 'posse' another. If with him the 'esse' and the 'posse' were the same, what he 'would' he 'could.' But with God it is not so that His substance 'to be' is one thing and His power to 'can' another. Whatever is His and whatever He is is consubstantial with Him, because He is God. It is not so that He in one way 'is' and in some other 'can.' He has the 'esse' and the 'posse' together, because to will and to do he has together.

In Joan. Evang. XX, 4.

176

For He is a certain form, a form not formed, but the form of all things formed; a form immutable, without flaw, without decay, without time, without place, surpassing all things, being in all things, at once a kind of foundation on which they are and a headstone under which they are.

Serm. (de Script. N. T.) CXVII, ii, 3.

III. WHOLE

177

On earth, a fountain is one thing, light another. Thirsting, thou seekest a fountain and that thou mayest come to the fountain thou seekest light . . . that fountain is the light itself; to the thirsty a fountain; to the blind light. Let the mouth of the heart be opened that it may drink of the fountain. That which thou drinkest thou seest, thou hearest. God becomes everything to thee, for he is to thee the whole of those things which thou lovest.

In Joan. Evang. XIII, 5.

178

Peace shall be thy gold. Peace shall be thy silver. Peace shall be thy life. Peace shall be thy God. Peace shall be to thee whatsoever thou dost desire. For here what is gold cannot be silver to thee; what is wine cannot be bread to thee; what is light to thee cannot be drink to thee. Thy God shall be all to thee. Thou shalt eat of Him so that thou shalt never hunger. Thou shalt drink of Him so that never more shalt thou thirst. Thou shalt be illumined by Him, so that thou shalt be no more blind.

Thou shalt be stayed by Him, so that thou shalt not fail. He shall possess thee whole, entire, Himself whole, entire. Thou shalt not be straitened for room in dwelling with Him with whom thou dost possess all. Thou shalt possess the whole of Him, and He shall possess the whole of thee also; for thou and He shall be one, which one He who possesses you shall possess the whole.

In Ps. XXXVI, *Serm.* i, 12.

179

This good and that good: take away the 'this' and 'that,' and regard good itself, if thou canst. Thus wilt thou see God, not good by a good other than Himself, but the good of all good. For in all these good things, whether those which I have enumerated, or any others that may be discerned or imagined, we could not say that one was better than another, if we are to judge truly, unless a conception of good itself had been impressed upon us, by reference to which we might approve something as good, and prefer one good to another. So God is to be loved, not this and that good, but good itself.

De Trin. VIII, iii, 4.

180

Briefly in one word the praise of the Lord our God is explained. 'The Lord is good' (Ps. cxxxiv, 3). But good not in the same manner as the things which He hath made are good. For God made all things not merely good, but very good (Gen. i, 31). He made the heaven and the earth and all things which are in them good, and He made them very good. If He made all these things good, of what kind is He who made them? And yet since He made them good, and He who made is much better than the things which He made, you can find nothing better to speak of Him than that 'the Lord is good,' if at any rate you understand Him to be good in a peculiar sense, from whom all other good things proceed. For He made all things good, He Himself is good, whom no one made. He is good by His own goodness, not by any good derived from elsewhere. He by His own good, that is Himself, is good, not by adhering to some other good. But for me it is good to adhere to God (Ps. lxxii, 28), Who never needed one by whom He might be made good, but all other things needed Him, that they might be made good. Would you hear how He is good singularly? The Lord when asked said, 'No one is good, save God alone' (Matt. xix, 17). I would not briefly pass over this singularity of His goodness, and yet I have not the power fitly to commend it to you. I fear lest I be found unthankful if I pass over it rapidly; and withal I fear lest, when I undertake to expound it, I may be oppressed by the vast burden of the Lord's praises. Yet so, my brethren, accept me, who praise and yet am incompetent, that the worship of my praise may be accepted, though the exposition of His praise be not fulfilled. And may He approve of my will, and pardon my failure.

In Ps. CXXXIV, 3.

181

I am filled with ineffable sweetness when I hear that 'the Lord is good' (Ps. cxxxiv, 3), and after examining and surveying all things that I see without, although these things please me, for they are all from Him, yet I return to Him from whom they are, to understand that 'the Lord is good.' And when I penetrate towards Him as near as I can, I find Him deeper within and higher than I can reach, for the Lord is in such sort good, as to need in no wise these things to make Him good. Lastly, I do not praise these things apart from Him. Him, however, I find to be perfect without them, needing nothing, immutable, seeking no good of another whereby He may be increased, fearing no evil whereby He may be diminished. And what more shall I say? In creation I find that the sky is good, the sun is good, the moon is good, the stars are good, the earth is good; the things which are brought forth in the earth, and are rooted there, are good; those which walk and move are good; those which fly in the air and swim in the waters are good. I say too that man is good, for 'the good man out of the good treasure of his heart bringeth forth good' (Matt. xii, 35). I say that an angel is good, if he have not fallen by pride and become a devil, but remains obedient to Him by whom he was made. I say all these things are good, but yet coupled with their names, as the good sky, a good angel, a good man; when, however, I turn me towards God, I think I can say nothing better than good. For truly the Lord Jesus, who Himself used the words 'a good man,' said also, 'No one is good, save God alone' (*id.*, xix, 17). Did He not urge us to seek and distinguish what that good is which is made good by another good, and that Good which is of itself good? How good must That be from which all good things proceed? You can find no good at all which is not good from Him. As He is properly *the* Good which makes things good, so He is properly *the* Good. For neither is it true that these things which He made are not, nor is any wrong done to Him when we say that the things which He made *are* not. Why then did He make them, if, when He has made them, they *are* not? Or what did He make, if that which He made *is* not? But since these things which He made have being, we come still to the comparison of Him with them. And as though He alone had being, He said, 'I AM WHO AM' and 'Thus thou shalt say to the children of Israel: HE WHO IS, hath sent me to you' (Exod. iii, 14). He did not say, the Almighty Lord God, the merciful, the just; though He would have said what was quite true, had he so spoken. Everything being taken away by which God might be named and called, He answered that He is called Very Being; and as though this were His name He said, 'this thou shalt say to them: HE WHO IS hath sent me.' For HE IS in such wise, that, compared with Him, things which are, *are* not. If He be not compared with them, they are, because they are from Him; but compared with Him they are not, because to *be* truly is to *be* immutably, and this HE IS alone. For what is, is; just as the good of goods, is good.

In Ps. CXXXIV, 4.

IV. ABOVE US AND IN US

182

God, . . . who abideth for ever, for whose presence no one has to wait, whose absence no one has to fear, for the very reason that He truly *is*, is ever present.

De ord. II, ii, 6.

183

For, my Brethren, we neither draw nigh through space to God, who is everywhere and is contained in no space, nor do we draw apart from Him through space. To draw nigh to Him is to become like Him, to draw apart from Him is to become unlike Him.

In Ps. XXXIV, *Serm.* ii, 6.

184

Thy God is whole everywhere: if thou fall not off from Him, He never falleth away from thee.

In Joan. Evang. XXXIV, 6.

185

Neither is this present day spent in Thee, and yet, after a sort, it is spent in Thee; because even all these transitory things are in Thee, nor could they have their ways of passing, unless Thou didst contain them. And, because 'Thy years do not fail' (Ps. ci, 28), Thy years are the present day; and . . . our days and our fathers' days have now passed by this one day of Thine, and have taken their measure thence, and received a kind of being, as others also shall pass and receive their measure also and their kind of being. 'But Thou art always the selfsame' (*ibid.*); to-morrow, with all that is to follow, and yesterday, with all that is past, in this day of Thine Thou shalt make, and Thou hast made.

Conf. I, vi, 10.

186

Thou dost precede all times past by the sublimity of Thy ever present eternity; and Thou dost pass all future times, because they are future now, and when they shall have come they will be past. 'But Thou art always the selfsame, and Thy years shall not fail' (Ps. ci, 28). Thy years neither go nor come; but ours do both go and come, that they may come in their order. Thy years stand all at the same time because they stand; neither are they that pass excluded by others that come, because they do not pass; but these years of thine shall be ours, when time shall be no more. Thy years are one day (cf. 2 Pet. iii, 8); and Thy day is not every day, but to-day; because Thy to-day neither gives place to to-morrow, nor comes it in place of yesterday. Thy to-day is eternity.

Conf. XI, xiii, 16.

187

What is more ancient than God, who is before all things, and is without end and without beginning? He becomes new to thee when thou returnest to Him; for it was by departing from Him that thou hadst become old.

In Ps. XXXIX, 4.

188

Most constant and incomprehensible; immutable, yet changing all things; never new and never old, yet renewing all things, and drawing such as are proud into decay, although they mark it not. Ever in action, and ever quiet; heaping up, yet needing nothing; upholding, filling, and protecting, creating, nourishing, and perfecting all things, though nothing is wanting to Thee. . . . Thou dost change Thy works without changing Thy decree; Thou takest what Thou findest, yet didst Thou never lose anything. . . . If we give Thee more than Thou dost claim, Thou becomest our debtor; yet who hath anything but of Thy gift? Thou payest debts, yet owest nothing; Thou forgivest debts, yet losest nothing.

Conf. I, iv, 4.

189

Of all things that are He is the Creator, of whom, by whom, in whom are all things (Rom. xi, 36), that is, the immutable first cause, immutable wisdom, immutable charity, one true and perfect God, who never was not, never will not be, never has been other, never will be other; than whom nothing is more hidden, nothing more present; hard to discover where He is, still harder to discover where He is not; with whom to be is not possible for all, and without whom no one can be; and whatever thing still more incredible and yet more fitting and apt which we as men can say of Him, He is that.

De quant. an. xxxiv, 77.

190

God . . . is Himself in no interval nor extension or place, but in His immutable and pre-eminent might is both interior to everything because all things are in Him, and exterior to everything because He is above all things. So too He is in no interval nor extension of time, but in His immutable eternity is older than all things because He is before all things, and younger than all things because the same He is after all things.

De Gen. ad litt. VIII, xxvi, 48.

191

God is then diffused through all things, as indeed He Himself says through the prophet: 'Do I not fill heaven and earth?' (Jer. xxiii, 24.) And His wisdom 'reaches therefore from end to end mightily, and ordereth all things sweetly' (Wis. viii, 1). Again it is written: 'The Spirit of the Lord hath filled the whole world' (Wis. i, 7), and the Psalmist says: 'Whither shall I go from thy spirit? or whither shall I flee from thy face? If I ascend into heaven thou art there: if I descend into hell, thou art present' (Ps. cxxxviii, 7 *sq*.). But God is not diffused through all things as a quality of the world but as the creative substance of the world which He governs and maintains without labour or effort. Yet he is not diffused through space like a diffused mass, with one half of Himself in one half the world and the other in the other half, and thus the whole of Himself in the whole. For He is wholly complete in heaven and on earth, complete both in heaven and on earth. No space contains Him, but He is everywhere complete in Himself. . . .

But what is more marvellous is the fact that God, though everywhere complete, does not dwell in all men. For it is not to all men that the Apostle could say: 'Know you not that you are the temple of God, and that the Spirit of God dwelleth in you?' (1 Cor. iii, 16). On the contrary, to some he says: 'Now if any man have not the Spirit of Christ, he is none of His' (Rom. viii, 9). . . . It must therefore be acknowledged that God is everywhere by the presence of His divinity but not everywhere by the in-dwelling of His grace. . . .

As then, God who is everywhere dwells not in all men, so too He does not dwell in all equally. . . . And if among all the saints some are more saintly than others, it is only because God dwells in them more abundantly. . . .

But God is not less Himself if he in whom He is present is less capable of receiving Him. For He is wholly complete in Himself, and He has no need of those in whom He dwells, as if He could not exist except in them. And in the same manner that God is not absent from him in whom He is not dwelling, and is indeed wholly present although He does not dwell in him, so too He is wholly present in those in whom He is dwelling, although they cannot contain Him wholly.

Nor does God divide Himself in the hearts or the bodies, giving to the latter one part of Himself, to the former another, as light does through the entrances and windows of houses, but rather like some sound, which is a corporeal and transient thing, is not heard by a deaf person and is not heard in its entirety by one hard of hearing, while among those whose hearing is good and are at the same distance from the sound, some hear more, others less, according to the fineness of their hearing, although the sound reaches them all equally at the place where they are. How much more excellently can God in His immaterial and immutably living nature, who unlike the sound is neither subject to time nor divisible and has no need of the air in order to come to us, and who lives in Himself in eternal stability, be wholly present in all things, and wholly complete in each one, although those in whom He dwells and whose hearts He forms by the grace of His goodness to be delectable temples for Him, possess Him in the proportion of their several capacities, some more fully, some less.

And indeed there are diversities of graces distributed through-out the members and parts of the one body, in which we are at once all one temple and, each one of us, separate temples. For God is not greater in all than He is in each one. And often it happens that one possesses Him more amply than the many. But when the Apostle said: 'Now there are diversity of graces,' he at once adds, 'but the same Spirit.' And again when he has enumerated the diversity of graces he goes on to say: 'But all these things one and the same Spirit worketh, dividing to every one according as He will' (1 Cor. xii, 4, 11). Dividing, that is to say, not Himself divided, for He is always one and the same. These diversities are indeed like those of the members in a body; for the ears have not the same function as the eyes, and so too in the case of the other members of the body which each perform their several offices in perfect concord.

When we are in good health the diversity of our organs does not prevent them from enjoying equally good health, without one member having more of it than another. Christ is the head of that body of which the unity is marked by our sacrifice, as the Apostle has briefly expressed in the words: 'We, being many, are one bread, one body' (1 Cor. x, 17). Through our Head we are reconciled to God, for in Him the divinity of the only-begotten Son is made participator in our humanity, that we may be participators in His immortality.

Ep. CLXXXVII, iv, 14–vi, 20.

192

I should not, therefore, be, O God, I could have no being at all unless thou wert in me; or rather, I should not be at all unless I were in Thee, 'of whom, and by whom, and in whom, are all things' (Rom. xi, 36). . . . Why then do I invoke Thee, since I am in Thee, or whence canst Thou come into me? For whither shall I go out of heaven and earth, that my God may come thence into me, He who hath said, 'Do not I fill heaven and earth'? (Jer. xxiii, 24).

Do therefore heaven and earth contain Thee, because Thou fillest them? Or dost Thou fill them so that there is still an overplus of Thee, because they are unable to comprehend Thee? And into what dost Thou pour whatsoever of Thee doth remain, after heaven and earth are filled? Or hast Thou no need to be contained by somewhat, Thou who containest all things, because those things which Thou fillest, Thou fillest by containing them? For those vessels which are full of Thee do not give any stability to Thee, nor, if they be broken, art thou poured out. When Thou art poured out upon us, Thou art not abased, but Thou dost raise us up (cf. Acts ii, 17). Neither art Thou scattered, but Thou dost gather us up.

Conf. I, ii, 2; iii, 3.

193

God's seat is thus in the hearts of men, that if man fall from God, God abides in Himself, nor does he fall like one not finding where to be. For rather doth He lift thee up, that thou mayest be in Him, than so lean on thee as to fall if thou withdraw thyself. If He withdraw, thou wilt fall; but if thou withdraw, He will not fall.

In Ps. XLV, 9.

194

'The spirit of God moved over the waters' (Gen. i, 2). Since a greedy and selfish love so loves that it is subject to what it loves, therefore when men speak of the spirit of God, whereby we have to understand His benevolence and love, He is said to be 'moving over' things, lest it should be thought that God loves the works He is to do rather from the need of His indigence than from the abundance of His benevolence. And mindful of this, the Apostle, when about to speak of charity, says that he will shew a yet more excellent way (1 Cor. xii, 31); and in another place, that the charity of Christ surpasseth all knowledge (Eph. iii, 19).

De Gen. ad litt. I, vii, 13.

195

It is a defect and a weakness of the soul so to delight in its own works as to rest in them, rather than in itself from them, since without any doubt there is something better in that through which works are done than the works themselves. Hence in that passage of Scripture which tells us that God rested from all his work which He had done (Gen. ii, 1), we are shewn that in none of His works He so rejoiced as if He felt the need to do them, or as if He would have been less if He had not done them, or happier for having done them; since in fact whatever is out of Him is so out of Him that it owes what it is to Him, whereas He owes it to nothing that is out of Him that He is happy. And so He set Himself before the things which He made in His love, not sanctifying that day on which He began His labours, nor that day on which He ended them, but the day on which He rested from them.

De Gen. ad litt. IV, xv, 26.

196

Thou shalt so repose in us, even as now Thou dost work in us; and so shall that rest be Thine through us, even as now these works of ours are Thine through us. But Thou, O Lord, dost ever work, and art ever at rest. Nor dost Thou see in time, nor art Thou moved in time, nor dost Thou rest in time; and yet thou makest all things that are seen in time, yea and the very times themselves, and even the rest that cometh out of time.

Conf. XIII, xxxvii, 52.

We shall mutually pardon one another the more easily if we know, or at any rate firmly believe and hold, that whatever is said of a nature immutable, invisible, and existing absolutely and being sufficient to itself, must not be measured after the custom of things visible, and mutable, and mortal, or not self-sufficient. But although we labour, and yet fail to grasp and know even those things which are within the scope of our bodily senses, or what ourselves are in the inner man, yet it is not an impertinence for faithful piety to burn after those divine and ineffable things which are above. And this piety is not puffed up by the arrogance of its own power, but is inflamed by the grace of its Creator and Saviour himself. For with what understanding can man apprehend God, if he does not yet apprehend that very understanding of his own, by which he desires to apprehend Him? And if he does already apprehend this, let him carefully consider that there is nothing in his own nature better than it; and let him see whether he can there see any outlines of forms, or brightness of colours, or greatness of space, or distance of parts, or extension of bulk, or any movements through intervals of space, or anything of the kind. Certainly we find nothing of all this in that, than which we find nothing better in our own nature, that is, in our own intellect, by which we apprehend wisdom according to our capacity. What, therefore, we do not find in that which is our own best, we ought not to seek in Him who is far better than that best of ours; that thus we may understand God, if we are able, and as far as we are able, as being good without quality, great without quantity, a creator though He lacks nothing, governing but from no position, sustaining all things without having them, in His wholeness everywhere, yet without location, eternal without time, making things that are mutable without mutation of Himself, and suffering nothing. Whoso thus thinks of God, though he cannot yet find out in all ways what He is, nevertheless piously takes heed, as much as he is able, to think nothing of Him that He is not.

De Trin. V, i, 2.

V. CREATURE—CREATOR

I. ALL-CREATING KNOWLEDGE

198

God, therefore, knew all things which He made before He made them. . . . He knew them, therefore, as things to be made, not as things made; He knew them that He might make them, not because He had made them. Hence although they were already known, for except by one knowing them they could not be made, yet those things, which were known that they might be made, did not begin to be until after they were made; and that they might be rightly made, were known before they were made.

Ad Orosium, viii, 9.

199

He knew beforehand, without any beginning, all things to come in time, and among them also what we should ask of Him and when, and to whom He would listen or not listen, and on what subjects. And with respect to all His creatures, both spiritual and corporeal, it is not because they are that He knows them, but they are because He knows them. For He was not ignorant of what He was to create; hence He created because He knew, He did not know because He created. Nor did He know them when created in any other way than He knew them when still to be created; for nothing accrued to His wisdom from them, but that wisdom remained as it was, while they came into being as it was fitting and when it was fitting.

De Trin. XV, xiii, 22.

200

The proposition holds that that which came into being through Him is to be understood as being life in Him, in which life He saw everything when He made it; and as He saw it, so He made it: not seeing anything except Himself, He enumerated in Himself all the things that He made. . . . If He knew them before He made them, assuredly before they were made they were in Him known in that fashion in which they eternally and immutably live, and are life; but they were made in that fashion by which each several creature in its species is.

De Gen. ad litt. V, xv, 33.

201

Because there is one Word of God, by which all things were made, and which is immutable truth, all things · are simultaneously therein, primarily and immutably; and not only those things which in this whole creation now are, but also those which have been, and those which are to be. And therein they neither have been, nor shall be, but only are; and all things are life, and all things are one, or rather it is one being and one life. For all things were so made by Him, that whatsoever was made in them was life in Him, and this life was not made.

De Trin. IV, i, 3.

202

When anything is to come into being, is as an eternal in the word of God, and it comes into being at that time when 'it ought to come into being,' is in that Word, in which there is no then and sometime, since this Word in its entirety is eternal.

De Gen. ad litt. I, ii, 6.

203

The Spirit of understanding is called in Holy Scripture manifold because its powers are many (cf. Wis. vii, 22), but all one with the essence and all included in one. And wisdom is not manifold but one, and in it are infinite and immeasurable treasuries of things intelligible, wherein are all the invisible and immutable causes of all things, both visible and mutable, which are thereby created. For God did nothing unwittingly; which cannot rightly be said of any human artificer. But if He made all things wittingly, then made He but what He knew. This appears as a wonder but yet as a truth to our minds: that this world could not be known to us, if it were not existing, but it could not have existed at all unless God had known it.

De civ. Dei XI, x, 3.

204

And his wisdom being simply multiple and uniformly multiform can comprehend all incomprehensible things with such incomprehensible comprehension that whatsoever thing that is new and unlike to all other He should ever please to create, it could not be irregular or unforeseen by Him, nor would He foresee it a little while before, but contain it in His eternal prescience.

De civ. Dei XVIII (Trübner ed. XIX).

205

What man is there who can comprehend that wisdom by which God knows all things, in such wise that neither what we call things past are past therein, nor what we call things future are therein looked for as coming, as though they were absent; but both past and future things together with those actually present are all present; nor again are things thought severally, so that thought passes from one to another but all things are simultaneously at hand in one mental view—what man, I say, is there that comprehends that wisdom, and the like precedence and knowledge, since in truth even our own wisdom is beyond our comprehension? Sometimes, indeed, we are able to behold the things that are present to our senses or to our understanding; and to be sure things that are absent but once were present we know by memory, if we have not forgotten them. And we conjecture, too, not the past from the future, but the future from the past, nevertheless with no sure cognition. For some of our thoughts, although of the future, we discern, as it were, with greater plainness and certainty as being very near; and this we do by means of memory, when we are able to do it and as much as we ever are able, though memory seems to belong not to the future, but to the past. And this may be tried in the case of any words or songs, the due order of which we render by memory, for we certainly should not utter each in proper succession, unless we foresaw in thought what came next. And yet it is not foresight but

memory that enables us to foresee it, for up to the very end
of the words or the song, nothing is uttered except as foreseen
and anticipated. Nevertheless in doing this, we are not said
to speak or sing by foresight, but by memory; and if anyone
is more than commonly capable of rendering many pieces in
this way, he is usually praised, not for his foresight but for
his memory. We know, and are absolutely certain, that all
this takes place in our mind or by our mind; but how it takes
place, the more attentively we wish to scrutinize, the more do
our words break down, and our purpose itself fails, when by
our understanding, if not by our tongue, we would attain to
some measure of clearness on the subject. And do such as we
are think that in so great infirmity of mind we can comprehend
whether the foresight of God is the same as His memory and
His understanding, He who does not regard in thought each
several thing, but embraces all that He knows in one eternal,
immutable, and ineffable vision? In this difficulty, then, and
strait, we may well cry out to the living God, 'Thy knowledge
is become wonderful to me: it is high and I cannot reach it'
(Ps. cxxxviii, 6). I understand, indeed, by myself, how wonderful
and incomprehensible is Thy knowledge, by which Thou
didst create me, when I cannot even contemplate myself
whom Thou has made! And yet, 'in my meditation a fire
flamed out' (Ps. xxxviii, 4), so that I seek Thy face evermore,
(Ps. civ, 4).

De Trin. XV, vii, 13.

II. ALL-EFFECTING WILL

206

How do I know that thou art alive, whose soul I see not?
How do I know? Thou wilt answer, Because I speak, because
I walk, because I work. Fool! by the operations of the body
I know thee to be living, canst thou not by the works of creation
know the Creator?

In Ps. LXXIII, 25.

207

The very order, disposition, beauty, change, and motion
of the world and of all visible things silently proclaim that

it could only have been made by God, the ineffably and invisibly great and the ineffably and invisibly beautiful.

De civ. Dei XI, iv, 2.

208

Ask the loveliness of the earth, ask the loveliness of the sea, ask the loveliness of the wide airy spaces, ask the loveliness of the sky, ask the order of the stars, ask the sun making the day light with its beams, ask the moon tempering the darkness of the night that follows, ask the living things which move in the waters, which tarry on the land, which fly in the air; ask the souls that are hidden, the bodies that are perceptive; the visible things which must be governed, the invisible things which govern—ask all these things, and they will all answer thee, Lo, see we are lovely. Their loveliness is their confession. And these lovely but mutable things, who has made them, save Beauty immutable? Lastly, men put their question in man himself, so that they might be able to understand and recognize God, the Creator of the whole universe, in man himself; I say, they asked soul and body, they put the question to that which they themselves bore; they saw the body, the soul they did not see. Yet they did not see the body except by means of the soul. They saw, indeed, through the eyes, but there was that within which looked through these windows. Moreover, when the householder leaves the house, the house falls; when the ruler departs, the ruled falls; and since it falls (*cadit*), it is called a corpse (*cadaver*). But are not the eyes still untouched? Even though they be open, they see nothing. The ears are still there, but the head is departed elsewhere; the organ of the tongue remains, but the musician who played on it is gone away. You have examined, then, these two things, the body which is visible and the soul which is invisible, and you have found that that which is not seen is better than that which is seen; that the hidden soul is the better, the visible body the inferior.

Men saw these two things, pondered them, investigated both of them, and found that each is mutable in man. The body is mutable in its several ages, in its corruption, its ailments, its reflections and its defections, its life, its death. They passed to the soul, which they certainly comprehended as being the better, and also wondered at as being invisible. But they found it too to be mutable, now willing something, again not willing; now knowing, again not knowing; now remembering, again forgetting; now fearing, again daring; now advancing in wisdom, again relapsing into folly. They saw that it was mutable, they left it, too, and went in search of something that should be immutable. And thus they arrived at a cognition of God the Creator by means of the things which He created.

Serm. CCXLI, ii, 2; iii, 3.

209

All things are subject to the will of God, to whom all wills are subject, since they have no power but what He gives them. The cause, therefore, that makes all and is not made itself is God. Other causes both effect and are effected; such are all created spirits, chiefly the rational ones. But corporal causes, which are rather effects than otherwise, are not to be counted among efficient causes, because they can but do that which the will of the spirit within them causes them to do.

De civ. Dei V, ix, 4.

210

For how can we deny that all things which are created are now the work of God's hand when the Lord has said, 'My Father worketh unto now'? (John v, 17). Hence the cessation from work on the seventh day must be understood to refer to the creation of the natures themselves and not to their regiment. When, therefore, the nature of things is governed by the Creator, and all things come into being in due order at the times and places preappointed by Him, God 'worketh unto now.'

Ep. CCV, iii, 17.

211

Indeed the power of the Creator and His omnipotent and all-swaying strength is for each and every creature the cause of its continued existence; and if this strength were at any time to cease from directing the things which have been created,

at one and the same time both their species would cease to be
and their whole nature would perish. . . . Since we are other
than He, we are not in Him for any other reason except that
He caused it, and this is His work, whereby He contains all
things. . . . And by this disposition, 'in Him we live and move
and are' (Acts xvii, 28). Whence it follows that if this His working
were withdrawn from things, we should neither live nor move
nor be.

De Gen. ad litt. IV, xxii, 22, 23.

212

The will of God, which maketh His angels spirits and His
ministers a burning fire (Ps. ciii, 4), presiding among spirits
which are joined together in perfect peace and amity, and
kindled into one will by a kind of spiritual charity, seated as
it were on an exalted, holy and secret throne, as in its own
house and its own temple, thence diffuses itself through all
things by certain perfectly ordered movements of created
things, firstly spiritual, then corporeal, and puts all to the
service of the immutable bidding of its purpose, whether they
be incorporeal or corporeal things, whether rational or irrational
spirits, whether good by God's grace, or evil through their own
will. But as the more gross and inferior bodies are governed
in a certain order by the more subtile and powerful ones, so
too all bodies are governed by the living spirit, the irrational
living spirit by the rational, the rational living spirit that makes
default and sins by the living and rational spirit that is pious
and just, and the last by God himself, and thus the whole of
creation by its Creator, from whom and through whom and
in whom it is created and established (Col. i, 16). And so it
comes to pass that the will of God is the first and supreme cause
of all corporeal forms and movements. For nothing is done
visibly or sensibly, unless either by command or permission from
the inner judgment hall, invisible and intelligible, of the supreme
Ruler, according to the ineffable justice of rewards and punishments, of grace and retribution, in that abounding and boundless
commonwealth of the whole creation.

De Trin. III, iv, 9.

For it is one thing to form and direct the creature from the most profound and ultimate pole of causation, and he who does this is alone the Creator, God; but it is quite another thing to apply some operation from without in proportion to the power and faculties assigned by Him, so that at this time or that, and in this or that way, the thing created may emerge. All these things, indeed, have originally and primarily already been created in a kind of web of the elements; but they make their appearance when they get the opportunity. For just as mothers are pregnant with their young, so the world itself is pregnant with things that are to come into being, things which are not created in it, except from that highest essence, where nothing either springs up or dies, has a beginning or an end. But the application from without of adventitious causes, which although they are not natural, are yet to be applied according to nature, in order that those things which are contained and hidden in the secret bosom of nature may break out and be outwardly created in some way by the unfolding of their proper measures and numbers and weights which they have received from Him who has 'ordered all things in measure, and number, and weight' (Wis. xi, 21), this is in the power not only of bad angels, but also of bad men.

De Trin. III, ix, 16.

214

As in the seed there are invisibly and at one time all the things which in course of time will grow into a tree, so the universe must be conceived—since God created all things at the same time—as having had at the same time all the things which were made in it and with it, when the day of creation came, not only the heavens with the sun and the moon and the stars, whose species remains in their rotary motion, and the earth and the deeps, which suffer changing movements, and joined together below produce the other part of the world; but also those things which earth and water produced potentially and causally, before in the course of time they came into being in the shape in which they are now known to us in those works which God 'worketh until now' (John v, 17).

De Gen. ad litt. V, xxiii, 45.

III. ALL-BEARING BEING

215

So is the verse also beautiful in its manner, although two syllables cannot by any possibility be pronounced together. For the second cannot be uttered if the first be not passed away; and thus we come in due order to the end, so that the last syllable sounds alone, and those that were sounding before are not heard with it, yet, woven into the texture of what has gone before, it perfects the metrical form and beauty of the verse. Nevertheless the art by which a verse is fashioned, is not to this extent subject to time, that its beauty is distributed over measured intervals; but it possesses at one time all the things requisite to the making of a verse, though the verse does not possess all this together, but brings into prominence the later things by what is gone before. Nevertheless it is beautiful for the reason that it displays the ultimate imprints of that beauty, which art preserves immovably and immutably.

And so, as there are some misguided people who love the verse more than the art by which the verse is composed, because they have surrendered themselves to the ear rather than to the intelligence; so there are many who love temporal things, but do not seek after the divine providence which creates and directs the circumstances of the time, and for very love of temporal things are unwilling to pass beyond that which they love, and are as ridiculous as one who in the recitation of a glorious poem would want to hear some one syllable repeated over and over again. However, people who thus listen to verse are not to be found, whereas the world is full of people who judge things in this manner, for the reason that there is nobody who cannot easily hear not only a whole verse but also a whole poem, but no man can perceive the whole order of the ages. Moreover, we are not parts of a verse, but owing to the curse of sin laid upon us we are made parts of the ages. Therefore a poem is recited and submitted to our judgment, while the ages are consummated by our toil. To the vanquished the public games are no pleasure, and yet they are skilful and beautiful in spite of his want of skill; and this may be taken as some sort of imitation of truth. And only for this reason are we forbidden such spectacles, lest deceived by the shadows of things, we should stray away from the things themselves of which they are but shadows. Thus the condition and regiment of this universe is displeasing only to the impious and damned souls; but, in spite of the misery of these souls, to the many souls whether victorious on earth or safely looking on in heaven, it is pleasing; for nothing just displeases the just.

De vera relig. xxii, 42–43.

216

Even those things which are corruptible are good. For they could not be corrupted if they were the Supreme Good, nor yet could they be corrupted if there were not some good in them. Because, if they were the Supreme Good they would be incorruptible, and if they were not good at all, there would be nothing in them which could be corrupted.

Conf. VII, xii, 18.

217

Just as these antitheses add beauty to the saying, so is the beauty of the world composed of antitheses, not of expressions but of things.

De civ. Dei XI, xviii.

218

By the decession and succession of things the beauty of the ages is woven.

De Gen. ad litt. I, viii, 14.

219

Wherefore, in regard to all temporal things which are so set in the order of things that unless they disappeared, nothing future could succeed to the past, so that the beauty of the ages in its several degrees must be accomplished as a whole, it were absurd to say that such things should not pass away. For as much as they receive, so much they perform, and render back to Him to whom they owe their being, in so far as they are.

De lib. arb. III, xv, 42.

220

And however much these created things decline and thus tend towards not-being, nevertheless something of form remains to them, that in some degree they may be. But whatever form remains to any thing thus declining, is from that Form which cannot decline and pass, and does not suffer the very motions of things advancing and passing away to overstep the laws of their rhythms. And if any thing praiseworthy is noticed in the nature of things, whether this be judged worthy of slight praise or great, it must be applied to the most excellent and ineffable praise of the Creator.

De lib. arb. II, xvii, 46.

221

Whatever is, however insignificant it be in kind, necessarily is. Thus even the minutest good will yet be a good, and will be from God. For since the highest kind is the highest good, that which is of the least kind is the smallest good. But all good is either God himself or is from God. Therefore even the least kind is also from God. What we have said of kind can clearly also be said of form. For it is not without good reason that the highest in kind and the highest in form are equally objects of praise. That out of which God has created all things is what possesses neither species nor form; and this is nothing other than nothing. For that which in comparison with completed things is called formless, is, if it have any form however slight, however inchoate, not quite nothing, and consequently this also, in so far as it is, is only from God. Wherefore, even if the universe was created out of some formless matter, this very matter was created from something which was wholly nothing. For that which is not yet formed, but is nevertheless in an inchoate state, so that it can be given form, is formable by the goodness of God; for it is a good to have form. Consequently the capacity to be formed is also some good. Hence the Author of all good, who gives the form, also gives the power to receive the form. Thus everything that is, in so far as it is, and everything which not yet is, but which can be, holds this from God. To put this in other words: Everything which has form, in so

far as it has form, and everything which has not yet form, in so
far as it is capable of receiving form, holds what it has from
God.

De vera relig. xviii, 35–36.

222

For the mutable state of mutable things is itself capable of
all those forms whereinto things mutable are changed. And
this mutability, what is it? . . . If a man might say a 'nothing-
something,' or an 'is is-not,' I would say this were it, and yet
in some way it was, even then, seeing that it could receive these
visible and compound figures.

Conf. XII, vi, 6.

223

I beheld all other things that are beneath Thee, and I saw
that they had neither any absolute being, nor that they had
absolutely no being at all. They have a being because they
are of Thee; and they have no being, because they be not
that which Thou art. For that truly is, which doth immutably
remain.

Conf. VII, xi, 17.

224

I was sure that Thou art, and that Thou art infinite, . . .
and that thou truly art, because Thou art always the same,
and art not ever different or otherwise either in any part or in
any motion; and that all other things have their being from
Thee, which thing is demonstrated most firmly by the very
fact that they are.

Conf. VII, xx, 26.

225

In Thy presence do stand the causes of all things that are
unstable and even of all things that are changeable—the
unchangeable roots remain with Thee, and the eternal reasons
of things which are temporal and irrational do live.

Conf. I, vi, 9.

Commend unto this Truth whatsoever it hath imparted unto thee . . . and they shall stay with thee and shall stand fast for ever in God's own presence, who is immutable and eternal.

Conf. IV, xi, 16.

IV. ALL-OVERCOMING GOOD

227

All sins are contained in this one category, that one turns away from things divine and truly enduring, and turns towards those which are mutable and uncertain. And although the latter are rightly placed each in its order, and work out that beauty proper to them it is nevertheless the mark of a perverted and ungoverned mind to be in subjection to them as things to be pursued, when by the divine order and law it is set above them as things to be directed.

De lib. arb. I, xvi, 35.

228

The will that turns away from the immutable good common to all and turns towards its own good, whether outward to itself or downward, sins. It turns towards its own when it wills to be its own master; towards outward good, when out of curiosity it strives to know things which are the property of others, or which do not pertain to itself; to the lower good, when it loves the pleasures of the body. And in this way man, having become proud and inquisitive and licentious, is taken captive by another life, which in comparison with the higher life is death. Yet this other life is governed by the administration of the divine Providence, which orders all things in their proper place, and apportions to each his due according to his merit. Thus it comes to pass that neither are the good things striven for by sinners in any way bad, nor is free will itself, which we are told should be counted as holding a middle place among good things; but that evil is the turning away of the will from the immutable good, and the turning towards mutable goods. And since this turning away and this turning to are not forced but voluntary

actions, it is meet and right that their consequence should be
the punishment of misery.

De lib. arb. II, xix, 35.

229

Since truly no one is above the laws of the almighty Creator,
the soul is not allowed not to pay back its debt. For either it
pays it by using well what it has received, or it pays by losing
that which it refused to use well. If therefore it does not pay
by working justice, it will repay by suffering misery. . . . If
it does not pay what it owes by works, it will pay what it owes
by suffering.

De lib. arb. III, xv, 44.

230

Let man choose for himself what he will; the works of the
Lord are not so constituted that the creature, constituted with a
free will, should transcend the will of the Creator, even though
he act contrary to His will. For God willeth not that thou shouldst
sin, since He forbiddeth it. Yet if thou hast sinned, think not that
a man hath done what he willed, and that that hath happened
to God which He did not will. For as He would that man should
not sin, so would He spare the sinner, that he may return and
live. So too is it His will finally to punish one who persisteth in
his sin, that the rebellious may not escape the power of justice.
Thus whatever choice thou hast made, the Almighty will not
be at a loss to fulfil His will concerning thee.

In Ps. CX, 2.

231

When God punishes sinners, He does not inflict His evil on
them, but leaves them to their own evil. 'Behold,' saith the
Psalmist, 'he hath been in labour with injustice, he hath conceived toil; brought forth iniquity. He hath opened a pit and
dug it: and he is fallen into the hole he made. His sorrow shall
be turned on his own head: and his iniquity shall come down
upon his crown' (Ps. vii, 15 *sqq.*). When therefore God punishes,
He punishes as a judge those that transgress the law, not by
bringing evil upon them from Himself, but by driving them on

to that which they have chosen, to fill up the sum of their misery.

In Ps. V, 10.

232

The ungodly are driven out from that inheritance which is possessed by seeing and knowing God; just as diseased eyes are driven out from the shining of the light, when what is gladness to others is pain to them. . . . To sinners the bread of truth is bitter. Whence they hate the mouth of him that speaketh the truth. These therefore have embittered God, who by sin have fallen into such a state of sickness, that, as if it were bitter gall, they cannot bear the food of truth, in which healthy souls delight.

In Ps. V, 14, 15.

233

Evil, therefore, is that which falls away from essence and tends to non-being . . . It tends to make that which is to cease to be.

De mor. Eccl. II, ii, 2.

234

It is indeed not possible to know that this [motion, that is, the turning of the will away from God] is nothingness. Hold thou therefore fast to thy unshakable piety, that no good thing may befall thee, whether by thy senses, or thy understanding, or thy thoughts of whatever kind, which is not from God. For no nature is met with which is not from God. Every thing in which thou seest measure and number and order, that thing attribute to God, the Artificer, without hesitation. Indeed, if thou completely takest away from it these three qualities, absolutely nothing will remain. For even if an inchoation of a form remained, in which you found neither measure, nor number, nor order; since everywhere where these are is perfect form, you must needs remove even this inchoation of a form, which as material to be perfected seems to lie under the hand of the Artificer. For if the perfection of the form is good, the inchoation of the form is already some good. It follows that if all the good has been completely removed, there will remain not something which is not nothing, but absolutely nothing.

De lib. arb. II, xx, 54.

235

He indeed always is, nor has He been and is not, nor is but has not been; but as He never will not be, so He never was not. And He is whole everywhere. And hence [the soul] 'lives, and moves, and is in Him' (Acts xvii, 28), and so it can remember Him. . . . But it is reminded of it, that it may turn to God, as to that light by which it was in some way touched, even when it was turned away from Him. Hence it is that even the ungodly think of eternity, and rightly blame and rightly praise many things in the conduct of men. And by what rules do they thus judge, except by those wherein they see how men ought to live, even though they themselves do not so live? And where do they see those rules? For they do not see them in their own nature; for though these things are without doubt seen by the mind, yet it is agreed that their minds are mutable; but these rules are seen as immutable by anyone who can see them at all. Nor again do they see them in the character of their own mind, since these rules are rules of justice, and their minds are confessedly unjust. Where indeed are these rules written, wherein even the unjust recognizes what is just, wherein he discerns that he ought to have what he himself has not? Where, then, are they written, unless in the book of that light which is called Truth? From this every just law is copied and transferred to the heart of the man that worketh justice, not by migrating to it, but by being as it were impressed upon it, as the impression from a ring passes into the wax, yet does not leave the ring. But he who worketh not justice, and yet sees how he ought to work, he is the man who is turned away from that light, which nevertheless touches him. He, however, who does not even see how he ought to live, sins indeed with more excuse, because he is not a transgressor of a law that he knows; but even he too is just touched sometimes by the splendour of the omnipresent truth, when after being admonished he confesses.

De Trin. XIV, xv, 21.

236

In so far, therefore, as anything that is, is good, so far plainly it still has some likeness to the supreme good, at however great a distance it be. And if it is a natural likeness, then certainly it is a right and ordered one; but if it is a faulty likeness, then certainly it is a base and perverse one. For souls in their very sins strive after nothing else but some kind of likeness to God, in a proud, preposterous, and, so to speak, servile liberty.

De Trin. XI, v, 8.

237

Whence a wonderful thing is brought to pass, that, whereas every nature, in so far as it is nature, is a good, nothing else would seem to be said when a faulty nature is called an evil nature, except that that is an evil which is a good; and that neither is there any evil but what is good, since every nature is a good; nor would anything be evil, if the thing itself that is evil were not a nature. There cannot therefore be evil, except it be some good. . . . Wherefore in those contraries which are called evils and goods, that rule of the dialecticians ceases to hold, by which, according to them, nothing has in it two contraries at the same time. . . . Though no one doubts that goods and evils are contraries, yet not only can they be at the same time, but evils cannot be altogether without goods, nor can they be except in goods; although goods can be without evils.

Enchiridion xiii, 4; xiv, 4.

238

We in our perversity want God to be merciful in such way as not to be just. Others again, trusting all too much in their own justice, would have God just in such a way that they do not wish Him to be merciful. God shows himself to be both; He is supremely both. His mercy does not prescribe His justice, nor does His justice sweep away His mercy. He is merciful and just.

Serm. XXII, v, 5.

239

For when men judge, sometimes overcome by mercy they act contrary to justice; and mercy but not justice seemeth to be in them: while sometimes when they wish to enforce a rigid judgment, they lose mercy. But God neither loseth the severity of judgment in the bounty of mercy nor in judging with severity loseth the bounty of mercy.

In Ps. CT, 1.

240

He foresees the good to come, and creates them; He foresees the wicked to come, and creates them; offering Himself to be enjoyed by the good, bestowing bountifully on the wicked also many of His gifts; mercifully forgiving, justly punishing; and again, mercifully punishing, justly forgiving; fearing nothing from the malice of anyone, wanting nothing of the justice of anyone; taking no thought for Himself even from the works of the good; taking thought for the good even from the punishments of the wicked.

De Gen. ad litt. XI, xi, 15.

241

This is proper to God; the contrary is characteristic of the wicked. For as the wicked make a bad use of the good works of God, so contrariwise God makes a good use of the bad works of the wicked. . . . All the good gifts of God . . . a bad man turns to bad use; on the other hand the good man turns the evils of evil men to a good use. And what so good as the One God? . . . Therefore by how much He is better, by so much the better use He makes of our evil deeds. . . . What the bad man effects by making a bad use is to hurt himself, not to contradict the goodness of God. The Artificer puts him to use; and the great Artificer, if He had not known how to put him to use, would not have permitted him to be.

In Joan. Evang. XXVII, 10.

242

It is manifest that all things, whether they offend or are offended against, whether they give delight or are given delight, publish and proclaim the unity of the Creator.

De lib. arb. III, xxiii, 70.

243

God, through whom all things, which of themselves were not, come to be.

God, who permittest not to perish even that which is mutually destructive.

God, who from nothing hast created this world which the eyes of all perceive to be most beautiful.

God, who dost not cause evil but causest that it become not most evil.

God, who to the few that flee for refuge to that which truly is, showest evil to be nothing.

God, through whom the universe, even with those things which are sinister in it, is perfect.

God, from whom dissonance to the extreme limit is nothing, since better things are brought in concert with worse.

God, who art loved knowingly or unknowingly by everything that is capable of loving.

God, in whom are all things, yet to whom neither the vileness of any creature is vile, nor its error erroneous.

Solil. I, i, 2.

244

I call upon Thee, O God, the Truth, in whom, by whom, and through whom those things are true which are true in every respect.

God, the Wisdom, in whom and by whom and through whom those things are wise which anywhere are wise.

God, the true and highest life, in whom and by whom and through whom those things live which anywhere live truly and supremely.

God, the Beatitude, in whom and by whom and through whom all things are happy which anywhere are happy.

God, the Good and the Beautiful, in whom and by whom and through whom those things are good and beautiful which anywhere are good and beautiful.

God, the intelligible Light, in whom and by whom and through whom those things intelligibly shine which anywhere intelligibly shine.

God, whose kingdom is a whole universe of which the senses have no knowledge.

God, from whose kingdom law is assigned even to those realms.

God, from whom to be turned away is to fall, to whom to be turned again is to rise again, in whom to abide is to stand secure.

God, from whom to depart is to die, to whom to return is to be restored to life, in whom to dwell is to live.

God, whom no one loses unless deceived, whom no one seeks unless stirred to do so, whom no one finds unless made pure.

God, whom to forsake is the same as to perish; whom to strive for is the same as to live; whom to see is the same as to possess.

God to whom faith urges us, hope raises us, charity joins us.

Solil. I, i, 3.

245

God, through whom we serve well and govern well.

God, through whom we learn that things which at one time we thought our own are another's, and things which at one time we thought to belong to others are our own.

God, through whom petty things do not lessen us.

God, who dost strip us of that which is not and dost clothe us with that which is.

God, who dost call us back into the way.

God, who dost lead us up to the door.

God, who dost cause it to be opened to them that knock.

Solil. I, i, 3.

246

God, whom all things serve, that serve; to whom every virtuous soul submits. By whose laws the poles rotate, the stars complete their courses, the sun oversees the day, the moon rules the night: the whole universe, day by day by the alternation of light and darkness; month by month by the waxings and wanings of the moon; year by year by due succession of spring, summer, autumn and winter; cycle by cycle as the sun completes its appointed path; orbit by orbit as the stars return to their place of rising, maintains, as far as sensible matter permits, an enduring harmony.

God, by whose eternal laws the unstable motion of mutable things is not allowed to be disturbed, but by the restraining force of recurring cycles is ever called back to a similitude of stability: by whose laws the will of the soul is free, and to the good rewards are given, to the evil punishments by wholly necessary connexion.

God, from whom flow to us all good things, by whom all evil things are kept from us.

God, above whom is nothing, beyond whom is nothing, without whom is nothing.

God, under whom all is, in whom all is, with whom all is.

Solil. I, i, 4.

VI. SPIRIT—GOD

I. TRUTH AND GOODNESS

247

For when we aspire from this depth to that height, it is a part of no small knowledge if, before we can know what God is, we can yet know what He is not. For certainly He is neither heaven nor earth; nor, as it were, heaven and earth; nor any such things as we see in the heavens; nor any such thing as we do not see, but which perhaps is in the heavens. Again, if you were to magnify in imagination the light of the sun as much as you can, either making it greater or brighter, a thousand times as much, or times without number, this too is not God. And if we think of the Angels as pure spirits animating celestial bodies, and changing and dealing with them after the will by which they serve God, and if we imagine them all—and there are 'thousands of thousands' (Apoc. v, 11; cf. Dan. vii, 10)—brought together into one, and become one, no such thing as this is God. And the same would be true if you were to think of these spirits as without bodies—a thing indeed most difficult for carnal thought to conceive. Behold and see, O soul pressed down by the corruptible body, and weighed down by the multitude and variety of earthly thoughts (Wis. ix, 15); behold and see, if thou canst, that God is truth. For it is written that 'God is light' (1 John i, 5); not in such way as the eyes see, but in such way as the heart sees, when it hears that He is truth. Ask not what is truth; for immediately the mists of corporeal images and the clouds of phantasms will put themselves in the way, and will disturb the calm which at the first moment shone forth to thee, when I said Truth, see what there remaineth, if thou canst, in that first moment in which thou wert dazzled as by a flash, when there was said, Truth. But thou canst not; thou wilt slip back into those familiar, earthly things. And what influence, pray, is it that will cause thee thus to slip back, unless it be the bird-lime of the stains of appetite thou hast contracted, and the errors of the wandering from the right path.

De Trin. VIII, ii, 3.

248

Thou certainly dost not love anything except what is good; for the earth is good with its lofty mountains and the ordered disposition of its hills, and the level surface of its plains; and good is an estate that is pleasant and fertile; and a house is good that is well-proportioned in its parts and is spacious and bright; and good are the animate bodies of animals; and good is the air that is temperate and salubrious; and food is good and wholesome; and health without pains and lassitude is good; and good is the countenance of man when it is well-proportioned and cheerful in expression and pleasantly coloured; and good is the mind of a friend in the sweetness of agreement and the confidence of love; and good is a just man; and good are riches, since they are readily useful; and good is the sky with its sun and moon and stars; and good are the Angels by their holy obedience; and good is a discourse that pleasantly teaches and aptly admonishes the hearer; and good is a form that is harmonious in its numbers and weighty in its sentiment. But why add more and yet more? This good and that good: Take away the 'this' and 'that', and regard good itself, if thou canst. Thus wilt thou see God, not good by a good other than Himself, but the good of all good. For in all these good things, whether those which I have enumerated, or any others that may be discerned or imagined, we could not say that one was better than another, if we are to judge truly, unless a conception of good itself had been impressed upon us, by reference to which we might approve something as good, and prefer one good to another. So God is to be loved, not this and that good, but good itself. For the good that must be sought for the soul is not one over which it is to fly by judging, but one to which it is to cleave by loving. And what can this be except God? Not a good mind, or a good Angel, or a good heaven, but the good good. But perhaps what I wish to say may be more easily perceived in this way. When, for example, a mind is called good, as there are two words, so from these words I understand two things—one by which it is a mind, the other by which it is good. And indeed to be a mind it did nothing of itself, for there was nothing as yet to cause it to be; but to make itself to be a good mind must, I see, be the work of the will; not because that by which it is mind is not itself something good,—for why otherwise is it called, and rightly called, better than the body?—but it is not yet called a good mind, for the reason that the action of the will by which it is to become more excellent, is still wanted; and if it has neglected this, then is it justly blamed, and is rightly called not a good mind. For it then differs from the mind which does take this action; and since the latter is praiseworthy, the former, which does not so act, is undoubtedly blamable. But when it takes this action of set purpose, and becomes a good mind, it nevertheless cannot attain to being so, unless it turn itself to something which itself is not. But to what can it turn itself that it may become a good mind, save to the good which it loves, and seeks, and obtains? And if it reverts from this, then by the very act of turning away from the good, unless that good from which it turns away remain in it, it cannot again turn back thither if it should wish to amend.

Wherefore there would be no mutable good things unless there were an immutable good. When therefore thou hearest of this and that good thing, which things can also in other respects be called not good, if, setting aside those things which are good by the participation of the good, thou canst discern that good by the participation of which they are good (for when this or that good thing is spoken of thou understandest together with them the good itself also): if, then, I say thou canst remove these things and discern the good *per se*, thou wilt have discerned God. And if thou adhere to it with love, thou shalt be forth-with blessed. But, since other things are not loved save because they are good, it were a shame in cleaving to them not to love the good itself whence they are good. That also which is a mind, only because it is a mind, while it is not yet also good by the turning itself to the immutable good, but, as I have said, is only a mind, whenever it so pleases us that, if we understand aright, we prefer it even to all corporeal light, it does not please us in itself, but in that skill by which it was made. For it is thence approved as made, wherein it is seen to have been to be made. This is truth and simple good; for it is nothing other than the good itself, and therefore also the supreme good. For no good can be diminished or increased, except that which is good from some other good. Therefore the mind turns itself, in order to be good, to that by which it comes to be a mind. Therefore the will is then in harmony with nature, that the mind may be perfected in the good, when that good is loved by the turning of the will to it, whence that other good also comes which is not lost by the turning away of the will from it. For by turning itself from the supreme good, the mind loses the being a good mind, but it does not lose the being a mind. And this, too, is already a good, and one better than the body. The will therefore loses that which the will obtains. For the mind already was, that could wish to be turned to that from which it was; but that as yet was not which could wish to be before it was. And this is our good, when we see whether the thing ought to have been or to be, respecting which we comprehend that it ought to have been or to be, and when we see that it could not have been unless it ought to have been, of which we also do not comprehend in what manner it ought to have been. This good therefore 'is not far from every one of us,' for in it 'we live, and move, and are' (Acts xvii, 27 *sq.*).

De Trin. VIII, iii, 4–5.

249

When indeed I wish to speak of Carthage, I seek within myself what to speak, and I find within myself an image of Carthage; but I have received this through the body, that is through the senses of the body, since I have been present in that city in the body, and I saw and perceived it, and retained it in my memory, so that I might find within myself a word concerning it, whenever I might wish to speak of it. For its word is the image itself of it in my memory, not that sound of two syllables when Carthage is named, or even when that name itself is thought of from time to time, but that which I discern in my mind, when I utter that dissyllable with my voice, or even before I utter it. So, also, when I wish to speak of Alexandria, which I never saw, an imaginary image of it is present with me. For whereas I had heard from many and believed that it was a great city, I formed an image of it in my mind, as far as I was able, from the description which could be given me; and this is with me its word when I wish to speak of it, before I utter with my voice the five syllables which make up the name that almost everybody knows. And yet if I could transmit that image from my mind to the eyes of men who knew Alexandria, certainly either all would say, That is not it, or if they said, That is it, I should greatly wonder; and as I gazed at it in my mind, that is, at the image which was as it were its picture, I should yet not know it to be it, but would believe those who retained an image they had seen. But I do not thus ask what it is to be just, nor do I thus find it, nor do I thus gaze upon it when I utter it, nor am I thus approved when I am heard, nor do I thus approve when I hear; as though I had-seen such a thing with my eyes, or learned it by some bodily sense, or heard it from those who had thus learned it. For when I say, and wittingly say, that that mind is just which with full knowledge and purpose assigns to everyone his due in life and character, I do not think of any absent thing such as Carthage, or imagine it, as I am able to do, in the case of Alexandria, whether that be so or not; but I discern something present, and I discern it within myself, though I am not that which I discern, and many if they hear me will approve. And whoever hears me and consciously approves, discerns this same thing within himself, though he too be not what he discerns. But when a just man says this, he discerns and says that which he himself is. And whence also does he discern it, except within himself? But this is not wonderful, for where should he discern himself, except within himself? The wonderful thing is that the mind should see within itself that which it has seen nowhere else, and should see truly, and should see the actual just mind, and should itself be a mind, and yet is not the just mind, which nevertheless it sees within himself. Is there another mind which is just in a mind that is not yet just? Or if there is not, what does he see when he sees and says what a just mind is, nor sees it anywhere else but in itself, when itself is not a just mind? Is that which it sees an inner truth present to the mind which has the power to behold it? Yet all have not that power; and those who have the power to perceive it are not all that which they perceive, that is, they are not themselves just minds, though they are able to see and to say what a just mind is. And whence will they be able to be this except by cleaving to that very same form which they behold, so that they may thence be formed and may be just minds; not only discerning that the mind is just which with full knowledge and purpose assigns to every one that which is his due in life and character, but also, that they themselves may live justly and be just in character, assigning to every one his due, so as to 'owe no man anything, but to love one another.' (Rom. xiii, 8.) And how can any adhere to that form except by loving it? Why then do we love another whom we believe to be just, and do not love that form wherein we see what a just mind is, that we also may be able to be just? Is it that unless we loved that also, we should not love him at all, whom because of it we love, although, not being just ourselves, we love that form too little to allow of our being just? The man, therefore, who is believed to be just, is loved through that form and truth which he who loves discerns and understands within himself; but that form and truth cannot be loved from any other source than itself. For we do not find any such thing besides itself which by believing we might love though unknown, from the fact that we already know another such thing. For whatsoever of such kind one may have seen, is itself; and there is not any other such thing, since itself alone is such as itself is. . . .

And except we loved above all else that form which we discern to be always stable and immutable, we should not love Him for the reason that we hold fast to the belief that His life, when He was living in the flesh, was adapted to and in harmony with His form. But somehow we are stirred up the more to the love of this form itself through the faith by which we believe that someone so lived, and to the hope which leads us not to despair at all that we also, who are men, are able so to live; and this from the fact that some men have so lived; with the result that we both desire this the more ardently and pray for it the more confidently. So that the love of that form, according to which they are believed to have lived, makes the life of these men to be loved by us, and their life thus believed stirs up a more burning love for that same form. Hence the more ardently we love God, the more certainly and the more serenely do we see Him, because we behold in God the immutable form of justice, according to which in our judgment man ought to live. Therefore faith avails to the knowledge and to the love of God, not as though of one wholly unknown or not loved at all, but to the end that He may be known more clearly and loved more steadfastly.

De Trin. VIII, vi, 9; ix, 13.

II. BEING, KNOWING, WILLING

250

But as far as relates to the discerning in some way by the understanding of that supreme, ineffable, incorporeal, and unchangeable nature, the sight of the human mind can nowhere better exercise itself, provided only it be governed by the rule of faith, than in that which man himself has in his own nature better than the other animals, better also than the other parts of his own soul, namely, the mind itself, to which has been assigned a certain sight of things invisible, and to which, as though it were honourably presiding in a higher and inner place, the bodily senses also bring word of all things on which judgment is required, and than which there is nothing higher, to which, as subject to it, it must be governed, except God.

De Trin. XV, xxvii, 49.

251

We have attempted by our disputation to raise the purpose of the mind to an understanding of that most excellent and immutable nature, which our mind is not. And we contemplated this nature as to picture it as not far from us, and as above us, not in place, but by its own awful and wonderful excellence, and in such wise that it appeared to be with us by the presence of its own light.

De Trin. XV, vi, 10.

I could wish that men would but consider these three things that are in themselves, . . . namely, to Be, to Know, and to Will. For indeed I am, and I know, and I will. I am, both knowing and willing. I know myself both to be and to will. And I am willing both to be and to know. Let him therefore that can reach to it, comprehend in these three, how inseparable is life: one life, one mind, one essence; yet at the end how inseparable is the distinction; yet there is a distinction. . . . But when he shall have discovered and said anything about these things, let him take heed of thinking that he hath found out that Unchangeable, which is above all these things; which is unchangeably, and knoweth unchangeably, and willeth unchangeably; or that he hath found out whether there is a Trinity also because of these three; or whether all three be in each one so that all three belong to each; or whether both ways at once in a manner admirable, simple, and manifold; infinite to itself yet a limit to itself, whereby it *is*, and is known unto itself, and *sufficeth* unto itself, unchangeably the self-same by the most plentiful abundance of its Unity.

Conf. XIII, xi, 12.

252

253

Because we are men made in the image of our Creator, whose eternity is true, eternal truth, eternal and true charity, . . . we as it were run through all things beneath us which He has created of such wonderful stability and which could not by any possibility exist nor take any form nor arrive at or keep any order unless they had been made by Him who supremely is, who is supremely wise and supremely good, let us gather here more, there less, distinct marks of His essence; and beholding His image in ourselves let us like that prodigal son in the gospel return to our proper selves and rise and go back to Him from whom by sinning we had departed. There our being will have no death, our knowledge no error, our love no offence.

De civ. Dei XI, xxviii.

254

For the essence of God, whereby He is, has absolutely nothing mutable in it, neither in eternity, nor in truth, nor in will, since in it truth is eternal, charity is eternal; and in it charity is true and eternity is true; in it, too, eternity is loved and truth is loved.

De Trin. IV, 1 (procemium).

255

In Him is the cause of continued existence, the light of understanding, and the rule of life. . . . If then man was so created that by that in him which excels he may approach that which is above all things, namely, the one, true, almighty God, without whom no nature can have being, no teaching can instruct, and no use can assist, let him seek Him in whom all things are joined, in whom all things have security for us. Let him behold Him in whom is all our certainty; let him love Him in whom is all our morality.

De civ. Dei XIII, 4.

256

All these things which are made by the divine craftsmanship, show in themselves a certain unity, and form, and order. For each of them is both some one thing, as are the several natures of bodies and dispositions of souls; and is fashioned in some form, as are the figures or qualities of bodies, and the various learning or skill of souls; and seeks or preserves a certain order, as are the several weights or collocation of bodies, and the loves or delights of souls. When therefore we contemplate the Creator, who is understood by the things that are made (Rom. i, 20), we must needs understand the Trinity, of whom, as is fitting, there appear traces in the creature. For in that Trinity is the supreme source of all things, and the most perfect beauty, and the most blessed delight. Those three, therefore, both seem to be mutually determined to each other, and are in themselves infinite. Now here, in corporeal things, one thing alone is not as much as three together, and two are something more than one; but in that supreme Trinity one is as much as the three together, nor are two anything more than one. And in themselves they are infinite. So both each are in each, and all in each, and each in all, all in all, and all are one.

De Trin. VI, x, 12.

257

There is no nature, and, indeed, there is no substance, which does not contain within itself and exhibit these three things: first, that it *is;* next, that it is *this* or *that;* and third, that as far as possible it *persists* as it is. The first of these displays the original cause of nature from which all things exist; the second presents the species according to which all things are fashioned and formed in a particular way; the third exhibits a certain permanence, so to speak, in which all things are. Now, if it be possible that a thing *be,* and yet be not *this* or *that,* and not *persist* in its own generic form, or that a thing be *this* or *that,* and yet not *be,* and not *persist* in its own generic form, so far as it is possible for it to do so; or that a thing *persist* in its own generic form by the form belonging to it, and yet not *be,* and not be *this* or *that,* then it is also possible that in that Trinity one Person can do something in which the others have no part. But if you see that whatever *is* must forthwith be *this* or *that,* and must *persist* so far as possible in its own generic form, you will see also that those Three do nothing in which all have not a part.

Ep. XI, 3.

258

The whole Trinity is revealed to us in its works, and hence is the origin, the informing, and the blessedness of the holy city. . . . If it be asked whence it is, God founded it; or how it has wisdom, God enlightened it; or whence is its bliss, the enjoyment of God, who controls its existence, illumines its contemplation, gives joy to its perseverance; that is to say, it lives, contemplates, loves; blossoms in the eternity of God, shines in His truth, and joys in His goodness.

De civ. Dei XI, xxiv.

259

To know Thee fully as Thou art, Thou only knowest;
Who art unchangeably, and knowest unchangeably, and
willest unchangeably. And Thy essence doth know, and doth
will unchangeably; and Thy knowledge both is and doth will
unchangeably.

Conf. XIII, xvi, 19.

260

O eternal truth, and true Charity, and lovely Eternity!
Thou art my God, to Thee do I sigh day and night.

Conf. VII, x, 16.

III. SELF-MINDFUL, SELF-ATTENTIVE, SELF-SENSIBLE, SELF-UNITY

261

The mind cannot love itself, unless it also know itself; for
how can it love what it does not know? Again, if any one say
that the mind, from either special or general knowledge, believes
itself to be such as it has by experience found others to be, and
for this reason loves itself, he speaks most foolishly. For whence
does a mind know another mind if it does not know itself? . . .
As the mind gathers knowledge of corporeal things through the
senses of the body, so it gathers that of incorporeal things
through itself. . . .

But as these are two things, the mind and the love of it, when
it loves itself; so there are two things, the mind and the knowledge of it, when it knows itself. Therefore the mind itself, and
the love of it, and the knowledge of it are three things, and these
three are one; and when they are perfect, they are equal.
For if one loves himself less than is his due,—as for example,
suppose the mind of a man loves itself as much as the body of
a man ought to be loved, whereas the mind is more than the
body,—then it is in fault, and its love is not perfect. Again,
if it loves itself more than is its due, as if, for instance, it loves
itself as much as God is to be loved, whereas the mind is incomparably less than God,—here too it is exceedingly in fault, and
the love it has for itself is not perfect. . . . Also, if knowledge

is less than that thing which is known, and which can be fully known, then that knowledge is not perfect; but if it is greater, then the nature which knows is above that nature which is known. . . . But when the mind knows itself, its knowledge does not rise above itself, because itself knows, and itself is known. When therefore it knows itself entirely, and no other thing with itself, then its knowledge is equal to itself. . . .

In these three, when the mind knows itself and loves itself, there remains the trinity, mind, love, knowledge; and this trinity is not confounded by any commingling, although they are each severally in themselves, and mutually all in all, or each severally in each two, or each two in each. Therefore all are in all. For the mind certainly is in itself, since it is called mind in relation to itself; although it is called knowing, or known, or knowable, relatively to its own knowledge; although as loving, or loved, or lovable, it is referred to the love with which it loves itself. And knowledge, though it is referred to the mind that knows, or is known, nevertheless it is spoken of as knowing and known in relation to itself; for the knowledge by which the mind knows itself is not unknown to itself. And although love is referred to the mind that loves, whose love it is; nevertheless it is also love in respect to itself, so that it also is in itself; since love too is loved, and it cannot be loved with anything else but love, that is with itself. Thus these things are severally in themselves. But so they are in each other, because the mind that loves is *in* love, and love is *in* the knowledge of him that loves, and knowledge is *in* the mind that knows. And each severally is likewise in each two, because the mind which knows and loves itself is in its own love and knowledge; and the love of the mind that loves and knows itself, is in the mind and in its knowledge; and the knowledge of the mind that knows and loves itself is in the mind and in its love, because it loves itself that knows, and knows itself that loves. Hence too each two is in each severally, since the mind which knows and loves itself is together with its own knowledge in love, and together with its own love in knowledge; and love itself, also, and knowledge are together in the mind which loves itself and knows itself. But in what way all are in all, we have already shown above; since the mind loves itself as a whole, and knows itself as a whole,

and knows its own love wholly, and loves its own knowledge
wholly, when these three things are perfect in relation to themselves. Therefore these three things are marvellously inseparable
from each other; and yet each one of them is everally a substance, and all together they are one substance or essence,
whilst they are mutually predicated relatively. . . .

Parturition by the mind is preceded by a certain desire, by
which, through seeking and finding what we wish to know,
the offspring, namely, knowledge itself, is born. And consequently, that desire by which knowledge is conceived and
brought forth, cannot rightly be called the parturition and the
offspring; and the same desire which led us to long for the
knowing of the thing, becomes the love of the thing when known,
while it holds and embraces its accepted offspring, that is,
knowledge, and unites it to its begetter. And so there is a kind
of image of the Trinity in the mind itself, and the knowledge
of it, which is its offspring, and love as the third, and these
three are one, and one substance.

De Trin. IX, iii, 3; v, 8; xii, 18.

262

When [the mind] seeks to know itself, it already knows itself
as seeking. Therefore it knows itself. For it cannot altogether
not know itself, when certainly it does so far know itself in that
it knows that it does not know itself. But if it does not know itself
as not knowing itself, then it does not seek to know itself. Hence,
in the very fact that it seeks itself, it is clearly convicted of being
more known to itself than unknown. For it knows itself as seeking
and as not knowing itself, in that it seeks to know itself. . . .

Why then is it enjoined to know itself? I suppose, in order
that it may reflect upon itself, and live according to its own
nature, that is, seek to be ordered according to its own nature,
namely, under Him to whom it ought to be subject, and above
those things to which it is to be preferred,—under Him by whom
it ought to be ruled, above those things which it ought to
rule. . . .

Therefore let the mind learn to know itself, and not seek
itself as if it were absent, but fix upon itself the intention of the
will, by which it was wandering among other things, and let

it reflect upon itself. Thus it will see that at no time did it not love itself, but that by loving some other thing together with itself, it has confounded itself with it and in some sense has grown one with it. . . . Let it not therefore seek to discern itself as though absent, but take pains to discern itself as present. Nor let it acquire knowledge of itself as if it did not know itself, but let it distinguish itself from that which it knows to be another. . . .

In three things [memory, understanding, will,] we may commonly also discern the quality of the abilities of the young. For the more tenaciously a boy remembers, and the more acutely he understands, and the more ardently he studies, the more laudable he is in point of ability. But when the question is about anyone's learning, then we do not ask how solidly and easily he remembers, or how shrewdly he understands, but what it is he remembers, and what it is he understands. And because the mind is held to be praiseworthy not only as being learned but also as being good, we take note not only of what he remembers and what he understands but also of what he wills; not how ardently he wills, but first what it is he wills, and next how greatly he wills it. For the mind that loves eagerly is worthy of praise only when that which it loves ought to be loved eagerly. Where therefore we talk of the three things, ability, knowledge, use, the first of these is to be considered under the three heads of what a man can do by memory, understanding and will. The second of them is to be considered in regard to that which any one has in his memory and in his understanding, to which he has attained by the assiduity of his will. But the third, namely, use, lies in the will, which handles those things that are contained in the memory and understanding, whether it refer them to something further, or rest satisfied with them as an end. For to use, is to take up something into the power of the will; to enjoy, is to use with the joy, not now of hope but of the actual thing. Accordingly, every one who enjoys, uses; for he takes up something into the power of the will and is satisfied with it as an end. However not every one who uses, enjoys, if he has sought after that which he takes up into the power of the will, not on account of the thing itself, but on account of something else. . . .

By what is the mind removed, except by itself? And where is it placed so as to be in its own sight, except before itself? . . . It appears, therefore, that the beholding of the mind is something pertaining to its nature, and is recalled to that nature when it thinks itself, not by a movement through space, as it were, but by an incorporeal return to it. But when it is not thinking itself, it appears that it is indeed not in its own sight, nor is its own perception formed from it, but yet it knows itself as though it were to itself a memory of itself. . . . Therefore the trinity which we were setting first was conceived thus: first that there be placed in the memory that by which the perception of the percipient was formed; next the conformation, or as it were the image which is impressed thereby, and lastly love or will as that which combines the two. When therefore the mind beholds itself in thought, it understands, and has cognition of, itself. Hence it begets its own understanding and cognition. For an incorporeal thing is seen as understood, and by understanding cognition of it is had. Yet certainly the mind does not so beget this knowledge of itself, when it beholds itself as understood by conception, as though it had been before unknown to itself; but it was known to itself in the way in which things are contained in the memory; just as we say that a man knows letters, even when he is thinking of other things, and not of letters. And these two things, the begetter and the begotten, are joined together by a third, namely, love, which is nothing other than will seeking for or holding fast to something that is to be enjoyed. . . .

For the mind is not adventitious to itself; as though from somewhere else there came to itself, already existing, that same self not already existing, from somewhere else or did not come from somewhere else, but that in the mind already existing, there was born that same mind not already existing; just as faith, which before was not, arises in the mind which already was; or as if the mind saw itself set up, as it were, in its own memory subsequent to its cognition of itself, as though it were not there before it knew itself; whereas actually, from the time when it began to be, it had never ceased to remember, to understand, and to love itself. . . .

Wherefore, as in relation to things past that is called memory which makes it possible to recall and remember them, so in a thing present, as the mind is to itself, that may not reasonably be called memory which makes the mind at hand to itself, so that it can be understood by its own thought, both be joined together by love of itself. . . .

Since, therefore, memory, understanding, will, are not three lives, but one life; not three minds, but one mind; it follows as a certainty that they are also not three substances, but one substance. Since memory, which is called life, and mind, and substance, is so called in respect to itself; but relatively to something else it is called memory. And I should say the same also of understanding and of will, since they are called understanding and will relatively to something else; but each in respect to itself is life, and mind, and essence. And hence these three are one, in that they are one life, one mind, one essence, and whatever else they are severally called in respect to themselves, they are called also together, not plurally, but in the singular number. But they are three in that wherein they are mutually referred to each other; and if they were not equal, and this not only each to each, but also each to all, they certainly could not mutually contain each other; for not only is each contained by each, but also all by each. For I remember that I have memory, and understanding, and will; and I understand that I understand, and will, and remember; and I will that I will, and remember, and understand; and I remember together my whole memory, and understanding, and will. For that of my memory which I do not remember, is not in my memory; and nothing is so much in the memory as memory itself. Therefore I remember the whole memory. Again, whatever I understand I know that I understand, and I know that I will whatever I will; but whatever I know I remember. Therefore I remember the whole of my understanding and the whole of my will. Similarly, when I understand these three things, I understand them together as whole. For there is none of things that are intelligible which I do not understand, except that which I do not know; but what I do not know, I neither remember, nor will. Therefore whatever of intelligible things I do not understand, I consequently neither remember nor will. And whatever of intelligible things I remember and will, I consequently understand. My will also embraces my whole understanding and my whole memory, while I am using the whole that I understand and remember. Hence, while all are mutually comprehended by each, and as wholes, each as a whole is equal to each as a whole, and each as a whole at the same time to all as wholes; and these three are one, one life, one mind, one essence. . . .

But that is a still more hidden depth of our memory, wherein we found this also first [to be true] when we thought of it, and wherein an interior word is begotten such as belongs to no tongue,—knowledge, as it were of knowledge, vision of vision, and understanding, which shows itself in thought, of understanding which had indeed already existed in the memory, but was latent there; although, unless the thought itself had also some sort of memory of its own, it would not return to those things which it had left in the memory while it turned to think of other things. . . .

As there are both understanding and love in that primary memory wherein we find provided and stored up that at which we can arrive by thought, because we find also those two things there, when we find by thinking that we both understand and love anything; which things were there too when we were not thinking of them; and as there are memory and love in that understanding which is formed by thought; which true word we say inwardly without the tongue of anything, when we say what we know; for the gaze of our thought does not return to anything except by remembering it, and does not care to return unless by loving it; so love, which combines the vision set up in the memory and the vision of the thought formed thereby, as, so to speak, parent and offspring, would not know what to love rightly, unless it had a knowledge of what was to be desired, and this it cannot have without memory and understanding.

De Trin. X, iii, 5; xi, 6; XIV, vi, 8; xi, 14;
X, xi, 18; XV, xxi, 40, 41.

263

Experience has shown that the mind could never be in such a case as not to remember, understand and love itself, although it might not always think of itself. But when it did think of itself, it did not in the same act of thought distinguish itself from corporeal things. . . .

For that [outer] man also is not called man to no purpose; but because there is in it some likeness of the interior man. . . . As testimony to this let us use that of the eyes in preference. For this bodily sense far surpasses the others, and, with all its difference in kind, is nearer akin to the sight of the mind. . . .

Vision is produced from a thing that is visible; but not from that alone, unless there be present also one who sees. Wherefore vision is produced from something visible and someone seeing, in such a way, indeed, that on the part of him who sees there is the sense of the eyes and the intention of looking at and observing the object. Yet that information of the sense, which is called vision, is imprinted only by the body which is seen, that is, by some visible thing; and if this is taken away, no form remains of that which was in the sense so long as that which was seen was present. Yet the sense itself remains which existed also before anything was perceived; just as the trace of a thing in water lasts so long as the body itself, which is impressed on it, is in the water; but if this is taken away there will no longer be any such trace, though the water remains, which existed also before it took the form of that body. And therefore we cannot say that a visible thing produces the sense; nevertheless it produces the form, its own likeness, so to speak, which comes to be in the sense, when we perceive anything by seeing. . . .

This being the case, let us remember how these three things following, though diverse in nature, are tempered together into a kind of unity; that is to say, the shape of the body which is seen, and the image of it impressed on the sense, which is vision, or sense informed, and the will of the mind which applies the sense to the sensible thing, and retains the vision itself in it. The first of these, that is, the visible thing itself, does not belong to the nature of the living being, except when we discern our own body. The second, however, belongs to that nature to this extent, that it is wrought in the body, and through the body in the soul; for it is wrought in the sense, which is neither without the body nor without the soul. But the third is of the soul alone, for it is the will. Although, however, the substances of these three are so different, yet they coalesce into such a unity that, even with the intervention of the reason as arbiter, a distinction can scarcely be made between the two former, namely, the form of the body which is seen, and the image of it which is wrought in the sense, that is, vision. And the will has such power to combine these two, that it both applies the sense to be informed to the thing which is seen, and holds it when informed in that thing. . . .

If the form of the body which was corporeally perceived, is withdrawn, its likeness remains on in the memory, to which the will may again direct its eye, so as to be formed thence from within, as the sense was formed from without by the sensible body exposed to it. And thus that trinity is produced from memory, from internal vision, and from the will, which unites both of these. And when these three things are coacted (*coguntur*) into one, from that very coaction it is called cogitation (*ab ipso coactu cogitatio dicitur*). Nor is there any longer in these three any diversity of substance. For neither is the sensible body there, which is wholly distinct from the nature of the living being, nor is the bodily sense there informed, so as to produce vision, nor does the will itself act so as to apply the sense to be informed to the sensible body, and to hold it when informed in it. But in place of that bodily species which was perceived from without, there succeeds the memory retaining that form which the soul absorbed through the bodily sense; and in place of that vision which was outward when the sense was informed by the sensible body, there succeeds a similar vision within, since the eye of the mind is informed by that which the memory retains, and the bodies thought of are absent. And the will itself, just as before it applied the sense to be informed to the body exposed to it from without, and united it thereto when informed, so now it turns the eye of the recollecting mind to the memory, in order that it may be informed by that which the memory has retained, and that there may be in the thought a like vision. . . .

What therefore a body in place is to the bodily sense, that the similitude of the body in the memory is to the eye of the mind; and what the vision of the percipient is to that form of the body by which the sense is informed, that the vision of the concipient is to the image of the body established in the memory, by which the eye of the mind is informed; and what the intention of the will is to the body seen and the vision to be combined with it, in order that a kind of trinity of the three things may therein take place, although their nature is diverse, this the same intention of the will is towards combining the image of the body, which is in the memory, and the vision of the concipient, that is the form which the eye of the mind returning to the memory took, in order that here too a kind of trinity of three things may take place, not distinguished by diversity of nature, but of one and the same substance; since this whole is now within, and the whole is one mind. . . .

In this distribution, therefore, when we begin from the form of the body and arrive finally at the form which comes into being in the vision of the concipient, we find four forms born, as it were, step by step one from the other, the second from the first, the third from the second, the fourth from the third; since from the form of the body which is perceived there arises that which comes to be in the sense of the percipient, and from this that which comes to be in the memory, and from this that which comes to be in the mind's eye of the concipient. Hence the will thrice combines, as it were, parent and offspring: first, the form of the body with that which it begets in the sense of the body; and that again with that which from it comes to be in the memory; and thirdly this also with that which is begotten by it in the vision of the concipient's mind. But the intermediate combination, which is the second, although nearer to the first, is yet not so like the first as the third is. For there are two kinds of vision, the one perceptive, the other conceptive. But in order to make the conceptive vision possible, there is wrought in the memory by the perceptive vision something like it, to which the mind's eye may turn in evoking its conception; just as the glance of the eyes turns in perceptive vision to the bodily object. I have, therefore, chosen to put forward two trinities in this class; one when the perceptive vision is formed from the bodily object, the other when the conceptive vision is formed from the memory. But I have refrained from putting forward an intermediate one, because we do not commonly call it vision, when the form which comes to be in the sense of the percipient is entrusted to the memory. Yet in no case does the will appear except as the combiner as it were of parent and offspring, and therefore, proceed whence it may, it can be called neither parent nor offspring. . . .

But because things which are impressed on the memory singly can be conceived according to number, measure seems to belong to the memory but number to the vision; for, though the multiplicity of such visions is innumerable, yet a limit not to be transgressed is prescribed for each in the memory. Measure, therefore, appears in the memory, number in the visions; just as there is in the visible bodies themselves some measure, to which the sense of the beholders is most multifariously adapted, and from one visible object there is formed the sight seen by many percipients, so that even a single person commonly sees a single object under a double appearance on account of the number of his two eyes. . . . In those things, therefore, from which visions are expressed, there is a certain measure; but in the visions themselves, number. But the will, which unites these things and regulates them, and combines them in a kind of trinity, and does not find pleasure in setting its desire on perceptive or conceptive vision, except in those things whence the visions are formed, resembles weight. Wherefore I would just notice by way of anticipation those three things, measure, number, weight, which are to be perceived in all other things also. . . .

He lives badly and degenerately who lives according to the trinity of the outer man, because it is the purpose of using sensible and corporeal things that has also brought forth that trinity, which though it imagines interiorly, nevertheless imagines exterior things. For no one could use those things even well, unless the images of things perceived by the senses were retained in the memory. And unless the will dwells for the greatest part in the higher, interior things, and unless that will itself, which is accommodated either to bodies without or to their images within, relates whatever it receives in them to a better and truer life, and rests in that end by the aspect of which it judges that these things ought to be done, what else do we do but that which the Apostle forbids us to do, when he says, 'Be

not conformed to this world' (Rom. xi, 12)? And therefore
that trinity is not an image of God, since it is produced in the
soul itself through a bodily sense, from the lowest, that is, the
corporeal creature, than which the soul is higher. And yet it
is not altogether dissimilar; for what is there that has not, in
proportion to its species and measure, a likeness of God, seeing
that God made all things exceeding good (Ecclus. xxxix, 21),
for no other reason but that He Himself is supremely good?
In so far, therefore, as anything that is, is good, so far clearly
it has still some likeness of the supreme good, at however far a
distance; and if this is natural, it is certainly a right and well-
ordered one; but if it is a faulty likeness, then it is certainly a
debased and distorted one. For souls even in their very sins
strive after nothing else but a kind of likeness of God, in a proud
and perverse, and, so to speak, servile liberty.

De Trin. XV, iii, 5; XI, i, 1; ii, 3, 5;
iii, 6; iv, 7; ix, 16; xi, 18; v, 8

264

As we leave behind those things which belong to the exterior
man and desire to ascend interiorly from those things which
we have in common with the beasts, before we come to the cognition of the things intelligible and supreme, which are eternal,
the rational cognition of temporal things presents itself. . . . It
belongs to all men to will to be blessed, yet the faith by which
the heart is cleansed, and thus blessedness attained to (cf. Matt.
v, 8), is not the possession of all men. And so it comes about that
by means of the faith, which not everyone wishes to have, we
must reach out to the blessedness which no one can exist without
wishing for. That they wish to be blessed all see in their own
heart. And so great is the agreement of human nature on this
subject, that the man is not deceived who from his own mind
conjectures this concerning the mind of another; in short we
know ourselves that all wish this. But many despair of being
able to be immortal, though in no other way can anyone be
what all wish to be, that is, blessed. Yet all would be immortal
if they could, but through not believing that they can be, they do
not live so that they may be. Faith is therefore necessary to the

attainment of blessedness in all the good things of human nature, that is, both of the soul and of the body. . . .

If, then, anyone have committed to memory the words of this faith in their sounds alone, not knowing what they mean, as those who do not know Greek commonly hold in memory Greek words, or similarly Latin ones, or words of any other language of which they are ignorant, has not he a sort of trinity in his mind? For firstly, those sounds of words are in his memory, even when he is not thinking of them, and next, the mental vision of his act of recollection is formed from them when he thinks of them; and the will of him who remembers and thinks of them unites both. Yet we should on no account say that the man in so doing, does it in relation to a trinity of the interior man, but rather of the exterior; because he remembers, and when he wills, contemplates as much as he wills, that alone which belongs to the sense of the body, which is called, hearing. Nor in such an act of thought does he do anything else than deal with images of corporeal things, in this case sounds. But if he holds and recollects what those words signify, now indeed something of the interior man is brought into action. However, he ought not yet to be said or thought to live according to a trinity of the interior man, unless he loves those things which are there declared, enjoined, and promised. . . .

Wherefore, since, as it is written, 'While we are in the body we are absent from the Lord. For we walk by faith and not by sight' (2 Cor. v, 6 sq.); certainly so long as 'the just man liveth by faith' (Rom. i, 17), however much he live according to the interior man, although by this same temporal faith he strive after truth and reach out to things eternal, nevertheless in the retention, contemplation, and love of this same temporal faith, there is not yet such a trinity as may be called an image of God; lest that should seem to be constituted in things temporal which ought to be constituted in things eternal. For when the human mind sees its own faith, whereby it believes what it does not see, it does not see anything eternal. For that will not always exist, which certainly will not then exist, when this pilgrimage in which we are absent from God, so that it is necessary to walk by faith, shall be ended, and that sight shall have succeeded it whereby we shall see face to face (1 Cor. xiii, 12); just as now, though we do not see, yet because we believe, we shall deserve to see, and shall rejoice at having been brought through faith to sight. For then it will no longer be faith, by which that is believed which is not seen, but sight, by which that is seen which is believed. At that time, therefore, although we remember this mortal life that is passed, and call to mind by recollection that we once believed what we did not see, yet that faith will be reckoned among things past and done with, not among things present and ever continuing. And hence that trinity also which now consists in the memory, contemplation and love of this same faith present and continuing, will then be found to be done with and past, and not enduring. From which it may be gathered, that if that trinity is indeed an image of God, then this very image would have to be reckoned not among things which exist always, but among transient things. . . .

Things which are known are, as it were, adventitious in the mind, either wrought into it in the form of historical knowledge, such as facts and sayings, which are accomplished in time and are transient, or which in the nature of things are set in their own place and region; or they arise in the man himself, not having been there before, either through the teaching of others or by his own meditation, such as faith . . . or as the virtues, by which, if they are true, man lives righteously in this mortal state, so that he may live blessed in that eternity which is promised him by God. These and such like things have their due order in time, and in that order we discerned more readily a trinity of memory, vision, and love. For some of these things anticipate the cognition of the learner; for they are knowable before there is cognition of them, and they beget in him cognition of themselves. And they either exist in their own proper places, or they have happened in the past; although things that are past do not themselves exist, but only certain signs of them as being past, the sight or hearing of which makes it known that they have been and are passed away. And those signs are either situate in places, such as monuments of the dead and the like; or they exist in written books worthy of credence, as is all history which is serious and of approved authority; or they are in the minds of those who already know them, since what is already known to them is certainly knowable by others also, whose knowledge they have anticipated, and who are able to know it on the information of those who already know it. And all these things when they are learned also produce a kind of trinity, namely, by their own proper species, which was knowable also before it was known; and by the cognition of the learner applied to this, which then begins to exist when he learns them, and by the will as a third which combines both. And when these are known, another trinity is produced in the recollection of them, and this now inwardly in the mind itself, from those images which, when they are learned, were impressed upon the memory, and from the information given by thought when the look has been turned on them by recollection, and from the will which as a third combines these two. But the things which arise in the mind, not having been there before, such as faith and other things of the kind, although they seem to be adventitious, since they are implanted by teaching, yet they are not situate without or transacted without, such as those things which are believed, but began to have being wholly within the mind itself. For faith is not that which is believed, but that by which it is believed; and the former is believed, the latter seen. Nevertheless because it began to be in the mind, which was already a mind before these things began to be in it, it seems to be somewhat adventitious, and will be reckoned among things past, when sight shall have succeeded and itself shall have ceased to be. And it now makes by its presence, retained as it is, and beheld, and loved, a different trinity from that which it will then make by means of some trace of itself, which in passing it will have left behind in the memory.

De Trin. XII, xv, 25; XIII, xx, 25, 26; XIV, ii, 4; viii, 11.

265

But when the human mind knows and loves itself, it does not know and love something immutable; and each individual man, when considering what takes place in himself reveals his own mind by speech in one manner, but defines the human mind by special or general knowledge in another. . . . But we contemplate inviolable truth, by which to define perfectly, so far as we can, not of what sort the mind of any particular person is, but of what sort it ought to be in the eternal scheme of things. . . .

In that eternal truth, therefore, out of which all temporal things have come into being, we see by the sight of the mind the form according to which we are, and according to which we do anything by true and right reason; and we have, thence conceived, the true knowledge of things, as it were as a word within us; and by speech we beget it from within, nor being born does it depart from us. And when we speak to others, we apply to the word, remaining within us, the ministry of the voice or of some bodily sign, that by some kind of sensible remembrance a similar notion may come into being also in the mind of the hearer, similar, that is, to that which does not depart from the mind of the speaker. We do nothing, therefore, through the members of the body, in our deeds or words, by which the behaviour of men is either approved or reprehended, which we do not anticipate by a word uttered within ourselves. For no one does anything by an act of will, which he has not first said in his heart. . . .

The word conceived and the word born are, however, one and the same, when the will finds complete rest in the knowledge itself, as is the case in the love of spiritual things. . . . The word, therefore, is knowledge with love. And so, whenever the mind knows and loves itself, its word is joined to it by love. And since the mind loves knowledge and knows love, the word is in the love, and the love is in the word, and both are in him who loves and speaks. . . .

When the mind knows and approves itself, this same knowledge is in such way its word that it is altogether on a par and equal with it, and conversely; since it is neither the knowledge of an inferior essence, such as the body, nor of a higher one, such as God. And whereas knowledge bears a likeness to the thing which it knows, that is, of which it is the knowledge, this knowledge has perfect and equal likeness, by which the mind itself, which knows, is known. And so it is both image and word, because it is an expression of that mind, to which it is equalled in knowing, and that which is born is equal to the begetter. . . .

When we seek the trinity [in the mind], we seek it in the whole mind, not separating the action of reason in things temporal from the contemplation of things eternal, so as thus to seek some third thing by which a trinity may be completed. But this trinity must needs be discovered in the whole nature of the mind in such form that, even if action upon temporal things were wanting, for which work help is necessary with a view to which some part of the mind is diverted in order to deal with these inferior things, yet a trinity would still be found in the one wholly undivided mind. And when this distribution has been already made, not only a trinity may be found, but also an image of God in that part alone which pertains to the contemplation of things eternal; while in that other part, which is diverted from it in the dealing with temporal things, although there may be a trinity, yet there cannot be found an image of God.

It is in the soul of man, that is, the rational or intellectual soul, that we must find that image of the Creator which is immortally implanted in its immortality. For as the immortality itself of the soul is spoken of with a qualification, since the soul too has its death proper to it when it lacks a blessed life, which is what the true life of the soul must be called—though it is called immortal, because it never ceases to live with some life or other, even when it is most miserable, so, although reason or intellect be at one time dormant in it, at another appears to be small, and at another great, yet the human soul is never anything but rational or intellectual. Hence, if it is made after the image of God in respect to this, that it is able to use reason and intellect for the understanding and beholding of God, then from the very moment when that nature so marvellous and so great began to be, whether this image be so worn down as to be almost none at all, whether it be obscure and defaced or bright and beautiful, assuredly it always is. Furthermore, pitying the defaced condition of its dignity, divine Scripture tells us that 'although man walketh as an image, yet he is disquieted in vain. He storeth up: and he knoweth not for whom he shall gather these things' (Ps. xxxviii, 17). It would not therefore attribute vanity to the image of God, unless it perceived it to have been defaced. Yet it sufficiently shows that such defacing does not extend to the taking away its being an image, by saying, 'Although man walks as an image.' Wherefore in each of two ways that sentence can be truthfully enunciated; namely as it was said, 'Although man walketh as an image, yet he is disquieted in vain,' and with equal truth, 'Although man is disquieted in vain, yet he walketh as an image.' For although the nature of the soul is great, yet it can be corrupted, because it is not the highest nature, yet because it is capable of the highest nature and can partake of it, it is a great nature. . . . For although the human mind is not of that nature of which God is, yet the image of His nature, than which nature none is better, is to be sought and found in us, where too our nature has nothing better. . . For it is His image for the very reason that it is capable of Him and can be a partaker of Him. . . .

This trinity of the mind, therefore, is not the image of God for the reason that the mind remembers itself, and understands and loves itself, but because it can also remember, understand, and love Him by whom it was made; . . . so that a trinity appears in the image of God, which is man in respect to his mind, which mind is renewed unto the knowledge of God, according to the image of Him who created man (Col. iii, 10) to His own image (Gen. i, 27); and thus obtains wisdom wherein is the contemplation of things eternal. . . .

The human mind, therefore, is so constituted that at no time does it not remember and understand and love itself. But since he who hates anyone seeks to do him an injury, not undeservedly is the mind of man said to hate itself when it injures itself. For it wills ill to itself unconsciously, in that it does not think that what it wills is prejudicial to it; but it none the less does will ill to itself, when it wills what would be prejudicial to it. And hence it is written, 'He that loveth iniquity hateth his own soul' (Ps. x, 6). He, therefore, who knows how to love himself, loves God; but he who does not love God, even if he does love himself—a thing implanted in him by nature—yet is not inaptly said to hate himself, inasmuch as he does that which is adverse to himself, and assails himself as though he were his own enemy. . . .

And in this image of God within itself the mind has such power as to be able to cleave to Him whose image it is. For it is so established in the order, not of place, but of natures, that there is none above it save Him. And when, finally, it shall altogether adhere to Him, then it will be one spirit (cf.

1 Cor vi, 17); . . . and this by its drawing near to partake
of His nature, truth, and blessedness, yet not by His increasing
in His own nature, truth, and blessedness. In that nature,
then, it will live immutably, and will see as immutable all
that it does see. Then, as divine Scripture promises, its desire
will be satisfied with good things (Ps. cii, 5), good things immutable, the very Trinity itself, its own God, whose image it is.
And that it may thenceforth never in any way suffer wrong,
it will be hidden in the secret of His face (Ps. xxx, 21), filled
with such rich measure of His fulness, that sin will never more
delight it.

De Trin. IX, vi, 9; vii, 12; ix, 14; x, 15; xi, 16; XII, iv, 4;
XIV, iv, 6; viii, 11; xii, 15; XIV, xiv, 18, 20; XV, iii, 5.

266

These three things are in man in such wise that they are
not themselves man. For man, as the ancients defined him,
is a rational mortal animal. These things are the chief things
in man, but are not themselves man. And any one person, that
is, each individual has these three things in his mind. Again,
if we define man in the words, Man is a rational substance
consisting of soul and body, then without doubt man has a
soul that is not body, and a body that is not soul. Hence these
three things are not man, but belong to man, or are in man.
Further, if we take away the body and think of the soul by
itself, the mind is something belonging to the soul, as it were
its head, or eye, or countenance; but these things are not to
be thought of as bodies. It is therefore not the soul, but that
which is the chief thing in the soul, that is called the mind.
But can we say that the Trinity is in such a way in God as to
be something belonging to God, but not itself God? Hence
each individual man, who is called the image of God, not
in respect to all the things that pertain to his nature, but in
respect to his mind alone, is one person, and is an image of
the Trinity in his mind. But that Trinity of which he is the
image is in its totality nothing else than God, is nothing else
in its totality than the Trinity. Nor does anything pertain
to the nature of God so as not to pertain to that Trinity; and

the three Persons are of one essence, not as each individual man one person.

There is moreover a wide difference in this point also, that whether we speak of the mind in a man and of its knowledge and love, or of memory, understanding, will, we remember nothing of the mind except by memory, nor do we understand anything except by understanding, nor love anything except by love. But in that Trinity, who would dare say that the Father understands neither Himself nor the Son, nor the Holy Spirit except through the Son, or loves them except through the Holy Spirit; and that He remembers only by Himself either Himself, or the Son, or the Holy Spirit; and in the same way that the Son remembers neither Himself nor the Father, except by the Father, nor loves them except by the Holy Spirit; but that by Himself He only understands both the Father and the Son and the Holy Spirit; and similarly that the Holy Spirit remembers by the Father both the Father and the Son and Himself, and the Son understands both the Father and the Son and Himself; but by Himself only loves both Himself and the Father and the Son;—as though the Father were both his own memory, and that of the Son and of the Holy Spirit; and the Son were the understanding both of Himself, and the Father and the Holy Spirit; and as though the Holy Spirit were the love both of Himself, and of the Father and of the Son? . . .

We must go on to that word of man, to the word of the rational animal, to the word of that image of God, that is not born of God, but created by God, which is neither utterable in sound nor capable of being conceived under the likeness of sound, such as must needs be with the word of any tongue, but which precedes all the signs by which it is signified, and is begotten of the knowledge which continues in the mind, when that same knowledge is spoken inwardly, such as it really is. . . . For when it is uttered by sound, or by any bodily sign, it is not uttered according as it really is, but as it can be seen or heard by the body. When, therefore, that is in the word which is in the knowledge, then it is a true word, and is truth, such as is expected of man; namely, that what is in the know-ledge is also in the word, and what is not in the knowledge is not in the word; and here 'Yea, Yea: No, No' (Matt. v, 37) is seen to exist. And in this way this likeness of the image that is made approaches as nearly as is possible to that likeness of the image that is born, by which God the Son is declared to be of like substance with the Father. . . . But now, in this glass, in this dark manner (1 Cor. xv, 12), in this likeness, such as it is, who can explain how great also the unlikeness is? . . .

Wherefore, since seeing in this 'dark manner' we have found now so great an unlikeness to God and the word of God, wherein nevertheless there was before found some likeness, this, too, must be admitted, that even when 'we shall be like Him,' when 'we shall see Him as He is' (1 John iii, 2),—and certainly he who said this was aware without doubt of our present unlikeness—not even then shall we be equal to Him in nature. For that nature which is made is always less than that which makes. And at that time indeed our word will not be false, since we shall neither lie nor be deceived. Perhaps, too, our thoughts will not be in a state of flux, passing and repassing from one thing to another, but we shall see all our knowledge at once and in one glance. Still, even when this shall have come to pass, if indeed it come to pass, though the creature that was formable will have been formed, so that nothing will be wanting of that form to which it ought to attain, yet it will not be equatable to that simplicity wherein there is not anything formable, whether formed or reformed, but simply Form. And this being neither formless nor formed is eternal and immutable substance. . . .

We have urged those who demand a reason on such subjects to observe and understand the 'invisible things' of God, so far as they may, by 'the things that are made' (Rom. i, 20), and especially by the rational or intellectual creature which is made after God's image; through which glass, so to speak, they might discern as far as they could, if they could, the Trinity which is God, in our memory, understanding, will. And if anyone alertly explores these three things as by nature divinely appointed in his mind, and remembers by memory, contemplates by understanding, embraces by love, how great that thing in his mind is whereby even the eternal and immutable nature can be recollected, beheld, desired, that man assuredly finds an image of that supreme Trinity. And to the remembering, seeing, loving this supreme Trinity he ought to refer all that he experiences in life, in order that he may recollect, contemplate, find his joy in it. But let him not so compare this image thus wrought by that Trinity and by his own fault changed for the worse, to that same Trinity as to think it in all points like to it, but let him rather discern in that likeness, of whatever sort it be, a great unlikeness also. . . .

These three things, memory, understanding, and love, are mine, not their own; neither do they do what they do for themselves, but for me; or rather I do it through them. For it is I who remember by memory, understand by understanding, love by love; and when I direct the eye of thought to my memory, and thus say in my heart the thing I know, and a true word is begotten of my knowledge, both are mine, the knowledge assuredly and the word. For it is I who know, I who say in my heart the thing I know. And when by thinking I come to find in my memory that I now understand, that I now love anything, which understanding and love were there also before I thought thereon, it is my own understanding and my own love that I find in my memory, whereby it is I who understand, I who love, and not they. Likewise, when my thought is mindful, and wills to return to those things which it had left in the memory, and to contemplate and understand them, and to say them inwardly, it is my memory that is mindful, and it is with my will, not its own, that it wills. When, too, my very love itself remembers and understands what it ought to try to get and what it ought to avoid, it remembers by my memory, not its own, and understands whatever it intelligently loves by my understanding, not its own. Which can be put shortly thus: By all these three things it is I who remember, I who understand, I who love, I who am neither memory, nor understanding, nor love, but who have them. These three things can therefore be expressed as by one person, which has these three, but is not itself these three. In the simplicity, however, of that supreme Nature, which is God, although there is one God, yet there are three Persons, the Father and the Son and the Holy Ghost.

The thing itself, therefore, which is a trinity differs from the image of a trinity in another thing; by reason of which image, at the same time that also in which these three are is called an image; just as both a panel and the picture painted on it are at the same time called an image; but by reason of the picture which is on it, the panel also is called by the name of image. But in that supreme Trinity, which is incomparably superior to all things, the indivisibility is so great that while a trinity of men cannot be called one man, in that supreme Trinity there both is said to be and is one God, and it is not *in* one God but is one God. Nor again, as the image in the case of man having those three things is one person, is this so in the case of the Trinity; but in it there are three persons, the Father of the Son, the Son of the Father, and the Spirit of both Father and Son. For although the memory in the case of man, and especially that memory which the beasts do not have (that is, the memory by which intelligible things are so comprehended that they have entered it through the bodily senses), has, in its own small measure, in this image of the Trinity a likeness of the Father incomparably inferior, yet a likeness of some sort, whatever it be; likewise man's understanding, which by the intention of the thought is formed when that which is known is said, and there is a word of the heart which is of no tongue, has in its own great disparity some likeness to the Son; and love in man, proceeding from knowledge, and combining memory and understanding, as though common to parent and offspring, whereby it is understood to be neither parent nor offspring, has in this image a likeness, although incomparably inadequate, to the Holy Ghost; it is nevertheless not the case that in this image of the Trinity these three things are not one man, but belong to one man, so in the supreme Trinity these three belong to one God, for they are one God, and there are three Persons, not one Person. And it is something wonderfully ineffable, or ineffably wonderful, that while this image of the Trinity is one person, and the supreme Trinity itself is three Persons, yet that Trinity of three Persons is more indivisible than this of one. For that Trinity in the nature of its Divinity or, better expressed, deity is that which it is, and is mutually and for ever immutably equal; and there was no time when it was not, or when it was otherwise; nor will there be any time when it will not be, or when it will be otherwise. But these three which are in the inadequate image, although they are not separate in place, for they are not bodies, yet are now in this life mutually separate in magnitude. For that there are therein no several masses does not hinder us from seeing that memory is greater than understanding in one man, but the contrary in another, and that in yet another these two are overtopped by the greatness of love, and this whether the two themselves are or are not equal to one another. And so each two by each one, and each one by each two, and each one by each one, the less are surpassed by the greater. And when, healed from every infirmity, they are mutually equal, not even then will that thing which by grace will not be changed, be made equal to that which by nature cannot be changed, because the creature cannot be equated to the Creator, and when it shall be healed from every infirmity, will be changed.

De Trin. XV, vii, 11–12; xi, 20, 21; xvi, 26; xxii, 42; xxiii, 43.

267

I do not say that the Father is memory, the Son understanding, and the Holy Ghost will. . . . I do not say that these things are to be equated by analogy as it were to the Holy Trinity, that is to say are to be arranged according to some exact rule of comparison. This I do not say. But what do I say? See. I have discovered in thee three things which are exhibited separately, whose operation is inseparable; and of these three every single name is produced by the three together; yet does this name belong not to the three but to some one of those three. In the Trinity, then, believe what thou canst not see, if in thyself thou hast heard, and seen, and retained it. For that which is in thyself thou canst know, but what is in Him who made thee, whatever it be, how canst thou know? And if thou shalt ever be able, thou canst not yet. And even when thou shalt be able, wilt thou be able to know God as He knoweth Himself?

Serm. (*de Script. N. T.*) LII, x, 23.

Let no one, then, wonder that we have trouble to see anything
at all, even in the manner of seeing which is granted to us in
this life, that is, 'through a glass in a dark manner' (1 Cor.
xiii, 12). For the phrase 'dark manner' would not be heard
here, if sight were easy. And this is a still greater enigma,
that we do not see what we cannot but see. For who does not
see his own thought? And yet who does see his own thought,
I do not say with the eyes of the body, but with that interior
vision of his? Who does not see it, yet who does see it? For
thought is indeed a kind of sight of the mind, whether those
things are present which are also seen by the bodily eyes, or are
perceived by the other senses, or whether they are not present,
but their likenesses are discerned by thought, or whether neither
of these is the case, but things are thought of which are neither
bodily things nor likenesses of bodily things, such as virtues and
vices, or indeed thought itself is thought of; or whether they
be those things which are conveyed by instruction in the liberal
sciences, or whether the higher causes and governing principles
of these things in the immutable nature are pondered; or
whether it be even evil and vain and false things we are thinking
of, with the sense not consenting, or erring in its consent.

De Trin. XV, ix, 16.

269

When the vision, which is promised anew to us face to
face, shall have come, we shall see this not only incorporeal
but also absolutely indivisible and truly immutable Trinity
far more clearly and certainly than we now see that image of
it which we ourselves are. And yet, they who see through this
glass and in this dark manner, as it is permitted in this life to
see, are not those who see in their own mind the things we have
explained and impressed on them, but those who see it as if an
image, so as to be able in some way or another to refer what
they see to Him whose image it is, and also by conjecturing to
see that which by beholding they see through the image, since
they cannot yet see face to face. For the Apostle does not say,
We see now a glass, but, 'We see now through a glass' (1 Cor.
xiii, 12).

They, then, who see their own mind, in whatever way that is possible, and in it that Trinity, . . . and yet do not believe or understand it to be an image of God, but so far do not see through the glass Him who is now to be seen through the glass, so that they do not even know the very glass which they see to be a glass, that is, an image. And if they knew this, perhaps they would feel that He too whose glass this is, should be sought by it, and by it somehow provisionally be seen, an unfeigned faith cleaning their hearts (1 Tim. i, 5), that He who is now seen through a glass, may be able to be seen face to face.

De Trin. XV, xxiii, 44; xxiv, 44.

270

Do Thou give me strength to seek, who hast made me find Thee, and hast given the Hope of finding Thee more and more. My strength and my infirmity are in Thy sight; preserve the one, heal the other. My knowledge and my ignorance are in Thy sight, where Thou hast opened to me, receive me as I enter; where Thou hast closed, open to my knocking. May I remember Thee, understand Thee, love Thee. Increase these things in me, until Thou amendest me wholly.

De Trin. XV, xxviii, 51.

VII. GOD—MAN

271

That God is some kind of eternal life, immutable, intelligible, intelligent, having wisdom, and giving wisdom, this some philosophers of this world have seen. That there is an immovable truth, enduring, indeclinable, wherein are all the governing principles of all created things, this too they have seen indeed, but from afar. They saw, but they were set in error, and therefore they never found by what road that so great and ineffable, and beatific possession could be reached. . . . The Son of God who in the Father is ever the truth and the life, became, by taking upon Himself man's nature, the way. . . . By Him thou goest, to Him thou goest. Seek not to come to Him by any other way than Him. For if He had not willed to be the way, we should ever stray.

Serm. CXLI, i, 1; iv, 4.

272

There is One invisible, from whom as the Creator and prime cause all things seen by us derive their being; and He is supreme, eternal, immutable, and comprehensible by none save Himself alone. There is One by whom the supreme Majesty reveals and proclaims Himself, namely, the Word, not inferior to Him by whom it is begotten and revealed. There is One who is Holiness, the sanctifier of all that becomes holy, who is the inseparable and undivided communion between this immutable Word through whom that Prime Cause is revealed and that Prime Cause which reveals Himself by the Word which is His equal. But who is able with perfectly calm and pure mind to contemplate this whole essence—whom I have attempted to describe without naming, instead of naming without describing—and to draw blessedness from that contemplation, and losing himself in such contemplation to become, as it were, oblivious of self, and to press on to that of which the sight is beyond our perception, in other words, to be clothed with immortality and obtain eternal salvation? . . . Who, I say, can do this but he who, confessing his sins, shall have levelled with the dust all the vain swellings of pride and prostrated himself in meekness and humility to receive God as his teacher?

Since, therefore, it is necessary that we be first brought down from the vanity of pride to humility of spirit, that rising thence we may attain to real exaltation, it was not possible for this spirit to be produced in us by any manner at once more glorious and more gentle, subduing our haughtiness by persuasion instead of violence, than that Word, through whom God the Father reveals Himself to the angels, and who is His power and wisdom; who could not be discerned by the human heart so long as it was blinded by desire for visible things, should condescend so to reveal and to exercise His personality in human form as to make men more afraid of being elated by the pride of man than of being brought low after the example of God. Therefore the Christ Who is preached throughout the world is not Christ adorned with an earthly crown, nor Christ rich in earthly treasures, but Christ crucified. This was ridiculed at first by multitudes of proud men, and is still ridiculed by a remnant. It was the object of faith at first to the few but now to multitudes; for when at first, notwithstanding the ridicule of the multitude, Christ crucified was preached to the few who believed, the lame received power to walk, the dumb to speak, the deaf to hear, the blind to see, and the dead were restored to life. Thus, at length, the pride of this world was convinced that, even among the things of this world, there is nothing more powerful than the humility of God (cf. 1 Cor. i, 23 *sqq.*); so that beneath the shield of a divine example that humility, which it is most profitable to men to practise, might find defence against the contemptuous assaults of pride.

Ep. CCXXXII, 5, 6.

273

Wherefore the Word of God, which is also the Son of God, co-eternal with the Father, the power and the wisdom of God (cf. 1 Cor. i, 24), reaching from end to end mightily, and ordering all things sweetly (cf. Wis. viii, 1), from the highest limit of rational beings to the lowest limit of material creation, present and hidden, nowhere confined, nowhere divided, nowhere distended, but without dimensions, everywhere present in totality—this Word of God took to Himself, in a manner wholly different from that in which He is present to other creatures, the nature of man, and made by union of Himself therewith the one man Christ Jesus, the mediator of God and men (cf. 1 Tim. ii, 5), equal to the Father in His divinity, in His flesh, i.e. in His human nature, inferior to the Father, immutably immortal in respect of the divine nature, in which He is equal to the Father, and yet mutable and mortal in respect of the infirmity which was His through His kinship to us. In this Christ there came to men, at the time which He knew to be most fitting and which He had determined before the world began, the teaching and the help necessary to the obtaining of eternal salvation. Teaching came by Him that those truths which to men's advantage had been spoken before that time, not only by the holy prophets (all whose words were true) but also by philosophers and even poets and authors in all branches of letters (for who will deny that they mixed much truth with what was false?), presented by His authority in the flesh, might be confirmed as true for the sake of those who could not perceive and distinguish them in the light of essential Truth, which Truth was, even before He took upon Himself human nature, present to all who were capable of receiving truth. Moreover, by the example of His incarnation, He taught this above all else for our benefit, that whereas very many men thirsting for the Divine, thought, from pride rather than piety, that they must not approach God directly, but through celestial powers which they regarded as gods, and through various illicit rites which were not religious but sacrilegious, in which worship devils, through the bond of pride between them and men, take the place of the holy angels, now men might understand that the God whom they regarded far off and were approaching through mediatory powers, was actually so near to the pious longings of men after Him, that He had condescended to take upon Himself human nature in such a way as to be united with it as the body is joined to the soul in man, save that whereas both body and soul have a common progressive development, He does not participate in this because it implies mutability, a property alien to God. Again, in this Christ the help necessary to salvation was brought to men. For without the grace of that faith which is from Him, no one can either subdue concupiscence or be cleansed by pardon from the guilt of any sinful desire which he may not have wholly vanquished. As to what relates to His teaching, is there now even an imbecile, however weak, or a silly woman, however degraded, that does not believe in the immortality of the soul and the reality of a life after death? Yet these are truths which, when Pherecydes the Assyrian for the first time maintained them in discussion among the Greeks of old, moved Pythagoras of Samos so deeply by their novelty as to make him turn from the games of the athlete to the studies of the philosopher. But now what Virgil said we all behold: *Assyrium vulgo nascitur amomum*, the balsam of Assyria grows everywhere (Ecl. iv). And as to the help given through the grace of Christ, in Him truly are the words of the same poet fulfilled.

> *Quo duce si qua manent sceleris vestigia nostri,*
> *Irrita perpetua solvent formidine terras.*
>
> (*Virgil*, Ecl. iv).
>
> *Ep.* CXXXVII, iii, 12.

274

There is a certain discipline necessary for men, by which they may be trained and formed after some model. We cannot, however, say regarding that which is accomplished in men by this training, either that it does not exist or that it is a thing not to be desired; but we seek first to know what it is, for in knowing this we know that by which we may infer that it is something, and in which we may remain. Hence the first thing necessary was that some norm and pattern of discipline be demonstrated. And this was done by the divinely appointed method of the Incarnation, which is properly to be ascribed to the Son, in order that from it should follow both our knowledge, through the Son, of the Father Himself, i.e. of the one prime cause whence all things have their being, and a certain interior and ineffable charm and sweetness of remaining in that knowledge, and of despising all mortal things—a gift and work which is properly ascribed to the Holy Ghost.

Ep. XI, 4.

275

And all these things which the Word made flesh did and endured for us in time and place, pertain . . . to knowledge, not to wisdom. And as the Word is without time or place, it is co-eternal with the Father and is in its totality everywhere; and if anyone can, and so far as he can, speak truly about this Word, then his discourse will pertain to wisdom. And hence the Word made flesh, which is Christ Jesus, holds the treasures both of wisdom and of knowledge. For, writing to the Colossians, the Apostle speaks of . . . 'the mystery of God, which is Christ Jesus; in whom are hid all the treasures of wisdom and knowledge' (Col. ii, 2 *sq.*). To what extent the Apostle knew those treasures, how much of them he had penetrated, to how great things he had attained in them, who can know? Yet for my part, according to that which was written, 'Now the manifestation of the Spirit is given to each one of us unto profit; to one indeed, by the Spirit, is given the word of wisdom: and to another, the word of knowledge, according to the same Spirit' (1 Cor. xii, 7 *sq.*), if these two are in such wise to be distinguished from each other, that wisdom is to be assigned to divine things, knowledge to human, then I acknowledge both in Christ, and so with me do all His faithful. And when I read, 'the Word was made flesh, and dwelt among us,' I understand by the Word the true Son of God, I acknowledge in the flesh the true Son of man, and both together joined into one Person of God and man, by an ineffable outpouring of grace. And on this account the Apostle goes on to say, 'And we saw His glory, the glory as it were of the only begotten of the Father, full of grace and truth' (John i, 14). If we refer grace to knowledge and truth to wisdom, we shall, I think, not be inconsistent with that distinction between these two things which we have recommended. For in those things that have their origin in time, this is the supreme grace, that man was joined to God in unity of person; but in things eternal the supreme truth is rightly attributed to God. But that the same is Himself the only begotten of the Father, full of grace and truth, this was brought about in order that He himself in things done for us in time should be the same for whom we are cleansed by the same faith, that we may contemplate Him steadfastly in things eternal. But those distinguished philosophers of the heathen, who have been able to see and understand 'the invisible things of God by the things that are made,' have yet, as is said of them, 'detained the truth of God in injustice,' because they philosophized without a Mediator, that is, without the man Christ, whom they neither believed to be about to come, on the word of the prophets, nor to have come, on that of the Apostles. For set as they were in these lowest things, they could not but seek some media, through which they might attain to those things which they had perceived in their minds to be sublime. And so their thoughts turned to evil, deceptive spirits, through whom it came to pass that 'they changed the glory of the incorruptible God into the likeness of the image of a corruptible man and of birds, and of fourfooted beasts and of creeping things' (Rom. i, 20, 18, 25). And in such forms, in fact, they set up or worshipped idols. Christ is therefore our knowledge, and the same Christ is also our wisdom. He Himself implants in us faith concerning temporal things, He Himself shows forth the truth concerning eternal things. Through Him we proceed to Him; and through knowledge we strive towards wisdom; yet we do not withdraw from the one and the same Christ, 'in whom are hid all the treasures of wisdom and of knowledge.'

De Trin. XIII, xix, 24

276

Unless, also, in the nature of the rational soul something should come into being in time, that is to say, unless something began to be which previously was not, there could never be any passing from a life of utter corruption and folly to one of wisdom and true goodness. And thus as truth in the contemplative lies in the enjoyment of things eternal, while faith in the believer is what is due to things created, man is purified through the faith which is conversant with temporal things, so that he may be receptive to the truth of things eternal. . . . In order, therefore, that we may be called away from the lowest objects and that that which is created may attain to the eternal, we must come to truth through faith. And because all contraries are reduced to unity by some middle factor, and because also the iniquity of time was alienating us from the eternal justice, there was need of some mediatorial justice in time, which middle factor might be temporal in respect to the lowest things, just in respect to the highest; and thus by adapting itself to the former without cutting itself off from the latter, might bring back those lowest objects to the highest. Accordingly Christ was called the mediator of God and man, standing between the immortal God and mortal man, Himself both God and man (1 Tim. ii, 5), reconciling man to God, continuing to be what He (formerly) was, but made also what (formerly) he was not. And the same Person is for us at once the faith in things created and the truth in things eternal.

De cons. Evang. I, xxxv, 53.

277

Since we were not fit to grasp things eternal, and since we were weighed down by the foulness of sins, gathered on us by the love of temporal things, and as it were naturally implanted in us by the seed of mortality, it was needful that we should be cleansed. But cleansed we could not be, so as to be attuned to things eternal, except through things temporal, to which we were already attuned and by which we were held fast. For health is at the opposite extreme from disease; but the intermediate process of healing does not lead us to perfect health, unless it be congruent to the disease. Things temporal that are useless merely deceive the sick; things temporal that are useful bear up those who are to be healed and bring them healed to things eternal. And as the obligation to contemplate things eternal rests on the rational mind when it is cleansed, so the obligation rests on it to have faith in temporal things when it is still to be cleansed. One even of those who in former days were held wise among the Greeks has said that 'the truth bears the same relation to faith as eternity does to that which has begun to be.' . . . And we ourselves also are of this latter class, not only in respect to the body, but also in respect to the mutability of the soul. For that is not properly called eternal which undergoes any degree of change. Therefore, in so far as we are mutable, in so far we stand apart from eternity. But life eternal is promised us through the truth, from the clear knowledge of which, again, our faith stands as far apart as mortality does from eternity. We therefore now apply our faith to things done in time for our sake, and by that very faith we are cleansed; in order that when we have attained to sight, as truth succeeds faith, so eternity may succeed mortality. And hence, since our faith will become truth, when we have attained to that which is promised to us who believe,—and that which is promised us is eternal life, for the Truth (not that which will come to be according as our faith shall be, but that truth which ever is, because in it is eternity) has said, 'Now this is eternal life: that they may know Thee the only true God, and Jesus Christ, whom Thou hast sent' (John xvii, 3); —When our faith by seeing is become truth, then eternity shall possess our transmuted mortality. And until this take place, and in order that it may take place,—for we adapt the faith of belief to things which have come into being, as in things eternal we hope for the truth of contemplation, lest the faith of mortal life should be dissonant with the truth of eternal life—the 'Truth' itself, coeternal with the Father, 'is sprung out of the earth' (Ps. lxxxiv, 12), when the Son of God so came as to become the Son of man, and to take to Himself our faith, that He might thereby lead us on to His own truth, who so took upon Himself mortality, as not to lose His own eternity. . . . It therefore behoves us to be so cleansed, that we may come to have such a beginning as remains eternal, that we may not have one beginning in faith, and another in truth. Nor could we pass from the state of having a beginning to things eternal, unless we were transferred, by the union of the eternal to ourselves, through our own beginning to His own eternity. . . . Since therefore in Him that also which had a beginning has passed over to eternity, in ourselves also it will so pass over, when faith shall have arrived at truth. For to those who already believe, that they might remain in the work of faith, and being thence led on to the truth, and through that to eternity, might be freed from death, He thus speaks: 'If you continue in my word, you shall be my disciples indeed.' And as though they should ask, With what reward? He goes on to say, 'And you shall know the truth.' And again, as though they should say, Of what good is truth to mortal men? He says, 'And the truth shall make you free' (John viii, 31 *sq.*). From what, except from death, from corruption, from mutability? Since truth remains for ever immortal, incorrupt, immutable. But true immortality, true incorruptibility, true immutability, is eternity itself.

De Trin. IV, xviii, 24.

278

While man is properly understood or at any rate held to be made in the image of God, in that part of him of course which excels those inferior parts which he has in common with the beasts of the field; yet because the mind itself, in which reason and understanding are naturally inherent, is darkened by the mist of inveterate error and disenabled not only to enjoy by inherence but even to endure that immutable light, it must gradually be purified and healed and made fit for such happiness, and must first be instructed by faith and purged. And in the mind truth itself, the Son of God, taking on our manhood without any loss of His divinity, founded and established faith, that the way of man to God should be through the God made man.

De civ. Dei XI, ii.

279

We indeed confess that the whole nature of the body is given it by God the omnipotent creator. And therefore whencesoever Our Lord took a body He assuredly took it from His creature. However He willed rather to take it from a woman, as one who, humble, had come to set free His lost creatures, who through a woman were fallen. Hence, willing to lead each sex to the hope of restoration and reparation, He chose the male sex in which to be born, the female of which to be born.

Serm. XII, xii, 12.

That you may know that no creature of God is bad but that unregulated pleasure perverteth it, when in the beginning I made man, I made them male and female. I do not condemn the creature which I made. Behold, I have been born a man, and was born of a woman. It is therefore not the creature which I made that I condemn, but the sins which I did not make. Let each sex then at once see its honour and confess its iniquity; and let each hope for salvation.

Serm. (de Script. N.T.) LI, ii, 3.

281

If our first fall took place when the woman received in her heart the venom of the serpent, it is not to be wondered at that our salvation was brought about when a woman conceived the flesh of the Almighty in Her womb. . . . Through a woman we were sent to destruction; through a woman salvation was restored to us.

Serm. CCLXXXIX, 2.

282

It was first seen by women, and then announced to men. First the women saw the risen Lord, and the evangel was made known by the women to the future evangelists, the apostles, and by the women was Christ announced to them. Now, evangel is in Latin good tidings. . . . What tidings could we call as good as that Our Saviour rose from the dead; and what greater thing could they preach than that which the women made known to them? But why did woman announce the evangel? Because through a woman death was amended. For the woman giving tidings of life consoled the woman giving tidings of death, since she was dead, giving the cup of death. By the woman was Adam seduced, so that he fell into death, by woman was Christ proclaimed as being risen and never more to die.

Serm. XLV, 5.

The women came to the sepulchre; they found not the body
in the sepulchre; they heard from the Angels that the Lord
was risen, and they told these things to the men. And . . .
'these words seemed to them as idle tales' (Luke xxiv, i–12).
But when Eve told what the serpent had said, she was at once
listened to. To the lying woman credence was given, that we
should die; to the women speaking true words, that we should
live, no credence was given. If women ought not to be believed,
why did Adam believe Eve? If woman ought to be believed,
why did not the disciples believe the holy women? And therefore
in this fact the benign dispensation of Our Lord is to be carefully noticed. For it is this which the Lord Jesus Christ did, that
the feminine sex should be the first to proclaim that He was
risen. Since through the feminine sex man fell, through the
feminine sex man was reinstated, for Christ was born of a
Virgin, a woman proclaimed that He was risen. Death through
the woman, through the woman life.

Serm. CCXXXII, ii, 2.

284

He who gave thee form is formed in thee, He is made in thee
through whom thou wast made, indeed, through whom heaven
and earth were made, by whom all things are made, He becomes
in thee the Word of God made flesh, by taking upon Himself
flesh, but without losing His divinity. And the Word is joined
to the flesh, and the Word becomes one with the flesh; and the
bride-chamber of this so great marriage is thy womb; of this
so great marriage, I repeat, that is, of the Word and the flesh,
thy womb is the bride-chamber, whence He, the bridegroom
comes out (Ps. xviii, 6). He found thee a Virgin when He was
conceived, He left thee a virgin when He was born. He gives
thee fecundity, He takes not away thy spotlessness. How came
this for thee? . . . Thou askest me, how came this to me? I
am shy of giving my treasure as an answer. Hear the salutation
of the Angel, and recognize in me thy salvation. Believe Him,
whom I have believed. Thou askest me whence this came to me?
Let the Angel reply. Tell me, O Angel, how did this come to

Mary? I have already told this when I saluted her with the words: 'Hail, full of grace' (Luke i, 28).

Serm. CCXCI, 6.

285

Beautiful as a bridegroom, strong as a giant, lovable and terrible, severe and serene, beautiful to the good, harsh to the wicked, remaining in the bosom of the Father, He made pregnant the womb of the Mother.

Serm. CXCV, 3.

286

Immediately after the words, 'He, as a bridegroom coming out of his bride-chamber, hath rejoiced as a giant to run his way,' there follows, 'His going out is from the end of heaven' (Ps. xviii, 6 *seq.*). What you have just heard: 'Truth is sprung out of the earth' (Ps. lxxxiv, 12), is a dignity conferred, not a creating; is a compassion, not misery (*dignatio est, non conditio; misericordia est, non miseria*). For truth in order to spring out of the earth descends from heaven; of the Bridegroom, in order to come out of his bride-chamber, His going out is from the end of heaven. From there it is that He is born to-day, a day than which there is none shorter on earth, but one after which the days take on their increase. He who bent down to us to raise us up, chose the shortest days, but one after which the light increases; admonishing us by the very manner of his coming, silently yet as it were with the noise of a great shout, that we should learn to be rich in Him, who for our sakes made Himself poor, who for our sakes took the form of a servant, that in Him, who for our sakes sprang out of the earth, we might possess heaven.

Serm. CXCII, iii, 3.

287

The Word of the Father, by whom all the cycles of time were made, when He was made flesh, caused the day of His birth to take place in time; and in this human genesis willed to have one day, when no day opens without His divine command. With the Father He precedes all the ages of the world, by the Mother He set Himself on this day in the courses of the years. The Maker

of man was made man, that the Ruler of the stars might suck at
the breast; that the Bread might be hungered; the Fountain,
thirst; the Light, sleep; the Way, be wearied by the journey;
the Truth, be accused by false witnesses; the Judge of the living
and the dead, be judged by a mortal judge; the Chastener, be
chastised with whips; the Vine, be crowned with thorns; the
Foundation, be hung upon the tree; strength, be made weak;
Health, be wounded; Life, die. To suffer these and suchlike things,
undeserved things, that He might free the undeserving, for neither
did He deserve any evil, who for our sakes endured so many
evils, nor were we deserving of anything good, we who through
Him received so great good things; to suffer these, He who was
before all the ages, without any beginning of days, Son of God,
deigned in these days just past to be the Son of man; and He who
was begotten of the Father, not made by the Father, was 'made'
in the mother whom He had made; that here and now He
might spring from Her, who, except through Him could no-
when and no-where have been.

Serm. CXCI, i, 1.

288

The fact that He took rest in sleep, and was nourished by food,
and experienced all the feelings of humanity is the evidence to
men of the reality of the man's nature which He assumed but
did not consume. This indeed was a fact, and yet there are
heretics who, by a perverted admiration and praise of His
power, have refused absolutely to acknowledge the reality of
His human nature, in which is the guarantee of all that grace
by which He saves those who believe in Him, containing vast
treasures of wisdom and knowledge, and imparting faith to the
minds which He leads on to the eternal contemplation of the
immutable truth. What if the Almighty had created the man
Christ not by causing Him to be born of a mother but by some
other way, and had presented Him suddenly to the eyes of
mankind? What if He had not passed through the stages of
growth from infancy to manhood, and had taken neither food
nor sleep? Would not this have confirmed the erroneous opinion
above referred to, and have made it impossible to believe that
He had taken upon Himself true human nature? And, while

leaving what was marvellous would it not have eliminated the element of mercy from His actions? But now He has so appeared as the Mediator between God and men that, uniting both natures in one person, He both exalted what was ordinary by what was extraordinary and tempered what was extraordinary by what was ordinary in Himself.

Ep. CXXXVII, iii, 9.

289

He who so loved us, that for our sakes He was made in time, through whom all times were made; was in the world less in age than His servants, though older than the world itself in His eternity; was made man, who made man; was created of a mother, whom He created, was carried by hands which He formed; sucked at breasts, which He had filled; cried in the manger in wordless infancy, He the Word, without Whom all human eloquence is mute.

Serm. CLXXXVIII, ii, 2.

290

He lies in the manger, but contains the world; He sucks at the breasts, but feeds the Angels; He is wrapped in swaddling clothes, but vests us with immortality; He is suckled, but adored; He found no place in the inn, but makes for Himself a temple in the hearts of believers. For in order that weakness might become strong, strength became weak.

Serm. CXC, iii, 4.

291

He it is by whom all things were made, and who was made one of all things; who is the revealer of the Father, the creator of the Mother; the Son of God by the Father without a mother, the Son of man by the Mother without a father; the great day of the Angels, little in the day of men; the Word who is God before all time, the Word made flesh at a fitting time; the maker of the sun, made under the sun; ordering all the ages from the bosom of the Father, hallowing a day of to-day from the womb of the Mother; remaining in the former, coming forth from the latter; author of the heaven and the earth, sprung under the

heaven out of the earth; unutterably wise, in His wisdom a babe
without utterance; filling the world, lying in a manger; ruling
the stars, feeling for the breasts with His infant lips; great in the
form of God, tiny in the form of a servant, in such a way that
neither was that greatness minished by His tininess, nor was
this tininess oppressed by that greatness. For when He took upon
Himself human members, He did not abandon divine works, nor
did He cease from reaching from end to end mightily and ordering all things sweetly (Wis. viii, 1). When having put on the
weakness of the flesh He was received in the womb of the Virgin,
He was not confined there, so that the good of wisdom was not
withdrawn from the Angels, and we might taste and see how
sweet the Lord is (Ps. xxxiii, 9).

Serm. 'CLXXXVII, i, 1.

292

The maker of Mary, He was born of Mary; the son of David,
He is David's Lord; the seed of Abram, before Abraham was
He is; the maker of the earth, made on the earth; the Creator
of Heaven, He was created under Heaven. He is Himself the
day which the Lord made, and the day of our heart, that is the
Lord.

Serm. CLXXXVII, iv, 4.

293

O food and bread of Angels, the Angels are filled by Thee,
are satisfied by Thee, but not to the point of satiety; they live
by Thee, they have wisdom by Thee, by Thee they are blessed.
Where art thou for my sake? In a mean lodging, in a manger.
For whom? He who rules the stars, sucks at the breast; He who
speaks in the bosom of the Father, is silent in the Mother's lap.
But He will speak when He reaches suitable age, and will fill
for us the gospel. For our sakes He will suffer, for us He will die;
as an example of our reward He will rise again; He will ascend
into heaven before the eyes of His disciples, and He will come
from heaven to judge the world. Behold Him lying in the
manger; He is reduced to tininess, yet He has not lost anything
of Himself; He has accepted what was not His, but He remains

what He was. Lo, we have the infant Christ, let us grow with Him.

Serm. CXCVI, iii, 3.

294

For behold, God is above us, behold, we are beneath Him, vast spaces lie between, and most of all the intervening space of sin separates us far from Him and casts us down. In so great a distance as His, since we must come to God, how are we to come? God himself remains God; man is added to God, and there is made one person, so that there is not a semi-God, as it were in one part God and in one part man, but wholly God and wholly man; God the liberator, man the mediator, so that we come through Him to Him, not through anyone else, and still to Him; but through that which we are in Him, we come to Him by whom we were made.

Serm. CCXCIII, 7.

295

What is so far, so remote as God from man, the immortal from mortals, the just from sinners? Not far off in place, but in unlikeness. For thus we are wont to speak of two men when their characters are different: this one is far removed from the other. Even though they be standing side by side, even though they dwell in close neighbourhood, even though they be bound by one chain, the godly is far from the ungodly, the innocent is far from the guilty, the just is far from the unjust. If this is said of two men, what of God and man? For as much then as He who is immortal and just was far from us, as mortals and sinners, He came down to us so that He who is far might be made very nigh unto us . . . very nigh not that which we are, but nigh us. . . . In thy two ills one is guilt, the other is penalty: the guilt is that thou art unrighteous, the penalty, that thou art mortal. That He might be very nigh He took thy penalty; He did not take thy guilt. And if He took it, He took it to efface not to incur it. Just and immortal, He is far from the unjust and mortal. O mortal sinner, thou wert far from Him who is just and immortal. He was not made a sinner as thou, but He was made mortal, as thou art. While remaining just,

He was made mortal. By taking the penalty and not taking the guilt, He effaced both the guilt and the penalty. *The Lord, therefore, is nigh, be nothing solicitous* (Phil. iv, *ssq.*). Although in body He is ascended above the heavens, He hath not withdrawn in His majesty. He is everywhere present, who made all things.

Serm. (de Script. N.T.) CLXXI, iii, 3.

296

'The prince in the midst of them' (Ezech. xxxiv, 24). And therefore Mediator of God and Man; since He is God with the Father, man with men: not a man-mediator without a divine nature, nor a God-Mediator without a human nature. Behold the mediator! Divinity without humanity is not a mediator; humanity without divinity is not a Mediator; but between divinity alone and humanity alone there is as mediator the human divinity and the divine humanity of Christ.

Serm. XLVII, xii, 21.

297

The grace of God could never be more gracefully displayed than when the only-begotten Son of God remaining immutably Himself took on man's nature, and by becoming man gave the Spirit of His love to men, by which they might come to Him who was so far removed from men, immortal while they are mortal, immutable while they are mutable, just while they are sinful, blessed while they are wretched. And because He has implanted in us the natural desire to be eternally blessed, He remaining blessed, and putting on our mortal nature to give us what we desired, taught us by His patience in suffering to despise what we feared.

De civ. Dei X, xxix, 1.

298

Whereas it needed both that man be imitated, and that our hope be not set on man, what could be done on the part of God more full of kindness and grace, than that most pure, eternal, immutable Wisdom of God, to whom it behoves us to adhere, should deign to take upon Himself human form? Who not only might do what should invite us to follow God, but also might suffer what used to deter us from following God.

De util. cred. xv, 33.

299

It is said, *the flesh profiteth nothing* (John vi, 64), as in like manner it is said that 'knowledge puffeth up' (1 Cor. viii, 1). Ought we then straightway to hate knowledge? Far from it. And what does 'knowledge puffeth up' mean? Knowledge of itself, without charity. Therefore he added 'but charity edifieth.' Add then to knowledge charity, and knowledge shall be profitable; not by itself but through charity. So too now, 'the flesh profiteth nothing,' but this means of itself. Let the spirit be added to the flesh, as charity is added to knowledge, and it profiteth much. For if the flesh profited nothing, the Word had not been made flesh that it might dwell in us. If through the flesh Christ has greatly profited us, how does the flesh profit nothing? But it is through the flesh that the Spirit acted for our salvation. The flesh was the vessel. Consider what it held, not what it was. The apostles were sent; did their flesh profit us nothing? If the flesh of the apostles profited us, can the flesh of the Lord have profited nothing? For how should the sound of the Word come to us except by the voice of the flesh? Whence the pen of the writer, whence the writing? These all are works of the flesh, but only when the spirit moves it, as if it were its organ.

In Joan. Evang. XXVII, 5.

300

That this may be remedied, seeing that those things which are mortal and impure cannot from their depths rise to the heights of immortal purity, we must have a mediator who, joined to us in our depths by the mortality of His body yet of an immortal righteousness of spirit, whereby, not by distance of space but by excellence of similitude, He remains on high, should give us His truly divine help in our cure from corruption and captivity. Far be it from this incorruptible God to fear the corruption of that man which He put on or of those men with whom as man he abode.

De civ. Dei IX, xvii.

301

He, being God, for this cause became Man, that man might acknowledge himself to be but man. . . . Being God He is made man; and man does not acknowledge himself to be man, that is, does not acknowledge himself to be mortal, does not acknowledge himself to be frail, does not acknowledge himself to be a sinner, does not acknowledge himself to be sick, that as sick he may at least seek a physician; and what is still more perilous, he fancies himself to be in good health.

Serm. (de Script. N.T.) LXXVII, vii, 11.

302

Lo, thou art far from God, O man, and God is far above man. Between them the God-man placed Himself. Acknowledge Christ, and through Him as Man ascend to God.

Serm. (de Script. N.T.) LXXXI, 6.

303

He is at once above, and below: above in Himself, below in His people; above with the Father, below in us. . . . Fear Christ above, recognize Him below. Have Christ above bestowing His bounty, recognize Him here in need. Here He is poor, there He is rich. . . . So then Christ is rich and poor. As God He is rich, as Man poor. Yea, rich too now as Very Man, He hath ascended into heaven, and sitteth at the right hand of the Father; yet is He still poor here, is a-hungered and athirst and naked.

Serm. (de Script. N.T.) CXXIII, iv. 4.

304

For what man knoweth the treasures of knowledge and wisdom which are hidden in Christ and concealed in the poverty of His flesh? For 'He became poor for our sakes, that through His poverty we might become rich' (2 Cor. viii, 9). For when He took on himself mortality, and 'swallowed up' death, He shewed Himself in poverty; He promised riches hereafter, He did not lose those which He had put off. How great is the multitude of His sweetness, which He hath hidden for them that fear Him; which He hath wrought for them that hope in Him (Ps. xxx, 20). For now we know in part, until that which is perfect is come (cf. 1 Cor. xiii, 9 *seq.*). And that we might be made fit to understand this, He, the equal of the Father in the form of God, and made in the form of a servant like to us, remakes us to the likeness of God; and He, the unique Son of God, made the Son of man, makes the sons of men sons of God, and the servants whom He nourished through the visible form of a servant, He perfects in freedom that they may see the form of God. . . .

Until this comes to pass, until He shews us what may suffice us, until we drink our fill of Him, the fountain of life, let us meanwhile, while we are walking in faith, exiled from Him, while we are hungering and thirsting after justice, and with unspeakable longing are yearning for the beauty of the form of God, celebrate in devout allegiance, the birthday of the form of a servant. We cannot yet have in full contemplation the fact that He was begotten by the Father before the morning star was given being, but let us ever celebrate the fact that He was born of a Virgin in the hours of the night. Not yet can we grasp that 'His name continueth before the sun' (Ps. lxxi, 17), but let us recognize that His tabernacle is set in the sun. We do not yet see the Only-begotten for ever remaining in the Father; let us call to mind the bridegroom coming out of His bride-chamber (Ps. xviii, 6). We are not yet fit to be guests at the banquet of our Father; let us give recognition to the manger of Our Lord Jesus Christ.

Serm. CXCIV, iii, 3; iv, 4.

305

Man was lost by free-will; the God-Man came by liberating grace. Dost thou ask what power for evil free-will hath? Call to mind man sinning. Dost thou ask what power to aid He who is God and Man hath? Mark in Him the liberating grace. In no way could it be so shewn what is the power of man's will, if unaided by God, in avoiding evil; it could not be better shewn than in the case of the first man. . . . Verily, in no way doth the benevolence of God's grace and the bounty of His omnipotence so plainly appear as in the Man who is the 'mediator of God and men, the Man Christ Jesus' (1 Tim. ii 5).

Serm. (de Script. N.T.) CLXXIV, ii, 2.

306

In order, therefore, that as by one man came death, so also by one man might come also the resurrection of the dead (1 Cor. xv, 22);—for men strive more to avoid that which they could not avoid, namely, the death of the flesh, than the death of the spirit, that is, the punishment more than the desert of the punishment (for not to sin is a thing about which men either take no thought or too little thought, whereas not to die, though a thing not attainable, is yet eagerly sought after); the Mediator of life, making it plain that death is not to be feared, which by the condition of humanity cannot now be escaped, but rather ungodliness, which can be guarded against through faith, meets us at the end to which we have come, but not by the way by which we came. For we, indeed, came to death through sin, but He through justice; and therefore, as our death is the punishment of sin, so His death became a sacrifice for sin.

Wherefore since the spirit is to be set above the body, and the death of the spirit means that God has left it, but the death of the body that the spirit has left it; and since herein lies the punishment in the death of the body, that the spirit leaves the body against its will, because it left God of its own will; so that, whereas the spirit left God because it would, it leaves the body although it would not, nor leaves it when it would, unless it has done violence to itself, whereby the body is slain: the spirit of the Mediator showed how it was through no punishment of sin that He came to the death of the flesh, because He did not leave it against His will, but because He willed, and when He willed, and as He willed.

De Trin. IV, xii, 15; xiii, 16.

307

If all men of necessity must be miserable whilst they are mortal, then must a mediator be found which is not only man but also truly God, who by means of His blessed mortality may lead men from their state of mortal misery to that of immortal blessedness; and this mediator must be born mortal but not remain so. He became mortal not by any weakening of the divinity of the Word but by taking on Himself the weakness of our flesh. He did this in the mortality of that flesh since he raised Himself from the dead; for the fruit of His mediation is that those to liberate whom He became mediator, might not remain in the eternal death of the flesh. Accordingly it was necessary for the mediator between God and us to have a temporary mortality and an eternal beatitude; so that by that which is transient He might be congruent with mortal men and by that which is eternal He might rescue them from mortality.

De civ. Dei IX, 15.

308

God died, that a kind of celestial exchange might be made, that men might not see death. . . . Forasmuch as He is both God and man, wishing that we should live by that which was His, He died by that which was ours. For He had nothing himself whereby He could die, nor had we anything whereby we could live. . . . Seek for anything in God by which He may die and thou wilt not find it. But we all die, who are flesh, being men bearing on them sinful flesh. Seek for that whereby sin may live; it hath nothing. So then neither could He have death by that which was His, nor we life by that which was ours; but we have life by that which is His, and He death by what is ours. What an exchange!

Serm. (de script. N.T.) LXXX, v.

309

Our enlightening is the partaking of the Word, namely, of that life which is the light of men, . . . that we may be cleansed through Him, made as He was what we are by nature, and what we are not by sin, that we may contemplate God, which by nature we are not. For by nature we are not God; by nature we are men, and by sin we are not just. For which reason God,

made a just man, interceded with God for us man the sinner.
For the sinner is not congruent to the just, but man is congruent
to man. By joining therefore to us the likeness of His humanity,
He took away the unlikeness of our iniquity; and by being made
partaker of our mortality, He made us partakers of His divinity.
For the death of the sinner arising from the necessity of condemnation is deservedly abolished by the death of the Just One arising
from the free choice of His compassion; while His single [death
and resurrection] is congruent to our double [death and resurrec-
tion]. For this congruence, or accord, or concord, or consonance,
or whatever more suitable word there may be, whereby one is
[united] to two, is of great weight in all compacting or, perhaps,
better, co-adaptation of the creature, . . . which the Greeks
call ἁρμονία, . . . and which is found especially in us, and so
naturally implanted by us (and by whom, except by Him who
created us?), that not even the unskilled can fail to perceive it,
whether when singing themselves, or listening to others. For by
this it is that voices of higher and lower pitch are concordant,
so that if any one produces a discordant note, he seriously
offends not only against the science [of music], of which most
people understand nothing, but against the very sense of
hearing. . . .

We certainly, as no Christian doubts, are dead both in soul
and body; in soul, because of sin; in body, because of the
punishment of sin, and consequently in the body also because
of sin. But to each of those two parts of ourselves, both to soul
and to body, there was need of a remedy and of resurrection,
that what had been changed for the worse might be renewed
for the better. . . . Therefore to this double death of ours our
Saviour applied His own single death, and to bring about both
our resurrections, He appointed beforehand and set forth in
a sacrament and type His own one resurrection. . . . The
one death of our Saviour brought, therefore, salvation to our
double death, and His one resurrection wrought for us two
resurrections; since His body in both cases, that is, both in His
death and in His resurrection, was ministered to us by a kind
of remedial harmony, both as a sacrament of the inner man
and as a type of the outer.

De Trin. IV, ii, 4; iii, 5, 6.

310

He was made sharer in our mortality, that we might also be made partakers in His divinity. We were made partakers in One unto life, He a partaker in many unto death.

In Ps. CXVIII, *Serm.* xix, 6.

311

We know, . . . and hold with the most steadfast faith, . . . that Christ died for us, the just man for sinners, the Lord for servants, the free man for the captives, the physician for the sick, the blessed for the miserable, the rich for the needy, the seeker for the lost ones, the redeemer for the bond slaves, the shepherd for the flock, and, what is more wonderful than all, the Creator for the creature; keeping, nevertheless, what He for ever is, the God hidden, man in appearance, quickening by His power, dying in weakness, immutable in His divinity, sensitive to suffering in His flesh, 'who,' as the Apostle says, 'was delivered up for our sins and rose again for our justification' (Rom. iv, 25).

Serm. CCXX.

312

The Lord Jesus, the only begotten of the Father and co-eternal with the begetter, equally invisible, equally immutable, equally omnipotent, equally God, for us . . . was made man, taking upon himself human shape, not losing His divinity, the Mighty One hidden, reappearing in weakness, . . . was born that we might be reborn, died that we might not die for ever and ever. . . . On the third day He rose again . . . He shewed Himself to be seen by the eyes of the disciples, and to be touched by their hands; convincing in regard to that which He had been made, not relinquishing anything of that which He ever was. He companied with them for forty days . . . coming and going, eating and drinking, no longer now in want, but in His full power, and manifesting to them the truth of the flesh, the weakness in the cross, immortality by the sepulchre.

Serm. CCLXII, i, 1.

313

For to this end was He 'God with us,' that we might be with Him. For He who came down to us to be with us, maketh us ascend to Him, that we may be with Him.

In Ps. CXLV, 1.

314

In His words and deeds Christ ever acted so that He should be believed to be God and man; God that made us; man that sought us. . . . For He would not have sought man whom He had made had He not Himself become that which He had made.

In Joan. Evang. XXVIII, 1.

315

As for those who say, What, had God no other way by which He might free man from the misery of this mortality, that He should will the only-begotten Son, God co-eternal with Himself, to become man by putting on a human soul and flesh, and being made mortal to endure death? It is not enough to refute them by asserting that the manner by which God deigns to free us through the Mediator of God and man, the man Christ Jesus, is good and in accord with the dignity of God; but we must also show not indeed that no other mode was possible to God, to whose power all things are equally subject, but that there neither was nor need have been any other mode more appropriate for curing our misery. For what was so necessary for the building up of our hope, and for the freeing the minds of mortals, cast down by the very condition of mortality, from despair of immortality, than that it should be demonstrated to us at how great a price God rated us, and how greatly He loved us? But what is more manifest and evident in this so great proof hereof, than that the Son of God, immutably good, remaining what He was in Himself, and receiving from us and for us what He was not, apart from any loss of His own nature, and deigning to enter into this fellowship of ours, should first, without any evil desert of His own, bear our evils, and so with unobligated munificence should bestow His own gifts on us, who now believe how much God loves us, and who now hope that of which we used to despair, without any good deserts of our own, nay, with our evil deserts too going before. Since those also which are called our deserts are His gifts.

De Trin. XIII, x, 13–14.

316

And after the pattern of [the Son], who is the Image, let us too not depart from God, since we, also, are the image of God. . . . We are this because we are enlightened by the light, but that Image, because it is the Light that enlightens; and it, because it is without pattern, is to us a pattern. For He does not imitate any one preceding Him, in respect to the Father, from whom He is never separable at all, since He is of the very same substance with Him from whom He is. But we by striving imitate Him who abides, and follow Him who stands still, and walking in Him we reach out to Him, because He is made a way in time for us, by His humility, which is to us an eternal abiding place by His divinity. For since to pure intellectual spirits, who have not fallen through pride, He affords a pattern in the form of God, and as equal with God, and as God, so, in order that He might also give Himself as an example to fallen man, who on account of the uncleanness of sins and the punishment of mortality cannot see God, 'He emptied himself,' not by changing His divinity, but by assuming our mutability, and 'taking the form of a servant' (Phil. ii, 7), 'He came into this world' to us (1 Tim. i, 15), and 'He was in the world,' because 'the world was made by Him' (John i, 10), that He might be an example upwards to those who see God, an example downwards to those who wonder at man, an example to the healthy to persevere, an example to the sick to be made whole, an example to those about to die that they may not fear, an example to the dead that they may rise again, 'He in all things holding the primacy' (Col. i, 18). For since man ought not to follow any save God to attain to blessedness, and yet could not perceive God, by following God made man, he might follow at once Him whom he could not perceive, and whom he ought to follow.

De Trin. VII, iii, 5.

317

It was much for thee to taste the sweetness of God, because it was too remote and lofty, thou too abject and grovelling here below. In this so great a severance there was sent a Mediator. Being man thou couldst not come to God, and God was made man, that as man thou couldst come to Man, when thou couldst not come to God; and mightest come to God through Man; and there was made a 'mediator of God and men, the man Christ Jesus' (1. Tim. ii, 5). But if He were man alone, by following what thou art thou wouldst never reach Him; if He were God alone, for lack of comprehending what thou art not, thou wouldst never reach Him. So God was made man, that by following man, which thou canst do, thou mightest reach God, which thou hadst not been able to do. He is the Mediator, and therefore is made sweet. What is sweeter than the bread of angels? How can the Lord not be sweet, since 'man ate the bread of angels?' (Ps. lxxvii, 25). For men and angels live not on different food. This is truth, this is wisdom, this is the goodness of God; but thou canst not enjoy it in a like manner with the angels. For how do they enjoy it? As it is written: 'In the beginning was the Word: and the Word was with God: and the Word was God.... All things were made by Him.' But thou, how dost thou reach it? Because 'the Word was made flesh and dwelt among us' (John i, 1, 3, 14). That man might eat the bread of angels, the Creator of the Angels was made man.

In Ps. CXXXIV, 5.

318

In Christ thou hast all. Dost thou wish to love God? Thou hast Him in Christ. 'In the beginning was the Word, and the Word was with God, and the Word was God.' Dost thou wish to love thy neighbour? Thou hast him in Christ. 'The Word was made flesh.'

Serm. CCLXI, viii, 8.

319

The one Son of God became 'the mediator of God and men' (1 Tim. ii, 5), in that the Word of God, God with God, both laid aside His majesty down even to the level of the human, and raised human lowliness up even to the height of the divine, that He might be the mediator of God and men, and men through God transcend men.

Expos. Ep. ad Gal. 24.

320

'No man hath ascended into heaven, but He that descended from heaven, the Son of man who is in heaven' (John iii, 13). . . . Christ, therefore, is one: word, soul, and flesh, one Christ, Son of God always, Son of man in time; yet one Christ in regard to unity of person.

In Joan. Evang. XXVIII, 4.

321

If, then, the form of a servant was so taken that the form of God was not lost, since both in the form of a servant and in the form of God, He is the same only-begotten Son of God the Father, in the form of God equal to the Father, in the form of a servant the Mediator of God and man, the man Christ Jesus; is there any one who cannot perceive that He himself in the form of God is also greater than Himself, but in the form of a servant also less than Himself?

De Trin. I, vii, 14.

322

The Creator received the creature into Himself; the Creator was not changed into the creature, He took upon Him that which He was not, He did not lose that which He was.

Serm. XLVII, xi, 20.

323

He who was God was made man, by taking what He was not, not by losing what He was: thus was God made man. . . . Let Christ, therefore, lift thee up by that which is man, let Him lead thee by that which is God-man, let Him guide thee through to that which is God.

In Joan. Evang. XXIII, 6.

324

From the very beginning of the human race no one passes to death but through Adam, and no one through Adam but passes to death; and no one attains to life but through Christ, and no one through Christ but attains to life. . . . For if some are saved without Christ, and some are justified without Christ, then Christ died to no purpose.

Contra Julianum VI, xxiv, 80, 81.

325

There was one man, there is one man; one man through whom was downfall, another man through whom there is the building up; through the former downfall, through the latter, a building up. He who did not endure, fell; He who did not fall, raised up. That one fell to destruction because he renounced Him who endures; He who endures came down to him who was lying in ruin.

Serm. XXX, iv. 5.

326

We put on the image of the earthly man by the propagation of sin and corruption, which are ours by our generation, but we put on the image of the heavenly man by the grace of pardon and of eternal life. And this our regeneration gives us only through the mediator of God and men, the man Christ Jesus; . . . for as no one dies in his animal body save in Adam, so no one is made alive in a spiritual body save in Christ.

De civ. Dei XIII, xxiii.

327

. . . Adam, of whom Christ received the flesh. Christ therefore is in Adam and Adam in Christ.

In Ps. CI, *Serm.* i, 4.

VIII. THE WAY, THE TRUTH, THE LIFE

328

And I began to search how I might get me the strength sufficient and fit for the enjoyment of Thee. But I could meet with none, until I embraced the 'mediator of God and men, the man Christ Jesus, God blessed for ever' (1 Tim. ii, 5; Rom. ix, 5).

Conf. VII, xviii, 24.

329

'I am the way, and the truth, and the life' (John xiv, 6). Truth and life doth every man desire, but the way is not found by every man. That God is a certain Life eternal, immutable, intelligible, intelligent, wise, and making wise, some philosophers even of this world have seen. The fixed, settled, unwavering truth, wherein are all the governing principles of all created things, they saw indeed, but afar off. They saw, but amid the error in which they were placed, and hence they did not find the way by which to attain to that so great and ineffable and beatific possession. . . . But Christ, in that He is with the Father the truth and the life, . . . and we had no way by which to go to the truth, as the Son of God, who in the Father is ever the truth and the life, by assuming man's nature became the way. Walk by Him the Man, and thou comest to God. By Him thou goest, to Him thou goest. Look not for any way except Himself by which to come to Him. For if He had not vouchsafed to be the way, we should have always gone astray. Therefore He became the way by which thou shouldest come. I do not say to thee, seek the way. The way itself is come to thee; arise and walk.

Serm. (de Script. Nov. Test.) CXLI, i, 1; iv, 4.

330

For whatever the lower place where thou hast stood before coming home to Christ, the divine discourse has but this to say to thee: Draw near, not yet is the place where there is security.

In Ps. LV, 1.

331

Thou wast walking in thy own ways a vagabond; straying through wooded places, through rough places, torn in all thy limbs. Thou wast seeking a home, that is, a sort of settlement of thy spirit, where thou mightest say, it is well; and might say this in security, at rest from all uneasiness, from every trial, in a word from every captivity; and thou didst not find it. What shall I say? Did one come to thee to shew thee the way? There came to thee the Way itself, and thou wast set therein by no preceding merits of thine; for clearly thou wast straying. What? since the time thou didst set foot therein, dost thou now direct thyself? Doth He that hath taught thee the way now leave thee?

In Ps. LXX, *Serm.* ii, 3.

332

It is one thing to lead to the way, another to guide in the way. Behold man is everywhere poor, everywhere in need of help. . . . While thou leadest I shall not err, if thou let go of me, I shall err. Pray therefore that He let not go of thee, but lead thee to the end. How doth He lead thee? By ever admonishing, ever giving thee His hand. . . . For in giving His Christ He giveth His hand; in giving His hand, He giveth His Christ. He leadeth to the way by leading to His Christ; He leadeth in the way by leading in His Christ; now Christ is truth. 'Conduct me,' then, 'O Lord, in Thy way, and I will walk in Thy truth' (Ps. lxxxv, 11), in Him verily who said 'I am the way, and the truth, and the life' (John iii, 6). For Thou who leadest in the way and the truth, whither leadest thou, but unto life? In Him therefore, unto Him thou leadest. 'Conduct me, O Lord, in Thy way and I will walk in Thy truth' (Ps. lxxxv, 11).

In Ps. LXXXV, 15.

333

By men a thing can be recalled to the mind by the use of word-signs, but it is incorruptible Truth itself that teaches, the one true, the sole interior Master. He became an exterior Teacher also, that He might recall us from exterior to interior things, and taking the form of a servant, He deigned to appear in lowliness to the lowly, that His sublimity might become clear to those rising up to Him.

Contra ep. fund. xxxvi, 41.

334

They profess that that sun which we see scatters its rays through all dregs and filth in bodies, and preserves those rays everywhere clean and pure. If then visible clean things can be touched by visible unclean things and yet not be polluted, how much more hath the invisible and immutable Truth, having through the Spirit taken a soul, and through the Soul a Body, having, that is, assumed the whole of manhood, set that manhood free from all weaknesses without any contamination to Itself.

De ag. christ. xviii, 20.

335

'The temple of God is holy, which you are' (1 Cor. iii, 17), that is all who believe in Christ, and so believe as to love; not as the devils believed (Jas. ii, 19), who loved not; and therefore, though th~y believed, cried, 'What have we to do with Thee, Jesus Son of God?' (Matt. viii, 29). But we, let us so believe that we may believe on Him, loving Him, and may not say, What have we to do with Thee? but may rather say, Unto Thee we belong; Thou hast redeemed us.

In Ps. CXXX, 1.

336

The end therefore of our purpose is Christ, for however much we attempt, in Him we are made perfect, and this is our perfection, that we come home to Him. More thou seekest not; He is thy end. For in like manner the end of thy life is the place whither thou art tending; and when thou hast arrived there, then thou wilt stay. So the end of thy study, of thy purpose, of thy attempt, of thy intention, is He to whom thou art tending, and when thou hast come home to Him, thou wilt desire nothing further, since thou canst have nothing better. He therefore Himself hath set forth in this life an example of living, and will give us in the future life the reward of living.

In Ps. LVI, 2.

337

How are we to imitate the ways of Christ? Are we to imitate Him in the glorious power which He had as God in the flesh? . . . Is it to govern with Him heaven and earth and all that is therein, that He calls men? . . . He does not say that to thee. Thou shalt not be my disciple unless thou hast walked upon the sea (Matt. xiv, 25), or raised one who was four days dead (John xi, 38 *sqq.*), or opened the eyes of one blind from birth (*id.* ix, 1 *sqq.*). Nor this either. . . . What then doth He say? 'Learn of me, because I am meek, and humble of heart' (Matt. xi, 29). That which He became for thy sake is what thou shouldst attend to in Him, that thou mayest imitate Him. . . . To what doth He exhort thee? To imitate Him in those works which He could not have done had He not been made man. For how could He endure sufferings, unless He had become man? How could He otherwise have died, been crucified, been humbled? Thus then do thou, when thou sufferest the troubles of this world. . . . Be strong, be long-suffering, thou shalt abide under the protection of the Most High.

In Ps. XC, *Serm.* i, 1.

338

Whatever other thing thou here seekest, if thou seekest worldlily, if thou seekest in love of the earth, if thou seekest with relish for the earth, thou seekest to the end that thou mayest be happy, but nothing earthly can make thee happy. . . . 'O ye sons of men, how long will you be dull of heart?' (Ps. iv, 3). Do not you wish to be dull of heart, you who burden your hearts with the earth? How long were men dull of heart? Before Christ came, before Christ rose again, men were dull of heart. . . .

Christ came to share our miseries: He hungered, He thirsted, He was wearied, He slept, He worked wonders, He suffered wicked ills, He was scourged, He was crowned with thorns, He was spat upon, He was buffeted, He was nailed to the tree, He was pierced by the spear, He was placed in the tomb; but on the third day He rose again, His labours finished, and death dead. . . . He shewed thee what thou shouldst occupy thy mind with, if thou wouldst be happy; for here thou canst not be this. In this life thou canst not be happy; no one can. . . . If Christ had this here, so canst thou also. In the land of thy death mark what He found. Coming from another region what did He find here but what abounds here? He ate with thee of that which abounds in the storehouse of thy misery. He drank vinegar here, gall He had here. See, that is what He found in thy storehouse. But He has invited you to His own table, the table of heaven, the Angels' table, where He himself is the bread. . . . He gave us His death as earnest of what He would give, as though He would say, I invite you to My life, where no one dies, where truly the blessed life is, where the food suffers no corruption, where it restores, nor ever fails. Look whither I invite you, to the land of the Angels, to the friendship of the Father and the Holy Ghost, to the eternal feast, to brotherhood with me; finally I invite you to Myself, to my life. Are you not willing to believe that I will give you My life? Hold my death as security. Now, therefore, while we are living in this corruptible flesh, let us by reforming our lives die with Christ, and by loving justice live with Christ, for we shall not receive the blessed life until we have come to Him, who came to us, and in Him have begun to be, who died for us.

Serm. CCXXXI, iv, 4; v, 5.

339

The Son of God took upon Himself man, and therein suffered the things which belong to man. This Medicine is for men so great that thought cannot reach to it. For what pride can be healed, if it be not healed by the humiliation of the Son of God? What avarice can be healed, if it be not healed by the poverty of the Son of God? What anger can be healed, if it be not healed by the long-suffering of the Son of God? What ungodliness can be healed, if it be not healed by the charity of the Son of God? Finally, what fearfulness can be healed, if it be not healed by the resurrection of the body of the Son of God? Let the human race lift up its hope, and learn to know its own nature; let it see how great a place it holds in the works of God. Men, despise not yourselves; the Son of God took upon Him the nature of man. Women, despise not yourselves; the Son of God was born of a woman. Yet love not the things of the flesh, for in the Son of God we are 'neither male nor female' (Gal. iii, 28). Love not temporal things, for if it were well to love them, the manhood which the Son of God assumed would love them. Do not fear insult, the cross, death, for if they were harmful to man, the manhood which the Son of God assumed, would not suffer them. . . . If we think much of ourselves, let us be worthy to imitate Him who is called the Son of the most High; if we think little of ourselves let us dare to imitate the fishermen and publicans who imitated Him. . . . Who shall now set himself up against the Son of God? Who shall despair of himself, for whom the Son of God was willing to be so humble? Who shall judge that a happy life consists in those things which the Son of God hath taught us are to be despised? To what adversities shall he give way, who believes that man's nature was in the person of the Son of God guarded in so great persecutions? Who shall think that the kingdom is shut against him, when he understands that publicans and harlots followed the Son of God? From what perversity shall not he be free, who contemplates and loves and follows the words and deeds of that Manhood, wherein the Son of God offered Himself to us as an example of life?

De ag. christ. xi, 12.

340

But the Teacher of humility, the partaker of our infirmity, giving us to partake of His own divinity, coming down for the purpose that He might teach the way and become the way (cf. John xiv, 6), deigned to recommend chiefly His own humility to us.

In Ps. LVIII, *Serm.* i, 7.

341

He to whom the Father hath delivered all things, and whom no one knoweth but the Father, and who alone (and he to whom it shall have pleased Him to reveal Him) knoweth the Father, saith not 'learn of me' to make the world, or to raise the dead, but 'because I am meek, and humble of heart' (Matt. xi, 27, 29).

De scta. virg. XXXV, 35.

342

The Apostle himself seeing not only whither to ascend but also whereby to ascend—for many have seen whither, but have not seen whereby, have loved the country of exaltation, but have not known the way of humiliation—the Apostle, I say, knowing and reflecting and meditating beforehand not only whither but also whereby, saith: 'God forbid that I should glory, save in the cross of our Lord Jesus Christ' (Gal. vi, 14). He could have said, in the wisdom of our Lord Jesus Christ, and said true. He could have said, in the Majesty, and said true; but he said, 'in the cross of Christ' . . . 'By whom,' he continues, 'the world is crucified to me, and I to the world' (Gal. vi, 14). How could the world be crucified to thee, had not He been crucified for thee, by Whom the world was made? Wherefore, 'he that glorieth, let him glory in the Lord' (2 Cor. x, 17; cf. 1 Cor. i, 31; Jer. ix, 23 *seq.*). In what Lord? In Christ crucified. Where there is humility, there is majesty; where there is infirmity, there is power; where there is death, there is life. If thou wouldest attain to the one, despise not the other.

Serm. (de Script. N.T.) CLX, 4.

343

For it was not enough for God to give in His Son one who should show the way, He made Him the way, so that walking by Him thou mightest go under His governance.

In Ps. CIX, 2.

344

Let us therefore so walk as if we were on the way; for the King of our country himself hath been made the way. The King of our country is our Lord Jesus Christ, and there He is the

Truth, but here He is the Way. Whither do we go? To the Truth. By what path do we go? By faith. Whither do we go? To Christ. By what path do we go? By Christ. For He Himself hath said, 'I am the way, and the truth, and the life' (John xiv, 6). But He had once said to those that believed in Him: 'If you continue in my word, you shall be my disciples indeed. And you shall know the truth: and the truth shall set you free' (John viii, 31 *sq.*). And you shall know the truth, He saith, but only if you continue in my word. In what word? As the Apostle saith: 'This is the word of faith, which we preach' (Rom. x, 8). First therefore is the word of faith, and if we continue in this word of faith, we shall know the truth, and the truth shall make us free. Truth is immortal, truth is immutable; Truth is that Word of which it was said, 'In the beginning was the Word, and the Word was with God, and the Word was God' (John i, 1). And who can see this unless his heart be cleansed? How are hearts cleansed? 'And the Word was made flesh, and dwelt among us' (*id.* i, 14). In that therefore the Word continueth in Itself, it is Truth to which we are coming, and which will make us free. But inasmuch as the word of faith is preached, in which the Lord wisheth us to continue, that we may know the truth, it is this: 'The Word was made flesh, and dwelt among us.' Thou believest in Christ born in the flesh, and thus wilt come to Christ born of God, God with God.

In Ps. CXXIII, 2.

345

Vanity and truth are directly contrary to one another. The desires of this world are vanity; but Christ, who freeth us from the world, is truth. He is the way, too, wherein [the Psalmist] wisheth to be quickened (Ps. cxviii, 37), for He is also the life. 'I am the way, and the truth, and the life,' are His own words. . . . And they live rather in Him than under the sun who do not heedlessly hear what the Apostle saith: 'Seek the things that are above, where Christ is sitting at the right hand of God. Mind the things that are above, not the things that are upon the earth. For you are dead: and your life is hid with Christ in God' (Col. iii, 1–3). Therefore if our life is there where Truth is, our life is not under the sun, where is vanity. But this

so great blessing we have rather in hope than possess in deed.
. . . And in the hope wherein we hope that we shall adhere
to the contemplation of the Truth, we are meanwhile made
subject to vanity. For all creation, spiritual, animal, and
bodily is in man; indeed, is man. It sinned of its own free will,
and became an enemy to truth; but that it might justly be
punished, it was not of its own free will made subject to vanity.
. . . As long as we are here according to the flesh, whose
adoption and redemption we here wait for in the patience of
hope; so long, in that respect in which we are under the sun,
we are made subject to vanity.

In Ps. CXVIII, *Serm.* xii, 1.

346

He came to us and was despised among us, first by us, afterwards with us; He taught us to be despised, because He was
despised; taught us to endure, because He endured; taught us
to suffer, because He suffered; and promised that we should
rise again, because He rose again, showing in Himself what we
ought to hope for.

In Ps. CXXV, 1.

347

As our Leader He leadeth us down, He leadeth us on Himself
as the Way, and He bringeth us to Himself as our home. . . .
In Him thou seest both thy labour and thy reward; labour in
His passion, reward in His resurrection.

In Ps. LX, 4.

348

'I am the way, and the truth, and the life' (John xiv, 6).
If thou seekest the truth, keep thou the way; for that same
is the way which is the truth. The way thou art going is the
same as the whither thou art going. Thou art not going by a
way as one thing to an object as another thing, not coming to
Christ by something other than Christ; thou comest through
Christ to Christ . . . through Christ the man to Christ God,

through the Word made flesh to the Word which in the beginning
was God with God.

In Joan. Evang. XIII, 4.

349

Through the man Christ thou stretchest out to the God Christ.
In relation to thee God is far removed, but God was made man.
That which was far from thee, by being made man is close
to thee. Where thou abidest, that is God, the road by which
thou goest, that is Man; the same Christ Himself is both the
way by which thou goest, and the place whither thou goest. . . .
There appeared the man, God was hidden. The Man was slain,
the God was struck; but the man rose again, and God was found.

Serm. CCLXI, vi, 7.

350

Through Me thou comest, unto Me thou comest.

In Ps. CIII, *Serm.* iv, 6.

351

We are Christians, we belong to Christ.

Serm. (de Script. N.T.) CXXX, 4.

352

For the name of Christ is on the lips of all: it is invoked by
the just man in the service of justice, by the perjurer for the sake
of deceiving, by the King to confirm his rule, by the soldier
to nerve himself for battle, by the husband to establish his
authority, by the wife to confess her submission, by the father
to enforce his authority, by the son to declare his obedience, by
the master in support of his rule, by the slave in performing his
duty, by the humble in quickening piety, by the proud in
stimulating ambition, by the rich man when he gives and by
the poor when he receives an alms, by the drunkard at his
wine-sup, by the beggar at the gate, by the good man in dis-
charging his obligations, by the wicked man in failing to do so;
all invoke the name of Christ, the Christian with true reverence,
the pagan with feigned respect; and they shall all undoubtedly
give to that same Person whom they invoke an account both
of the spirit and of the language in which they repeat His name.

Ep. CCXXXII, 4.

To our hearts God is light, and sound, and odour, and food; and He is all of these things for the reason that He is none of these things, and He is none of these things for the reason that He is the Creator of all these things. He is light to our hearts, to whom we say, 'In Thy light we shall see light' (Ps. xxxv, 10). To our hearts He is sound, to whom we say, 'To my hearing thou shalt give joy and gladness' (Ps. l, 10). Odour to our hearts is He of whom it is said, 'We are the good odour of Christ' (2 Cor. ii, 15). But if you seek food, because you are fasting, 'Blessed are they that hunger and thirst after justice' (Matt. v, 6). But of the Lord Jesus Christ himself it is said that He 'is made unto us wisdom and justice' (1 Cor. i, 30). Behold the feast is prepared. Justice is Christ and it nowhere is wanting; it is not prepared by cooks. It is not like foreign fruits brought to us by merchants from lands beyond the sea; He is the food which everyone can savour who has a healthy palate, He is the food of the interior man. . . . He is food which restores and does not fail; He is food which we take into ourselves but do not consume; He is food which fills the hungry, yet remains undiminished. . . .

This light is seen by all, it feeds the eyes of all, and the sight of the beholder is restored, and the light continues undiminished. If two see it, it remains as great as it was; if more see it, it remains the same. The rich man may see it, the poor man may see it, it is equal for all. No one has set bounds to it; the want of the poor man is made full, the avarice of the rich man is left empty. For does he see more, who has more? and does he by the offer of money, forestall the poor man, and buy for himself what he may see, so that the other may not have it? If then such is the food to our eyes, what is God himself to our minds? . . .

As soon as a sound has struck the air and touched the ear, it passes away; nor does it return, nor sound any more. For thus syllables follow one another in sequence the one after the other, so that the second will not sound unless the first shall have passed away. Nevertheless in this kind of passing there is a great wonder. For look you, if you are hungry and I put bread before you, it would not all go to each of you singly; you would divide the whole quantity I had put down, and the more in numbers you were, the less you would each have. But as I now deliver my sermon, you do not divide among yourselves the words and syllables, nor do you cut up my sermon, so that one may take this part, another that, and thus what I am saying reach you piecemeal in little bits to each of you; but one hears the whole thing, two hear the whole thing, several hear the whole thing, and as many as come to listen hear the whole thing. And it is sufficient for all, and it is undiminished for each one; thine ear is made for the purpose of hearing, nor does another ear in the neighbourhood rob it of any part. If this happens with the word which sounds, what happens with the Word which is almighty? For as this voice of ours is audible as a whole to each single ear of all who are listening, and is this to each one of them; and there are not as many voices of mine as there are ears among you, but one voice fills all the ears, undivided, and complete to all, so conceive the Word of God as whole in the heavens, whole on earth, whole among the Angels, whole with the Father, whole with the Virgin, whole in eternity, whole in the flesh, whole in hell, since He visited it, whole in Paradise, whither He bore the thief. . . .

I utter a sound, but when I have uttered it, I do not recall it again, but if I wish to be heard, I utter another sound, and when it has passed away, yet another; otherwise silence will follow. But again I put some conception before them, and I keep it with me, and thou findest what thou hast heard, and I do not lose what I have said. . . . A conception while remaining in my heart, travels to thine, yet it does not leave mine. Nevertheless when the conception is present in my heart, and I wish it to be in thine, I seek by what way a sound as a vehicle for it may pass to thee. And I take up the sound and, as it were, put into it the conception, and I utter it and bring it before thee, and I teach it yet do not lose it. If my conception could do this by my voice, could not the Word of God do it by His flesh? For behold, the Word of God, God with God, the Wisdom of God abiding immutably with the Father, that He might go forth to us, sought flesh to be as it were the sound, and implanted Himself in it, and came forth to us, yet did not withdraw from the Father. Understand, savour this that you have heard, ponder how great and of what nature it is, and feel greater things about God. For He surpasseth all light, He surpasseth all sound, He surpasseth all understanding. Our desire must be for Him, and in love and longing must our gaze be set on Him, so that the heart of them may rejoice that seek the Lord (Ps. civ, 3).

Serm. XXVIII, 2-5.

354

Be not ashamed to be God's beast of burden. Thou wilt carry Christ, thou wilt not go astray; thou walkest by the way, He is sitting on thee. Let the Lord sit on us and guide us whither He will; let us be His colt, let us go to Jerusalem. By His sitting on us we are not weighed down, but are raised up. With Him guiding us we shall not go astray. Let us go through Him to Him.

Serm. CLXXXIX, iv, 4.

355

Christ is never conquered. . . . He hath conquered in thy behalf, and He hath conquered for thee, and He hath conquered in thee.

In Ps. CXLIX, 10.

IX. HEAD AND BODY

I. UNITY, MULTIPLICITY

356

There is nothing in the world so sociable by nature and so jarring by vice as man is . . . God created him single, from him to propagate all the rest of the human race, so as to admonish us to preserve concordant unity among its multitudes.

De civ. Dei XII, xxvii (Trübner xxviii), I.

357

Because by the iniquity of ungodliness we had recoiled and fallen away in discord from the one true and supreme God, and in respect of many things had sunk to nothing, distracted by many things and attaching ourselves to many things, it was necessary, by the decree and command of God in His mercy, that these same many things should join in proclaiming the One that was to come, and that the One so proclaimed by these many things should come, and that these many things should join in attesting that this One was come; and that, freed from the burden of these many things, we should come to that One, and dead as we were in our souls by many sins, and destined to die in the flesh on account of sin, that we should love that One who, without sin, died in the flesh for us; and by believing in Him now raised again, and by rising again with Him in the spirit through faith, that we should be justified by being made one in the one Just One, . . . and through Him as Mediator reconciled to God, we should cleave to the One, and enjoy the One, and abide one for ever.

De Crin. IV, vii, 11.

358

Thus the Son of God Himself, the Word of God, Himself also the Mediator of God and man (1 Tim. ii, 5), equal to the

Father by unity of Godhead, and partaker of us by the taking upon Himself human nature, making intercession for us with the Father in that He was man, . . . prays . . . 'that they may be one, as Thou, Father in me, and I in thee; that they also may be one in us: and the world may believe that thou hast sent me. And the glory which thou hast given me, I have given to them: that they may be one, as we also are one' (John xvii, 20 *sq*.).

He did not say, I and they are one thing; although in that He is the head of the Church and the Church is His body (Eph. i, 22 *sq*.), He could have said, I and they are, not one thing, but one person, because the head and the body is one Christ; but declaring His own Godhead to be consubstantial with the Father, . . . in His own Kind, that is, in the consubstantial parity of the same creature, He wills His own to be one, but in Himself, since this they could not be in themselves, disunited as they are from one another owing to the diverse pleasures and desires and uncleannesses of sin, from which they are cleansed through the Mediator, that they may be one in Him, not only through the same nature in which all from being mortal man are made equal to the Angels, but also through the same will harmoniously conspiring to the same blessedness, and fused in some way by the fire of charity into one spirit. For this is the force of His words, when He says, 'That they may be one, as we also are one,' namely, that as the Father and Son are one, not only in equality of substance, but also in will, so those also may be one, between whom and God the Son is Mediator, not only in that they are of the same nature, but also through the same union of love.

De Trin. IV, viii, 12; ix, 12.

359

If the divine substance, though a far more distant object, and more sublime in its incomparable diversity, was able for our sakes so to take upon itself the substance of man as to become one Person, and whilst appearing as the Son of man on earth in the weakness of the flesh, was at the same time in heaven in the divinity which partook of the flesh; how much easier it is to believe that other men, who are his faithful saints, become one

Christ with the man Christ, so that when all ascend by His grace and fellowship, the one Christ himself ascends to heaven who came down from heaven. It is in this sense that the Apostle says, 'as in one body there are many members; and all the members of the body, whereas they are many, are one body, so also is Christ' (1 Cor. xii, 12). He did not say, 'so also is Christ's,' that is, Christ's body, or Christ's members, but 'so also is Christ,' thus calling the head and the body one Christ.

De peccat. meritis I, xxxi, 60.

360

. . . Redeeming us by His blood, incorporating us with Himself, making us His own members, that in Him we also might be Christ. . . . We all are in Him both Christ's and Christ, since in some manner the whole Christ is the Head and the body.

In Ps. XXVI, *En.* ii, 2.

361

We are not ignorant of the slurs cast upon themselves by those men who take their joy in dissensions founded on calumnies. We learn to know Christ in the Scriptures and it is in the Scriptures that we learn to know the Church. . . . Where we apprehend Him of whom the Apostle said: 'To Abraham were the promises made and to his seed. He saith not, *And to his seeds*, as of many: but as of one, *And to thy seed*, which is Christ' (Gal. iii, 16), then we apprehend the Church, of which God said to Abraham: 'In thee shall all the kindred of the earth be blessed' (Gen. xii, 3). Where we apprehend Christ in the psalm which says in prophecy of Him: 'The Lord hath said to me: Thou art my son, this day have I begotten thee,' there, too, in the same psalm we find the Church: 'Ask of me and I will give thee the Gentiles for thy inheritance, and the utmost parts of the earth for thy possession' (Ps. ii, 7 *sq.*) Where we recognize Christ in the words, 'The God of Gods, the Lord hath spoken,' there we recognize the Church in what follows: 'And he hath called the earth. From the rising of the sun to the going down thereof' (Ps. xlix, 1). Where we recognize Christ in the words: 'And he as a bridegroom coming out of his bride-chamber, hath rejoiced as a giant to run the way,' there too we find the Church in the preceding words: 'Their sound hath gone forth into all the earth: and their words unto the ends of the world. He hath set his tabernacle in the sun' (Ps. xviii, 5, 6). It is the Church herself that is set in the sun to be manifest to all unto the ends of the earth. Where we recognize Christ in the words: 'They have dug my hands and feet. They have numbered all my bones. And they have looked and stared upon me. They parted my garments amongst them; and upon my vesture they cast lots,' there too we find the Church a little further on in the same psalm: 'All the ends of the earth shall remember, and shall be converted to the Lord: And all the kindreds of the Gentiles shall adore in his sight. For the Kingdom is the Lord's; and he shall have dominion over the nations' (Ps. xxi, 17–19, 28, 29). Where we recognize Christ, as in the words, 'Be thou exalted, O God, above the heavens,' there too we recognize the Church in the words which follow: 'And thy glory above all the earth' (Ps. lvi, 6). When we find Christ in the words: 'Give to the King thy judgment, O God; and to the King's son thy justice,' there too in the words which occur later do we find the Church: 'And he shall rule from sea to sea, and from the river unto the ends of the earth. Before him the Ethiopians shall fall down: and his enemies shall lick the ground. The Kings of Tharsis and the islands shall offer presents: the Kings of the Arabians and of Saba shall bring gifts. And all Kings of the earth shall adore him: all nations shall serve him' (Ps. lxxi, 2, 8–11).

When we recognize Christ in the scripture of the stone which was cut out of the mountain without hands, and struck and broke all the Kingdoms of the earth, that is, all those given over to the worship of demons; there, too, we shall find in the same passage the Church, when it is told that the stone itself grew and became a great mountain and filled the whole earth (cf. Dan. ii, 34 sq.). When we find Christ in the words: 'The Lord shall be terrible upon them, and shall consume all the gods of the earth,' there too we find the Church in the next sentence: 'And they shall adore him every man from his own place, all the islands of the Gentiles' (Sophon. ii, 11). When we find Christ in the words: 'God will come from the South, and the holy one from mount Pharan: his glory covered the heavens,' then too in what follows we find the Church in the words 'and the earth is full of his praise' (Hab. iii, 3). For Jerusalem is situated in the South as we read in the book of Josue (xv, 8), and from there the name of Christ has spread over the world; there too is the wooded hill, the mount of Olives, whence He ascended into heaven, that His power might cover the heavens, and the Church throughout the whole world might be filled with his praise. When we recognize Christ in the words: 'He shall be led as a sheep to the slaughter, and shall be dumb as a lamb before his shearer, and he shall not open his mouth'; there too we find the Church when it is written: 'Give praise, O thou barren, that bearest not: sing forth praise, and make a joyful noise, that thou didst not travail with child: for many are the children of the desolate, more than of her that hath a husband, said the Lord. Enlarge this place of thy tent, and stretch out the skins of thy tabernacles, spare not: lengthen thy cords, and strengthen thy stakes. For thou shalt pass on to the right hand, and to the left: and thy seed shall inherit the Gentiles, and shall inhabit the desolate cities. Fear not, for thou shalt not be confounded, nor blush: for thou shalt not be put to shame, because thou shalt forget the shame of thy youth, and shalt remember no more the reproach of thy widowhood. For he that made thee shall rule over thee, the Lord of hosts is his name: and thy Redeemer, the holy one of Israel, shall be called the God of all the earth' (Is. liii, 7; liv, 1 *sqq.*).

Ep. CV, iv, 14, 15.

362

For Christ is not simply in the head and not in the body, but Christ whole is in the head and in the body. What therefore His members are, that He is; but what He is, it does not follow that His members are.

In Joan. Evang. XXVIII, 1.

363

Hold this fast and keep it entirely fixed in your memory, as children of the Church's training and of the Catholic Faith, that you may perceive Christ to be the Head and the Body, and the same Christ to be also the Word of God, the Only-begotten, equal to the Father, and so may see how great is the grace whereby you pertain to God, that He, Who is one with the Father, has willed to be one with us. . . . Christ and the Church are two in one flesh. The 'two' you must refer to the distance of His Majesty from us. Clearly there are two. For we are not also the Word; we are not also God in the beginning with God: we are not also He by Whom all things were made (John i, 1–3).

In Ps. CXLII, 3.

364

He who puts on a garment is not turned into the garment, but remains wholly himself within; and if a senator put on a servile garment, perhaps not being able to go and console some-one lying fettered in prison if he wears his senatorial robe, and therefore adopts the prison dress, he is because of his humanity to outward view squalid; but within, the sena-torial dignity remains all the more unimpaired the greater mercy he shewed in wishing to clothe himself in humility. So too the Lord remaining God, remaining the Word, remaining Wisdom, remaining divine strength, remaining in the governance of the heavens, remaining in the regiment of the earth, filling the Angels, is whole everywhere, whole in the universe, whole in the Patriarchs, whole in the Prophets, whole in all the saints, whole in the womb of the Virgin, in putting on the garment of flesh, in joining it to himself as it were a spouse, so that as a bride-groom He might come forth out of His bride-chamber, so that He might betroth Himself to the pure virgin which is the Church.

Serm. CCLXIV, 4.

365

'Behold, thus shall the man be blessed that feareth the Lord' (Ps. cxxvii, 4). . . . For there is a certain Man who is thus blessed; and no one feareth the Lord, except he be in the mem-bers of this Man. And there are many men, and there is one Man; for there are many Christians and there is one Christ. The Christians themselves with their Head, Who hath ascended into heaven, are one Christ. He is not One and we many, but we who are many are one in that One. Christ therefore is one Man, the Head and the Body.

In Ps. cxxvii, 1, 3.

366

All mankind is in Christ one man, and the unity of Christians is one Man.

In Ps. XXIX, *En.* ii, 5.

367

When I call Christians many, I understand them to be one in Christ. Therefore ye are many and ye are one; we are many and we are one. How are we many and yet one? Because we cleave to Him whose members we are; of which the head is in Heaven, so that the members may follow.

In Ps. CXXVII, 4.

368

Since all are in His body, as it were one man speaketh; and he is one who is also many. For in themselves they are many, but they are one in Him Who is One.

In Ps. CXXX, 1.

369

. . . as it were one Man, yet is He not one man, but even as one, the Unity . . . but for this reason one because Christ is one, of whom we are all members.

In Ps. LX, 1, 2.

370

Our Lord Jesus Christ is as one whole perfect man, both head and body. We acknowledge the Head in that Man who was born of the Virgin Mary, suffered under Pontius Pilate, was buried, rose from the dead, ascended into heaven, sitteth at the right hand of the Father, from thence we look for Him to come to judge the living and the dead. This is the Head of the Church (Eph. v, 23). The body of this Head is the Church, not the church of this country only, but of the whole world; not that of this age only, but from Abel himself down to those who shall to the end be born and shall believe in Christ, the whole assembly of Saints belonging to one City, which City is Christ's body, of which Christ is the head.

In Ps. XC, *Serm.* ii, 1.

371

The whole Christ is Head and Body, which truth I doubt not you know well: the Head is our Saviour Himself. . . . But His body is the Church, not this one or that, but spread throughout the whole world. Nor is it only that which now is among men who are living in the present life, but it is in those belonging to it who have been before us and in those who are to come after us, even unto the end of the world. For the whole Church, which consists of all the faithful, since all the faithful are members of Christ, hath that Head set in Heaven, and it governeth His body. And although it is separated from our vision, yet is it joined together in charity. Hence the whole Christ is Head and its body.

In Ps. LVI, 1.

372

All who from the beginning of the world have been righteous have Christ for their Head. For they believed that He was to come, Whom we believe to have now come; and it was in faith of Him in whose faith we have been made whole, that they were made whole also; so that He should be in His own person the head of the whole of the City of Jerusalem. And all the faithful from the beginning unto the end were included in the number, to whom the legions and the armies of the Angels were also joined, so that it might become one City under one King, and, as it were, one Province under one Governor, happy in perpetual peace and security, praising God eternally and happy eternally. Now the Body of Christ, which is the Church (Col. i, 18, 24), like an individual man, was once indeed young; and, behold! she is now in a fruitful old age; for it was of her that it was said, 'They shall still increase in a fruitful old age' (Ps. xci, 15). She hath multiplied herself through all nations, and her voice is as that of an individual man reflecting on her first period and on this her latest. She looks back over it all, since all ages are known to her by the Scriptures; and she says exultingly to warn us, 'once was I young' in the first ages of the world, 'and, lo! now am I old,' I am even now in the last ages of the world.

In Ps. XXXVI, *Serm.* iii, 4.

Since you have said that all religions by diverse highways
and byways aspire to that one dwelling place, I fear lest, perchance, while supposing that the way in which you are now set
tends thither, you should be somewhat reluctant to embrace
the way which alone leads men to heaven. Observing, however,
more carefully, the word which you used, I think it not presumptuous of me to expound its meaning somewhat differently.
For you did not say that all religions by diverse highways and
byways reach heaven, or reveal, or find, or enter, or secure
that state, but by saying in a phrase, deliberately weighed and
chosen that all religions aspire to it, you have indicated not
the fruition but the desire of attaining to it as common to all
religions. You have, in three words, neither excluded that one
religion which is true, nor admitted other religions which are
false; for certainly the way which brings us to the goal aspires
thitherward, but not every way which aspires thitherward brings
us to the place wherein all who are brought thither are
unquestionably blest. Now we all wish, that is, we aspire to be
blest; but we cannot all achieve what we wish, that is, we do
not all obtain what we aspire to. That man, therefore, obtains
heaven who walks in the way which not only aspires thitherward,
but actually brings him thither, separating himself from others
who keep to the ways which aspire heavenward, without in
the end reaching heaven. For there would be no wandering,
if men aspired to nothing, or if the truth aspired to were obtained.
If however by 'diverse ways' you meant me not to understand
contrary ways but different ways in the sense in which we speak
of diverse precepts, which yet all tend to build up a holy life,
one enjoining chastity, another patience or faith or mercy, and
the like, in highways and byways which are only in this sense
diverse, that country is not only aspired to but actually found.
For in the Holy Scriptures we read both of ways and a way.
Of ways, for instance, in the words: 'I will teach the unjust thy
ways: and the wicked shall be converted to thee' (Ps. l, 15);
and of a way in the prayer: 'Conduct me, O Lord, in thy way,
and I will walk in thy truth' (Ps. lxxxv, 11). Those ways and
this way are not different, but all make up one way, of which

in another place Holy Scripture saith: 'All the ways of the Lord are mercy and truth' (Ps. xxiv, 10).

Ep. CIV, iv, 12.

374

Since we affirm that Christ is the Word of God, by whom all things were made, and is the Son because He is the Word, not a word uttered and completed in the part, but one abiding immutably with the immutable Father, Who is Himself immutable, and under whose rule the whole universe, spiritual and material, is ordered in the way best suited to different times and places; and that He has perfect wisdom and knowledge as to what should be done, and when and where everything should be done in the controlling and ordering of the universe—most certainly both before He gave being to the Hebrew nation, by which through sacraments fitting to the time He prefigured the manifestation of Himself in His advent, and during the time of the Israelitish Kingdom, and, after that, when He manifested Himself in mortal form to mortal men in the body which He received from the Virgin, and thenceforward even to our own day, in which He is fulfilling all that He predicted of old by the prophets, and from this time on to the end of the world, when He shall separate the holy from the wicked, and give to every man his due reward—in all these successive ages He is the same Son of God, co-eternal with the Father, and the immutable Wisdom, by whom universal nature was created, and by participation in whom every rational soul is blessed.

Therefore, from the beginning of the human race, whoever believed in Him and in any way knew Him, and led a pious and just life according to His commandments, was undoubtedly saved by Him, in whatever time and place He may have lived. For as we believe in Him both as dwelling with the Father and as having come in the flesh, so the men of old believed in Him both as dwelling with the Father and as destined to come in the flesh. And the nature of faith is not changed, nor is the salvation made different in our age, but in the fact that in consequence of the difference between the two epochs, that which was then foretold as future is now proclaimed as past. Moreover, we are not under necessity to suppose different things and different kinds of salvation to be signified, when the self-same thing is by different sacred acts and sacraments announced in the one case as fulfilled, in the other as to come. As to the manner and time, however, in which anything that pertains to the one salvation common to all believers and pious persons is brought to pass, let us ascribe wisdom to God, and for our part submit ourselves to His will. Wherefore the true religion, although formerly set forth and practised under other names and with other rites than it now has, and formerly more obscurely revealed and known to fewer persons but now more clearly and to many, is one and the same in both periods. . . . Thus the salvation provided by this religion, by which alone, as alone true, true salvation is truly promised, was never wanting to any one who was worthy of it, and he to whom it was wanting was unworthy of it.

Ep. CII, 11, 12, 15.

375

Therefore it is not true to say that what has once been done rightly must in no respect whatever be changed. For if the circumstances of time which occasioned anything be changed, true reason in almost all cases demands that what had in the former circumstances been rightly done be now so altered that, although they may say that it is not rightly done if it be changed, truth, on the contrary, protests that it is not rightly done unless it be changed, because at both times it will be rightly done if it accords with the different circumstances of the times. For just as in the case of different persons it may happen that, at one and the same time, one man may do with impunity what another may not, because of a difference not in the thing done but in the person who does it, so in the case of one and the same person at different times, that which it is right to do at one time is not right at another, not because the person who does it is different from his former self, but because the time at which he does it is different.

The wide range opened up by this question may be seen by any one who is competent and careful to observe the contrast between the beautiful and the suitable, examples of which are scattered throughout the universe. For the beautiful, to which the ugly and deformed are opposed, is estimated and praised for what it is in itself. But the suitable, to which the incongruous is opposed, depends on something else to which it is as it were bound, and is estimated not by what it is in itself, but by that with which it is connected. The contrast also between becoming and unbecoming is either the same or at any rate so regarded. . . . The divine institution of sacrifice was suitable in former times, but it is not so now. For the change suitable to the present age has been prescribed by God, Who knows infinitely better than man what is fitting to each age, and who, whether He give or add, abolish or curtail, increase or diminish, is the immutable Governor as He is the immutable Creator of mutable things, ordering all things, until the beauty of the completed course of time, the component parts of which are the dispensations suited to each successive age, shall be finished, like the great melody of some ineffable great master of song, and until those pass into the eternal contemplation of God, who here, though it is a time of faith and not of sight, are acceptably worshipping Him. . . .

For as the man is not fickle who does one thing in the morning and another in the evening, one thing this month and another in the next, one thing this year and another thing next year, so there is no variableness with God, though in the former period of the world's history He enjoined one kind of offerings and in the latter period another, therein ordering the symbolical actions pertaining to the most profitable doctrine of the true religion in harmony with the changes of successive epochs without any change in Himself. For in order to let those whom these things perplex understand that the change was already in the divine counsel, and that, when the new ordinances were appointed, it was not because the old had lost the divine approbation through inconstancy in His will, but that this had already been fixed and determined by the wisdom of that God to whom, in reference to much greater changes, these words are spoken in Scripture: 'Thou shalt change them, and they shall be changed. But thou art always the self-same' (Ps. ci, 27 sq.), it is necessary to convince them that this change in the sacraments of the New Testament from those of the old had been predicted by the voices of the prophets. For thus they will see, if they can see anything, that what is new in time is not new in relation to Him who has appointed the times, and Who possesses, without succession of time, all those things which according to their variety He assigns to the several ages.

Ep. CXXXVIII, i, 4–7.

376

This the disciples did not yet see, namely, the Church throughout all nations, beginning at Jerusalem. They saw the Head and they believed the Head in the matter of the Body. By this which they saw they believed that which they did not see. We too are like to them; we see something which they did not see, and we do not see something which they did see. What do we see which they did not? The Church throughout all nations. What is it we do not see, which they saw? Christ present in the flesh. As they saw Him and believed concerning the Body, so do we see the Body; let us believe concerning the Head. Let what we have respectively seen help us. The sight of Christ helped them to believe in the future Church; the sight of the Church helps us to believe that Christ has risen. Their faith was made complete, and ours is made complete also. Their faith was made complete by the sight of the Head; ours is made complete by the sight of the Body. Christ was made known to them wholly, and to us is He so made known. But He was not seen wholly by them, nor has He been seen wholly by us. By them the Head was seen, the Body believed. By us the Body has been seen, the Head believed. Yet to none is Christ lacking. In all He is complete, though to this day His Body remains imperfect.

Serm. (de Script. N.T.) CXVI, vi, 6.

377

The Church is spread throughout the whole world: all nations have the Church. Let no one deceive you; it is the true, it is the Catholic Church. Christ we have not seen, but we have her; let us believe as regards Him. The Apostles on the contrary saw Him, they believed as regards her. . . . They saw Christ, they believed in the Church which they did not see; and we who see the Church, let us believe in Christ, whom we do not yet see.

Serm. CCXXXVIII, 3.

378

For the Church shall increase till it filleth every tongue. That which you have abandoned, how great hath it grown! Advance with us whithersoever it hath approached, that with us you may reach places whither it hath not yet approached. I dare to say to thee that I speak in the tongues of all men. I am in the Body of Christ, in the Church of Christ. If the Body of Christ now speaketh in the tongues of all men, I also am in all tongues: mine is the Greek, mine the Syrian, mine the Hebrew, mine the tongues of all nations, because I am in the unity of all nations.

In Ps. CXLVII, 19.

379

Christ Jesus was to come to the nation of the Jews to be seen and slain and to gain from among them those whom He foreknew. For that people was not wholly condemned but winnowed. There was among them a great quantity of chaff, but there was also the hidden worth of the grain. There was among them that which was to be burnt and also that wherewith the barn was to be filled.

Serm. (*de Script. N.T.*) LXXVII, ii, 2.

380

To Peter alone was it given to play the part of the whole Church, and because of His part, which of the whole Church he alone took, it was given him to hear the words, 'I will give to thee the keys of the kingdom of heaven' (Matt. xvi, 19). Now it was not one man but the unity of the Church that received those keys. By this fact the pre-eminence of Peter was proclaimed, in that he bore the figure of the very universality and unity of the Church. . . .

Therefore the strength of the Church is set forth in Peter, because he followed the Lord when He went to His passion, and a weakness was also observed, since when questioned by the maid-servant, he denied the Lord. Behold the lover suddenly become the denier. He found himself, who had presumed on himself. . . . But what happened then? At once the Lord looked at him. . . . 'The Lord looked on him, and he went out and wept bitterly' (Luke xxii, 61, 62). He 'went out,' that is, to make confession. He 'wept bitterly,' who knew what to love meant. Sweetness followed in love, of which the bitterness had gone before in grief.

Serm. CCXCV, ii, 2.

381

As Christ is the Shepherd, is Peter not a shepherd? On the contrary, Peter is also shepherd, and so are all of such kind without any doubt shepherds. For if he be not shepherd, why should it be said to him, 'Feed my sheep' (John xxi, 17)? Yet it is the true shepherd who feeds his own sheep. Now it was said to Peter, not, Feed thy sheep, but *my* sheep. Hence Peter is shepherd not in himself, but in the body of the Shepherd. For if he fed his own sheep, they would immediately become goats which he was feeding.

Serm. CCLXXXV, 5.

382

I find all good shepherds in the one Shepherd (cf. Ezech. xxxiv, 1–16). For in very truth good shepherds are not wanting, but they are in the one Shepherd. There are many who are divided; here one is proclaimed, since unity is being commended. And indeed, it is not the case that shepherds were passed over in silence and a Shepherd spoken of for the reason that the Lord had not found one to whom to entrust His sheep; for the same reason He commended it at the time because He found Peter. Indeed, it was precisely in Peter himself that He laid emphasis on unity. There were many disciples, and only to one there is said, 'Feed my sheep.' . . . They feed, Christ feeds. For the friends of the bridegroom do not name their own voice, but 'rejoice with joy because of the bridegroom's voice' (John iii, 29). Therefore it is He Himself who

225

feeds, when they feed; and He says, I feed; because His voice is in them, and in them is His charity. For He willed Peter himself, to whom He was entrusting His sheep, as one to another, one with Himself, so that He entrusted the sheep to him in such wise that He himself should be head, Peter bear the form of the body, that is of the Church, and that, as Bridegroom and Bride, they two should, be one flesh. Accordingly, what did He first say to Peter, so that He might not be entrusting the sheep to him as to another? Peter, lovest thou Me? and he replied, I love; and a second time He asked, lovest thou Me? and he answered, I do love; and a third time, lovest thou Me? and he answered, I love. He established the love in order to confirm the unity. . . . This it is to feed by Christ, this it is to feed in Christ, and to feed with Christ, and not to feed for oneself except through Christ.

Serm. XLVI, xiii, 30.

383

Because thou hast said to me, 'Thou art Christ, the Son of the Living God, . . . I say to thee that thou art Peter' (Matt. xvi, 16, 18). . . . For because Christ is petra (the rock), Peter is the Christian people. For 'Petra' is the original name. Therefore Peter is so called from 'petra' not 'petra' from Peter; just as Christ is not called Christ from the Christians, but the Christians from Christ. . . . Upon Myself, the Son of the Living God, will I build my Church, I will build thee upon Myself, not Myself upon thee.

Serm. (de Script. N.T.) LXXVI, i, 1.

384

And if one should say to you, 'Dost thou worship Peter?' answer as Eulogius did about Fructuosus: I do not worship Peter, but I worship God, whom Peter also worships. Then Peter loves you. For if you wished to have Peter for God, you offend the rock (*petram*), and take care lest by offending the rock you bruise your foot.

Serm. CCLXXIII, vii, 7.

HEAD AND BODY

385

. . . Christ, but, as you who are learned in His school are wont to understand, Christ is both head and body. Do not therefore hear anything spoken in the person of Christ, as though it did not concern you, who are members of Christ.

In Ps. CXLIII, 1.

386

For in Christ thou wast being tempted, since Christ had of thee flesh, and for thee of Himself salvation; of thee He had death, and for thee of Himself life; of thee He had revilings, for thee of Himself honours; wherefor of thee He had temptation, and for thee of Himself victory. If in Him we have been tempted, in Him we overcome the devil. . . . Acknowledge thyself to be tempted in Him, and acknowledge thyself to be conquering in Him.

In Ps. LX, 3.

387

Therefore in Him who is our Head let there appear to us the very fountain of grace, whence, according to the measure of every man, He diffuses Himself through all His members. It is by that grace that every man from his beginning is made a Christian; and it is by that grace that that Man from his beginning became Christ. The former is born again of the same Spirit of which the latter was born. The remission of sins is effected in us by the same spirit as that by which it was effected that He should have no sin. . . . As, therefore, that one Man was predestinated to be our Head, so we being many are predestined to be His members. . . . He truly made us to believe in Christ, who made for us a Christ on whom we believe. He makes in men the beginning and the completion of faith in Jesus, who made the man Jesus 'the author and finisher of faith' (Heb. XII, 2).

De praed. sanct, XV, 31.

388

When Christ hath begun to dwell in man's heart by faith (cf. Eph. iii, 17), and hath begun when invoked to possess him that hath confessed, there is made up the whole Christ, the Head and the Body, and out of many One. . . . But whether the Head speak or the members, Christ speaketh. He speaketh in the person of the Head, He speaketh in the person of the Body . . . Christ is preaching Himself; He is preaching Himself even in His members now existing, in order that He may guide unto Himself others, that they may draw near that were not, and may be united with those of His members through whom His gospel has been preached, and that there may be made one Body under one Head, in one spirit and in one life.

In Ps. LXXIV, 4.

389

The Divine lessons are all so connected with one another, as if they were one lesson; for they all proceed from one mouth. The mouths of those who carry on the ministry of the word are many; but the mouth of Him who filleth the ministers is one.

Serm. (de Script. N.T.) CLXX, i, 1.

390

No greater gift could God have given to man than in making His Word, by which He created all things, their head, and joining them to Him as His members; that the Son of God might become also the Son of man, one God with the Father, one Man with men. So that when we speak to God in prayer for mercy, we do not separate the Son from Him; and when the Body of the Son pray, it does not separate its Head from itself; and it is one Saviour of His body, our Lord Jesus Christ, the Son of God, who prays for us, and prays in us, and is prayed to by us. He prays for us, as our Priest; He prays in us, as our Head; He is prayed to by us, as our God.

In Ps. LXXXV, 1.

'For the temple of God is holy, which you are' (1 Cor. iii, 17); that is, all who believe in Christ, and so believe as to love. . . . Now this is the temple, that is, men themselves, wherein God is prayed to, and hears. For whosoever except he be the temple of God, prays to God, is not heard unto that peace of the heavenly Jerusalem, although he is heard for certain temporal things, which God has given to the heathen also. For the devils themselves were heard when they asked that they might enter the swine (Matt. viii, 31 *sq.*). To be heard unto eternal life is another thing, nor is it granted save to him who prays in the temple of God. Now he prays in the temple of God who prays in the peace of the Church, in the unity of Christ's body; which body of Christ consists of the many in the whole world who believe. And therefore he who prays in the temple is heard. For he prays in spirit and in truth who prays in the peace of the Church, not in that temple wherein was the figure.

In Ps. CXXX, 1.

392

For as if they were one single man, one single poor man and beggar, the members of Christ, who are the Body of Christ extended everywhere, are asking of God.

In Ps. XXXIX, 28.

393

Herein therefore shall the saints rejoice, herein the priests shall rejoice; because all that is good in themselves is not of themselves, but of Him who hath the power of baptizing. Fearlessly therefore doth every one who hath received baptism come into His temple; because it is not man's, but His in whom the horn of David was raised up (*v.* Ps. cxxxi, 17).

'But upon him shall my sanctification flourish' (*ibid.*, 18). Upon whom? Upon My anointed. For when He saith 'My anointed,' it is the voice of the Father, who saith: 'Blessing I will bless her widow: I will satisfy her poor with bread. I will clothe her priests with salvation: and her saints shall rejoice with exceeding great joy' (*ibid.*, 15 *sq.*). He who saith,

'There will I bring forth a horn to David,' is God. He himself saith, 'I have prepared a lamp, for My anointed' (*ibid.*, 1) because the Christ is both ours and the Father's. He is our Christ when He saveth us and ruleth us, as He is also our Lord. He is the Son of the Father, but both our Christ and the Father's. For if He were not the Father's Christ, it would not be said just before: 'For thy servant David's sake, turn not away the face of thy anointed. But upon him shall my sanctification flourish' (*ibid.*, 10, 18). It flourisheth upon Christ. Let none among men assume this to himself, that he himself sanctifieth. . . . The sanctification of Christ in Christ himself is the power of the sanctification of God in Christ. . . . Why hath the world yielded to this beauty? Because it flourisheth in Christ. For, put it in the power of man, and how doth it flourish? Since all flesh is grass and all the splendour of the flesh is as the flower of the grass (*v*. Is. xl, 6).

In Ps. CXXXI, 27, 28.

394

That true mediator, inasmuch as, taking the form of a servant, He was made mediator of God and man, the man Christ Jesus, He receives sacrifices as God with the Father, with whom He is one God, yet in the form of a servant He preferred rather to be a sacrifice than to receive one. For this reason He is also the Priest, Himself offering the sacrifice and Himself the oblation.

De civ. Dei X, xx.

395

Christ is for us both the Victor and the Victim unto Thee, and therefore the Victor because He is the Victim; He is for us unto Thee both the offering and the Priest that offers it, and therefore the Priest because He is the offering.

Conf. X, xliii, 69.

396

They do not understand that not even the very proudest of spirits could rejoice in the honour of sacrifices, unless a true sacrifice were done to the one true God in whose stead they desire to be worshipped; nor do they understand that this cannot be rightly offered, except by a holy and just priest; or unless that which is offered be received from those for whom it is offered; and unless also it be without blemish, so that it may be offered for the cleansing of the blemished. This at least all desire who wish a sacrifice to be offered to God for them. Now who can be so just and holy a priest as the only Son of God, who needed not to offer sacrifices for the purging of His own sins, neither original, nor those which are added during human life? (Heb. vii). And what could be so agreeably chosen by man to be offered for them as human flesh? And what so fitting for this immolation as mortal flesh? And what so clean for cleansing the blemishes of mortal man as flesh born in and from the womb of a virgin without any contamination of carnal concupiscence? And what could be so acceptably offered and received as the flesh of our sacrifice, made the body of our priest? So that, since there are four things to be considered in every sacrifice, namely, to whom it is offered, by whom it is offered, what is offered, for whom it is offered, the same one and true Mediator himself, reconciling us to God by the sacrifice of peace, might remain one with Him to whom He was offering, might make one in Himself those for whom He was offering, and Himself might be in one person both He who was offering and what He was offering.

De Trin. IV, xiv, 19.

397

Those sacrifices, as being but expressions of a promise, have been abrogated. What is it that has been given as its fulfilment? . . . 'Sacrifice and oblation,' says the Psalmist, 'Thou didst not desire' (Ps. xxxix, 7). What then? Are we left at this present time without a sacrifice? God forbid! A body hast Thou perfected for me (cf. Heb. x, 5). It was for the reason that Thou mightest perfect this that Thou didst not desire the others. Before Thou didst perfect this, Thou didst desire the others. The fulfilment of the promise has done away with the words that express the promise. . . . The signs that convey the promise are done away, because the Truth that was promised

231

is revealed. We are in this Body; we are partakers of this Body, we know what we are receiving. . . . A Body has been perfected for us; let us be made perfect in that Body.

In Ps. XXXIX, 12.

398

A true sacrifice is every work which brings about that we cleave to God in holy association; is related, that is to say, to that end by which we may be truly blessed . . . whence in so far as man himself, consecrated by God's name and dedicated to God, dies to the world that he may live for God, he is a sacrifice. . . . It follows truly that the whole body of the redeemed, that is the congregation and society of the saints, be offered to God by that great Priest, for He offered himself as an oblation for us, that we might be members of so great a head in the form of a servant. . . . This is the Christian sacrifice that 'we, being many, are one body in Christ' (Rom. xii, 5). This the Church celebrates in the Sacrament of the altar, so well known to the faithful, wherein is shown that in that oblation the Church is offered.

De civ. Dei X, vi.

399

My flesh for the life of the world (John vi, 52). . . . That is called flesh, which flesh receiveth not; and for this reason the more the flesh receiveth it not, because it is called flesh. . . . The faithful know the body of Christ if they neglect not to be the body of Christ. Let them become the body of Christ if they wish to live by the spirit of Christ. None lives by the spirit of Christ save the body of Christ. . . . Tell me which lives of the other: does thy spirit live of thy body, or thy body of thy spirit? . . . My body, of course, lives by my spirit. Wouldst thou then also live by the spirit of Christ? Be thou in the body of Christ. For doth my body live by thy spirit? Mine lives by my spirit and thine by thy spirit. The body of Christ cannot live but by the spirit of Christ. O sacrament of piety! O mark of unity! O bond of charity! He who would live has where to live and by what to live. Let him draw nigh, let him believe; let him be incorporated, that he may be quickened. Let him not shrink from the body, into which the members are compacted, let him not be a rotten member that deserves to be cut off, let him not be a deformed member to be ashamed of; let him be a beautiful, proper, and sound member; let him cleave to the body, let him live for God by God; let him now labour on earth, that hereafter he may reign in heaven.

In Joan. Evang. XXVI, 13.

400

He would have, then, this meat and drink to be understood as being the fellowship of His body and members, which is the holy Church, in His predestinated and called and justified and glorified saints and His faithful. Of these the first is already effected, namely predestination; the second and third, that is vocation and justification, have taken place, are taking place, and will take place; but the fourth, namely the glorifying, is now in hope, while in the reality it is of the future. The Sacrament of this thing, that is of the unity of the body and blood of Christ, is prepared on the Lord's Table in some places every day, in some places at certain intervals of days, and from the Lord's Table it is taken by some to life, by some to destruction. But the thing itself, of which it is the Sacrament, is for every man to life, for none to destruction, whosoever shall have been partaker thereof. . . . For whilst by meat and drink men seek to attain to this, neither to hunger nor to thirst, there is nothing that truly affords this save only this meat and drink which maketh them by whom it is taken immortal and incorruptible, namely the very fellowship of the saints, where shall be peace and unity full and perfect. For to this end, as men of God before us have also understood, did Our Lord Jesus Christ betoken His body and blood in things which from being many are reduced to some one thing. For out of many grains several are made into one thing and out of many grapes several flow together into one thing.

In Joan. Evang. XXVI, 15, 17.

401

'He that eateth my flesh, and drinketh my blood, abideth in me, and I in him' (John vi, 57). The sign that one has eaten and drunk is this, if he abideth and is abode in, if he inhabiteth and is inhabited, if he cleaveth that he be not deserted. This then it is that He hath taught us and admonished us in mystical words, that we may be in His body, in His members under Himself the head, eating His flesh, not forsaking the unity of Him. . . . But we abide in Him when we are His temple. That we may be His members unity joins us together. And what but love can effect that unity join us together? And the love of God, whence is it? . . . 'By the Holy Ghost which is given us' (Rom. v, 5). Therefore 'it is the spirit that quickeneth,' for the spirit makes living members. Nor does the spirit make any living members save those which the spirit itself finds in the body which it quickens. For the spirit which is in thee, O man, whereby it consists that thou art man, does it quicken a member which it finds separated from thy flesh? . . . Let all this avail us to this end, that we eat not the flesh and blood of Christ merely in the Sacrament, as many evil men do, but that we eat and drink to the participation of the Spirit, that we abide as members in the Lord's body to be quickened by His spirit.

In Joan. Evang. XXVII, 1, 6, 11.

402

He who suffered for us entrusted to us in His Sacrament His own body and blood, and this too He makes us also; for we are become His body, and we are that which we receive through His mercy. Remember this, that you both were not and were created. You have been brought to the Lord's threshing-floor, by the labours of the oxen, that is of those preaching the Gospel; you have been threshed. When as catechumens you were set apart, you were stored in the granary. You have your names; you began to be ground in the mill of fasting and exorcism. Afterwards you came to the water, and you were moistened, and were formed into one; by the heat of the Holy Spirit which came to you you were baked, and you became the bread of the Lord. Look what you have received. As then you see what was made as one thing, so be you one, by loving one another, by holding one faith, one hope, undivided charity. . . . So too the wine was in many clusters of grapes and now is one thing. It is one in the sweetness of the chalice, after it has been pressed out in the winepress. And you, after those fasts, those labours, after abasement and grinding, are now come in the name of Christ as it were to the chalice of the Lord; and there you are on the table, there you are in the chalice. You are now of our company. For we take this together, we drink it together, because we live together.

Serm. CCIX.

403

If then you wish to understand the body of Christ, hear what the Apostle says to believers: 'Now you are the body of Christ and members' (i Cor. xii, 27). If therefore you are the body of Christ and members, your divine mystery is set on the table of the Lord; you receive your mystery. To that which you are, you answer Amen, and by so answering give your assent. For thou hearest, the Body of Christ, that thy Amen may be true. Why then in bread? . . . Let us again and again hear what the Apostle himself says, when speaking of this Sacrament: 'We, being many, are one bread, one body' (*id.* x, 17). Understand and rejoice: unity, truth, piety, charity. One bread, who is this one bread? Being many, one body. Remember that bread is not made of one grain but of many. When you were exorcized, it was as if you were ground in the mill; when you were baptized, it was as if you were moistened with water; when you received the fire of the Holy Spirit, it was as if you were baked. Be what you see and receive what you are. This the Apostle has said about the bread. And what we should understand about the Chalice, though not actually expressed, he sufficiently shows. For just as, in order that the visible shape of bread may exist, many grains are moistened together into one mass, as in the case of the believers, of whom Holy Scripture says, 'they had but one soul and one heart unto God' (Acts iv, 32), so it is with the wine. Brethren, remember from what the wine is made. Many grapes hang on the vine, but the juice of the grapes is mingled into a unity. Thus also has Christ the Lord designated us. He willed that we should belong to Him, and consecrated the mystery of our peace and of our unity on His table.

Serm. CCLXXII.

'The poor shall eat and shall be filled. . . . All the fat ones of the earth have eaten and have adored' (Ps. xxi, 27, 30). The latter have indeed been brought to Christ's table, and receive of His body and His blood, but they only adore, they are not filled, since they do not imitate Him. For they eat of Him Who was poor, and they refuse to be poor like Him, forgetting that Christ suffered for us, leaving us an example that we should follow His steps (cf. 1 Pet. ii, 21). Yet the rich disdain the fact that He humbled Himself, becoming obedient unto death; even to the death of the cross, and they refuse to endure similar things not from true greatness but from pride, from weakness not from true strength. But because God hath raised Him from the dead 'and hath given him a name which is above all names: that in the name of Jesus every knee should bow, of those that are in heaven, on earth, and under the earth' (Phil. ii, 8–10), and the fame of His greatness and the glory of His name are in the Church spread throughout the world, the rich also are moved to come to His table; they eat and adore, but yet they are not filled, for they do not 'hunger and thirst after justice': for only those who do so eat 'shall have their fill' (Matt. v, 6). Although to have our complete fill will only be possible in that eternal life when we shall have ended our pilgrimage and shall have passed from faith to vision, from seeing 'through a glass in a dark manner' to seeing 'face to face,' from what is an enigma to what is transparent truth, yet it is not unmete to call him filled by the poverty of Christ who, for His justice, that is to say in order to participate in the eternal Word, which he has begun to do by faith, not only despises all temporal goods but also patiently suffers the ills.

Of such were the fishermen and the publicans; for 'the weak things of the world hath God chosen, that He may confound the strong' (1 Cor. i, 27). It is of them that it was said; 'the poor shall eat and shall be filled.' But because they could not contain this fulness within themselves they had the praise of the Lord for ever on their lips and they preached Him seeking His glory and not their own and burning in love for Him; so that the whole world has been moved by their preaching, and 'all

the seeds of the earth shall remember and shall be converted
to the Lord, and all the kindreds of the nations shall adore in
his sight. For the Kingdom is the Lord's; and He shall have
dominion over the nations' (Ps. xxi, 28 *sq.*). By this continual
enlarging of the Church the proud, too, that is to say, the rich
of the earth, are drawn to Him and eat of His table, and though
they are not filled, yet they adore.

Ep. CXL, xxvii, 66, 67.

405

As for those who think that visible sacrifices are fitting to
other gods, but to Him as being invisible they should be invisible,
as the greater to the greater and the better to the better, such
being the duties of a pure heart and a holy will, such men
assuredly do not see that the former are symbols of the latter,
just as the sounds of words are symbols of things. Wherefore as
in our praise and prayer to Him we speak audible words but
offer the contents of our hearts which the words symbolize,
even so in our sacrifices we know that the visible sacrifice may
be offered only to Him, to whom our hearts must be the
invisible sacrifice.

De civ. Dei X, xix.

406

Come now, brethren, where did the Lord will to be recognized?
In the breaking of bread. We are untroubled, we break the
bread, and we recognize the Lord. Whosoever thou art that
believes, whosoever thou art that callest thyself not idly a
Christian, whosoever thou art that not without cause comest
into the Church, whosoever thou art that heareth the word
of God with fear and hope, let the breaking of bread be thy
consolation. The absence of God is not absence. Have faith,
and He whom thou dost not see is with thee.

Serm. CXXXIII, ii, 3.

III. VIRGIN AND MOTHER

407

We are Holy Church. But I did not say 'we' as if I meant
we who are here present, you who are now listening to me. I

do mean the many faithful Christians as are by God's favour here in this Church, that is in this city, as many as are in this province, as many as are across the sea, as many as are in the whole wide world, for 'from the rising of the sun unto the going down of the same, the name of the Lord is praised' (Ps. cxii, 3). Thus is constituted the Catholic Church our true mother, the true spouse of that Bridegroom. . . . Great is the dignity conferred by the Bridegroom; He found a harlot, and made her a virgin. That she was a harlot she must not deny, lest she forget the mercy of Him who freed her. How could she not be a harlot when she went a-whoring after idols and evil spirits? Fornication of the heart was in all, in a few according to the flesh, in all according to the heart. He came, and made her a virgin. . . . In faith she is a virgin. In the flesh she has few holy virgins. In the faith she is in duty bound to have all virgins, both women and men. For there must be chastity and purity and sanctity. . . . A virgin is the Church . . . and she is a virgin and she brings forth. She imitates Mary who bore the Lord. Did not the holy Virgin Mary both bear a Son and remain a virgin? So too the Church, for she both brings forth and is a virgin. And if thou wilt consider the matter, she brings forth Christ, since His members are those who are baptized. 'You are,' says the Apostle, 'the body of Christ and members' (1 Cor. xii, 27). If therefore she gives birth to members of Christ, she is most like to Mary.

Serm. CCXIII, vii, 7.

408

The holy virgin the Church celebrates the birth by the Virgin. The Apostle indeed says to her, 'I have prepared you for one husband, that I may present you as a chaste virgin to Christ' (2 Cor. xi, 2). How a 'chaste virgin' in so many peoples made up of both sexes, in so many not only boys and girls but also married fathers and mothers? How, I say, a chaste virgin, except in faith, hope, and in the completeness of charity? Christ, therefore, in order to make the virginity of the Church in the heart, preserved the virginity of Mary in the body. In human wedlock, indeed, the woman is given over to the bridegroom, so that she may not continue to be a virgin. The Church, however, could not be a virgin unless she had found the Bridegroom to whom she was given over to be the Son of a virgin.

Serm. CLXXXVIII, iii, 4.

409

The lance of him who pierced the sacred side betokens the piercing of our conscience which we have as a result of sin. . . . Eve, who was the cause of the beginning of sin, was taken from the side of the man to be fashioned. The man was lying asleep, when this was done; he was hovering in death, when this was done. Two related things are sleep and death: side and side; the Lord was pierced in the place of sins. But from the one side Eve was made, who by sinning brought death to us men; from the other the Church came into being, which by giving birth to us quickens us.

Serm. CCCXXXVI, v, 5.

410

Each sex is called woman, because each is the Church; and each sex, that is, the Church, is called a virgin. 'I have espoused you to one husband, that I may present you as a chaste virgin to Christ' (2 Cor. xi, 2). And have virginity in the flesh; all ought to have it in the heart. Virginity of the flesh is a body unsullied; virginity of heart is a faith uncorrupted. The whole Church therefore is called 'a Virgin', and, in the masculine gender, 'the people of God,' and 'one people,' and 'a single people.'

In Ps. CXLVII, 10.

411

That birth of one Holy Virgin is the ornament of all holy virgins, and these with Mary are mothers of Christ, if they do the will of His Father. For Mary also is on this account the Mother of Christ in a way more full of praise and blessing, since He said, 'Whosoever shall do the will of my Father that is in heaven, he is my brother, and sister, and mother' (Matt. xii, 50). All these kinships to Himself He shews forth in a spiritual manner, in the people whom He hath redeemed; as sisters and brothers

He hath the holy men and holy women, for as much as they all are joint heirs in the heavenly inheritance. His mother is the whole Church, since she herself by the grace of God assuredly gives birth to His members, that is His faithful. Again His mother is every pious soul doing with most fruitful charity the will of His Father, in them of whom it is in labour, until He himself be formed in them (Gal. iv, 19). Mary, therefore, doing the will of God, is after the flesh only the mother of Christ, but after the spirit she is both His sister and His mother.

And on this account that one woman is both a mother and a virgin, not only in the spirit but also in the flesh. In the spirit, indeed, she is not the mother of our Head, which is the Saviour himself, of whom rather she was born after the Spirit—forasmuch as all, who have believed in him, among whom she herself also is, are rightly called 'children of the Bridegroom' (Matt. ix, 15)—but she is clearly the mother of His members, which we are, in that she co-operated by charity, that faithful ones should be born in the Church, who are members of that Head. In the flesh, however, she is the mother of the Head himself. For it was meet that our Head should by means of an extraordinary miracle be born after the flesh of a virgin, that He might thereby signify that His members would be born after the the Spirit of a virgin, the Church. Hence Mary alone both in spirit and in flesh is a mother and a virgin—both the mother of Christ and a virgin of Christ—but the Church, in the saints who shall possess the kingdom of God, is indeed in the Spirit as a whole the mother of Christ, and as a whole a virgin of Christ, but in the flesh not as a whole, but in some a virgin of Christ, in some a mother, but not of Christ. And truly faithful women who are married and virgins dedicated to God, of holy manner of living and 'charity from a pure heart, and a good conscience, and an unfeigned faith' (1 Tim. i, 5), are after a spiritual sense mothers of Christ, because they do the will of the Father. But those who in married life give birth to children after the flesh, give birth not to Christ, but to Adam; and, since they know what they have given birth to, they make it their care that, imbued by His sacraments, they become members of Christ.

De scta. virg. v, 5; vi, 6.

Is there any thought which a virgin of God may truly have, which would make her not dare to set herself before a faithful woman, not only a widow but even married? I do not say a reprobate virgin, for who does not know that an obedient woman is to be preferred to a disobedient virgin? But where both are obedient to God's commands, is she to fear to prefer holy virginity to even chaste marriage, and continence to wedded life, to set the fruit an hundred-fold before the thirty-fold? No, let her not hesitate to prefer the former to the latter; yet let not any particular virgin, who obeys and fears God, dare to set herself before this or that woman, who is also obedient and God-fearing, otherwise she will not be humble, and 'God resisteth the proud' (Jas. iv, 6). What, therefore, shall she have in her thoughts? Assuredly the hidden gifts of God, which nothing but the questioning of trial makes known to each, even in himself. For, to pass over the rest, whence doth a virgin, however 'solicitous for the things that belong to the Lord, know how she may please the Lord' (1 Cor. vii, 32), but that perchance, by reason of some weakness of mind unknown to herself, she be not as yet ripe for martyrdom, whereas that woman to whom she rejoiced to prefer herself, may already be able to drink the chalice of the Lord's humiliation, which He set before His disciples who had shown themselves enamoured of high places (v. Matt. xx, 22)?

De scta. virg. xliv, 45.

413

I venture to say that it is good for those who observe continence and are proud of it to fall, that they may be humbled in that very thing for which they extol themselves. For what benefit is it to anyone in whom is the virtue continency, if pride holds sway in him? He is but despising that whereby man is born, and striving after that which led to satan's fall. . . . Holy virginity is a better thing than conjugal chastity. . . . But if we add two other things, pride and humility, . . . which is the better, pride or humility? . . . I have no doubt that a humble married woman is to be preferred to a proud virgin. . . . A mother will hold a lesser place in the kingdom of heaven, because she has been married, than the daughter, seeing that she is a virgin. . . . But if thy mother has been humble and thou proud, she will have some sort of a place, but thou none.

Serm. CCCLIV, ix, 9.

414

[The Apostle] doth not say that [the unmarried woman or virgin] is solicitous for the things which make for security in this world, so that she may pass her time without the weightier troubles; nor doth he say that a woman unmarried and a virgin is divided, that is distinguished and separated from her who is married, to the end that the unmarried woman may be without care in this life, in order to avoid the temporal troubles, from which the married woman is not free; but she 'thinketh', he saith, 'on the things of the Lord, how she may please the Lord: that she may be holy both in body and in spirit' (1 Cor. vii, 34). Unless, perchance, each be foolishly contentious to the point of essaying to assert that we wish to 'please the Lord' not on account of the Kingdom of heaven but on account of this present world, or that it is on account of this life, not on account of life eternal, that we wish to be 'holy both in body and spirit.' To believe this, what is it but to be miserable above all men? For so the Apostle saith: 'If in this life only we have hope in Christ, we are of all men most miserable' (1 Cor. xv, 19).

De scta. virg. xxii, 22.

415

Husband and wife love one another in that they see each other; and what they see not, that they fear in each other. Nor have they sure delight in what is visible, whilst in what is concealed they usually suspect what is not. In Him, whom you see not with the eyes, but behold by faith, you have neither what is real to blame, nor have you need to fear lest perchance you offend Him by what is false. If therefore you should owe great love to husbands, how greatly ought you to love Him, for whose sake you would not have husbands. Let Him be fixed

in your whole heart, who for you was fixed on the cross. Let
him possess in your soul all, whatever that be, which you wished
not to be occupied by marriage. It is not lawful to give a little
love to One for whose sake you have not loved even what were
lawful.

De scta. virg. lv, 56.

416

He hath said as of universal application: 'If any man will
follow me, let him deny himself' (Mark viii, 34). For it is
not that the virgins ought to give ear to this and the married
women not; or that the widows ought and those who still have
husbands ought not; or that monks ought, and married men
ought not; or that the clergy ought, and the laity ought not;
but let the whole Church, the whole body, all the members
distinguished and distributed throughout their several offices,
follow Christ. Let the whole Church follow Him, the one
Church, let the dove follow Him, let the spouse follow Him,
let her who has been redeemed and endowed with the blood
of the Bridegroom, follow Him. There virgin purity hath its
place; there widowed continence hath its place; there married
chastity hath its place; but adultery hath no place for itself
there; and no place there hath lasciviousness, unlawful and
meet for punishment. But let these several members which
have their place there, in their kind and place and measure,
follow Christ. Let them deny themselves; that is, let them
presume nothing of themselves; let them take up their cross;
that is, let them in the world endure for Christ's sake whatever
the world may bring upon them. Let them love Him who alone
doth not deceive, who alone is not deceived, alone deceiveth
not. Let them love Him, for that is true which He doth
promise. . . .

Let not the virgin say, 'I alone shall be there,' for Mary
shall not be there alone, but the widow Anna shall also be
there. Let not the married woman say, 'the widow will be
there, but not I.' For Anna will not be there and Susanna not
there. But by all means let them who would be there prove
themselves hereby, that they who have a lower place envy
not, but love in others the better place. . . . To whatever

point anyone has been able to reach let him fear to look back thence, and let him walk in the way, let him follow Christ. Forgetting the things that are behind and stretching forth to those that are before, let him by an earnest inward intuition press towards the prize of the vocation of God in Christ Jesus (cf. Phil. iii, 13 *seq.*). Let them that are married regard the unmarried as above themselves; let them acknowledge them to be better; let them love in them what they themselves have not, and let them love Christ in them.

Serm. (*de script. N.T.*) XCVI, vii, 9; viii, 10.

417

In Mary holy virginity gave birth to Christ; in Anna aged widowhood recognized Christ in the Child; in Elizabeth conjugal chastity and the fecundity of one advanced in years did service for Christ. All ranks of the faithful members have contributed to the Head that which by His grace they have been able to contribute. Therefore since Christ is truth and peace and justice, conceive Him by faith, bring Him forth by works; so that what Mary's womb did in the flesh of Christ, your heart may do in the law of Christ. For how can you not pertain to the Christ's birth of a Virgin when you are His members? Mary gave birth to your Head, the Church gives birth to you. For she also is both virgin and mother; mother in the bowels of charity, virgin in the integrity of faith and piety. She brings forth peoples, but they are members of One of whom she herself is both body and spouse, in this also bearing a likeness to that Virgin, since she, too, is in the many the mother of unity.

Serm. CXCII, ii, 2.

418

The Church, in imitation of the mother of her Lord, whereas she could not be this according to the body, is yet both mother and virgin according to the mind. In no degree whatever did Christ deprive His mother of her virginity by being born of her, who, by redeeming His Church from the fornication of evil spirits, made her a virgin. And, O holy virgins begotten of her undefiled virginity, . . . He who has brought to you

what you should love, did not take away from His mother
what you love. He who is healing in you that which you
derived from Eve, would be the last to mar that which you
have loved in Mary. . . . You who could not indeed bring
Him forth as a son in the flesh, have found Him as a Bridegroom in your hearts, and such a bridegroom as your happiness
may hold to as a Redeemer, without your virginity having to
fear Him as a ravisher. For He who did not deprive the mother
of her virginity by being born of her according to the body,
preserves this in you all the more by His spiritual embrace.
Nor must you deem yourselves sterile because you remain
virgins; for that very purity of the flesh conduces to fertility
of the mind. Do as the Apostle tells you: do not think on the
things of the world how you may please your husbands, but
be solicitous for the things that belong to God: how you may
please Him in all ways (1 Cor. vii, 32 sq.), that you may have
not a womb fruitful in offspring, but a soul fruitful in virtues.
. . . What you look with admiration on in Mary's flesh,
that do in the sanctuaries of your soul. He who with the heart
believes unto justice, conceives Christ; he who with the mouth
makes confession unto salvation (Rom. x, 10), brings forth
Christ. Thus both fecundity will abound in your minds and
your virginity will endure.

Serm. CXCI, ii, 3; iii, 4.

419

The Mother bore Him in her womb, let us bear Him in our
hearts. The Virgin was pregnant by the incarnation of Christ;
let our hearts be pregnant by our faith in Christ. The Virgin
gave birth to the Saviour; let our souls give birth to salvation,
and let us bring forth praise. Let us not be sterile; let our souls
be fertile to God.

Serm. CLXXXIX, iii, 3.

420

The joy of a virgin of Christ is of Christ, in Christ, with Christ,
through Christ, for Christ.

De scta. virg. xxvii, 27.

Without Him we are nothing; but in Him are Christ Himself
and we. And how is this? Because the whole Christ is Head
and Body. . . . And that you may know that the Head
and His Body are called one Christ, He says Himself when
speaking of marriage, 'they two shall be one flesh. Therefore
now they are not two, but one flesh' (Matt. xix, 5 *sq.*). But,
perchance, He may be saying this of any marriage. Hear the
Apostle Paul when he says: 'And they shall be two in one flesh.
This is a great sacrament; but I speak in Christ and in the
Church' (Eph. v, 31 *sq.*). There is therefore formed as it were
out of two one person: from the Head and the Body, from
the Bridegroom and the Bride. . . . Christ may therefore
speak, since the Church speaks in Christ, and Christ in the
Church; both the Body in the Head and the Head in the Body.
. . . Therefore we all are together with our Head, Christ,
being worth nothing without our Head. . . . O Lord, if
without Thee there is nothing, in Thee there is all. For whatever He works by us, we seem to work. He can do much, indeed
all, without us; without Him we can do nothing.

In Ps. XXX, *En.* II, *Serm.* i, 3, 4.

IV. HEAVEN AND EARTH

422

Since then the whole Christ is Head and Body . . . the
members of Christ understand, and Christ in His members
understands, and the members of Christ understand in Christ,
that Head and members are one Christ. . . . We are with
Him in heaven through hope; He is with us on earth through
love.

In Ps. LIV, 3.

423

Our Lord Jesus Christ Himself said, 'No man hath ascended
into heaven, but He that descended from heaven, the Son
of man who is in heaven' (John iii, 13). He seems to have
spoken of Himself alone. Did then the rest remain below,

because He who alone descended, alone ascended? What ought the rest to do? To be united with His body, that the Christ who descended and ascended may be one. The Head descended and ascended with the Body, clothed with His Church, which He presented to Himself, 'not having spot or wrinkle' (Eph. v, 27). He therefore alone ascended. But we also ascend, when we are in such wise with Him that we are His members in Him, and He with us is alone, and therefore One, and One evermore. Unity bindeth us with the One. . . . We ought not to exclude the hope, nay, we ought rather confidently to trust, that, if through charity He is Himself with us on earth, we also are with Him in heaven through the same charity. . . . He therefore is still here below and we are already above—He is here below through the compassion of charity, we are above through the hope of charity.

In Ps. CXXII, 1.

424

Paul the Apostle . . . went on to say, 'Wherefore he saith: he ascended on high, he led captivity captive, he gave gifts to men' (Eph. iv, 8). . . . In the psalm, however, this reads, 'Thou hast ascended on high; thou hast led captivity captive; thou hast received gifts in men' (Ps. lxvii, 19). . . . But while the Prophet said, 'thou hast received gifts in men,' the Apostle preferred to say, 'he gave gifts to men'; and this in order that the fullest meaning might be yielded by both expressions, since in each resides the authority of the divine utterance. For each is true, both that He gave to men, and that He received in men. He gave to men, as the head of His own members; he, the same who gave, received in men, at least as in His own members, on account of which members of His He cried out from Heaven, 'Saul, Saul, why persecutest thou me?' (Acts ix, 4); and of His own members He saith, 'As long as you did it to one of these my least brethren, you did it to me' (Matt. ·xxv, 40). Christ therefore himself both gives in heaven and receives on earth.

De Trin. XV, xix, 33.

425

Christ, inasmuch as He is the Head, the Saviour of the Body, . . . who sitteth at the right hand of the Father and is inter-

ceding for us, is also here in His Body which is the Church. The
Body is conjoined to the Head thereof, . . . and the Body is
in the Head thereof. . . . And we are sitting there, and He is
labouring here. We are sitting there in accordance with hope;
He is here with us in accordance with charity.

In Ps. LV, 3.

426

We, imagining that we shall see the Lord present and clothed in
the flesh, may say to Him, Lord, if Thou wilt show Thyself at
this time, when 'wilt thou 'restore again the kingdom to
Israel?' . . . And what did He answer to those who put this
question to Him? . . . 'It is not for you to know the times
which the Father hath put in His own power' (Acts i,
6 *sq.*). . . .

Note the order and method of teaching of the good Master,
the unique Master, the one Master. He did not give an answer
to what they had asked, but He did to what they had not asked.
For He knew that it was not expedient that they should know
what they had asked; but what He knew was expedient to them
to know, even though they had not asked it, that He told them.
'It is not for you,' He said, 'to know the times.' What are the
times to thee? Thy concern is to escape from time, and thou
askest the time. 'It is not for you to know the times, which the
Father hath put in His own power'. . . . But what is it for
you to know? . . . 'You shall be witnesses unto me.' And
where? 'In Jerusalem,' where I was slain, 'and in all Judæa
and Samaria, and even to the uttermost part of the earth'
(*ibid.*). Mark this well, see that you grasp it. Be you the spouse,
and await the Bridegroom with untroubled minds. The Church
is the spouse . . . the glorified Lord on His resurrection commends the Church; at His ascension to glory He commends the
Church; in sending the Holy Ghost from Heaven He commends
the Church.

Serm. CCLXV, iii, 4; v, 6; x, 12.

427

For because He himself, being 'the first begotten of the dead'
(Apoc. i, 5), made a road to the Kingdom of God to life eternal

for His Church, to which He is the head in such way as to make the body immortal, He was therefore created [as regards the form of a servant] in the beginning of the ways of God in His work (Prov. viii, 22).

De Trin. I, xii, 24.

V. CATHOLIC

428

Let us rejoice and give thanks, that we are made not merely Christians but Christ. Do you understand, brethren, do you take in the grace of God upon us? . . . . We are made Christ. For if He is the head, we are the members. The whole man is He and we. . . . The fulness of Christ is head and members, . . . Christ and the Church.

In Joan. Evang. XXI, 8.

429

. . . so that it could not in any wise be doubted that Christ is Head and Body, Bridegroom and Bride, the Son of God and the Church, the Son of God made Son of Man for our sakes, that He might make the sons of men sons of God.

In Ps. XXX, *En.* II, *Serm.* ii, 1.

430

No one, indeed, attains to salvation and eternal life except he who has Christ as his Head. But no one can have Christ as Head, except he who is in His body, which is the Church.

Ep. ad Cath. contra Donat. xix, 49.

431

Repudiating therefore all those who seek neither philosophy in sacred things nor holiness in philosophy, . . . we must hold fast to the Christian religion and to communion with that Church which is Catholic, and is called Catholic, not only by its own members but also by all its enemies. For whether they will or not, even heretics and schismatics when talking, not among themselves but with outsiders, call the Catholic Church nothing else but the Catholic Church. For otherwise they would not be understood unless they distinguished the Church by that name which she bears throughout the whole world.

De vera relig. vii, 12.

432

There are mountains that we love, lofty mountains, preachers of the truth, whether Angels, or Apostles, or Prophets. They are round about Jerusalem (Ps. cxxiv, 2); they encircle her, and as it were form a wall for her. . . . They are the mountains that are enlightened by God; and they are enlightened in the first place, that light may descend from them into the valleys or onto the hills, because they are not of so great height as are the mountains. . . . But because the mountains themselves are not protected by themselves, and it is not of themselves that they provide for us, and our hope ought not to be in the mountains lest a curse come upon us for putting our trust in man (Jer. xvii, 5), after saying, 'I have lifted up my eyes to the mountains, from whence help shall come to me' the Psalmist added, 'My help is from the Lord, who made heaven and earth' (Ps. cxx, 1, 2). They are the mountains of which he again says, 'Let the mountains receive peace for the people: and the hills justice' (Ps. lxxi, 3). . . . . He did not say, they have peace from themselves, or they make peace, or generate peace; but, they receive peace. The Lord is the source whence they receive peace. So therefore lift up thine eyes to the mountains for the sake of peace, that thy help may be from the Lord, Who made heaven and earth.

'I have lifted up my eyes to the mountains, from whence help shall come to me'; and lest thou shouldst remain there, he adds, 'my help is from the Lord, Who made heaven and earth.' Again, 'Let the mountains receive peace for the people'; in the word, 'receive,' he shews that there is another source of peace whence they receive. Again, 'enlightening from the hills'; but thou, he said, 'Thou enlightenest wonderfully from the eternal hills' (Ps. lxxv, 5). Again in this passage after saying that mountains are round about Jerusalem, lest again thou shouldst tarry in the mountains, he at once added, 'So the Lord is round about His people'; that thy hope might not rest in the mountains but on

Him who enlightens the mountains. . . . But love such mountains, wherein the Lord is. Then do those very mountains love thee, if thou hast not placed thy hope in them. . . . If thou would be loved by good mountains, place not thy hope even in good mountains. For how great a mountain was Paul! Where is one like him to be found? (we speak of the greatness of men). Can anyone readily be found of so great grace? Nevertheless he feared lest that sparrow should place hope in him, and what does he say: 'was Paul crucified for you?' (1 Cor. i, 13). But lift up your eyes to the mountains from whence help may come to you; for 'I have planted, Apollo watered, but God gave the increase' (*id*. iii, 6).

In Ps. CXXIV, 4, 5, 6.

433

We do not say that you should believe us for the reason that we are in the Church of Christ, because Optatus of Milevi, or Ambrose of Milan, or countless other bishops of our communion, have commended this Church to which we hold; or because she is made known by the Councils of our associates in office, or because in holy places throughout the whole world so many miracles are wrought whether by the answering of prayers or by the healing of the sick. . . . Whatever things of this kind are done in the Catholic Church, they must be approved because they are done in the Catholic Church; but the Catholic Church herself is not manifested by the fact that these things are done in her.

Ep. ad Cath. contra Donat. xix, 50.

434

Rightly, O Catholic Church, most true mother of Christians, thou dost not only teach that God alone, to attain whom is the most blessed life, must be worshipped in perfect purity and chastity, bringing in no creature as an object of adoration whom we should be required to serve—and from that incorrupt and inviolable eternity, to which alone man should be subject, in cleaving to which alone the rational soul escapes misery, excluding everything that is made, that is liable to change, that is under the power of time; without confounding what eternity and truth and, indeed, peace itself keeps separate, or, on the other hand, separating what a common majesty unites: but thou dost also embrace love and charity to our neighbour in such a way that for the diverse diseases with which souls are for their sins afflicted, there is found with thee a medicine of prevailing efficacy. Thy training and teaching are childlike for children, forcible for youths, gentle for the aged, taking into account not only the age of the body but also that of the mind.

De mor. Eccl. I, xxx, 62-63.

435

O brethren, O children, O ye Catholic buds, O ye holy and supernal seeds, O ye who are regenerate in Christ and born from above, . . . sing with your voices, sing with your hearts, sing with your lips, sing in all that you do, 'sing ye to the Lord a new canticle' . . . 'Let His praise be in the church of the saints.' Praise in singing is the singer himself. Do you wish to utter praise to God? Be yourselves what you are saying! . . . Dost thou ask for what thou mayest rejoice when thou singest? 'Let Israel rejoice in Him that made him' (Ps. cxlix, 1 *sq.*). And he finds no place whence his joy springs except God.

Serm. XXXIV, iii, 6.

X. THE CITY OF GOD

I. ONE BODY OF MANY MEMBERS

436

For μόνος means one; not one in any manner, for a man in a crowd is one. But though he can be called one along with the many, he cannot be μόνος, for μόνος means 'one alone.' Those who live together in such wise that what is written they really possess, namely, 'but one heart and one soul' (Acts iv, 32)—many bodies, but not many souls; many bodies but not many hearts—can rightly be called μόνος, that is, 'one alone.'

In Ps. CXXXII, 6.

437

The Scripture saith, 'They were but one heart and one soul toward God' (Acts ii, 41; iv, 4, 32, 35). But many, so as not to make a place for the Lord, seek their own things, love their own things, delight in their own power, are greedy for their private interests. Whereas he who would make a place for the Lord, should rejoice not in his private good but in the common good. They did this with their private goods; they made them common. Did they lose what they had of their own? If they held their goods alone, and each man had his own, he would have that only which he had of his own; but when he made that which was his special property common, those things also which belonged to others were made his own. Let your charity consider this; that on account of those things which we individually possess there exist lawsuits, enmities, discords, wars between men, tumults, dissensions against one another, scandals, sins, iniquities, murders. On account of what? On account of what we each possess. Do we litigate for the sake of what we possess in common? Blessed therefore are they who so make a place for the Lord, as not to rejoice in their private goods. . . . Because thou wilt thyself be the place of the Lord, and thou wilt be one with those who shall be the Lord's place. Let us therefore, brethren, abstain from the possession of private property, or from the love of it, if we may not from its possession, and we make a place for the Lord. It is too much for me, saith some one. Consider who thou art, who art about to make a place for the Lord. . . . Desire the friendship of Christ without fear. He wishes to be entertained at thy house; make a place for Him. What is make a place for Him? Love not thyself, love Him. If thou love thyself, thou shuttest the door against Him; if thou love Him, thou openest it. And if thou open and He enter, thou shalt not be lost by loving thyself, but shalt find thyself with Him who loveth thee.

In Ps. CXXXI, 5, 6.

438

Think not those only poor, who have no money. Attend to every man in that wherein he wanteth; for perhaps thou art rich in this, wherein he is poor, and thou hast wherewith to help him. Perhaps thou lendest him thy limbs, and this is more than if thou shouldst lend him money. Lo, thou dost not toil, nor dost thou lose anything; thou givest counsel, and thou hast given alms. Now, my brethren, while we are speaking, ye are as it were poor, compared with us; and since God hath deigned to give unto us, we bestow therefrom upon you; and we all receive from Him, who alone is rich. Thus then the body of Christ maintaineth itself; thus the kindred members are held together and made one in charity and in the bond of peace, when each man giveth what he hath to him who hath it not; in that which he hath he is rich; in that which the other hath not, he is poor. Thus love ye, thus be ye affectioned to one another. Attend not solely to yourselves, but to those who are in want around you.

In Ps. CXXV, 13.

439

We will minister to you that which it [the feast of St. John Baptist] has yielded, remembering and bearing in mind the obligation of our servantship, so that we speak, not as master but as minister, not to pupils but to fellow pupils; since we speak not to servants but to fellow servants. For we have one Master, whose school is on earth and whose cathedral is in heaven.

Serm. CCXCII, i, 1.

440

If you wish to have the Holy Spirit, mark this well, my brethren. Our spirit by which man is a living being is called the soul, . . . so you see what the soul does in the body. It gives life to all the members; it sees through the eyes, it hears through the ears, it smells through the nostrils, it talks through the tongue, it works through the hands, it walks through the feet; it is present at one and the same time to all the members so that they may live; to each it gives life, to each it assigns its duty. The eye does not hear, nor the ear see, nor the tongue see, nor does the ear or eye talk; but yet it lives, the ear lives, the tongue lives; their duties are diverse, life they share in common. So is the Church of God: in some saints she works miracles, in other saints she preaches the truth, in others she protects virginity, in yet others she preserves conjugal chastity, in some she does one thing, in others another; all do that which is severally proper to them, but all share life in an equal degree. Now what the soul is to the body of man, that the Holy Spirit is in the body of Christ, which is the Church. The Holy Spirit does that in the whole Church, which the soul does in all the members of a single body. . . . If therefore you wish to live by the Holy Spirit, hold fast to charity, love truth, long for unity, so that you may attain to eternity.

Serm. CCLXVII, iv, 4.

441

The eye seeth, and heareth not; the ear heareth, and seeth not; the hand worketh, but it neither heareth nor seeth; the foot walketh, but it heareth not, nor seeth, nor doth what the hand doth. But if there be health in one body, and the members contend not against one another, the ear seeth in the eye, the ye heareth in the ear; nor can it be objected to the ear that it seeth not, so as to say to it: You are nothing, you are inferior; can you see and discern colours, as the eye doth? For the ear answereth from the peace of the body, and saith: I am where the eye is, I am in that body; in myself I see not, in that wherewith I exist I see. So when the ear saith, My eye seeth; the eye saith, My ear heareth; the eyes and ears say, Our hands work for us; the hands say, the eyes and the ears see and hear for us; the eyes and ears and hands say, the feet walk for us; while all members do their work in one body, if there be health therein and the members be in concord, they rejoice, and rejoice with one another. And if there be any trouble in any member, they forsake not one another, but suffer with one another. . . . Thus then, brethren, whosoever in the body of Christ cannot restore the dead to life, let him not seek this power, but let him seek that he may not be at discord in the body; just as there might be discord if the ear should seek to see. . . . When therefore a man who is progressing heareth this, as it were a calumny cast in his teeth by ignorant heathens, by men who know not what they speak of; in the sodality of the Body of Christ let him answer and say: Thou who sayest, thou art not righteous because thou dost not work miracles, thou couldst also say to the ear, thou art not in the body for thou seest not. You, he saith, should do what Peter did. But Peter did it for me also, since I am in that body wherein Peter wrought it. In him, from whom I am not divided, I can do what he can. In that I can do less, he suffereth together with me; and in that he can do more, I rejoice with him. The Lord himself cried from on high in behalf of His Body, 'Saul, Saul, why persecutest thou me?' (Acts ix, 4), and no man was touching Him. But the Head cried from heaven for the body suffering on earth.

In Ps. CXXX, 6.

442

When we reflect on the repose which you enjoy in Christ, we also, although engaged in manifold and arduous labours, find rest in your charity. For we are one body under one Head, so that you share our toils, and we share your repose.

Ep. XLVIII, 1.

443

He who hath received less seemeth to walk more safely; but if he do not perversely seek for what he hath rightly not received, let him seek that without which he cannot be in Christ's body, or without which he is there to his own hurt. For a sound finger is safer than a blear eye. The finger is a small thing; the eye is a great thing, it hath great power. Yet it is better to be the finger and be sound, than to be the eye and to be disordered, to be bleared, to be blind. Let therefore every man seek nothing in the Body of Christ save soundness. According to soundness let him have faith; by means of faith his heart is cleansed, by the cleansing of his heart he will see the face, of which it hath been said, 'Blessed are the clean of heart, for they shall see God' (Matt. v, 8; cf. Acts xv, 9). But he who hath wrought miracles as also he that hath not wrought miracles ought not to rejoice, save in the countenance of God.

In Ps. CXXX, 8.

444

These [Donatists] venture to insult us, because the brethren, when they see men, say, 'Thanks be to God'. . . . Consider whether a brother ought not to thank God when he sees his brother. Is it not indeed cause for rejoicing when they who dwell in Christ see one another?

In Ps. CXXXII, 6.

445

'We will adore in the place where his feet stood' (Ps. cxxxi, 7). Except it be one of His house, God heareth not unto eternal life. Now he belongeth to God's house who hath in charity been built in with living stones. But he who hath not charity falls into ruins, but though he be a ruin, the house stands. . . . And so, brethren, the house of God is in those whom He has pre-destined, and who He foreknew would persevere. Of these it was said, 'Where His feet stood.' For there are those who persevere not, and His feet stand not in them. They therefore are not the Church; they belong not to that which is now a tabernacle, but will then be the house. . . . 'But he that shall persevere to the end, he shall be saved' (Matt. xxiv, 13). Lo, in those where His feet have stood, in that place adore, that is, be thou among those in whom the Lord's feet have stood.

In Ps. CXXXI, 13.

446

Therefore only those in whom the charity of Christ is perfected dwell together to become one. For those in whom the charity of Christ is not perfected, even when they are together, are full of hatred, troublesome, turbulent; by their worrying they disturb the others, and they seek what they may say of them; just as a restive horse in a team, not only does not draw, but breaks with his hoofs that to which he is harnessed.

In Ps. CXXXII, 12.

447

There are some who hold pastoral chairs that they may shepherd the flock of Christ, others fill them that they may enjoy the temporal honours and secular advantages of their office. It must needs happen that these two kinds of pastors, some dying, others succeeding them, should continue in the Catholic Church to the end of time and the judgment of the Lord. If, then, in the times of the apostles there were men such that the Apostle should in his grief say that he had been 'in perils from false brethren' (2 Cor. xi, 26), yet he did not haughtily cast them out, but patiently bore with them, how much more must such arise in our own times, since the Lord has said most plainly concerning this age which is drawing to a close, that 'because iniquity hath abounded, the charity of many shall grow cold.' The words which follow ought, however, to cheer and exhort us, for He adds: 'But he that shall persevere to the end, he shall be saved' (Matt. xxiv, 12, 13).

But just as there are good shepherds and bad, so also in the flock itself there are good and bad. The good are represented by the name of sheep, but the bad are called goats. They feed, nevertheless, side by side in the same pasture until the Chief Shepherd, who is called the One Shepherd (John x, 16), shall come and, according to His promise, 'separate them one from another, as the shepherd separateth the sheep from the goats'

(Matt. xxv, 32). On us He has laid the duty of gathering the flock; to Himself He has reserved the work of final separation, because it pertains properly to Him Who cannot err. For those presumptuous servants who have lightly dared to separate before the time which the Lord has reserved to Himself, have only succeeded in separating themselves from Catholic unity. For how could those have a clean flock who have by schism become unclean?

Ep. CCVIII, 2, 3.

448

For what else are we to say to those heretics, save, learn peace, love peace. You call yourselves just, but if you were just, you would groan as grain among the chaff. For since there are grains of wheat in the Catholic Church, and they are true grains, they endure the chaff until the floor be threshed . . . The Catholic Church saith: Unity must not be lost, the Church of God must not be cut up. Hereafter God will judge of the wicked and the good. If the evil cannot now be separated from the good, they must be suffered for a season. The wicked may be with us on the threshing floor, in the barn they cannot be. And perhaps those who to-day appear evil, to-morrow will be good, and those who to-day pride themselves on their goodness, will to-morrow be found to be evil. Whoever therefore beareth with the wicked for a season humbly, he shall attain to eternal rest. This is the Catholic voice. But what is the voice of those who 'understand neither the things they say, nor whereof they affirm' (1 Tim. i, 7)? 'Touch no unclean thing' (Is. lii, 11), and 'He that toucheth an unclean thing shall be defiled' (*v*. Lev. xxii, 5); let us separate ourselves that we be not mingled with the wicked. But we say to them: Love peace, love unity. Are you ignorant from how many good men you are separated, while you slanderously call them wicked? . . . Love peace, love Christ. For if they love peace, they love Christ. . . . For the Apostle saith of Christ, 'He is our peace, who hath made both one' (Eph. ii, 14). If then Christ is peace because He hath made both one, why have you made two of one?

In Ps. CXIX, 9.

449

If thou belongest to Christ's members, come within, cleave to the Head. Suffer the cockle if thou art wheat, . . . suffer the chaff if thou art grain (cf. Matt. xiii, 30). Suffer the bad fish if thou art a good fish. Why dost thou fly away before the time of winnowing? Why before the time of harvest dost thou root up the grain also with thyself? Why before thou art come to the shore hast thou broken the nets?

In Ps. XL, 8.

450

Where is the Christian to live apart, that he may not groan among false brethren? Whither is he to go? What is he to do? Is he to seek solitudes? Scandals follow him. Is he who is well advanced to separate himself, that he may not have to suffer any man? What if no one wished to endure this very man before he lived in right manner? If therefore, because he is living well, he will not endure any man, by this very fact he is convicted of not living well. Mark these words of the Apostle, beloved: 'Supporting one another in charity. Careful to keep the unity of the Spirit in the bond of peace' (Eph. iv, 2, *sq.*). Hast thou nothing for another to support in thee? I am surprised if it is not so; but suppose it be not thus; for that reason thou art the stronger to support others, in proportion as thou hast no longer what others must support in thee. Thou art not supported, support others. I cannot, thou sayest. Thou hast what others must support in thee: 'Supporting one another in charity.' Thou forsakest human affairs, and separatest thyself, so that no one may see thee; whom wilt thou profit? Wouldst thou have advanced so far, had no one profited thee? Because thou seemest to have had speedy feet in passing over, wilt thou cut off the bridge? . . . I will live apart with a few good men, saith some one. With them it will be well with me. For to do good to no man is wicked and cruel. . . . I will not admit any wicked man, any wicked brother to my society. With a few good men it will be well with me. How dost thou recognise the person whom perhaps it is thy wish to exclude? That he may be known to be wicked, he must be tested within; how then dost thou shut out one about to enter, who must be proved afterwards, and who cannot be proved unless he has entered? Wilt thou repel all the wicked? Thou sayest so, and thou knowest how to inspect them. Do all come to thee with their hearts bare? Those who are about to enter do not know themselves; how much less dost thou know them? For many have promised themselves that they were about to fulfil that holy life, in which all things are in common, where no man calleth anything his own, where all have one heart and one soul in God (Acts iv, 32, 35). These have been put into the furnace, and have cracked. How then dost thou know him who is unknown even to himself? Wilt thou shut out wicked brethren from the company of the good? Whoever thou art who thus speakest, exclude, if thou canst, all evil thoughts from thy heart; let not even an evil suggestion enter thy heart. Thou sayest, I do not consent. Yet it entered so as to make suggestion to thee. For we all wish to have our hearts fortified, that no evil suggestion may enter. But who knoweth whence it entereth? Every day, even, we fight within our own heart. Within his own heart one man is at strife with a multitude. Avarice suggests, lust suggests, gluttony suggests, popular rejoicing suggests, all things suggest. He restraineth himself from all, hath an answer to all, turneth away from all. It is difficult to avoid being wounded by one of them. Where then is security? Here nowhere, in this life nowhere, except solely in God's promise. But there, when we shall have attained thereto, is perfect security; when the gates of Jerusalem are shut and the bolts of her gates strengthened (Ps. cxlvii, 13). Truly full jubilance is there, and great delight. But feel not secure in praising any sort of life now; 'praise not any man before death' (Ecclus. xi, 30).

In Ps. XCIX, 9–11.

451

By this means men are deceived, so that they either do not undertake, or rashly attempt, a better life; because, when they wish to praise, they praise without mention of the evil that is mixed with the good; and those who wish to blame, do so with a mind so envious and perverse as to shut their eyes to the good and exaggerate only the evils which either actually exist there or are imagined to be there. Thus it happens that when any profession has been ill, that is incautiously, praised, if it has invited men by its own reputation, those who betake themselves to it discover some such as they did not believe to be there, and, offended by the evil, recoil from the good. . . . The Church of God, to speak generally, is being praised: Christians and Christians alone are great; the Catholic Church is great; all love each other, each and all do all they can for one another; they give themselves up to prayers, fastings, hymns; throughout the world with peaceful unanimity God is praised. Someone perhaps hears this, who does not know that silence is preserved about the wicked who are mingled with the good. He comes to it drawn by this praise; he finds mixed with the others bad men who were not mentioned to him before he came; he is offended by the false Christians and flees from the true Christians. Again, those who hate and slander them burst into vituperation. What sort of people are Christians? Who are the Christians? Covetous people, usurers! Are not the very persons who fill the churches on feast days the same who during the games and other spectacles fill the theatres and amphitheatres? They are drunken, gluttonous, envious, calumniators of one another. There are such, but not such only. And this slanderer in his blindness is silent about the good, while that eulogist in his want of caution says nothing about the bad. But if the Church of God is praised at this time as the Scriptures praise her—'as the lily among thorns, so is my love among the daughters' (Cant. ii, 2)—a man listens, thinks it over; the lily pleases him, he enters, adheres to the lily, bears with the thorns; and the lily will deserve the praise and embraces of the spouse, who says, 'As the lily among thorns, so is my love among the daughters.' So too is it with the clergy. The eulogists of the clergy point to the good ministers, the faithful stewards, who bear with all things, devote their very life blood for those whom they wish to profit, and seek not what is their own, but what is Jesus Christ's. They praise these things, but forget that the good men are mingled with bad. Again, those who blame the avarice of the clergy, the dishonest practices of the clergy, the litigations of the clergy, are loud against the coveters of other people's property, the gluttonous, and the drunken. Thou enviously blamest and thou praisest indiscreetly. Do thou when thou praisest speak of the wicked who are mingled with the good, and do thou who blamest, see the good there also. So too in that communal life of the brethren which exists in a monastery; great and holy men live therein, spending their time in hymns, prayer and the praises of God. Their occupation is reading; they labour with their own hands, and by this means support themselves. They seek nothing covetously; whatever is brought in for them by pious brethren, they use with contentment and charity; no one claims as his own what another has not: all love, all support one another mutually. He praises who does not know all. He, who knows not what goes on within, who knows not that even in harbour ships come into collision when the wind enters, joins the community as one looking for security, expecting to find no one whom he must put up with; he finds there evil brethren, who could not have been found to be evil if they had not been admitted (and they must needs at first be tolerated lest they should perchance reform; nor can they easily be excluded, unless they have first been endured), and finding them himself becomes impatient past endurance. Who asked me here? I used to think that charity was here. And, irritated by the annoyance caused by a few men, he becomes a deserter from his holy design, and guilty of not keeping his vows. And then, when he has himself gone forth thence, he too becomes a vituperator and a slanderer; and records those things only (sometimes real), which he asserts that he could not have endured. But the real troubles caused by the wicked ought to be endured for the sake of the society of the good. The Scripture saith to him, 'Woe to them that have lost patience' (Ecclus. ii, 16). And what is more, he belches abroad the evil odour of his indignation, as a means to deter those who are about to enter; because when he had endured, he could not persevere. Of what sort are they? Envious, quarrelsome, forbearing no one, covetous; saying, he did this on this occasion, he did that on that. Wicked man, Why art thou silent about the good? Thou sayest nothing about those who suffered thy wickedness. . . .

Let no man deceive you, brethren; if you wish not to be

deceived, and to love your brethren, know that every profession in the Church contains false members. There are wicked Christians, but there are also good ones. Thou seemest to see more wicked than good, because they are like chaff, which prevents you from seeing the grain; but there is grain there also; approach, test them, sift them, judge of them by their taste. Thou findest religious devoid of self-discipline; is the religious life for this reason to be blamed? Many remain not in their own houses; they go from house to house; they are busybodies, speaking things which they ought not to, proud, tattlers, given to drunkenness (1 Tim. v, 15). Though they are virgins, what profit is it that the flesh be whole if the mind is corrupt? Humble wedlock is better than proud virginity. For if such a woman were to marry, she would not have the name of virgin to puff her up, while she would have a curb to govern her. But are we, on account of wicked virgins, to condemn those who are 'holy both in body and in spirit' (1 Cor. vii, 34)? Or, on account of these praiseworthy ones, are we forced to praise those who merit censure?

In Ps. XCIX, 12, 13.

452

Let not the imperfect fear, only let them progress. Yet, because I have said, 'let them not fear,' let them not love their imperfection, and remain there where they are found. Let them progress, as far as in them lies. Daily let them add, daily let them approach; yet let them not fall back from the Body of the Lord; so that, compacted in one Body and among these members, they may be counted worthy of it being said of them: 'Thy eyes did see my imperfect being, and in Thy book all shall be written' (Ps. cxxxviii, 16).

In Ps. CXXXVIII, 21.

453

It is manifest, brethren; all who separate themselves from unity are 'brought to be few' (Ps. cvi, 39). For they are many, but in unity, as long as they are not parted from unity. For when the multitude of unity has begun no more to belong to them, in heresy and schism they are brought to be few.

In Ps. CVI, 14.

If a member is cut off from the body, does the spirit follow it?
And a member is recognized for what it is; it is a finger, a hand,
an arm, an ear; it has form if apart from the body, but life it does
not have. So is it with a man separated from the Church. Thou
askest of him the Sacrament, thou dost find it; thou seekest
Baptism, thou findest it; thou seekest the Creed, thou findest it.
The form is there; but except thou be quickened within by the
Holy Spirit, thou gloriest in vain in the outward form.

Serm. CCLXVIII, 2.

II. JERUSALEM AND BABYLON

455

Two loves have created these two cities, namely, self-love to the
extent of despising God, the earthly; love of God to the extent of
despising one's self, the heavenly city. The former glories in
itself, the latter in God. For the former seeks the glory of men
while to the latter God as the testimony of the conscience is the
greatest glory. The former lifts its head in self-glory, the latter
says to its God: 'Thou art my glory, and the lifter up of my
head' (Ps. iii, 4). The former dominated by the lust of sovereignty
boasts of its princes or of the nations which it may bring under
subjection; in the latter men serve one another in charity,
the rulers by their counsel, the subjects by their obedience. The
former loves its own strength in the person of its masters, the
latter says to its God: 'I will love thee, O Lord, my strength'
(Ps. xvii, 2). Hence the wise men of the former, living according
to the flesh, follow the good things either of the body, or of the
mind, or of both; and such as might know God 'have not glorified him as God or given thanks: but became vain in their
thoughts. And their foolish heart was darkened. For professing
themselves to be wise [that is extolling themselves proudly in
their wisdom], they became fools. And they changed the glory
of the incorruptible God into the likeness of the image of a
corruptible man and of birds, and of four-footed beasts and of
creeping things [for they were either the people's leaders or
followers in all these idolatries], . . . and worshipped and served

the creature rather than the Creator, who is blessed for ever'
(Rom. i, 21 *sqq.*). But in the heavenly city there is no wisdom
of man but only the piety by which the true God is fitly worshipped, and the reward it looks for is the society of the saints
. . . 'that God may be all in all' (1 Cor. xv, 28).

De civ. Dei XIV, 28.

456

There are two kinds of love; of these the one is holy, the other
impure; the one is social, the other selfish; the one consults
the common good for the sake of the supernal fellowship; the
other reducing the affairs of the commonality to their own
power for the sake of arrogant domination; the one subject
to God, the other endeavouring to equal Him; the one tranquil,
the other turbulent; the one working for peace, the other sedi-
tious; the one preferring truth to the praise of those who are in
error, the other greedy for praise however got; the one friendly,
the other envious; the one wishing for the neighbour what it
would wish for itself, the other wishing to subject the very
neighbour to itself; the one guiding the neighbour in the interest
of the neighbour's good, the other in that of its own. . . .
These two kinds of love distinguish the two cities established in
the human race, . . . in the so to speak commingling of which
the ages are passed.

De Gen. ad litt. XI, xv, 20.

457

In the whole propagation of man and the growth of these two
cities as men were born and died, the citizen of this world was
born first and afterwards the pilgrim in this world whose home is
the city of God, being by grace predestinate, by grace elect, by
grace a pilgrim here below, and by grace a citizen of heaven.
. . . First there was reprobation, from which state we must
needs begin, and afterwards goodness, to which state we may
progress and where, after attaining to it, we may make our
abode.

De civ. Dei XV, 1, 2.

458

Two loves make up these two cities: love of God maketh Jerusalem, love of the world maketh Babylon. Wherefore let each one question himself as to what he loveth; and he shall find of which he is a citizen. And if he shall have found himself to be a citizen of Babylon, let him root out cupidity and implant charity. But if he shall have found himself a citizen of Jerusalem let him endure captivity and hope for liberty.

In Ps. LXIV, 2.

459

This city too which is called Babylon has its lovers, who look for peace in this world and hope for nothing beyond, but fix their whole joy in this, end it in this; and we see them toil exceedingly for their earthly country. But whosoever lives faithfully even therein, if they seek not therein pride, and perishable elation, and hateful boasting, but exhibit true faith, such as they can, as long as they can, to those whom they can, in so far as they see earthly things, and understand the nature of their citizenship, these God suffers not to perish in Babylon; He has predestined them to be citizens of Jerusalem. God understands their captivity, and shews to them another city, for which they ought truly to sigh, for which they ought to make every endeavour, to win which they ought to the utmost of their power to exhort their fellow-citizens now their fellow-wanderers.

In Ps. CXXXVI, 2.

460

What then? Shall all perish who . . . marry, who give in marriage, who till the fields, who build houses? No, but those who put their trust in these things, who prefer them to God, who for the sake of these things are quick to offend God, these will perish. But those who either do not use these things, or who use them as though they used them not, trusting more in Him who gave them than in the things given, and understanding in them His consolation and mercy, and who are not absorbed in the gifts, lest they fall away from the Giver; these are they whom the day will not overtake as a thief, and find unprepared.

In Ps. CXX, 3.

Observe, however, beloved, 'the rivers of Babylon.' The rivers of Babylon are all things which are here loved, and pass away. For example, one man loves to practise husbandry, to grow rich by it, to employ his mind on it, to get his pleasure from it. Let him observe the issue and see that what he has loved is not a foundation of Jerusalem, but a river of Babylon. Another says, it is a grand thing to be a soldier; all farmers fear those who are soldiers, are subservient to them, tremble at them. If I am a farmer, I shall fear soldiers; if a soldier, farmers will fear me. Madman! thou hast cast thyself headlong into another river of Babylon, and that still more turbulent and sweeping. Thou wishest to be feared by thy inferior; fear Him Who is greater than thou. He who fears thee may on a sudden become greater than thou, but He Whom thou oughtest to fear will never become less. To be an advocate, says another, is a grand thing; eloquence is most powerful; always to have clients hanging on the lips of their eloquent advocate, and from his words looking for loss or gain, death or life, ruin or security. Thou knowest not whither thou hast cast thyself. This too is another river of Babylon, and its roaring sound is the din of the waters dashing against the rocks. Mark that it flows, that it glides on; beware, for it carries things away with it. To sail the seas, says another, and to trade is a grand thing—to know many lands, to make gains from every quarter, never to be answerable to any powerful man in thy country, to be always travelling, and to feed thy mind with the diversity of the nations and the business met with, and to return enriched by the increase of thy gains. This too is a river of Babylon. When will the gains stop? When wilt thou have confidence and be secure in the gains thou makest? The richer thou art, the more fearful wilt thou be. Once shipwrecked, thou wilt come forth stripped of all, and rightly wilt bewail thy fate in the rivers of Babylon, because thou wouldest not sit down and weep *upon* the rivers of Babylon.

But there are other citizens of the holy Jerusalem, understanding their captivity, who mark how human wishes and the diverse lusts of men, hurry and drag them hither and thither, and drive them into the sea. They see this, and do not throw themselves into the rivers of Babylon, but sit down upon the rivers of Babylon and upon the rivers of Babylon weep, either for those who are being carried away by them, or for themselves whose deserts have placed them in Babylon. But they sit, that is, humble themselves. 'Upon the rivers of Babylon, there we sat and wept: when we remembered Sion' (Ps. cxxxvi, i). O holy Sion, where all stands firm and nothing flows! Who has thrown us headlong into this? Why have we left thy Founder and thy society? Behold, set where all things are flowing and gliding away, scarce one, if he can grasp a tree, shall be snatched from the river and escape. Humbling ourselves, therefore, in our captivity, let us 'sit upon the rivers of Babylon,' let us not dare to plunge into those rivers, or to be proud and lifted up in the evil and sadness of our captivity, but let us sit, and so weep.

In Ps. CXXXVI, 3, 4.

462

Thou oughtest to weep, but in remembering Sion. If in remembering Sion thou weepest, it is meet that thou shouldst weep even when it is well with thee in Babylon. . . . It matters much whether thou findest tribulation, or art found by tribulation. . . . When sadness suddenly overtakes thee through trouble in thy worldly affairs, wherein thou didst delight; when sudden sadness of her own accord finds thee, befalls thee from some point, whence thou didst not think thou couldst be saddened, and thou art made sad; then the sorrow of hell has found thee (cf. Ps. xvii, 5 *sq.*). For thou thoughtest thyself aloft, whereas thou wast beneath; there hast thou found thyself beneath, where thou thoughtest thyself aloft. . . . But when it is well with thee, when all earthly things smile on thee, none of thy dear ones has died, no drought nor hail nor barrenness has assailed thy vineyard, thy cask has not turned sour, thy cattle have not failed to give increase, thou hast not been dishonoured in any high dignity of this world, wherein thou hast been placed, thy friends all around thee live and preserve their friendship for thee, dependants are not wanting, thy children obey thee, thy slaves tremble before thee, thy wife lives in concord with thee, thy house is called happy—then find affliction, if in any way thou canst, that, having found affliction thou mayest call upon the name of the Lord. The divine word seems perversely to teach that we should weep in joy and rejoice in sorrow. Mark how it rejoices in sorrow: 'We glory,' it says, 'in tribulations' (Rom. v, 3). But see it weeping in joy if it has found tribulation. Let each one mark his own happiness, wherein his soul has exulted and has puffed itself up in a manner with joy and elated itself, and said, 'I am happy.' Let him mark whether that happiness does not flow by, whether he can be sure of it that it endures for ever. But if he is not certain, but sees that that wherein he rejoices is fleeting, it is a river of Babylon; let him sit down upon it and weep. But he will sit down and weep if he remember Sion. O for that peace which we shall see in the presence of God! O for that holy equality with the Angels! O for that vision, that fair sight!

In Ps. CXXXVI, 5.

463

Observe two kinds of men: the one of those who labour, the other of those among whom they labour; the one of men thinking of earth, the other of men thinking of heaven; the one of those whose hearts are set on the depths, the other of men who join their hearts to the Angels; the one trusting in earthly things with which this world abounds, the other confiding in heavenly things, which God, who doth not lie, hath promised. But these kinds of men are mingled. We see now a citizen of Jerusalem, a citizen of the Kingdom of heaven, holding some office upon earth; as for example, wearing the purple, serving as magistrate, as ædile, as proconsul, as Emperor, directing the earthly republic, but he hath his heart above if he is a Christian, if he is of the faithful, if he despiseth those things wherein he is and trusteth in that wherein he is not yet. . . . Let us not therefore despair of the citizens of the Kingdom of heaven when we see them engaged in the affairs of Babylon, doing something terrestrial in a terrestrial republic; nor again let us forthwith congratulate all men whom we see engaged in celestial matters, for even the sons of the pestilence sit sometimes in the seat of Moses. . . . The former amid earthly things lift up their hearts to heaven; the latter amid heavenly words trail their hearts on the earth. But there will come a time of winnowing when they will be separated, the one from the other, with the greatest care, that no grain pass over into the heap of chaff which is to be burned, and that not one single straw pass over to the mass that is to be stored in the barn (cf. Matt. iii, 12). So long then as it is mingled, let us listen thence to our voice, that is, the voice of the citizens of the Kingdom of heaven (for to this we ought to aspire, to bear with evil men here rather than be suffered by good men), and let us join ourselves to this voice, both with ear and with tongue, with heart and with work. And if we have done this, we speak here in those things which we hear.

In Ps. LI, 6.

464

There is to-day, in this age, a terrestrial kingdom where dwells also the celestial kingdom. Each kingdom—the terrestrial kingdom and the celestial, the kingdom to be rooted up and that to be planted for eternity—has its various citizens. Only in this world the citizens of each kingdom are mingled; the body of the terrestrial kingdom and the body of the celestial kingdom are commingled. The celestial kingdom groans amid the citizens of the terrestrial kingdom, and sometimes (for this too must not be hushed) the terrestrial kingdom doth in some manner exact service from the citizens of the kingdom of heaven and the kingdom of heaven doth exact service from the citizens of the terrestrial kingdom.

In Ps. LI, 4.

465

You have heard and know that there are two cities, for the present mingled together in body, but in heart separated. One whose end is eternal peace is called Jerusalem, the other whose joy is temporal peace is called Babylon. . . . Jerusalem was held captive in Babylon, but not all; for the Angels also are its citizens. But as regards men predestined to the glory of God, to become by adoption joint-heirs with Christ, whom He has redeemed from this very captivity by His own blood; this part of the citizens of Jerusalem is held captive in Babylon on account of sin, but first begins to go forth thence in spirit by confession of sin and by the charity of justice, and then afterwards, at the end of the world, is to be separated in the body also. This we have set before you in that psalm which we first treated here with you, beloved, and which begins thus: *Te decet hymnus* (Ps. lxiv, 2).

In Ps. CXXXVI, 1.

466

For the Catholic Church has been vindicated by heretics, and those that think rightly have been proved by those that think wrongly. For many things lay hid in the Scriptures, and when the heretics had been cut off, they troubled the Church of God with questions; those things were then opened up which lay hid, and the will of God was understood. . . . For was the Trinity perfectly treated of before the Arians carped thereat? Was penance perfectly treated of before the Novatians raised their opposition? So too Baptism was not perfectly treated of before the rebaptizers who were cast out of the fold contradicted the teaching. Nor were the doctrines of the very oneness of Christ, which have been stated, clearly set forth save after their separation began to weigh upon the weak; so that, lest the weak be vexed with the questionings of the ungodly, those that knew should by their discourses and disputations bring out into open day the obscure things of the Law. Therefore they have been divided because of the anger of His countenance, and unto us for our proper understanding His heart hath drawn near.

In Ps. LIV, 22.

467

For you are not to suppose, brethren, that heresies could be produced through any little souls. None save great men have been the authors of heresies.

In Ps. CXXIV, 5.

468

But since, as has been most truly said, 'there must be many heresies; that they who are approved may be made manifest among you' (1 Cor. xi, 19), let us make use also of this act of beneficence of divine Providence. For heretics are made from the ranks of those who even if they were in the Church would go astray notwithstanding. Since they are outside the Church, they are of very great service, not by teaching the truth, of which they are ignorant, but by exciting the carnally minded Catholics to seek the truth, and the spiritually minded to disclose it. For there are innumerable men in Holy Church who are approved before God, but they are not made manifest among us, so long as we prefer to sleep in contentment with the darkness of our ignorance, than to gaze upon the light of truth. Wherefore many are roused from their slumber by heretics, that they may see the day of the Lord and rejoice (cf. John viii, 56).

De vera relig. VIII, 15.

469

Members of all the heretical sects are not to be found spread over the whole face of the earth, but yet there are heretics over the whole face of the earth. Some are in one place, some in another, yet in no place are they wanting, and they themselves do not know one another. . . . Nevertheless the Catholic mother herself, the Shepherd Himself in her, is everywhere seeking those who are straying, and is strengthening the weak, healing the sick, binding up the broken, some from these sects, some from those, which mutually do not know one another.
. . . She is like the vine which has in its growth spread everywhere; they are like useless twigs, which are lopped off by the husbandman's sickle, as their sterility deserves; to prune the vine, not to cut it all away. Those twigs therefore remain lying where they were lopped off. The vine, however, continuing its growth through it all, knows both the twigs that remain on her and those lying beside it which have been lopped off.
. . . Whether thou speakest of sheep straying from the flock, or of wood cut away from the vine, God is equally able to bring back the sheep, or to ingraft the wood again, for He is the Chief Shepherd, He is the true Husbandman.

Serm. XLVI, viii, 18

470

We already rejoice in the correction of many who hold and defend the Catholic unity with such sincerity, and are so glad to have been delivered from their error, that we admire them with great thankfulness and pleasure. And yet these same persons, under some indescribable force of custom, would in no way have thought of being changed to a better state, had they not, under the shock of fear, directed their minds earnestly to the study of the truth. . . . For if they were only made afraid and not instructed, this might appear to be an almost outrageous tyranny. Again, if they were instructed only, and not made afraid, there would be more difficulty in persuading them to embrace the way of salvation, hardened as they had become through inveterate custom. . . .

Not every one who is indulgent is a friend; nor is every one an enemy who smites. 'Better are the wounds of a friend, than the deceitful kisses of an enemy' (Prov. xxvii, 6). It is better to love with severity than to deceive with gentleness. More good is done by taking away food from the hungry, if secure of his food he is forgetful of righteousness, than by providing food for the hungry, that, being thereby bribed, he may consent to unrighteousness. He who binds a man who is in a frenzy, and he who stirs a man out of his lethargy, are alike vexatious to both, yet both are prompted by love. Who can love us more than God does? And yet He not only teaches us tenderly but also quickens us by salutary fear, and this unceasingly. Often adding to the soothing remedies by which He comforts men the sharp medicine of tribulation, He afflicts with famine even the pious and devout Patriarchs (v. Gen. xii, xxvi, xlii, and xliii), disquiets a rebellious people by more severe chastisements, and refuses, though thrice besought, to take away the sting in the flesh of the Apostle, that He might make his power perfect in infirmity (2 Cor. xii, 7 *sqq.*). . . .

You now see therefore, I suppose, that what must be considered when anyone is coerced is not the mere fact of the coercion, but the nature of that to which he is coerced, whether it be good or bad. Not that anyone can be good against his will, but that, through fear of suffering what he does not desire, he either renounces his hampering animosity, or he is compelled to examine a truth of which he had been ignorant; and under the influence of this fear repudiates the error which he was wont to defend, or seeks the truth of which formerly he knew nothing, and now willingly holds what he formerly rejected. . . .

Originally my opinion was that no one should be coerced into the unity of Christ, that we must act only by words, fight only by arguments, and prevail only by force of reason, lest we should have those whom we knew to be avowed heretics feigning themselves to be Catholics. But this opinion of mine was overcome not by the words of those who contraverted it, but by conclusive examples to which they could point.

Ep. XCIII, i, 1, 3; ii, 4; v, 16, 17.

471

For this Catholic Church, vigorously spreading far and wide throughout the whole world, uses all who are in error to her own advancement, and to their amendment, when they shall wish to awake from their error. She uses the heathen as material on which to work, heretics as a test of her teaching, schismatics as a proof of her stability, Jews as a comparison to show her beauty. Hence she invites some, thrusts out others, leaves others alone, and of others she takes the lead. To all, however, she gives the opportunity of participating in God's grace, whether it be that they have to be formed, or to be reformed, or to be brought back to the fold, or to be admitted to it. But the carnally minded of her own people, that is, those whose lives or sentiments are carnal, she bears with as chaff protecting the grain on the threshing floor, until the latter is stripped of this tegument. But because on this threshing floor each one is, according to his will, either chaff or grain, the sin or error of each one is borne with for just so long until he either find an accuser, or until he defend his perverse opinion with obstinate animosity. Those, however, who are thrust out either return penitent, or of their own free and evil will descend into iniquity, and serve as a warning to our diligence; or bring about a schism, to the exercise of our patience; or give birth to some heresy, to the proving or the calling into being of our intelligence. . . .

Often, too, the divine Providence allows even good men to be driven out of the Christian communion by the all too factious dissensions of carnally minded men. And if they bear this ignominy or injury patiently for the sake of the peace of the

Church, and do not give occasion to any new heresies or schisms, they will teach men, with what true affection and sincere charity God must be served. The intention of such men is either to return when the storms are stilled; or if this be not allowed them, whether because the same storm persists or because their return may give rise to a similar or more violent one, they hold to the will to have regard for the good of those very men even, owing to whose violences and disturbances they had withdrawn, and, without setting up any separate sect, to the day of their death defend and by their witness support that faith which they know to be preached in the Catholic Church. These the Father, who sees in secret, crowns in secret. Men such as these are seldom seen; yet examples are not wanting; indeed there are more than might be thought. Thus divine Providence uses all classes of men and examples for the cure of souls and the institution of a spiritual people.

De vera relig. vi, 10–11.

472

How many that are not ours are yet, as it were, within; and how many that are ours are still, as it were, without. 'The Lord knoweth who are his' (2 Tim. ii, 19). And they that are not ours, who are within, when they find their opportunities, go out, and they that are ours, who are without, when they find opportunities, return.

In Ps. CVI, 14.

473

For we are not to despair of anyone so long as the patience of God leadeth the ungodly to penance, and doth not seize him out of this life; for God doth not will that a sinner should die, but that he should be converted from his ways and live (*v.* Ezech. xviii, 23). He is a heathen to-day, but how knowest thou whether he may not believe in Christ to-morrow? He is a heretic to-day, but what if to-morrow he follow the Catholic truth?

Serm. (*de Script. N.T.*) LXXI, xiii, 21.

XI. THROUGH CHRIST-MAN TO CHRIST-GOD

I. . . . . ABIDING IN THE FLESH

474

Now it is not an infant but a grown child that is weaned.
The weakling in his earliest infancy, which is his true infancy,
is at his mother's breast; and if perchance he is deprived of
her milk, he perishes. . . . For all can be weaned by growing. He who grows and is thus weaned, it is good for him;
but it is hurtful for him who is still at his mother's breast. We
must therefore beware, my brethren, and be fearful, lest anyone
be weaned from milk before his time. For every full-grown
child is separated from milk. But let none be taken away from
milk, when he is at his mother's breast. But while he is carried
in his mother's arms, who has been carried in her womb (for
he was carried in her womb, that he might be born; he is carried
in her arms, that he may grow), he has need of milk; he is
still at his mother's breast. Let him not therefore wish to exalt
his soul, when perhaps he is not fit to take meat, but let him
fulfil the commandments of humility. He has that wherein
he may exercise himself: let him believe in Christ, that he
may be able to understand Christ. He cannot see the Word;
he cannot understand the equality of the Word with the Father;
he cannot as yet see the equality of the Holy Ghost with the
Father and the Word; let him believe this, that is, let him
suck. He is safe because, when he is grown, he will eat, which
he could not do before he grew by sucking, and he had a point
to stretch towards. 'Seek not the things that are too high
for thee, and search not into things above thy ability'; that
is, things which thou art not as yet fit to understand. But
what am I to do? thou sayest. Shall I remain thus? 'But the
things that God hath commanded thee, think on them always'

(Ecclus. iii, 22). What hath the Lord commanded thee? Do works of mercy; break not up the peace of the Church; place not thy hope in man; tempt not God by longing for miracles. If there is new fruit in thee, thou knowest that thou sufferest cockle together with the good wheat until the harvest; that thou canst be with the wicked for a season, not for eternity. The chaff is here mingled during this time on the threshing floor, it will not be with thee in the barn. 'These things that God hath commanded thee, think on them always.' Thou shalt not be taken away from milk as long as thou art upon thy mother's breast; lest thou perish of hunger before thou art fit to eat bread. Grow; thy powers will be strong; and thou wilt see what thou couldest not, and wilt understand what thou didst not understand.

In Ps. CXXX, 13.

475

Await therefore, be formed; do not ascribe to thyself a judgment which perchance thou knowest not. Carnal thou art as yet; conceived thou hast been. From the very time when thou didst receive the name of Christ, thou hast been born by a kind of sacrament in the bowels of thy mother. For a man is born not only out of bowels but also in bowels. He is first born in bowels that he may be able to be born of bowels. . . . Therefore there are born within the bowels of the Church certain little ones, and it is good that being formed they should come forth, so that they perish not by a miscarriage. Let the mother bear thee, not miscarry. If thou hast been patient until thou be formed, until there be in thee the sure doctrine of truth, the maternal bowels ought to keep thee. But if by thy impatience thou hast shaken the sides of thy mother, she expelleth thee with pain indeed, but more to thy loss than to hers.

In Ps. LVII, 5.

476

Hope in Him, the bond of union of the new commonalty; and, you people that are being born, whom the Lord has made, strive that you may be born to your salvation, and that there may be no miscarriage to your destruction. Behold Mother Church, see, she is groaning in labour, that she may bring you forth, and lead you into the light of the faith. Do not in your impatience impair the bowels of your mother and narrow the portal of your birth; you people that are being created, praise your God; praise Him, you who are being created, praise your God. Because you are being suckled, praise Him; because you are being nourished, praise Him; because you are being nursed, progress in wisdom and years. These delays in your temporal birth have been permitted by Him who grows neither less through the shortness of time, nor greater through any duration of time, but who from all the eternal days has excluded all straits of space and time. . . . Grow up in Christ that you may after the manner of youth increase to a perfect man. . . .

Love what you are to be. For you will be sons of God, and sons of adoption. This will be given you freely, and freely conferred upon you. You will abound the more amply and plentifully the more grateful you are to Him from whom you have received these things. Seek to gain Him who knows who His are. . . . God is the father, the mother is the Church. Very different is your procreation by them than when you were born of your parents in the flesh. It is not labour, not misery, not weeping, nor death that will enter into these births, but ease, happiness, joy, and life. By the former, generation is a cause of tears; by the latter, one to be desired. The former in giving us birth gives birth unto eternal punishment by reason of the old sin; the latter in regenerating us causes neither the punishment nor the sin to endure. This is that 'generation of them that seek him, of them that seek the face of the God of Jacob' (Ps. xxiii, 6). As humble seekers seek Him; and when you have found Him, you will come to the safe heights. Your first infancy will be innocence, your boyhood reverence, your youth virtue, your maturity merit, your old age nothing other than hoary and wise understanding. In passing over these stages or steps of your age you are not gradually unfolded, but abiding in the way you are renewed. For it is not that as the first dies the second follows, or that the rise of the third will be the destruction of the second, or that the fourth is now born that the third may die; nor that the fifth grudges the fourth a longer existence, nor that the sixth buries the fifth. Though all these ages do not come at the same time, nevertheless in a soul that is pious and justified they persist on equal and harmonious terms. These bring you to the seventh stage of everlasting rest and peace. Nevertheless, delivered, as we read, six times from the troubles of the fatal age, in the seventh evil shall not touch thee (Job v. 19). . . . . There there will be secure immortality, there immortal security.

Serm. CCXVI, vii, 7; viii, 8.

477

He is in bondage to a sign who uses or venerates any significant object without knowing what it signifies. On the other hand, he who uses or venerates a useful sign divinely appointed, whose force and significance he understands, does not venerate the sign which is visible and temporal, but rather that thing to which all such signs refer. Now such a man is spiritual and free even in the time of his bondage, during which it is not yet meet that there should be revealed to carnal minds those signs by subjection to which their carnal qualities are to be subdued. To this class of spiritual persons belonged the patriarchs and prophets and all those of the people of Israel through whom the Holy Spirit ministered unto us the aids and consolations of the Scriptures. But at the present time, after the proof of our liberty has shone forth so clearly in the resurrection of our Lord, we are not oppressed with the heavy burden of attending even to those signs which we now understand, but there have been handed down to us by our Lord himself and by Apostolic practice a few rites in place of many, and those at once very easy to perform, most august in their significance, and most pious in their observance. Such for example are the Sacrament of baptism and the celebration of the body and blood of the Lord. And as soon as one comprehends those observances he knows by his instruction to what they refer, and that they are to be venerated not in carnal bondage but in spiritual freedom. Now, as to follow the letter and to take signs for the things they signify is a mark of servile weakness; so, too, to interpret signs wrongly is the result of

being misled by error. He, however, who does not know what
a sign signifies, yet knows it is a sign, is not in bondage. And
it is better to be in bondage to unknown but useful signs than,
by interpreting them wrongly, to draw the neck from under
the yoke of bondage only to insert it in the coils of error.

De doct. christ. III, ix, 13.

478

'If thou desire wisdom, keep the commandments: and God
will give her unto thee' (Ecclus. i, 33); lest any one, proceeding
out of order, may wish, before he hath the humility of obedience,
to arrive at the height of wisdom, which he cannot reach,
unless he hath approached it in regular order. Let him therefore hearken to these words: 'Seek not the things that are too
high for thee, and search not into things above thy ability:
but the things that God hath commanded thee, think on them
always' (*id.* iii, 22). Thus doth man reach the wisdom of
hidden things through obedience to the commandments. But
when he had said, 'the things that God hath commanded thee,
think on them,' he added 'always,' because obedience must
be kept that wisdom may be received, and not be given up
when wisdom hath been received.

In Ps. CXCIII, *Serm.* XXII, 8.

479

Be not therefore impatient to hear what you are not yet
capable of receiving, but grow that thou mayest be so capable.

In Ps. XXXVIII, 3.

480

'Thou shalt see my back parts: but my face thou canst not
see' (Exod. xxxiii, 23). . . . . It is desire for this last sight
that seizes every rational soul, and the more ardently the purer
that soul is; and it is the more pure the more it rises again to
spiritual things, and it rises the more to spiritual things the
more it dies to carnal things. Now whilst we are absent from
the Lord, and walk by faith and not by sight (2 Cor. v, 6 *sq.*),
we ought to see the 'back parts' of Christ, that is, His flesh,
by that same faith, standing, that is on the solid foundation of

faith, which the rock (*petra*) stands for; and beholding it from such a wholly secure watch-tower, namely, in the Catholic Church, of which it is said, 'And upon this rock I will build my Church' (Matt. xvi, 18). For we love the more surely that face of Christ which we long to see, in proportion as we recognize in His back parts how much Christ loved us.

De Trin. II, xvi, 28; xvii, 28.

481

In the Church those who adhere to the truth proclaim the Truth by whom all things were made: the Truth that is the Word made flesh and dwelling among us; the Truth that is Christ begotten of God, One of One, only-begotten and co-eternal; the Truth that taking the form of a servant was born of the Virgin Mary, suffered, crucified and rose again, ascended into Heaven. Everywhere they proclaim the Truth, both those who, as being as it were of ripe age, understand, and those who, as it were little ones, cannot. The Truth is proclaimed both in the bread and in the milk, in the bread of the big, in the milk of the little ones. Indeed, the same bread, that it may become milk is passed through the flesh.

Serm. VIII, ii, 3.

482

You are sons of the Church, and have profited in the Church, and you who have not as yet profited in the Church will profit in the Church, and you who have already profited have to profit further in the Church.

In Ps. CXX, 8.

483

'In the beginning was the word: and the word was with God' (John i, 1). . . . He therefore is bread: thence the Angels live. Behold, the bread is prepared for thee; but grow by the means of the milk, that thou mayest come to the bread. And how, thou sayest, do I grow on milk? That which Christ became for thee for thy weakness, this first believe, and steadily hold. As then the mother, when she seeth her child unfit for taking meat, giveth him meat, but meat that hath passed through her flesh, for the bread upon which the infant feeds is the same bread as that whereon the mother feeds; but the infant is not fit for the table, he is fit for the breast, and therefore bread is passed from the table through the mother's breast, that the same aliment may thus reach the little infant; thus our Lord Jesus Christ, when He was the Word with the Father, through whom all things were made, Who, since He was 'in the form of God, thought it not robbery to be the equal with God' (Phil. ii, 6); such as the Angels might receive according to their degree, and whence the Powers and Virtues, intellectual spirits, might feed; while man lay weak and wrapped in flesh on earth, and the heavenly bread could not reach him; that man might eat the bread of Angels (Ps. lxxvii, 25), and manna might come down to the truer people of Israel, 'the Word was made flesh, and dwelt among us' (John i, 14).

On which account the Apostle Paul saith this to the weak, those whom he calleth natural and carnal (1 Cor. iii, 1): 'I judged not myself to know anything among you, but Jesus Christ: and him crucified' (id. ii, 2). For there was Christ, and not crucified. 'In the beginning was the Word, and the Word was with God, and the Word was God.' And because 'the Word was made flesh,' the Word was also crucified, but was not changed into man; man was changed in Him. Man was changed in Him, that he might become better than he was, not that he might be changed into the very substance of the Word. In that therefore He was man, God died; and in that He was God, Man was raised from the dead, and arose, and ascended into Heaven. . . .

Our Lord Jesus Christ, the bread, made Himself milk for us, being incarnate and appearing in mortal shape, that in Him death might be finished, and that, believing in the flesh which the Word was made, we might not wander astray from the Word. On this let us grow, by this milk let us be nourished. Let us not depart from our faith in the milk before we are strong enough to receive the Word.

In Ps. CXXX, 9–10, 11.

484

The mind of man . . . in which Christ dwells by faith . . . must hold fast to Him who is ever the Son of God but for our sakes became the Son of man, in order that His eternal power and divinity might be attempered to our weakness and mortality and, on the basis of what is ours, make a way for us in Himself and to Himself. To be kept from sinning man must be ruled by Christ the King. If he happen to sin, he may obtain remission from the same Christ the Priest. And thus, nurtured in the exercise of a good conversation and life, and borne out of the atmosphere of the earth on the wings of a twofold law, as on a pair of strong pinions, so may he be enlightened by the same Christ who is also the Lord, the Lord who was in the beginning, the Lord who was with God, and the Lord who was God (John i, 1). But although that will still be 'through a glass in a dark manner' (i Cor. xiii, 12), it will be nevertheless a sublime illumination far superior to every corporeal similitude.

De cons. Evang. IV, XX, 20.

485

Why dost thou not allow that Christ gives faith in order by His gift to make the Christian? Why dost thou not allow that Christ is the source and origin of the Christian, that the Christian infixes his root in Christ, that Christ is the Head of the Christian?

Contra litt. Petil. I, v, vi.

486

For all the better sort in the Church, for whom there has now remained no longer any man worthy of their imitation, since by the progress they have made, they had left all others behind, Christ Himself remains, as One whom they may follow even unto the end.

In Ps. XXXIX, 6.

II. . . . SUFFERING ON THE CROSS

487

The whole Church is one widow, whether in men or women, in married men or married women, in young men or in old, or in virgins. The whole Church is one widow, desolate in this world; if she feel this, if she is aware of her widowhood: then is help at hand for her.

In Ps. CXXXI, 23.

488

'We are saved by hope' (Rom. viii, 24). Already the flesh taken of us in the Lord is saved not in hope but in fact. For in our Head our flesh hath risen again and ascended whole, though in the members it yet hath to be made whole. The members rejoice fearlessly, because they have not been deserted by their Head. For He said to His members in trouble, 'Behold I am with you all days, even to the consummation of the world' (Matt. xxviii, 20). Thus was it done that we might be converted to God. For we had no hope save toward the world, and therefore were wretched slaves, and twice wretched, because we had placed our hope in this life, and had our face toward the world, and our back toward God. But when the Lord hath turned us, so that we begin now to have our face toward God and our back toward the world, we who are still on our journey, are striving to reach our home. And when perchance we suffer any tribulation, but yet keep on our way, and are supported by the Word, the wind indeed may be rough, but it is favourable; with toil indeed but quickly it carrieth us, quickly carrieth us home.

In Ps. CXXV, 2.

489

Let each one therefore think of his enemy. If he is a Christian, the world is an enemy to him. . . . Let no one say to himself, There have been troubles in our fathers' time but not in ours. If thou thinkest thyself not to have troubles, thou hast not yet begun to be a Christian. . . . If thou sufferest not any persecution for Christ, take heed lest thou hast not yet begun to live godly in Christ. But when thou hast begun to live godly in Christ, thou hast entered the wine press; prepare thyself for the pressings, but be thou not dry, lest from the pressing nothing come forth.

In Ps. LV, 4.

490

The Church grew, the nations believed, the princes of the
earth have been conquered under the name of Christ, that
they might be conquerors in the whole world. Their necks
were placed under the yoke of Christ. Formerly they persecuted
the Christians in defence of the idols, now they persecute the
idols in defence of the Christians. All had recourse to the help
of the Church in their every affliction, their every tribulation.
That grain of mustard seed has grown and is become greater
than all the herbs, and the birds of the air; the proud ones of
the world, come and find rest under its branches (Matt. xiii,
31 *sq.*). Whence comes this great excellence? It has sprung
from some root or other. . . . Let us seek that root. It was spat
upon, it was abased, it was scourged, it was crucified, it was
wounded, it was despised. There is no splendour here, yet the
glory of that root is all-prevailing.

Serm. XLIV, i, 2.

491

For one Man with His head and body is Christ Jesus, the
Saviour of the body and members of the body; two in one
flesh (cf. Gen. ii, 24; Eph. v, 31), and in one voice, and in one
passion; and, when all iniquity shall have ceased, in one rest.
The sufferings therefore of Christ are not in Christ alone; nay,
there are no sufferings of Christ save in Christ. For if thou
understandest Christ to be the Head and the Body, the sufferings
of Christ are not, save in Christ. But if thou understandest
Christ to be the Head alone, the sufferings of Christ are not in
Christ alone. . . . If therefore thou art in the members of Christ,
whatsoever man thou art, . . . whatsoever thing thou sufferest
from those that are not in the members of Christ, was wanting
in the sufferings of Christ. Therefore it is added because it
was wanting; thou fillest up the measure, but dost not cause it
to run over. Thou sufferest so much as was to be contributed
out of thy sufferings to the whole passion of Christ, who hath
suffered in our Head and doth suffer in His members, that is
in our own selves. To this so to speak common republic each
of us, according to our measure, payeth what we owe; and,
according to the powers we have, we contribute our quota

as it were of sufferings. The tale of all men's sufferings will not be completely made up, until the world shall have come to an end. . . . Whatever the Prophets have suffered, 'from the blood of Abel the just, even unto the blood of Zacharias' (Matt. xxiii, 35), hath been laid upon man, because there have preceded the advent of the Incarnation of Christ certain members of Christ; just as in the birth of some child a hand is put forth though the head hath not yet appeared (cf. Gen. xxxviii, 27), and yet the hand also is joined to the head.

In Ps. LXI, 4.

492

Whatever He hath suffered, therein we also have suffered; and that which we suffer, He also suffers in us. . . . In Him we are dead, and in Him we are risen again; and He dieth in us and in us riseth again; for He is the unity of the Head and the Body.

In Ps. LXII, 2.

493

Such is the unity of the body that if one member suffer, all the members suffer (1 Cor. xii, 26). Thou art in trouble to-day, I too; another is in trouble to-morrow, I too; after this generation other descendants, who succeed your descendants, are in trouble, I am in trouble; down to the end of the world, whoever are in trouble in My body, I am in trouble.

In Ps. CI, *Serm.* i, 3.

494

Do thou suffer in Christ's suffering; for Christ as it were sinned in thy infirmity. . . . As He willed our sins should be His own, on account of our being His body, let us also regard His sufferings as our own, on account of His being our Head.

In Ps. XXXVII, 16.

495

If He, our Head, without labour having been at first accomplished on earth, chose not to reign in heaven, nor to raise up the body, which He received from below, save by the way of tribulation, how dare the members expect that they can be more fortunate than their Head? . . . Let us not therefore look for a more easy way; by the road on which He preceded us, let us also go; let us follow by the road on which He has led us.

In Ps. LI, 1.

496

The deformity of Christ forms thee. If He had not willed to be deformed, thou wouldst not have recovered the form which thou hadst lost. Therefore deformed He hung upon the Cross. But His deformity is our comeliness. In this life, therefore, let us hold fast to the deformed Christ. . . . We carry the sign of this deformity on our forehead. Let us not be ashamed of this deformity of Christ. Let us hold to this way, and we shall arrive where we shall see Him; we shall see the perfect justice of God. And there there will be no longer need to say, Why does He help this one and not that? Why is this one brought by the piloting of God to be baptized, whereas that one though he lived rightly as a catechumen, died in a sudden catastrophe, and did not attain to baptism? And that one, though his life may have been spent in crime, though he may have been a riotous liver, an adulterer, a play actor, a fighter of beasts in the arena, falls ill, is baptized, dies—is sin in such a one overcome, is the sin in him wiped out? Seek merits, and you will only find punishment; seek grace, 'O the depth of the riches!' (Rom. xi, 33); Peter denies, the thief believes: 'O the depth of the riches!'

Serm. XLIV, vi, 6.

497

He himself toileth in thee, thirsteth in thee, is hungered and in tribulation in thee. He is still dying in thee; and thou in Him art already risen from the dead. . . . For having put on Christ, we are Christ together with our Head, inasmuch as we are the seed of Abraham. . . . In thy seed shall all nations be blessed. He saith not in thy seeds as of many; but as of one: And to thy seed, which is Christ. And to us he saith, 'you are the seed of Abraham (Gal. iii, 8, 16, 29). It is clear that we belong to

Christ; and because we are His members and His body, we are one man with our Head.

In Ps. C, 3.

498

'And we saw him, and there was no beauty in him, nor comeliness' (Is. liii, 2). Is then our Bridegroom unsightly? God forbid! For how then would the virgins love Him, who have not sought husbands on earth? He therefore seemed unsightly to his persecutors. And had they not thought Him loathsome, they would not insult Him, they would not strike Him with scourges, would not crown Him with thorns, would not defile Him with spittle; but because He seemed loathsome to them, they did these things to Him; for they had not the eyes whereby Christ could seem beautiful to them. To what sort of eyes did Christ seem beautiful? To such as Christ himself sought, when He said to Philip, 'Have I been so long a time with you and have you not seen me?' (John xiv, 9). These eyes must be cleansed, that they may be able to see that light; and though slightly touched by the splendour, they are kindled with love, that they may wish to be healed, and may become enlightened. For that you may know that Christ who is loved is beautiful, the Prophet saith, 'Beautiful above the sons of men' (Ps. xliv, 3). His beauty surpasseth all men. What is it we love in Christ? His crucified members, His pierced side, or His charity? When we hear that He suffered for us, what do we love? Charity is loved. He loved us that we might in turn love Him; and that we might return His love, He hath visited us with His Spirit.

In Ps. CXXVII, 8.

499

'And they that are Jesus Christ's have crucified their flesh, with the passions and concupiscences' (Gal. v, 24). On this cross, indeed, throughout the whole of this life which is spent in the midst of trials and temptations, the Christian must continually hang. For there is no time in this life to draw out the nails, of which it is said in the psalm, 'Pierce thou my flesh with the nails of thy fear' (Ps. cxviii, 120); the flesh is the carnal concupiscences; the nails are the commandments of justice;

with the latter the fear of the Lord pierces the former, and it crucifies us as an acceptable sacrifice to Him. Therefore in like manner the Apostle says, 'I beseech you therefore, brethren, by the mercy of God, that you present your bodies a living sacrifice, holy, pleasing unto God' (Rom. xii, 1). This cross, therefore, in which the servant of God not only is not confounded but even glories in the words, 'God forbid that I should glory, save in the cross of our Lord Jesus Christ: by whom the world is crucified to me, and I to the world' (Gal. vi, 14), this cross, I say, is not merely for forty days but for the whole of this life. . . . In this wise ever live, O Christian: if thou dost not wish thy steps to sink in the slime of the earth, descend not from this cross.

Serm. CCV, 1.

500

'My soul hath fainted after thy salvation: and in thy word I have hoped' (Ps. cxviii, 81). . . . But who saith this, save the chosen generation, the kingly priesthood, the holy nation the purchased people (1 Pet. ii, 9), longing for Christ from the beginnings of the human race even unto the end of this world, in the persons of those who, each in his own time, have lived, are living, or are to live here? . . . Neither at that time, then, had this longing of the saints found rest, nor is it now at rest in the body of Christ, which is the Church, until the end of time, until 'the desired of all nations shall come,' as is promised by the Prophet (Agg. ii, 8). Wherefore the Apostle saith, 'There is laid up for me a crown of justice which the Lord the just judge will render to me in that day: and not only to me, but to all them also that love His appearing' (2 Tim. iv, 8). This desire, therefore, of which we are now speaking, ariseth from the love of His appearing; of which he also saith, 'When Christ shall appear, who is your life, then you also shall appear with Him in glory' (Col. iii, 4). The first ages of the Church, therefore, had Saints, before the Virgin's delivery, who desired the advent of His incarnation; but these times, since He hath ascended into heaven, have Saints who desire His appearance to judge the living and the dead. Nor hath this desire of the Church had any rest from the beginning unto the end of the world, save during the short space when He was here in the flesh with His disciples, so that the voice of the whole Body of Christ groaning in this life may be comformably understood: 'My soul hath fainted after Thy salvation: and in thy word I have hoped,' that is, of Thy promise; and this hope causes that which is not seen by believers to be awaited with patience by them.

In Ps. CXVIII, *Serm.* xx, 1.

501

Neither are we going, whither Christ hath gone before us; and Christ is still journeying whither He has gone before. For Christ went before us in the Head, and Christ follows in the Body. Christ is still here toiling; here Christ suffered at Saul's hands. . . . Christ is still here in want; here Christ still journeys; Christ here is sick, Christ is here in bonds.

In Ps. LXXXVI, 5.

502

For thus He spoke: 'Behold, I cast out devils and do cures, to-day and to-morrow, and the third day I am consummated' (Luke xiii, 32); that is, I am perfected, when we all meet 'unto a perfect man,. unto the measure of the age of the fulness of Christ' (Eph. iv, 13). . . . This is the consummation of the Body of Christ on the third day, when the devils have been cast out, and cures perfected, even unto the immortality of the body itself, the everlasting reign of those who perfectly praise Him, because they perfectly love Him; and they perfectly love Him, because they behold him face to face.

In Ps: CV, 36, 37.

503

The root is living, but in winter time the vigorous tree looks just like a withered one. For in winter time, both the tree which is vigorous and which is withered, are both bare of the beauty of the leaves, both are empty of the adornment of fruit. Summer will come, and there will be a distinction between the trees. The living root puts forth leaves and is pregnant with fruit; the withered one will remain as barren in the heat of summer as it was in the winter. . . . So our summer is the coming of Christ;

our winter the occultation of Christ; our summer the revelation of Christ.

Serm. XXXVI, iv, 4.

III. . . . PASSING TO GLORY

504

The same Holy Scripture speaks in many places in as it were carnal terms, but the meaning is always spiritual. . . . While it is spiritual yet with carnal things it often proceeds as it were carnally. But it does not want them to remain carnal. Because the mother loves to nourish her little one, she does not on that account want him to remain little. She holds him in her lap, fondles him with her hands, soothes him with caresses, feeds him with her milk, does everything for the little one; but she wants him to grow, so that she may not always have to do these things.

Serm. XXIII, iii, 3.

505

There is one thing that is transitory in the Lord, another which is enduring. What is transitory is the Virgin birth, the Incarnation of the Word, the gradation of ages, the exhibition of miracles, the endurance of sufferings, death, resurrection, the ascent into heaven—all this is transitory. For Christ is no longer in a state of birth, or dying, or rising again, or ascending into heaven. Do you not see that these acts ran their course in time, exhibited to those on the way something that was transitory, so that they should not abide on the way but reach their country? Lastly, these blind men also were sitting by the way; and felt Him passing them, and stopped Him by their cries. In the way, therefore, of this world, the Lord did this transitory work of His, and this transitory work pertaineth to the Son of David. Thus they cried out to Him as He passed, 'O Lord, thou Son of David, have mercy upon us.' It is as if they said, We recognize the Son of David in Him who is passing; we learn that He became the Son of David in His passage. Let us also acknowledge Him and confess that He is the Son of David, that we may deserve to be enlightened. For we perceive the Son of David passing, and are enlightened by the Lord of David.

In Ps. CIX, 5.

506

Whoever desire to understand God the Word, let not flesh suffice them, because for their sakes the Word was made flesh, that they might be nourished with milk. And let not this holy day in which the Lamb was slain, suffice on earth; but let it be declared in the highways and byways, until, our minds being raised by God, we reach the inner divinity of Him who hath deigned to offer to us, who must be fed with milk, this outward humanity.

In Ps. CXVII, 22.

507

'Do not touch me: for I am not yet ascended to my Father' (John xx, 17). . . . . It is better not to touch with the hand and to touch with faith than to touch with the hand and not touch with faith. It was no great thing to touch Christ with the hand. The Jews touched Him when they seized Him, they touched Him when they bound Him, they touched Him when they hung Him up. They touched Him, and by touching wrongly, lost that which they touched. By touching with faith, O Catholic Church, faith makes thee whole. Do thou touch only by faith, that is, draw near in faith and steadfastly believe. If thou hast thought of Christ only as man, thou hast touched Him on earth. If thou hast believed Christ to be God equal to the Father, then thou hast touched Him when He is ascended to the Father. Therefore He is ascended for us, when we rightly understand Him. At that time He ascended once only, but now He ascends every day.

Serm. CCXLVI, 4.

508

It seems to me that the disciples were engrossed by the human form of the Lord Christ, and as men were held to the man by a human affection. But He wished them to have a divine affection, and thus to make them, from being carnal, spiritual;

and this man does not become except by the gift of the Holy
Spirit. Therefore He said to them, I send you a gift, by which
you will be made spiritual, namely, the gift of the Holy Spirit.
But you cannot become spiritual, except you cease from being
carnal. You will indeed cease from being carnal, if the form
of the flesh be removed from your eyes, so that the form of God
may be implanted in your hearts.

Serm. CCLXX, 2.

509

As though He should say to His Apostles, you do not want
to let me go (just as a man does not want to let his friend go,
and says, as it were, stay with us a space, our soul is refreshed
when we see thee); but it is better that you do not see this
flesh, but picture to yourselves the divinity. I remove Myself
from you outwardly, and I fill you with Myself inwardly.
Does Christ enter into the heart through the flesh and with
the flesh? It is according to His divinity that He takes possession
of the heart; according to the flesh He speaks to the heart through
the eyes, and outwardly brings Himself to our minds, indwelling
in us, that we may be converted inwardly, and may be quickened
by Him, and formed out of Him, since He is the unfashioned
form of all things.

Serm. CCLXIV, 4.

510

Mark this, that even when He, who is very Truth and the
Word by whom all things were made, had been made flesh
that He might dwell among us, the Apostle nevertheless says:
'And if we have known Christ according to the flesh: but
now we know Him so no longer' (2 Cor. v, 16). For He desiring
not only to give the possession to those who had completed
the journey, but also to be Himself the way for those who were
setting out on it, determined to take upon Himself our flesh.
Whence also the words: 'The Lord created me in the beginning
of His ways' (Prov. viii, 22), that is, that those who wished
to come might begin their journey in Him. Therefore the
Apostle, though still walking in the way, and following after
God who had called him to the prize of his supernal vocation,

yet forgetting the things that were behind and stretching forth himself to those that were before (cf. Phil. iii, 12 *sq.*), had already traversed the beginning of the way, that is, did not then stand in need of it; yet by this way all must commence their journey who desire to attain to the truth, and to rest for ever in eternal life. For He it is who says, 'I am the way, the truth, and the life,' (John xiv, 6), that is to say, by Me man comes, to Me he comes, in Me he rests for ever. For when we come to Him, we come to the Father also. For through an equal an equal is known; and the Holy Spirit binds and as it were seals us, so that we are able to rest for ever in the supreme and immutable good. And hence we may learn how necessary it is that nothing should detain us on the way, when not even the Lord himself, in so far as He has condescended to be our way, is willing to detain us, but wishes us rather to press on; and instead of weakly clinging to temporal things, even though these were put on and born by Him for our salvation, to pass over them quickly, that we may deserve to be carried and brought to Himself, who has freed our nature from the bondage of temporal things, and has set it down at the right hand of the Father.

De doct. christ. I, xxxiv, 38.

511

Since that flesh which rose again and, restored to life, ascended into heaven, received resurrection and eternal life, this too is promised to us. . . . So far, indeed, the whole body has not received this, since the head is in heaven, but the members are still on the earth. It is not the head alone that is to receive the inheritance, and the body be left to itself. The whole Christ is to receive the inheritance, the whole Christ according to man, that is the head and the body.

Serm. XXII, x, 10.

512

For the immutable Truth which is the Word of God, God with God, by Whom all things were made, 'remaining in herself the same, reneweth all things' (Wis. vii, 27). In order that we may see this Truth, a great and perfect purity of heart is necessary and this only cometh by faith. For the form of a servant having been shewn, this was put aside for the shewing of the form of God. . . . 'I will manifest myself,' He saith, 'to him.' This is the very clear light into which the Kingdom which is now gathering together in the transition of this world is being led, for it is being led to a certain ineffable sight, which the ungodly shall not merit. Nevertheless, while the form of a servant was here, it was seen by the ungodly; those who believed saw it, those also who killed Him saw it. Lest thou shouldst suppose that it was any great thing that that form should be seen, His friends saw it, His enemies saw it; and some who saw it slew Him, some who saw it not believed. Both the godly and the ungodly, then, shall see in the Judgment that form of a servant which both the godly and the ungodly saw in humiliation here . . . They shall see Him about to judge whom they mocked when He was judged. The form, therefore, of the servant will be conspicuous both to the just and the unjust, the godly and the ungodly, the faithful and the unbelieving. What then shall the ungodly not see? . . . 'And I will manifest Myself to him.' What is 'Myself?' Not the form of a servant. What meaneth 'Myself?' The form of God, in which I 'thought it not robbery to be equal with God' (Phil. ii, 6). What meaneth 'Myself?' 'Dearly beloved, we are now the sons of God: and it hath not yet appeared what we shall be. We know that when He shall appear we shall be like to Him: because we shall see Him as He is' (1 John iii, 2). This brightness of God is the ineffable light, a fountain of light that can never change, truth without defect, wisdom remaining in herself, renewing all things: this is the substance of God.

In Ps. CIX, 12.

513

'Philip, he that hath seen Me seeth the Father also' (John xiv 9). He saith 'he that hath seen Me,' not 'he that hath seen the form of a servant in Me,' who 'have hidden myself for those who fear me,' who 'have wrought for them that hope in me' (Ps. xxx, 20)—such a one hath seen the Father also. But since this sight will be hereafter, what shall we have instead of it now? . . . How shall I see Thee, if Thou appearest other-

wise than in the form of a servant? or how shall I see the Father,
I a weak mortal, dust and ashes? . . . 'Dost thou not believe,'
He said, 'that I am in the Father and the Father in me' (John
xiv, 10)? Believe what thou canst not yet see, that thou mayest
deserve to see it. When therefore the time shall be come that
we shall see, then it will be apparent that 'with Thee is the
principality in the day of Thy strength' (Ps. cix, 3). 'Of Thy
strength,' not of the strength of Thy weakness; for there is
strength there. 'Of Thy strength': men have now their own
virtues, in faith, in hope, in charity, in good works; but 'they
shall go from virtue to virtue' (Ps. lxxxiii, 8). 'With Thee,'
therefore, 'is the principality.' Thou shalt appear with the
Father, in the Father, as the Father is 'with Thee the principality
in the day of Thy strength,' of that strength of Thine which the
ungodly shall not see.

In Ps. CIX, 14.

514

In the synoptists you may see men who have their conversation
in a certain manner with the man Christ on earth, in John,
however, you perceive one who has passed beyond the cloud
by which the whole earth is covered and has reached the
lambent heaven whence, with clearest and steadiest mental
eye, he is able to look upon God the Lord, who was in the
beginning with God, by whom all things were made, and may
recognize Him who was made flesh that He might dwell among
us (John i, 1, 3, 14), namely, that He assumed flesh, not that
He was changed into flesh. . . . For he is like one who has
drunk in the secret of His divinity more richly and somehow
more familiarly than others, as if he drew it from the very
bosom of his Lord on which he was wont to lean when he sat
at meat.

De cons. Evang. I, iv, 7.

515

John the Evangelist, among his fellows and companions
the other Evangelists, received this special and peculiar gift
from the Lord . . . that he should tell those things concerning
the Son of God which may perhaps rouse the attentive minds
of the little ones, but cannot fill them since they are as yet not

297

capable of receiving them; while to minds of somewhat larger growth, which have reached man's estate in the interior life, he gives with his words something whereby they may be both exercised and fed.

In Joan. Evang. XVIII, 1.

516

The risen Christ has gone before us to something whence, though He comes to us, He does not withdraw, nor in preceding us thither does He abandon us. . . . There we shall see Him as He is, when we shall be like to Him (1 John iii, 2). . . . He shall be known in that eternity to which He will bring His servants by the form of a servant, that in liberty they may contemplate the form of the Lord.

De cons. Evang. III, xxv, 86.

517

Be Thou exalted, Thou who wast enclosed in the womb of the mother, Thou who wast made flesh in her, whom thou didst make; Thou who didst lie in the manger, Thou who like as a little babe didst suck into the veins of the flesh milk from the breast; Thou who though bearing the world wast carried by the mother; Thou whom the aged Simeon recognized as a little one and praised as great; Thou whom the widow Anna saw at the breast, and recognized as omnipotent; Thou who didst hunger for our sakes, thirst for our sakes, wast wearied on the road for our sakes (does then the Bread hunger, the Fountain thirst, the Way get tired?); Thou who didst endure all these things for our sakes: Thou who didst sleep, yet, keeping Israel, dost not slumber (Ps. cxx, 4); lastly, Thou whom Judas sold, whom the Jews bought, yet did not possess; Thou seized, bound, scourged, crowned with thorns, hung upon the tree, pierced with the spear; Thou dead, Thou buried, 'Be Thou exalted, O God, above the heavens,' . . . 'and Thy glory above all the earth' (Ps. lvi, 12), and over all the earth Thy Church, over all the earth thy bride, thy beloved, thy dove, thy spouse. She is Thy glory. . . . For if 'the woman is the glory of the man' (1 Cor. xi, 7), the Church is the glory of Christ.

Serm. CCLXII, iv, 4; vi, 5.

XII. MAN OF GOD

I. MAN FROM GOD

518

'With Christ,' he saith, 'I am nailed to the cross. And I live, now not I: but Christ liveth in me' (Gal. ii, 19 *sq.*). And what else is this than, My justice is not in me, which is of the law, wherein I was made a transgressor, but the justice of God, that is, which is of God to me (Phil. iii 9), not from me? Thus there liveth in me, not I myself, but Christ, 'who of God is made unto us wisdom and justice and sanctification.'

In Ps. CXVIII, *Serm.* xxv, 6.

519

For Christ is the life, and He dwells in our hearts, for the present by faith, but hereafter by direct sight. For 'we see now through a glass in a dark manner: but then face to face' (1 Cor. xiii, 12). Hence charity itself is practised here below in good works of love, and it seeks where it may help, and this is its *breadth*. It bears all adversity patiently and in that which it holds to be true it perseveres, and this is its *length*. It does all this in order to gain the eternal life which is promised it above, and this is its *height*. This charity, in which we are in some manner 'rooted and founded' (Eph. iii, 17 *sqq.*), exists by virtue of some secret force, and in it reside the impenetrable causes of the divine will, by the grace of which we are saved, 'not by the works of justice, which we have done, but according to His mercy' (Titus iii, 5). 'Of his own will hath he begotten us by the word of truth' (Jas. i, 18), and this His will remains secret. And awestruck by the depth of this secret the Apostle exclaims: 'O the depth of the riches of the wisdom and of the knowledge of God! How incomprehensible are his judgments, and how unsearchable his ways! For who hath known the mind of the Lord? Or who hath been his counsellor?' (Rom. xi, 33 *sq.*) And this is the *depth.* Height (altitude) designates both that which is lofty and that which is profound. When the word is employed in the sense of loftiness, it signifies sublimity; but used in the sense of profundity it signifies difficulty of investigation and cognition. And so the Psalmist says: 'O Lord, how great are thy works! thy thoughts are exceeding deep' (Ps. xci, 6), and again: 'Thy judgments are a great deep' (Ps. xxxv, 7). . . .

In this mystery the figure of the cross is revealed. For Christ died because He so willed it and He died as He willed it. It was not without motive that He chose that form of death. He chose it that there might be in it also the teaching of that breadth and length and height and depth. For the breadth is represented by that piece of wood which is set transversely, and this pertains to good works; for here the hands are held out in the act of giving. The length is represented by that piece of wood set into the ground which is visible; for here we have a certain standing, that is to say persistence and perseverance, attributes of longanimity. The height is in that part of the wood which rises above the transverse piece, that is to say where the head of the Crucified appears; for it is the supernal object for which the pious soul longs and hopes. Lastly that part of the wood set in the ground and invisible, whence the whole rises, signifies the depth of gratuitous grace. How many men of genius have worn themselves out in the attempt to probe its secret, only to end by its being said of them: 'O man, who art thou that repliest against God?' (Rom. ix, 20).

Ep. CXL, xxv, 62; xxvi, 64.

520

What is the breadth and length and height and depth (Eph. iii, 18.) . . . When wilt thou comprehend these things either in mind or body? Hear the Apostle himself saying to thee: 'But God forbid that I should glory, save in the cross of our Lord Jesus Christ' (Gal. vi, 14) . . . There we shall peradventure find both the breadth and the length and the height and the depth. For by these words of the Apostle the Cross is, so to speak, set

up before our eyes. For it hath the breadth, in which the hands
are fixed, it hath the length in the beam which reaches thence
to the ground; it hath the height again in that part where the
Head of the Crucified is placed which juts a little above the
transverse beam in which the Hands are fixed; and it hath
the depth, which is that part which is fastened in the ground
and is not seen.

Serm. (de Script. N.T.) CLXV, ii, 2; iii, 3.

521

It is in the heart of man that Christ dwells, for the time being
by faith, there to dwell by the presence of His Divinity, when
we have learnt to know what is the breadth and length and
height and depth, and have learnt the charity of Christ which
surpasseth all knowledge, that we may be filled unto all the
fulness of God (Eph. iii, 17 *seq.*) . . . . The breadth is in good
works; the length is in long-suffering and perseverance in
good works; the height is in the expectation of celestial reward;
and on account of this length thou art told to lift up thy hearts
. . . Strive eagerly for the depth: the grace of God is in the
hidden places of His will. . . . It is not without good cause,
therefore, that 'He chose the cross, on which to crucify thee
to this world. For the breadth is on the cross, the transverse
piece of wood, to which the hands are fastened, on account
of the signification of good works. The length is in that part
of the wood which extends from the transverse piece to the
ground. For there the body is crucified, and in some manner
stands, and the standing position itself signifies perseverance.
But the height is in that part of the wood which rises above
the same transverse piece, as an expectation of celestial things.
And the depth, where can it be but in that part which is fixed
in the ground? For grace is secret, and lies hidden in a concealed
place. It is not seen, but what emerges from it is seen. . . .
Stretch thyself out, therefore, if thou canst, to get an understanding of the charity of Christ which surpasses all knowledge.
If thou attainest to this, thou wilt be filled unto all the fulness
of God.

Serm. LIII, xiv, 15; xi, 16.

522

God may do something in such a way that thou dost not know wherefore He doeth it, yet He, with whom there is no iniquity, cannot do unjustly. . . . For whence knowest thou that this thing is unjust, unless thou know what is just? . . . Therefore I ask of thee, whence seest thou this thing to be just? Where, I say, seest thou this just thing, after seeing which thou censurest an unjust thing? Whence is that something wherewith thy soul is imbued (though in many ways being in the dark), which gleameth upon thy mind, whence this thing is pronounced just? Is it possible that it hath not its source? Hast thou that which is just from thyself, and canst thou give justice to thyself? Therefore when thou art unjust, thou canst not be just except by turning thee to a certain abiding justice, wherefrom if thou withdrawest, thou art unjust, and if thou drawest near to it, thou art just. If thou withdraw, it decreaseth not; nor doth it increase if thou draw near. . . . Look back therefore, rise to the heights, go to that place where once God hath spoken, and there thou wilt find the fountain of justice where is the fountain of life. 'For with Thee is the fountain of life' (Ps. xxxv, 10). For if out of a little dew thou wouldst judge what is just and what is unjust, is there anywise iniquity with God, from Whom, as it were from a fountain, justice floweth to thee, in so far as thou tastest what is just, since in many ways thou dost but evilly mistaste?

In Ps. LXI, 21.

523

For even this very thing that man can live justly, as far as man can live justly, is not the fruit of human merit, but of divine beneficence. For no man liveth justly, save he who is justified, that is made just; and it is by Him who can never be unjust that man is made just. For as a lamp is not lit of itself, so also the human soul doth not give itself light, but crieth unto God, 'Thou shalt light my lamp, O Lord' (Ps. xvii, 29).

In Ps. CIX, 1.

524

It will appear that to live a good life is the gift of God, not only because God has given to man free-will, without which

there is neither ill nor well-living; nor only because He has
given him a commandment to teach him how he ought to live;
but because by the Holy Ghost he pours forth charity in the
hearts of those whom He foreknew, in order to predestinate
them; whom He predestinated, that He might call them;
whom He called that He might justify them; whom He justified,
that He might glorify them (Rom. v, 5; viii, 29 *sq.*).

De spir. et litt. V, 7.

525

'We will go into His tabernacle' (Ps. cxxxi, 7). Whose?
that of the Lord God of Jacob. Those who enter to dwell
therein, are the very same who enter that they may be dwelt
in. Thou enterest into thy house that thou mayest dwell therein;
into the house of God that thou mayest be dwelt in. For the
Lord is better, and when He hath begun to dwell in thee, He
will make thee happy. For if thou be not dwelt in by Him,
thou wilt be miserable. That son who said, 'Father, give me
the portion of the patrimony that falleth to me,' wished to be
his own master. It was well kept in his father's hands, that it
might not be wasted with harlots. He received it, it was given
into his power; going into a far country, he squandered it all
with harlots. At length he suffered hunger; he remembered
his father; he returned, that he might have his fill of bread
(Luke xv, 12 *sqq.*). Enter therefore, that thou mayest be dwelt
in; and mayest be not thine own, so to speak, but His. 'We
will go into his tabernacle.'

In Ps. CXXXI, 12.

526

Justice, which lives in itself an immutable life, can be nothing
but God Himself. And just as this God, Who is life itself, becomes
our life when we in some manner are made participators of Him,
so, too, this same God, Who is justice itself, becomes our justice
when by uniting ourselves to Him we lead a just and holy life;
and we shall be more or less just according as we are united to
Him in greater or lesser measure. . . . This supreme God
is clearly true justice, or, put otherwise, this true God is supreme
justice. Since assuredly to hunger and thirst after this is our

justice, the consummation of our justice in eternity will be to be filled by it. Let us then not conceive God to be something semblable to our justice, but rather think of ourselves as being the more semblable to God the more just we are by a fuller participation of His grace.

Ep. CXX, iv, 19.

527

That in the soul by which the body is quickened is one thing, that by which the soul itself is quickened is another. . . . The life of the soul is God, and as the soul, while it is in the body, gives it vigour, comeliness, activity, the services of members, so while its life, which is God, is in it, He supplies to it wisdom, godliness, righteousness, charity. . . . When therefore the word comes and is infused into the hearers, and they are made not only to hear but also to obey, the soul rises from its death to its life; that is to say from unrighteousness, from foolishness, from ungodliness to its God, Who is to it wisdom and righteousness and light. . . . If then by coming thereto ye are enlightened, your light was not in yourselves but in your God. . . . If by coming to Him, ye live, and by going from Him ye die, your life was not in yourselves. The same is your life which is your light.

In Joan. Evang. XIX, 12.

528

God enjoineth this, that we be not men. . . . What then did He wish them to become, but that which is expressed in the Psalm, 'I have said: You are gods, and all of you the sons of the Most High' (Ps. lxxxi, 6). . . . 'Shall I then,' says he, 'not be a man?' No, assuredly. For to this thou hast been called by Him who for thy sake was made Man, that thou mayest not be man. . . . For God wishes to make thee a god, not by nature as He is whom He hath begotten, but by His gift and adoption. For as He by His humanity was made partaker of thy mortality, so by thy exaltation doth He make thee partaker of His immortality . . . so that the whole man deified may inhere in the eternal and immutable Truth.

Serm. (*de Script. N.T.*) CLXVI,
i, 1; ii, 2; iv, 4.

529

It is manifest then, that He hath called men gods, that are deified by His Grace, not born of His substance. For He doth justify who is just through His own self and not of another; and He doth deify who is God through His own self, not by the partaking of another. But He that justifieth doth Himself deify, in that by justifying He doth make sons of God. 'For He gave them power to be made the sons of God' (John i, 12). If we have been made sons of God, we have also been made gods; but this is the effect of adoptive grace, not of a generation by nature. For the only Son of God, God, and one God with the Father, our Lord and Saviour Jesus Christ, was in the beginning the Word, the Word with God, the Word that was God. The rest who are made gods are made by His grace, and not born of His substance that they should be the same as He, but that by favour they should come to Him and be 'joint heirs with Christ. . . . 'Behold,' saith the Apostle, 'what manner of charity the Father hath bestowed upon us, that we should be called and should be the sons of God.' And in another place, 'dearly beloved, we are now the Sons of God: and it hath not yet appeared what we shall be' . . . But 'we know that when He shall appear we shall be like to Him: because we shall see Him as He is' (1 John iii, 1, 2). The only Son is like Him by His begetting, we are like Him by our seeing.

In Ps. XLIX, 2.

530

I have given to men to do well, but of Me, He saith, not of themselves; for of themselves they are evil. They are sons of men when they do evil, My sons when they do well. For God doth this thing, out of sons of men He maketh sons of God; because out of the Son of God He hath made the Son of Man. Mark what this participation is. There hath been promised to us a participation of Divinity. He that hath promised lieth, if He is not first made participator of mortality. For the Son of God hath been made participator of mortality in order that mortal man may be made participator of Divinity. He that hath promised that His good is to be shared with thee, hath first shared thy evil with thee. He that hath promised divinity to thee, sheweth in thee charity. Take away therefore that men are sons of God, there remaineth that they are sons of men.

In Ps. LII, 6.

531

For it is not by themselves being so that men are gods, but they become gods by participation in that one God who is the true God.

In Ps. CXVIII, *Serm.* xvi, 1.

532

His divinity can in no wise be seen by human sight, but is seen by that sight with which those who see are no longer men, but beyond men.

De Trin. I, vi, 11.

533

Let them understand that if they are the sons of God, they are led by the Spirit of God (Rom. viii, 14) to do that which should be done; and when they have done it let them give thanks to Him by whom they do it. For they are acted upon that they may act, not that they themselves may do nothing. And in addition to this, it is shown them what they ought to do, so that when they have done it as it ought to be done, that is to say, with the love and delight of justice, they may rejoice in having received the sweetness which the Lord has given, that their land may yield its fruit (Ps. lxxxiv, 13). But when they do not act, whether by not doing at all, or by not doing from charity; let them pray that what as yet they have not, they may receive. For what shall they have which they shall not receive, or what have they which they have not received (1 Cor. iv, 7)?

De corrupt. et gratia II, 4.

534

For man is not anything of such kind that, having come into being, he can as of himself do anything rightly, if He who made

him withdraws Himself from him; but his whole good action
is to turn to Him by whom he was made, and to be made just
by Him, and pious, and wise, and happy. . . . Man therefore turns to God, not with the purpose of withdrawing himself
from Him when he has been made just, but with that of being
continually made just by Him. And from the fact that he does
not withdraw from Him, he will by His presence be justified,
illumined, and beatified. . . . We ought to be ever being
made by Him, and perfected; adhering to Him and persevering
in the turning of ourselves to Him.

De Gen. ad. litt. VIII, xii, 25, 27.

535

God needeth no good thing, and is Himself the supreme good,
and from Him is every good thing. To be good, therefore, we
need God, but God needeth not us in order to be good. . . .
For what would anything be, whatever besides there is, unless
He had made it? . . . But in order that man may be anything
at all he turneth himself to Him by whom he was created.
For by withdrawing he becometh cold, by drawing near he
waxeth warm, by withdrawing he is made dark, by drawing
near he is made light. . . . Therefore whosoever willeth to be
thus like unto God, so that he may stand near Him and keep,
as it is written, his strength to Him (cf. Ps. lviii, 10), and not
withdraw from Him; by cleaving to Him may be sealed as the
wax by a ring, being joined to Him may have His image, doing
that which is written; 'It is good for me to adhere to my God'
(Ps. lxxii, 28): this man doth truly keep the likeness and image
after which he was made. On the other hand if he shall have
perversely willed to imitate God, so that, just as God hath no
one by whom He is formed, hath no one by whom He is ruled,
he may so will to use his own power to live, like God, with no
one forming, no one ruling him; what remaineth, brethren, but
that withdrawing from His heat he grow benumbed, withdrawing
from Truth he becomes empty, withdrawing from that which
is supremely and immutably Being, he is changed for the worse
and sinks down.

In Ps. LXX, *Serm.* ii, 6.

536

Man is something so long as he adhereth to Him by whom man was created. . . . Do thou so take counsel through man, as that thou consider Him who doth enlighten man.

In Ps. LXXV, 8.

II. IN GOD'S POWER

537

Through Thy Son, our Lord Jesus Christ . . . by whom Thou didst seek us when we sought Thee not, and soughtest us to the end that we might seek Thee.

Conf. XI, ii, 4.

538

[God] promised what He himself would do, not what men would do. Because, although men do those good things which pertain to the worship of God, He himself makes them do what He has commanded; it is not they who cause Him to do what He has promised. Otherwise the fulfilment of God's promises would not be in the power of God, but in that of men; and thus what was promised by God would be given by men themselves.

De praed. sanct. xv, 19.

539

God loves us such as we shall be; not such as we are. . . . But by what merit, except that of faith, by which we believe before we see that which is promised? For by this faith we shall attain to sight; that He may love us such as He loves that we may be, not such as He hates, because we are; and He exhorts us and gives it to us to wish that we may not always be.

De Trin. I, x, 21.

540

Whence the Apostle desireth us to be known as the children of promise (Rom. ix, 8), lest we imagine that we are what we are of ourselves, and that we may attribute the whole to the grace of God. For Christ, he saith, 'of God is made unto us wisdom and justice and sanctification and redemption: that, as it is written: He that glorieth may glory in the Lord' (1 Cor. i, 30 *sq.*). In the words then, 'Quicken me in thy justice,' the Psalmist prayeth to be quickened in Christ, and this is the mercy which he prayeth may also come upon him (Ps. cxviii, 40, 41). . . . This was indeed promised by Him, who 'calleth those things that are not, as those that are' (Rom. iv, 17). For those to whom the promise was made were not yet in existence, so that no man might glory in his merits. And those to whom it was promised were themselves promised; so that the whole body of Christ may say, 'By the grace of God, I am what I am' (1 Cor. xv, 10).

In Ps. CVIII, *Serm.* xiii, 1.

541

In the mystery of His will, He placed the riches of His grace, according to His good pleasure, not according to ours, which could not possibly be good, unless He himself, according to His good pleasure, should aid it to become so.

De praed. sanct. xviii, 36.

542

Let us then understand the vocation by which they become chosen,—not those who are chosen because they believed, but those who are chosen that they may believe. . . . For if they had been chosen because they had believed, they themselves would assuredly have first chosen Him by believing in Him. . . . Therefore they were chosen before the foundation of the world with that predestination in which God foreknew what He himself would do. But they were chosen out of the world with that vocation whereby God fulfilled that which He predestinated. For those whom He predestinated, them also He called. . . . Not others, therefore, but those whom He predestinated, them He also called; not others, but those whom He thus called, them He also justified; not others, but those whom He predestinated, called, and justified, them He also glorified (Rom. viii, 30); assuredly to that end which has no end.

De praed. sanct. xvii, 34.

543

Among the number of the elect and predestined there are also those who have led a most evil life, but are brought to repentance by the goodness of God, and by His forbearance have not been removed from this life in the midst of their sins; in order that they and their joint-heirs may be shewn from what depths of evil the grace of God can liberate man . . . The other mortals, however, who are not of this number, and, though made of the same clay as they, are become vessels of wrath, are born for the benefit of the former. For God does not create anyone of these fortuitously and without purpose; nor is He ignorant of what good He will work from them; since He works good by the very fact that He creates a human nature in them and by them embellishes the order of the present world. Of these He brings none to health-giving and spiritual repentance, whether He shews them greater, or not unequal, forbearance. Although therefore all are from the same mass of perdition and damnation according to the hardness of their heart and their impenitent heart, and, so far as pertains to them, lay up for themselves wrath in that day of wrath when there is rendered to every man according to his works (Apoc. xxii, 12); yet God in His merciful goodness leads some of them thence to repentance, while others by His just judgment He does not so bring. For He has the power to lead and to draw, as the Lord himself saith, 'No man can come to me, except the Father, who hath sent me, draw him' (John vi, 44).

Contra Julianum V, iv, 14.

544

Why should grace deliver this one and that, why not this one and that; I would not that thou enquire of me. I am a man. I consider the depth of the cross. I do not penetrate it. I stand in awe. I do not search into it. Incomprehensible are His judgments, unsearchable His ways! (*v.* Rom. xi, 33). . . . 'Have mercy on me, O God, have mercy on me' (Ps. lvi, 2). Why so? Because I have any virtue by which to obtain thy favour? No. Why then? Because I have the power of will whereby desert of mine may precede Thy grace? No. But why? Because

'my soul trusteth in Thee' (Ps. lvi, 2). A great science is this
trust.

Serm. (de Script. N. T.) CLXV, vii, 9.

545

But it does not follow that nothing should be left to our free
will, because God knows the certain and set order of all causes.
For our very wills are in that order of causes, which God knows
so surely and has in His prescience, since human wills are the
causes of all human actions; so that He who has foreknowledge
of the causes of all things can certainly not ignore our wills
which he knows in advance to be the causes of our actions.
. . . Our wills are of as much power as God would have them,
and knew before that they should be. And therefore the power
that they have is theirs, free to do what they shall do truly and
freely, for He foreknew that they should have this power and
do these acts; and His foreknowledge cannot be deceived. . . .
Wherefore we are neither compelled to leave our freedom of
will by retaining God's foreknowledge, nor by holding to our
will's freedom to deny God's foreknowledge (which would be a
sin). We should hold to them and affirm them both, constantly
and truly, the former that we may believe well and truly, the
latter that we may live a good life.

De civ. Dei V, ix, 3, 4; x, 2.

546

Let us not defend grace in such a way as to seem to make away
with free will. On the other hand we may not assert freedom
of will in such manner as in our impious pride to be judged
ungrateful for the grace of God.

De pecc. meritis et remiss. II, xviii, 28.

547

Each of these, namely, faith and good works, is ours because
it is the result of the free choice of our will, and yet each is the
gift of the Spirit of faith and of Charity to us.

Retract. I, xxiii, 2.

III. IN GOD'S LAW

548

So great is the difference between the law and grace, that although the law is undoubtedly of God, yet the justice which is 'of the law' is not 'of God,' but the justice which is consummated by grace is 'of God' (cf. Phil. iii, 9). The one is called 'the justice of the law,' because it is done through fear of the malediction of the law; but the other which is bestowed through the beneficence of His grace is called 'the justice of God.'

De grat. Christi xiii, 14.

549

He who lives according to the justice which is in the law, without the faith of the grace of Christ, . . . must be accounted to have no true justice; not because the law is not true and holy, but because to wish to obey the letter which commands without the quickening Spirit of God, as if by the strength of free will, is not true justice.

Contra duas epist. Pelag. III, vii, 23.

550

The letter which forbids sin quickeneth not man but rather killeth him (*v.* 2 Cor. iii, 6), by increasing concupiscence, and aggravating iniquity by prevarication; unless indeed grace liberates us by the law of faith, which is in Christ Jesus, when 'the charity of God is poured forth in our hearts, by the Holy Ghost who is given to us' (Rom. v, 5).

De spir. et litt. xiv, 25.

551

Whatever we are forbidden by God's law, and whatever we are bidden to do, comes under two commandments . . . the general prohibition, 'Thou shalt not covet' (Exod. xx, 7); and the general precept, 'Thou shalt love' (Deut. vi, 5). . . . . By eschewing covetousness we put off the old man, and by showing love we put on the new. But no man can otherwise be continent except God give it (Wis. viii, 21), and 'the charity of God is poured forth in our hearts' not by ourselves but 'by the Holy Ghost who is given to us' (Rom. v, 5). This, however, takes place day by day in those who make progress by willing, believing, and praying, and who forgetting the things that are behind stretch forth themselves to those that are before (Phil. iii, 13). For the reason why the law inculcates all these precepts is that when a man has failed in fulfilling them, he may not be puffed up with pride, but may in very weariness betake himself to grace. Thus the law in its office of pedagogue (Gal. iii, 24) by terrifying man leads him to love Christ.

De perf. just. hominis v, 11.

552

When the law of God is declared, for it hath said, 'Thou shalt not covet,' (Exod. xx, 17), when, I say, the law of God is declared, . . . whosoever is puffed up and thinketh that he can fulfil it by his own strength, and doeth what the law enjoineth, not from love of justice but from fear of punishment, he is indeed according to the justice that is in the law, a man without blame (*v.* Phil. iii, 6). He doth not steal, he doth not commit adultery, he doth not bear false witness, he doth not covet his neighbour's goods. For what reason? For fear of punishment. Although he who coveteth not for fear of punishment doth, as I think, covet. By the overpowering terror of arms and weapons and perhaps of a multitude surrounding or approaching him, even the lion is called off from his prey. And yet he came a lion, and a lion he returns; he hath not carried off his prey, his malice he hath not laid aside. If thou art such an one there is as yet but that justice in thee by which thou takest thought with thyself that thou mayest not be tormented. Is it such a great thing to fear punishment? Who doth not fear it? What robber, what villain, what abominable person, but fears it? But there is this difference between thy fear and the robber's fear, that the robber fears the laws of men, and therefore commits robbery because he hopes to elude the laws of men; but thou fearest the law, thou fearest the punishment of Him whom thou canst not elude. For if thou couldst elude it, what wouldst thou not have done? Hence love doth not take away thy evil concupiscence, but fear represseth it. The wolf comes to the sheepfold;

owing to the barking of the dogs and the shouting of the shepherds the wolf retires from the sheepfold; yet he is ever a wolf. Let him be turned into a sheep. For it is also as the Lord doeth, but this is His justice, not thine. For as long as thou hast thine own thou canst fear punishment, thou canst not love justice. . . . For whoso believeth on Him shall not have his own righteousness, which is of the law, though it be a good law, but shall fulfil this law by a justice not his own but given by God. For 'Love is the fulfilling of the Law' (Rom. xiii, 10).

Serm (de Script. N.T.) CLXIX, vi, 8; viii, 10.

553

The law hath fear, grace hope . . . the law alarmeth him who relieth on himself, grace assisteth him who trusteth in God. . . . Why dost thou boast to me whosoever thou art who hearing this dost rely upon thyself, why dost thou boast to me of innocence? . . . Why dost thou inspect thyself all round without, and dost not inspect within? . . . Look in; why dost thou pass over thyself? Descend into thyself. Thou wilt see another law in thy members, fighting against the law of thy mind and captivating thee in the law of sin that is in thy members (*v.* Rom. vii, 23). . . . Why is this but that on receiving the commandment thou didst fear, not love? Thou didst fear punishment, thou didst not love justice. Whoso feareth punishment, wishes if it be possible, to do what pleaseth him and not to have what he feareth . . . Thou fearest the threatenings of God, thou dost not love His commandments. . . . If thou refrain from sin because thou abhorrest contamination, because thou lovest His precepts, that thou mayest obtain His promises, it is the grace which maketh saints that aideth thee. It is all of grace. Ascribe it not to thine own self, attribute it not to thine own strength. Thou actest from delight in it; it is well. Thou actest in charity: it is well. Charity worketh by thee when thou actest with thy will. At once dost thou taste sweetness if thou place thy hope on the Lord.

Serm. (de Script. N.T.) CXLV, 3.

554

Since the law, whether given in Paradise, or implanted by nature, or promulgated in writing, hath made all the sinners of the earth transgressors, 'therefore have I loved Thy testimonies' (Ps. cxviii, 119), which are in Thy law, of Thy grace; so that not my but Thy justice is in me, . . . and that not their justice, but that of God, that is given them by God, should be the resource of all. . . . For the law profiteth unto this end, that it send us forward to grace. For not only because it attesteth to the manifestation of the justice of God, which is without the law, but also by the very fact that it rendereth men transgressors so that the letter even killeth, it driveth us by fear to flee unto the quickening Spirit (2 Cor. iii, 6), by whom the whole of our sins may be blotted out, and the love of righteous deeds may be inspired.

In Ps. CXVIII, *Serm.* xxv, 5.

555

When man tries to live justly by his own strength without the help of the liberating grace of God, he is then conquered by sins. But in free will he has it in his power to believe in the Liberator and to receive grace, in order that, with Him, who gave him this, freeing and assisting him, he may not sin, and thus may seem to be under the Law, but with the Law or in the Law, fulfil by God's charity that law, which in fear he had not been able to do.

Expos. quarumdam prop. ex epist. ad Rom. xliv.

556

The law was therefore given that grace might be sought; grace was given that the law might be fulfilled. Now it was not through any fault of its own that the law was not fulfilled, but by the fault of the carnal mind; and this fault was to be demonstrated by the law, and healed by grace.

De spir. et litt. xix, 34.

557

Because men, desiring those things that are without, have become exiles even from themselves, there has been given also a written law. Not because it had not been written in the heart, but because thou wast a deserter from thy heart, thou art seized by Him who is everywhere, and art called back to within thyself.

In Ps. LVII, 1.

558

We conclude that a man is not justified by the precepts of a holy life but by faith in Jesus Christ. That is to say, not by the law of works, but by that of faith; not by the letter, but by the spirit; not by the merits of deeds, but by gratuitous grace.

De spir. et litt. xiii, 22.

559

Not that the law is itself evil, but because the commandment has its good in the demonstration of the letter, not in the assistance of the spirit; and if this commandment is kept from the fear of punishment and not from the love of righteousness, it is servilely kept, not freely, and therefore is not kept at all. For no fruit is good which does not grow from the root of charity.

De spir. et litt. xiv, 26.

560

Our will is by the law shown to be weak, that grace may heal its infirmity; and that our healed will may fulfil the law, not as established under the law, nor yet as lacking a law.

De spir. et litt. ix, 15.

561

'For the end of the law is Christ: unto justice to every one that believeth' (Rom. x, 4), that they may be 'justified freely by His grace' (*id.*, iii, 24); not like those who think they obey the law of their own strength, and are therefore, though by God's law, still seeking to set up their own justice, but as the child of promise, who hungers and thirsts after it (Matt. v, 6), by seeking, by asking, by knocking, is as it were a mendicant for it to the Father (*id.*, vii, 7), that by adoption he may receive it through His only-begotten Son.

In Ps. CXVIII, *Serm.* xx, 2.

562

The grace of God through Jesus Christ Our Lord must be understood as that by which alone men are delivered from evil, and without which they do absolutely no good thing, whether in thought, or will and affection, or in deed; not only in order that they may know by the manifestation of the same what should be done, but moreover in order that by its enabling they may do with love what they know.

De corrupt. et gratia ii, 3.

563

Whoever would separate himself from what is animal and carnal, and, consequently, justly reprehensible and worthy of condemnation in Judaism, must not limit himself to rejecting those ancient observances, which, since the revelation of the new Covenant and the accomplishment of these things which they prefigured, are no longer at all necessary; so that no man may be judged 'in meat or in drink, or in respect of a festival day, or of the new moon, or of the sabbaths, which are a shadow of things to come' (1 Col. ii. 16 *sq.*); but he must also avoid those things which the Law forbids to the betterment of the morals of the faithful, so that 'denying ungodliness and worldly desires, we should live soberly, and justly, and godly in this world' (Tit. ii, 12). It is for this reason that the Apostle commends from the Law the precept 'Thou shalt not covet,' and all other things which, without any sacramental figuration, are enjoined in the Law concerning the love of God and of our neighbour, for 'on these two commandments,' as Our Lord Jesus Christ Himself said, 'dependeth the whole law and the prophets' (Matt. xxii, 40). And the Apostle accepts, understands, and commends these commandments to the observance of Christians, who must not attribute the good which can derive from them to themselves, but to the grace of God by Jesus Christ Our Lord (Rom. vii, 25). . . .

Let us therefore be Jews of this sort, not of the flesh but of the spirit, as being of the seed of Abraham, not according to the flesh, as are those who with carnal pride glory in bearing his name, but according to the spirit of faith, which these are not. . . . 'For you are all,' says the Apostle, 'one in Christ Jesus.

And if you be Christ's, then are you the seed of Abraham, heirs according to the promise' (Gal. iii, 28 *sq.*).

According to this interpretation of the Apostle those Jews who are not Christians are not the children of Abraham, although according to the flesh they be descended from him. For when he says 'Know ye therefore, that they who are of the faith, the same are the children of Abraham' (Gal. iii, 7), he assuredly means that those who are not of the faith are not children of Abraham. . . . Is it not a most marvellous thing and a profound mystery that there should be many born of Israel who are not Israelites and many who are not children of Abraham though they be of his seed? How is it that they are not his children and that we are, unless it be that they are not 'the children of the promise' pertaining to the grace of Christ, but 'children of the flesh' bearing a meaningless name? This is why they are not Israelites as we are, and they are not Israelites as we are. For we are Israelites by regeneration according to the spirit, they by generation according to the flesh. . . .

However this may be, we ought not on that account ridiculously to change the established form of human speech or to confuse the accustomed words for distinguished things by giving the name of Jews to those who are Christians and whom it is the practice to call by this name. Nor should one who is a Christian and bears this name take pleasure in applying to himself the name of Israelite. He should be sparing in using a term which is only applicable in a mysterious sense, and he would display senseless affectation and, if I may say so, misapprehend knowledge if he chose to employ it in his daily speech.

Ep. CXCVI, ii, 8; iii, 10, 11; iv, 14.

564

The law by teaching and commanding that which cannot be fulfilled without grace, demonstrates to man his weakness, in order that the weakness thus proved may resort to the Saviour, by whose healing the will may be able to do what in its feebleness it found impossible. Thus the law brings us to the faith, faith obtains the Spirit in fuller measure, the Spirit sheds charity on us, and charity fulfils the law. . . . So 'the law is good, if a man use it lawfully' (1 Tim. i, 8); and he uses it lawfully who, understanding to what purpose it was given, betakes himself, under the pressure of its communications, to liberating grace. Those who ungratefully neglect this grace, by which the godless are justified, and trust in their own strength as if by it they could fulfil the law, 'not knowing the justice of God and seeking to establish their own, have not submitted themselves to the justice of God' (Rom. x, 3); and thus the law becomes to him not a help to absolution but a bond fastening his guilt to him. Not that the law is evil but that *sin*, as it is written, *worketh death for such by that which is good* (cf. Rom. vii, 13). For by reason of the commandment he sins the more grievously who, by the commandment, knows how evil are the sins which he commits.

It is vain, however, for anyone to think that he has gained the victory over sin, if he refrains from sin merely through fear of punishment, for though the outward action inspired by his evil desire be not performed, yet the evil desire itself within him is an enemy unsubdued. And who is found innocent in God's sight who is willing to commit the forbidden sin if only the punishment which is feared be removed? And consequently in the volition itself he is guilty of sin, who wishes to do what is unlawful but refrains from so doing because it cannot be done with impunity; for, as far as he is concerned, he would prefer that there were no justice forbidding and punishing sins. And assuredly, if he would prefer that there should be no justice, who can doubt that he would, if he could, abolish it altogether?

How then can a man be called just who is such an enemy of justice that, if he had the power, he would abolish its authority, that he might not be subject to its commination or its penalties? He, therefore, is an enemy to justice who refrains from sin only through fear of punishment; but he will be the friend of justice if through love of it he sin not, for then he will really be afraid to sin. For the man who only fears the flames of hell is afraid not of sinning but of being burned; but the man who hates sin as much as he hates hell is afraid to sin. This is 'the fear of the Lord,' which 'is holy, enduring for ever and ever' (Ps. xviii, 10). For that fear of punishment holds torment and is not in charity, and 'perfect charity casteth out fear' (1 John iv, 18).

Ep. CXLV, 3, 4.

565

For he who still doeth well for the reason that he feareth punishment, loveth not God, is not yet among His sons. Nevertheless would that he might even fear punishment. Fear is a slave, charity is free; and, if we may say so, fear is the servant of charity. That the devil may not possess thine heart, let the servant go before into thine heart and keep a place for the mistress who is to come. Act, act even from fear of punishment, if thou canst not yet from love of justice. The mistress will come, the servant depart, for 'perfect charity casteth out fear' (1 John iv, 18).

Serm. (de Script. N.T.) CLVI, xiii, 14.

566

He who passes to Christ, passes from fear to love, and by love he begins to be capable of what he could not do by fear; and he who used to tremble in fear, does not tremble in love.

Serm. XXXII, viii, 8.

567

This is the law of faith, whereby we believe and pray that it may be granted to us through grace, that we may effect that which we cannot fulfil through ourselves, lest we, not knowing the justice of God and seeking to establish our own, submit not ourselves to the justice of God (Rom. x, 3). In the law of works, therefore, is the justice of God who commandeth, but in the law of faith is the mercy of Him who succoureth.

In Ps. CXVIII, *Serm.* x, 5.

568

Let us therefore acknowledge our condition, that, although even now sons through grace, by creation we still are as servants, for the whole of creation serveth God.

In Ps. CXXII, 5.

569

He sets us free from all things; and to serve Him is the most profitable thing for all, and to please in His service is the one and perfect liberty.

De quant. an. xxxiv, 78.

570

The service of the Lord is free, a service of freedom, when not necessity but charity serveth. . . . Let charity make thee a slave, since Truth maketh thee free. . . . Thou art at the same time both bond and free; bond, because thou art created such; free, because thou art loved by God, by whom thou wast created.

In Ps. XCIX, 7.

571

It is one thing to be in the law, another to be under the law. Whoso is in the law acteth according to the law; whoso is under the law is acted upon according to the law. The former, therefore, is free, the latter a slave.

In Ps. I, 2.

IV. THROUGH GOD'S IMPULSE

572

Know . . . that that good will, that good work, without the grace of God which is given through the one Mediator of God and man, can be granted to no one; and by this alone can man be brought to the eternal gift and kingdom of God. As to all other things, therefore, which among men seem to have some praise due them, . . . this I know, so far as I am concerned, that good will does not do them, for an unbelieving and impious will is not good.

Contra Julianum, IV, iii, 33.

573

Although some hold them to be true virtues when they are desired only for their own sake and nothing else, yet even so they lead to vainglory and pride and must therefore be accounted not virtues but vices. For as it is something not of the flesh but above the flesh that gives life to the flesh, so too it is something not of man but above man which beatifies man.

De civ. Dei XIX, xxv.

574

If all your prudence by which you try to watch over human affairs; if all the resolution with which you meet without fear the iniquities of which you are a victim; if all the temperance by which you keep yourself uncorrupted in the welter of human corruption surrounding you; if all the justice by the right application of which you render to each one his due; if all this effort and striving have as their sole aim that those to whom you wish well may be sound in body and safe and untroubled by the wickedness of anybody, . . . yours will not be true virtues nor will the happiness of those for whom you exercise them be true happiness. . . .

But if understanding at whose hands you have received these virtues, you give thanks to Him and apply them to His glory even in the execution of the secular offices you may hold, you will, by the example of your religious life and by your zeal in direction whether by praise or blame, awaken and lead to the worship of God those submitted to your authority, and in all that you do for the security of their lives your only wish will be that they may thus merit the graces of Him in whom they will find a happy life. Then will your virtues be true virtues, and by the assistance of Him, by whose liberality they were given you, they will so grow and perfect themselves that they will lead you without any doubt to the one truly happy life, which is life eternal. And in that life there will be no need of prudence to distinguish the good from the bad, for the bad will not exist; in it there will be no need of fortitude in suffering adversities, for there will only be there what we love, nor will there be anything even to try our patience; in it there will be no need of temperance to curb our desires, for our souls will be for ever preserved from them; nor will our justice be called upon to give help to the indigent, for there will be there neither rich nor poor. In it there will be but one virtue, and that virtue and its reward will be one and the same thing, as was said in Holy Scripture by one who loved this unique good: 'It is good for me to adhere to my God' (Ps. lxxii, 28). In that life we shall have full and eternal wisdom, and it will be a life veritably happy. In attaining to that happiness we shall arrive at the eternal and supreme good, and in adhering to it we shall find the zenith of our good. And this one virtue may be called prudence, because it will be with the fullest deliberation that we shall adhere to the good which we can never lose; and fortitude, because we shall with all our strength adhere to the good from which nothing can separate us; and temperance, because we shall with a most chaste love adhere to the good which is incorruptible; and justice, because we shall with the fullest reason adhere to the good to which it is right that we be for ever subject.

In this life, although there is no virtue save that of loving what ought to be loved, prudence lies in choosing it; fortitude in not being turned from it by any troubles; to be allured from it by no seductions is temperance, and by no pride is justice. But what ought we to choose as the object of our principal love but that which we find to be better than anything else? This object is God; and to set anything above or even equal to Him is to show that we do not know how to love ourselves. For our good becomes the greater the more we approach Him than whom there is nothing better. But we approach not by walking but by loving. And the purer our love is for Him towards whom we are striving, the more present to us will He be; for no space either contains or restricts Him. To Him, therefore, who is everywhere present and everywhere whole, we must proceed not by our feet but by our moral virtues. But these virtues of ours are wont to be judged not by that which is the object of our knowledge but by that which is the object of our love; for they are good or evil affections which make good or evil morals.

Ep. CLV, iii, 10–iv, 13.

575

Every one of us now knows, now does not know, now rejoices, now does not rejoice, to begin, continue, and complete our good work, in order that he may know that it is due not to his own faculty but to the gift of God, that he either knows or rejoices. . . . A good work, moreover, affords greater joy in proportion as God is more and more loved as the supreme and immutable Good, and as the Author of all good things of every kind whatever.

De pecc. meritis II, xvii, 27.

576

Those who were presuming on their own strength alone, found that they were helpless without His aid.

In Ps. CVI, 10.

577

Paul did not labour that he might receive grace, but he received grace in order that he might labour. And thus when unworthy he gratuitously received grace, whereby he might become worthy to receive the due reward. Not that he ventured to claim even his labour for himself; for, after saying, 'I have laboured more abundantly than all they,' he at once added: 'Yet not I, but the grace of God with me' (1 Cor. xv, 10). O mighty teacher, confessor, and preacher of grace! What doth this mean, 'I laboured more abundantly, yet not I?' Where the will exalted itself ever so little, there piety was instantly on the watch, and humility trembled, because weakness recognized itself.

De gestis Pelagii xiv, 36.

578

It is certain that we keep the commandments if we so will; but because the will is prepared by the Lord, we must ask Him for such a force of will as suffices to make us act by willing. It is certain that it is we who will when we will, but it is He who makes us will what is good. . . . It is certain that it is we who act when we act; but it is He who makes us act by supplying efficacious powers to our will.

De grat. et lib. arb. xvii, 32.

579

Since we are exiled from the immutable joy, though we are neither cut off nor torn away from it so as not to seek eternity, truth, blessedness, even in these mutable and temporal things (for we wish neither to die, nor to be deceived, nor to be troubled), visions have been sent to us from heaven suitable to our state of pilgrimage, in order to admonish us that what we seek is not here, but that from this pilgrimage we must return to that place, whence unless we originated there, we should not seek these things here. And first we had to be persuaded how much God loved us, lest from despair we should not dare to raise ourselves up towards Him. And we needed to be shown also what manner of men we are whom He loved, lest being proud, as if of our own merits, we should recede the more from Him and fail the more in our own strength. And hence He so dealt with us that we might the rather progress by His strength, and thus in the weakness of humility the virtue of charity might be perfected. This is the meaning of the Psalm, when it is said, 'Thou shalt set aside for thy inheritance a free rein, O God; and it was weakened, but thou hast made it perfect' (Ps. lxcii, 10). For by 'free rein' nothing else is meant than grace, not rendered for merits, but gratuitously given, whence also it is called grace; for He gave it, not because we were worthy, but because He so willed. And knowing this, we shall not be trusting in ourselves; and this is the meaning of to be 'weakened.' But he himself makes us perfect, the same who said to the Apostle Paul, 'My grace is sufficient for thee' (2 Cor. xii, 9). Man therefore had to be persuaded how much God loved us, and what manner of men we were whom He loved; the former, lest we should despair; the latter, lest we should be proud. . . . So that through the same faith they might be humbled, and so 'weakened,' and being weakened they might be made perfect.

De Trin. IV, i, 2.

580

I would have thee conform thy life and behaviour to God's commandments, which we have received as the rule of right living, beginning with religious fear; for 'the fear of the Lord is the beginning of wisdom' (Ps. cx, 10), and there human pride is subdued and weakened.

Next, I would that, tamed by piety and meek, thou dispute not by excited argument even those things which thou dost not as yet understand, and those things which in the Sacred Scriptures appear to the inexperienced to be incongruous and contradictory, nor superimpose thy own meaning on the meanings of the divine books; but submit it, and meekly defer thy understanding of these things rather than roughly rail against what is hidden. Thirdly, when the infirmity of human nature begins to be revealed to thy perception, and thou hast learnt where thou tarriest, and how penal are the chains of mortality which, as of the seed of Adam, thou carriest about with thee, and how far thou hast wandered from God, and hast seen another law in thy members, fighting against the law of thy mind and leading thee captive in the law of sin that is in thy members, I would have thee exclaim, 'Unhappy man that I am, who shall deliver me from the body of this death?' (Rom. vii, 23 *sqq.*) so that 'the grace of God, by Jesus Christ our Lord,' promising thee this deliverance, may comfort thee in thy mourning (cf. Matt. v, 5).

Fourthly, long now to fulfil justice, and much more vehemently and fervently than the pleasures of the flesh are longed for by sinful men; save only that in the hope of divine help there is in that desire of thine a more tranquil warmth and a serener flame. In this fourth stage of life man must resort to earnest prayer, that those hungering and thirsting after justice may be granted their fill (*ibid.*, 6); so that it may not only not be burdensome but also truly a delight to abstain from the enjoyment of everything that may corrupt, whether himself or his neighbour, or even to struggle against it.

And that this may be the more easily granted by God, a fifth is added, the injunction that thou show mercy, that thou help the needy, in that which thou canst help, since in that which thou art not yet capable of, thou desirest to be helped by the Almighty. Now the gift of mercy is twofold since punishment is remitted, and humanity displayed. And these two the Lord thus briefly coupled together: 'Forgive and you shall be forgiven. Give and it shall be given to you' (Luke vi, 37 *sq.*).

Now this work is also powerful in the cleansing of the heart, that, as far as is allowed in this life, we may be able to perceive by pure intelligence the immutable substance of God. For there is something held against us to fetter us which must be unloosed that our sight may break through to the light; wherefor the Lord himself says, 'But give alms, and behold, all things are clean to you' (Luke xi, 41). Wherefor as the sixth stage there follows the cleansing of the heart itself. But that the sight may be directed rightly and purely to the true light, neither those things which we do well and laudably, nor those things which we investigate acutely and sagaciously, must be related to the end of pleasing men, or of supplying bodily necessities. For God wishes to be worshipped for no reward; since there is nothing for the sake of which we ought to strive after Him.

When by the stages of a good life we have reached that purity of intelligence, whether this be later or earlier, then we may venture to say that we can, in however small measure, touch with our mind the unity of the supreme and ineffable Trinity; and there there will be supreme peace; since nothing further can be looked for, when, reformed according to the image of their race, the sons of God, become this from being men, enjoy the immutability of the Father.

First then, 'Blessed are the poor in spirit,' where there is the fear of God.

Secondly, 'Blessed are the meek,' where there is docile piety.

Thirdly, 'Blessed are they that mourn,' where there is knowledge of their own infirmity.

Fourthly, 'Blessed are they that hunger and thirst after justice,' where there is fortitude in trying to hold the passions in subjection.

Fifthly, 'Blessed are the merciful for they shall obtain mercy,' where there is the injunction to give help that thou mayest merit to be helped.

Then we come to the sixth stage in which it is said, 'Blessed are the clean of heart: for they shall see God,' when the pure intellect, now apt to understand, cannot perceive the Trinity in however small measure, unless also we do not seek after the praise of men, however laudable our works.

Then we reach by the seventh stage the serenity of that peace which the world cannot give.

For if to those four virtues, which with noteworthy diligence, the philosophers of old also were able to explore, that is, prudence, fortitude, temperance, and justice, we add, in order to perfect religious culture, these other three, namely, faith, hope, and charity, we certainly arrive at the number seven. And they are rightly added, for those three may not be omitted, without which, as we know, no one can either worship God, or please Him.

Ep. CLXXXI. A.

581

God's dispensation in time, and the remedy His Providence applies to those who by sin have merited mortality, may thus be set out.

Let us first consider the nature and culture of any man born into the world. His first age, that of infancy, is spent in the nourishment of his body, and this is forgotten as he grows older. Boyhood follows, and from this time on we begin to remember something. To this succeeds adolescence, and nature now permits the propagation of offspring, and makes him a father. Youth then follows adolescence, and this age must be exercised in public duties, and tamed under the laws. It is in this age that the more forcible prohibition of sins, and the servile coercion of the punishment awarded to Simeon, beget more violent onslaughts of lust, and double all the transgressions. For it is not simple sin, not only the evil thing, but what is forbidden, that is committed. After the struggles of youth some peace is granted as the man grows older. From this time on until his death there lasts a more worn age, colourless, more subject to ailments, and frail. Such is the life of the man living according to the body, and fettered by the desires for temporal things. This is called the 'old' man, and the exterior and earthly man, although he may obtain what the multitude calls happiness, in a well-ordered earthly state, whether under kings, or princes or under laws, or under all these together; for otherwise a people cannot be well organized, even that people which pursue only earthly things. For it has itself also a certain measure of its own beauty.

There are some who, throughout their life from its rising to its setting, play the part of such a man, whom we have described as 'old' and exterior and earthly, whether moderated in kind, or exceeding even the measure of servile justice. There are some, on the other hand, who necessarily begin this life with it, but are interiorly reborn, and destroy the other parts of this life by their spiritual strength, and by their increase in wisdom, and kill them, and constrain them to submit to the laws of heaven, until after their visible death the whole is made over anew. This is called the 'new' man, and the interior and celestial man; and he too by analogy has his several distinct spiritual ages, not in years but in his degrees of progress.

The first age he spends at the breast of beneficial history, which nourishes him with good examples. The second age, already oblivious of things human, stretches out to the divine; and in this man is not held in the lap of human authority, but, supported by the steps of reason, strives after the supreme and immutable law. In the third there is greater self-confidence, and this age, by the strength of reason, takes the carnal appetite in wedlock, and inwardly rejoices in a kind of conjugal sweetness, since the soul is coupled to the mind, and is veiled with the veil of modesty, and now there is no compulsion felt to live justly, for even if all allow it, sin has no more any attraction. In the fourth age we find the same features much more confirmed and ordered, and man advances towards the perfect state, and becomes capable and adapted for all things, and to suffer and to subdue the persecutions and the storms and the commotions of this world. The fifth age finds itself at peace, and in tranquillity on every side, living a life amidst the riches and abundance of the immutable kingdom of the supreme and ineffable wisdom. The sixth age sees a complete change leading to eternal life, and, utterly oblivious of this temporal life, the passing to that perfect form which is made in the image and likeness of God. The seventh age is that of eternal rest and of perpetual bliss, in which there is no further distinction of ages. For as the end of the old man is death, so the end of the new man is life eternal.

De vera relig. xxvi, 48–49.

582

He makes a beginning by working in us so that we may have the will, and in perfecting works in us when we have the will. . . . He operates, therefore, without us in order that we may will; but when we will, and so will as to act, He co-operates with us. We can, however, do nothing to effect good works of piety without Him either working that we may will, or co-working with us.

De grat. et lib. arb. xvii, 33.

583

Just as no one has true wisdom or understanding, is endowed with the gifts of counsel and fortitude, is pious with perception or perceptive with piety, or fears God with chaste fear, unless he have received the Spirit of wisdom and understanding, of counsel and fortitude, of knowledge and piety and the fear of God; nor can he have true virtue, sincere charity, or religious continence, save through the Spirit of virtue and charity, and continence; so too no one without the Spirit of faith can believe

329

rightly, or without the Spirit of prayer pray advantageously. Not that there are as many spirits as there are graces, 'but all these things one and the same Spirit worketh, dividing to every one according as he will' (1 Cor. xii, 11), for 'the Spirit breatheth where he will' (John iii, 11). This however must be observed, that the Spirit helps in one way the heart where He has no dwelling place, in another way where He has. For the former He helps that they may become believers, whereas in helping the latter He is helping those who already believe.

What then is the merit which man has before grace by which he may obtain grace, since it is grace alone which works all that there is of merit in us, and since God in crowning our merits only crowns His own gifts to us? For just as from the time our faith begins to dawn we have been granted mercy, not because we were but that we might become believers, so at the end where life eternal is in store for us, He shall crown us as the Psalmist says, 'with mercy and compassion' (Ps. cii, 4). Thus they are not groundless, those words which we sing to God: 'His mercy shall prevent me,' and 'His mercy will follow me,' (Ps. lviii, 11; xxii, 6). Hence the life eternal which, at the end of time, we shall possess for ever and ever, is given us as a reward for the merits we have previously acquired; nevertheless, since these same merits for which they are given have not been acquired by us of our own sufficing but are the work of grace in us, this life is itself called a Grace, not because it is not given us for our merits but because those very merits for which it is given are the gift of God.

Ep. CXCIV, iv, 18; v, 19.

584

We do ourselves work; but we are co-workers with Him who does the work, because His mercy prevents us (Ps. lviii, 11). He prevents us, however, that we may be healed, and He will follow us that being healed we may also be invigorated. He prevents us that we may be called; He will follow us that we may be glorified. He prevents us that we may live righteously, He will follow us that we may always live with Him, since without Him we can do nothing (John xv, 5).

De nat. et gratia, xxxi, 35.

One will say to me, 'Then we are actuated, we do not act.'
I answer, 'Yes, truly, thou dost both act and art actuated;
and thus thou dost act well if thou art actuated by the good.
For the Spirit of God who actuateth thee is a helper to thee in
thy action. The very name of helper teacheth thee that thou
thyself also doeth something. . . . If thou wert not a worker, He
would not be a co-worker.'

Serm. (de Script. N.T.) CLVI, xi, 11.

586

All of God; yet not as though we were sleeping, not as though
we should make no effort, not as though we should have no
will. Without thy will the justice of God will not be in thee.
The will indeed is none but thine own, the justice is none save
God's. The justice of God can be without thy will, but it cannot
be in thee without thy will. . . . Thou wilt be the work of God
not only because thou art a man but also because thou art just.
For it is a better thing for thee to be just than to be a man. If
God made thee a man, and thou makest thyself just, thou
makest something better than God made. But God made thee
without thyself. For thou didst not give any consent that God
might make thee. How wert thou to consent, who wast not?
He then who made thee without thyself, doth not justify thee
without thyself. He made thee then without thy knowledge,
He justifieth thee with thy will.

Serm. (de Script. N.T.) CLXIX, xi, 13.

587

'I pray you,' saith the Apostle, 'not to faint at my tribulations
for you, which is your glory' (Eph. iii, 13). . . . He prays them
then not to be enfeebled, which he would not do unless he
wished to stir up their will. . . . If he did not know that there
was in them a consent of their own will, wherein they too might
themselves do something, he would not say, 'I pray you'. . . . .
But again, as he knew that man's will without God's help is
weak, he not only said 'I pray,' that they might not say, 'we
have no free choice of will,' but also, lest they should say this

free choice of will is sufficient for us, mark what he added: . . .
'For this cause I bow my knees to the Father of our Lord Jesus
Christ, of whom all paternity in heaven and earth is named:
that He would grant you.' 'Grant you' what? I pray He would
grant you what I desire of you. For I desire of you because of
the free choice of the will, I pray that He would grant you
because of the aid of His majesty . . . 'that he would grant you,
according to the riches of His glory, to be strengthened by His
Spirit with might' (ibid, 14 *sqq.*). What else is this but not to be
enfeebled? . . . Mark what he desires. He desires of God what
he requires of men; because, that God may be willing to give,
thou oughtest also to accommodate thy will to receive. How
dost thou wish to receive the grace of the divine goodness when
thou dost not open the bosom of the will? 'Would grant you,'
he says. For you have not, unless He grant you. 'Would grant
you to be strengthened by His Spirit with might.' For if He
shall grant you to be strengthened with might, He will thereby grant you not to be enfeebled.

Serm. (de Script. N.T.) CLXV, i, 1; ii, 2.

588

What then is 'thy will be done'? . . . For the will of God
will be done in thee, though it be not done by thee. . . . Whether
it be well or ill with thee, it will still be done in thee. But O that
it may be done by thee also! Why do I say then, 'Thy will
be done in heaven and on earth,' and do not say, 'Thy will be
done by heaven and earth'? Because what is done by thee,
He himself doeth in thee. Never is anything done by thee
which He himself doeth not in thee. Sometimes, indeed, He
doeth in thee what is not done by thee; but never is anything
done by thee, if He do it not in thee.

Serm. (de Script. N.T.) LVI, v, 7.

589

Nor art Thou, O God, compelled to do anything against
Thy will, because Thy power and Thy will are equal. But one
would be greater than the other, if Thou thyself wert greater
than thyself, for the Will and the Power of God is God himself.

Conf. VII, iv, 6.

590

Thou dost strive, it is clear, and therefore thou shalt be crowned, because thou wilt conquer. But see Who conquered first; see Who hath made you conqueror, even though in the second place. . . . We who are conquered in ourselves, have conquered in Him. He crowneth thee, because He is crowning His own gifts, not thy merits.

In Ps. CII, 7.

591

Lest haply thou shouldest say, 'I have deserved it and therefore have received,' deem not thyself to have received by deserving, thou who hadst not deserved if thou hadst not received. Grace went before thy dessert; grace is not from merit, but merit from grace. For if grace be from merit, thou hast bought, not freely received. 'For nothing,' saith the Psalmist, 'shalt Thou save them' (Ps. LV, 8). . . . Thou dost find nothing in them wherefore to save, and yet Thou savest. Freely Thou givest, freely Thou savest. Thou dost prevent all merits, that my merits may follow Thy gifts. Assuredly thou dost give freely and freely dost thou save, who dost find nothing wherefore to save and much wherefore to condemn.

Serm. (*de Script. N.T.*) CLXIX, ii, 3.

592

David himself vowed as though he had it in his power, and he prayeth God to fulfil his vow. There is devotion in the vow, but there is humility in the prayer. Let no man presume to think that by his own strength he fulfilleth what he hath vowed. He who exhorteth thee to vow, Himself aideth thee to fulfil.

In Ps. CXXXI, 3.

593

God willed that even in the matter of perseverance in goodness itself, His saints should not glory in their own strength, but in Himself, who not only gives them aid . . . without which they cannot persevere, even if they should will, but causes in them also the will; in order that, since they will not persevere unless they both can and will, both the capability and the will should be bestowed on them by the liberality of the divine grace. Their will is so much enkindled by the Holy Spirit that they can, because they so will. And they so will, because God works in them to will.

De corrept. et gratia, xii, 38.

594

Aid me that I may do that which thou chargest me; do Thou thyself give what Thou dost command. 'Quicken me in Thy justice' (Ps. cxviii, 40); for in myself I had that of which I should die, and I find not save in Thee whence I may live.

In Ps. CXVIII, *Serm.* xii, 5.

595

My desire is insufficient, unless in that which I have desired, Thou thyself leadest me.

In Ps. CXVIII, *Serm.* xi, 5.

V. LIFE AS LOVE

596

Because it is Thou who hast made me, let it not be Thy will to destroy me utterly. Scourge me so that I may be made better, not so that I cease to be; beat me so that I may be given a better shape, not so as to crush me to bits.

In Ps. XXXVIII, 16.

597

There [on Sinai] the people were deterred by a terrible fear from approaching the place where the law was being given (Exod. xix); but here at [Pentecost] the Holy Ghost came upon them as they were gathered together in one place waiting for His promised coming (Acts ii). On the former occasion it was on tables of stone that the finger of God operated; on the latter it was on the hearts of men. There the law was laid down outwardly, that the unjust might be terrified; here it was given inwardly, that they might be justified. For . . . 'if there be any other commandment,' such of course as was written on those tables, 'it is,' saith the Apostle, 'comprised in this word: Thou shalt love thy neighbour as thyself. The love of our neighbour worketh no evil. Love therefore is the fulfilling of the law' (Rom. xiii, 9, 10). This was not written on tables of stone, but 'poured forth in our hearts, by the Holy Ghost who is given to us' (*id.* v, 5). Charity, therefore, is the law of God.

De spir. et litt. xvii, 29.

598

It is therefore apparent what a difference there is between the old covenant and the new. In the former the law is written on tables, in the latter on hearts; so that in the one what alarms from without, in the other delights from within. And in the former man becomes a transgressor through the letter that killeth, in the other a lover through the spirit that quickeneth. We must therefore avoid saying that God helps us to work justice and 'worketh in us both to will and to accomplish, according to His goodwill' (Phil. II, 13), by externally addressing to our faculties precepts of justice; for He 'giveth the increase' internally (1 Cor. iii, 7), by pouring fourth charity in our hearts, by the Holy Ghost who is given to us (Rom. v, 5).

De spir. et litt. xxv, 42.

599

But they, not understanding the grace hidden in the Old Testament, a veil as it were interposing (this was signified when they were unable to gaze upon the face of Moses) (Exod. xxxiv, 33 *sqq.*; 2 Cor. iii, 13 *sqq.*), endeavoured to obey the commandments of God for the sake of an earthly and carnal reward; but they could not obey them because they loved not them but something else. Hence these were not the works of the willing, but rather the burdens of the unwilling. But when these commandments are loved more than gold and many precious stones (Ps. cxviii, 127; Ps. xviii, 11), all earthly reward compared with the commandments themselves is vile; nor are any other goods of man comparable in any respect with those goods whereby man himself is made good.

In Ps. CXVIII, *Serm.* xxvi, 8.

600

For we, as the Apostle saith, 'are the temple of the living God; as God saith: I will dwell in them and walk among them' (2 Cor. vi, 16). . . . If we be enlarged, God walketh among them; but that we may be enlarged, let God himself work. For if charity maketh this enlargement, which knoweth no straitness, mark how it is God who maketh for Himself the enlargement in us, as the Apostle himself saith: 'the charity of God is poured forth in our hearts, by the Holy Ghost who is given to us' (Rom. v, 5). Because of this enlargement, I say, God walketh among us.

Serm. (de Script. N.T.) CLXIII, i, 1.

601

The enlarging of the heart is the delight we take in justice. This is the gift of God, that we are not straitened in His commandments, through the fear of punishment, but enlarged through love, and the delight we have in justice. For He promiseth His own breadth, when He saith, 'I will dwell in them and walk among them' (2 Cor. vi, 16; Lev. xxvi, 12). For how broad is the place where the Lord walketh! And in this breadth is charity 'poured forth in our hearts, by the Holy Ghost who is given to us' (Rom. v, 15).

In Ps CXVIII, *Serm.* X, 6.

602

Justice must be loved; and in this justice which must be loved there are steps taken by those who progress. The first is that not all things which give delight be preferred to the love of justice; . . . that among all the things which give delight, justice itself should give thee more delight; not that other things should not give delight, but that it should give more. . . . Let justice in such wise delight as to overcome even lawful delights; and prefer justice to that delight wherewith thou art lawfully delighted. . . .

You have two servants, one deformed in person, the other very beautiful. . . . You have questioned the eyes of the flesh, and what report have they brought back to you? This one is beautiful, the other deformed. You have driven them away, have refused their testimony; you have lifted up the eyes of the heart on the faithful servant and on the unfaithful servant: The first you have found ugly of body, the other beautiful; but you have made the decision and said, 'What is more beautiful than faithfulness, what more deformed than unfaithfulness? . . .

For if thou hast interior senses, all those interior senses are delighted by the delight of justice. If thou hast interior eyes, see the light of justice. 'For with thee is the fountain of life; and in Thy light we shall see light' (Ps. xxxv, 10). . . . Again, if thou hast interior ears, hear justice. Such ears did He seek, who said, 'He that hath ears to hear, let him hear ' (Luke viii, 8). . . . If thou hast an interior sense of smell, hear what the Apostle says: 'We are the good odour of Christ unto God in every place' (2 Cor. ii, 15). If thou hast an interior sense of taste hear the Psalmist: 'O taste, and see that the Lord is sweet' (Ps. xxxiii, 9). If thou hast an interior sense of touch, hear what the bride singeth of the spouse: 'His left hand is under my head, and his right hand shall embrace me' (Cant. ii, 6.). . . .

Weigh justice and iniquity together. Is justice worthy of as much as iniquity was worth? Ought it so to be loved as iniquity was loved? God forbid that it should be so loved, but would that it were even so. More then? Assuredly more. . . . In injustice thou didst follow delight; for justice endure pain. . . . Give me beauteous justice, give me the beauty of faith; let her come forth, shew herself to the eyes of the heart, inspire fervour in her lovers. Now she says to thee, 'Wouldst thou enjoy me? Despise whatever else delighteth thee; despise it for me.' Behold thou hast despised it; it is not enough for her. . . . 'It is not enough that thou despisest whatever else delighte thee; despise whatever terrified thee: despise the prison, despise the chains, despise the rack, despise torture, despise death. If these thou hast overcome, thou hast found me.' In each step prove yourselves lovers of justice.

Serm. (de Script. N.T.) CLIX, ii, 2; iv, 4; vi, 7.

What then is God's law written by God himself on the hearts of men, but the very presence of the Holy Ghost, who is the finger of God, and by whose presence there is poured forth in our hearts the charity which is the fulfilling of the law and the end of the commandment? (Rom. v, 5; 1 Tim. i, 5).

De spir. et litt., XXI, 36.

604

There is no gift of God more excellent than this [of charity]. It alone distinguishes between the children of the everlasting kingdom and the children of everlasting perdition. Other gifts, too, are given by the Holy Ghost, but without charity they profit nothing. Unless therefore the Holy Spirit is imparted to each in such measure as to make him love God and his neighbour, he is not transferred from the left hand to the right. Nor is the Spirit properly called the gift except on account of Charity. And he who has not got it, though he speak with the tongues of men and of angels, is but sounding brass and a tinkling cymbal. And if he should have prophecy and should know all mysteries and all knowledge, and if he should have all faith, so that he could remove mountains, he is nothing; and if he should distribute all his goods, and if he should deliver his body to be burned, it profiteth him nothing (v. 1 Cor. xiii, 1 *sqq.*). How great then is that good without which such great goods lead no one to eternal life! But this very love or charity (for they are each the name of one thing), if a man have it, who speaketh not with tongues, nor hath prophecy, nor knoweth all mysteries and all knowledge, nor distributeth all his goods to the poor (whether because he hath nought to distribute or because he is prevented by some necessity), nor delivereth his body to be burned (supposing no test of such a suffering be presented), this charity bringeth him to the kingdom. So that faith itself is of no avail without charity. For without charity faith can indeed be, but can profit nothing.

De Trin. XV, xviii, 32.

605

Sight shall displace faith; and hope shall be succeeded by that beatitude to which we shall attain; but charity shall grow greater when those others fail. For if we love by faith that which as yet we do not see, how much more shall we love it when we begin to see? And if by hope we love that to which as yet we have not attained, how much more shall we love it when we do attain it? For there is this difference between things temporal and things eternal, that a temporal object is more valued before we possess it; for it becomes of less worth when we have obtained it, since it does not satisfy the soul, whose true and sure resting-place is eternity; whereas an eternal object is loved more ardently after it has been received than when it was an object of desire; for no one in his longing for it can set a higher value on it than really attaches to it, so that he should think it to have less worth once he had found it. On the contrary, however high the value set on it when he is on his way to possess it, he will find it, when it comes into his possession, of higher value still.

De doct. christ. I, xxxviii, 42.

606

Let them all sign themselves with the sign of the cross of Christ; let them all respond Amen; let all sing Alleluia; let all be baptized, let all come to church, let all build the walls of churches; there is no discerning of the children of God from the children of the devil, but only by charity. They that have charity are born of God; they that have it not, are not born of God. A mighty token, a mighty distinction! Have what thou wilt; if this alone thou have not, it profiteth thee nothing: other things if thou have not, have this, and thou hast fulfilled the law.

In Epist. Joannis ad Parthos, Tr. v, 7.

607

In the land of the living we ought to have a root. Let our root be there. That root is out of sight; its fruits may be seen, the root cannot be seen. Our root is our charity; our fruits are our works. It is needful that thy works proceed from charity; then is thy root in the land of the living.

In Ps. LI, 12.

608

Sometimes open sins are beaten down by secret ones which pride and disastrous self-conceit persuade men to regard as virtues. Sins therefore can only be said to be quelled when they are beaten down by the love of God, which love is given by Him alone, and only through the mediator of God and man, the Man Christ Jesus (1 Tim. ii, 5), who made Himself a participator of our mortality that He might make us participators of His divinity.

De civ. Dei. **XXI**, xvi.

609

God's commandments are commended to us as being not burdensome, in order that he to whom they are burdensome may understand that he has not yet received the gift which removes their burdensomeness. 'For God loveth a cheerful giver' (2 Cor. ix, 7; Ecclus. xxxv, 11). Nevertheless, when a man finds them burdensome, let him not be crushed by despair; let him rather force himself to seek, to ask, and to knock.

De perf. just. hominis x, 21.

610

Inchoate charity, therefore, is inchoate justice; progressing charity is progressing justice; great charity is great justice; perfect charity is perfect justice.

De nat. et gratia, **LXX**, 84.

611

Ask what proficiency thou hast made in charity, and what thine heart will answer thee, that thou mayest know the measure of thy profiting. . . . As the love increases in thee, so the loveliness increases: for love is itself the loveliness of the soul.

In Epist. Joannis ad Parthos, Tr. ix, 2, 9.

612

All our good works are one work of charity, for love is the fulfilling of the law (Rom. xiii, 10). . . . For 'the end of the

commandment is charity from a pure heart, and a good conscience, and an unfeigned faith' (1 Tim. i, 5). There is therefore
one work, in which are all, 'faith that worketh by charity'
(Gal. v, 6).

In Ps. LXXXIX, 17.

VI. LOVE AS PASSION

613

Love, and do what thou wilt; whether thou hold thy peace,
of love hold thy peace; whether thou cry out, of love cry out;
whether thou correct, of love correct; whether thou spare,
through love do thou spare; let the root of love be within, of
this root can nothing spring but what is good.

In Epist. Joannis ad Parthos, Tr. vii, 8.

614

Lest thou think much of the works of faith add unto it hope
and love, and think not what thou workest. Love itself cannot
be empty. For what is there in any man that worketh at all,
even to evil, except love? Shew me the love that is empty
and doth no work. Shameful deeds, adulteries, acts of violence,
murders, all excesses; doth not love work these? Cleanse therefore thy love. Turn the waters flowing into the drain into the
garden; whatever desires it had for the world, the same let
it have for the Creator of the world. Do we say to you love
nothing? Love, but take heed what you love. The love of
God, the love of our neighbour, is called charity; the love
of the world, the love of this life is called concupiscence. Let
concupiscence be bridled, charity stirred up.

In Ps. XXXI, *En.* II,

615

What man doth live without affections? And do you suppose,
brethren, that those who fear God, worship God, love God,
have no affections? Do you really suppose, and do you dare
suppose, that painting, the theatre, hunting, hawking, fishing,

341

engage the affections, and that meditation on God doth not engage certain interior affections of their own, when we contemplate the universe and place before our eyes the spectacle of the nature of things, and therein seek to discover the Creator, and find Him nowhere displeasing but pleasing above all things?

In Ps. LXXVI, 14.

616

If some are so strangely vain and inhuman as to take pride in being absolutely callous to everything and in being left unmoved and uninfluenced by any affection, they lose their whole humanity rather than find true tranquillity of mind. For because a thing is hard it is not therefore right, nor because a thing is stupid is it therefore wholesome.

De civ. Dei XIV, ix, 6.

617

Soundness hath no sickness, but nevertheless, when it is touched and molested, it feeleth pain. But torpor hath no pain, hath lost the sense of pain, and the more insensible it is the worse it is. Again, immortality hath no pain; for all corruption is swallowed up, and this corruptible hath put on incorruption, and this mortal hath put on immortality (v. 1 Cor. xv, 53 *sq.*) Hence there is no pain in an immortal body, and no pain in a torpid body. Let not a man without feeling think himself already immortal; the soundness of a man in pain is nearer immortality than the torpor of a man who feeleth not. Thou findest therefore a man proud in the most excessive vapouring, that hath persuaded himself that he feareth nothing. Dost thou deem him mightier than he who saith, 'combats without: fears within'? (2 Cor. vii, 5), mightier than the Head Himself, our Lord God, who said: 'My soul is sorrowful even unto death'? (Matt. xxvi, 38). This man is not more mighty. Let not his stupor please thee. He hath not been clothed with immortality, but stripped of feeling. But keep thou thy soul not without affection, for they have been blamed who are without affection, and say from thy feeling of soundness; 'Who is weak, and I am not weak? Who is scandalized, and I am not on fire?' (2 Cor. xi, 29).

In Ps. LV, 6.

618

As to that man, I say, that athlete of Christ, taught by Him, anointed by Him, crucified with Him, glorious in Him, in the theatre of this world made a spectacle both to angels and to men, fighting a great fight, pressing towards the mark, to the prize of the supernal vocation (cf. Gal. i, 12; 2 Cor. i, 21; Gal. ii, 19 *sq.*; 1 Cor. iv, 9; Phil. iii, 14), with what joy and gladness do we behold him with the eyes of faith 'rejoice with them that rejoice: weep with them that weep' (Rom. xii, 15), having 'combats without: fears within' (2 Cor. vii, 5), 'having a desire to be dissolved and to be with Christ' (Phil. i, 23), 'longing to see' the Romans, 'that he might have some fruit among them also, even as among the other Gentiles' (Rom. i, 11, 13), 'jealous' of the Corinthians and of that very jealousy fearing lest 'their minds should be corrupted and fall from the simplicity that is in Christ' (2 Cor. xi, 2 *sq.*), 'having great sadness and continual sorrow in his heart' for the Israelites (Rom. ix, 2), 'for they not knowing the justice of God and seeking to establish their own, have not submitted themselves to the justice of God' (Rom. x, 3); and telling his grief and distress over those 'that sinned before and have not done penance for the uncleanness and fornication and lasciviousness that they have committed' (2 Cor. xii, 21).

If those impulses, those affections arising from the love of the good and from holy charity are to be called vices, then let us call what are truly vices virtues.

De civ. Dei XIV, ix, 2, 3.

619

As impure love inflames the mind and summons the soul destined to perish to lust after earthly things, and to follow what is perishable, and precipitates it into the lowest places, and sinks it in the abyss; so holy love raiseth us to supernal things, and inflames us to what is eternal, and excites the soul to those things which do not pass away and die, and from the depths of hell

343

raiseth it to heaven. Yet all love hath a power of its own, nor can love in the soul of the lover be idle; it must needs draw it on. But dost thou wish to know of what sort love is? See whither it leadeth. We do not therefore warn you to love nothing; but that you love not the world, that you may freely love Him who made the world. For the soul when bound by the love of the earth, hath as it were birdlime on its wings; it cannot fly. But when purged from the sordid affections of the world, extending as it were its pair of wings, and freeing them from every impediment, flieth upon them, that is to say, upon the two commandments of love unto God and our neighbour. Whither will it fly, but by rising in its flight to God? For it riseth by loving. Before it can do this, it groaneth on earth, if it hath already in it the desire for flight; and saith, 'who will give me wings like a dove, and I will fly and be at rest' (Ps. liv, 7). . . . From the midst of offences, then, from the medley of evil men, from the chaff mingled with the grain, it longeth to fly, where it may not suffer the society of any wicked one, but may live in the holy company of angels, the citizens of the eternal Jerusalem.

In Ps. CXXI, 1.

620

It is as if thou didst ask, When doth He satisfy my desire with good things (v. Ps. cii, 5)? for at present I am not satisfied. Whatever I turn myself to becomes vile when I have acquired it, inflamed me when I desired it. When I despise, when I have them, which I love, when I have them not, what good thing will satisfy me? . . . I will not be satisfied with things perishable, with things temporal; let Him give me something imperishable, let Him grant me something everlasting. . . . But God is willing to give; only He giveth not except to him who asketh, lest He give to one who receiveth not. . . . I know that good of His which I am to desire; I know what is enough for me. I see this in Philip's 'Lord, shew us the Father; and it is enough for us' (John xiv, 8).

In Ps. CII, 9, 10.

621

Suppose our heart to be in anguish and we cry out. For what cause should our heart be in anguish? Not in consequence of those things which the wicked also suffer here; for example, if they suffer loss; for if the heart be in anguish on this account, it is ashes. By the will of God thou hast perhaps lost some one of thy kin. If thine heart is in anguish on this account, what great thing is this? From this cause the hearts of infidels also are in anguish; those who have not as yet believed in Christ suffer these things also. What maketh the heart of the Christian heavy? The fact that he is a pilgrim, and longeth for his own country. If thy heart be heavy on this score, thou dost groan, even though thou hast been fortunate in thy worldly affairs; and if all things combine to make thee prosperous, and this world smile on thee from every side, thou dost nevertheless groan, because thou seest that thou art set in a pilgrimage, and feelest that thou hast indeed happiness in the eyes of fools, but not as yet according to the promise of Christ. This thou seekest with groans, and seeking this thou longest, and by thy longing dost ascend.

In Ps. CXXII, 2.

622

For thy desire is thy prayer; and if thy desire is without ceasing, thy prayer will also be without ceasing. . . . There is interior prayer without ceasing, and this is your desire. Whatever else you do, if you do but long for that sabbath, you do not cease to pray. If you would never cease to pray, never cease to long after it. The continuance of your longing is the continuance of your prayer. You will be ceasing to speak if you cease to love. . . . The chilling of charity is the silence of the heart; the glowing of charity is the cry of the heart. If love is without ceasing, you are always lifting up your voice; if you are ever lifting up your voice, you are for ever longing after something; if you are longing, the rest you long for is in your mind.

In Ps. XXXVII, 4.

VII. INPOURING LOVE

623

In order that we might receive that love whereby we should love, we were ourselves loved, while as yet we had it not. . . .

For we would not have wherewithal to love Him, unless we received it from Him by His first loving us.

De grat. Christi xxvi, 27.

624

The love of a created thing to be enjoyed without the love of God is not from God. The love of God however by which we attain to God, is not, except it be from God the Father through Jesus Christ with the Holy Ghost. Through this love of the Creator, every one can make a good use even of created things.

Contra Julianum IV, iii, 33.

625

. . . By love . . . either of the creature or of the Creator, that is, either of mutable nature or of immutable truth; therefore, either by desire or by charity. Not that the creature ought not to be loved; but if that love is referred to the Creator, then it will not be desire but charity. For it is desire when the creature is loved for itself; and it does not then help the man who indulges in it, but corrupts him in the enjoyment of it. When therefore the creature is either equal to us or inferior, we must use the inferior agreeably to God, but enjoy the equal only in God. For as thou oughtest to enjoy thyself, not in thyself, but in Him Who made thee, so also thou shouldest enjoy Him whom thou lovest as thyself. Let us therefore enjoy in the Lord both ourselves and our brethren; and from this let us not dare to yield, and as it were relax, ourselves to ourselves in the downward direction.

De Trin. IX, vii, 13 – viii, 13.

626

This is the general fornication of the soul, . . . containing all sins entirely in itself, whereby there is no cleaving to God whilst there is a cleaving to the world. . . . But if a worldly man, cleaving to the world, removeth himself far from God, by going a-whoring from God himself, he sinneth against his own body; because by corporeal concupiscence the mind of man is by carnal affection and judgment distracted by and dissipated upon such things as are temporal and carnal, serving 'the creature rather than the Creator, who is blessed for ever' (*v.*

Rom. i, 24 *sq.*). . . . For only by the evil power of carnal and general concupiscence does the soul go a-whoring throughout all things away from God. Bound down and chained as it were to bodily and temporal desires and gratifications, it sinneth against its own body, and serving its concupiscence universally, it bows down to the world and is alienated from God. . . . This love of the world, then, which contains in itself the universal concupiscence of the world, is the general fornication whereby a man sins against his own body; in that the mind serves without ceasing all bodily and visible and temporal desires and pleasure, left in desolation and abandonment by the Creator himself of all things.

Serm. (*de Script. N.T.*) CLXII, 3, 4.

627

For the devil does not seduce or influence anyone, unless he finds him already in some part similar to himself. He finds him coveting something, and cupidity opens the door for the devil's suggestion to enter. He finds him fearing something, he advises him to flee what he found him fearing; he advises him to get possession of that which he found him coveting, and by these two doors, cupidity and fear, he gets an entrance.

Serm. XXXII, xi, 11.

628

Now Scripture enjoins nothing except charity and condemns nothing except lust, and in that way informs the practices of men. . . . I mean by charity that affection of the mind which aims at the enjoyment of God for His own sake and of one's self and one's neighbour for God's sake. By lust I mean that affection of the mind which aims at the enjoyment of one's self and one's neighbour without reference to God. . . . Now in proportion as the dominion of lust is pulled down, in the same proportion that of charity is built up.

De doct. christ. III, x, 15, 16.

629

Now there are some things which are to be enjoyed, others which are to be used, others still which we enjoy and use. The objects of enjoyment make us happy. Things which are the object of use help and as it were support us in our efforts after happiness so that we may attain to those things which make us happy and cling to them. We ourselves, again, who enjoy and use those things, and are set among both kinds of objects, if we set ourselves to enjoy what ought to be used, are hindered in our course, and sometimes even led away from it; so that, entangled by the love of lower things, we lag behind or even turn back from the pursuit of the proper objects of enjoyment. For to enjoy a thing is to cling to it with love for its own sake. To use, on the other hand, is to employ the means at one's disposal to obtain what one desires, always supposing it to be a proper object of desire.

De doct. christ. I, iii, 3; iv, 4.

630

Now this is our highest reward that we should fully enjoy God, and that all who enjoy Him should enjoy one another in Him. . . . But when you have joy of a man in God, it is God rather than the man whom you enjoy. For you enjoy Him by whom you are made happy, and you rejoice to have come to Him in whom you place your hope that you may come to Him. Accordingly St. Paul says to Philemon: 'Yes, brother. May I enjoy thee in the Lord!' (Philem. 20). For if he had not added 'in the Lord,' but had only said 'may I enjoy thee,' he would have implied that he set his hope of happiness in him, although even in the immediate context 'to enjoy' is used in the sense of 'to use with delight.' For when what we love is near us, it necessarily brings delight with it. But if you pass beyond this delight and make it a means to that in which you are to rest for ever, you are using it, and it is improper and an abuse of language to say that you enjoy it. But if you cling to it, and rest in it, placing in it the goal of your happiness, then you may truly and properly be said to enjoy it. And this we must never do except in the case of the Blessed Trinity, that is to say of the supreme and immutable good.

De doct. christ. I, xxxii, 35; xxxiii, 37.

For a man is never in so good a state as when his whole life
is a journey towards the immutable life, and his affections are
entirely set upon it. If, however, he loves himself for his own
sake, he does not look at himself in relation to God, but turns
his mind in upon himself, and so is not occupied with anything
that is immutable. And thus he does not enjoy himself at his
best, because he is better when he is wholly set upon and wrapped
up in the immutable good than when he turns from that to
enjoy himself. If therefore you ought not to love even yourself
for your own sake, but only for His in whom your love finds
its most worthy object, no other man has a right to be angry
if you love him too for God's sake. For this is the divinely
ordained rule of love: 'Thou shalt love thy neighbour as thyself'; but 'thou shalt love the Lord thy God with thy whole
heart and with thy whole soul and with thy whole mind'
(Lev. xix, 18; Deut. vi, 5; Matt. xxii, 37 *seq.*); so that you
are to concentrate all your thoughts, your whole life, and all
your intelligence upon Him from whom you derive all that
you bring. For when He says, 'With thy whole heart and with
thy whole soul and with thy whole mind,' He means that no
part of our life is to be unoccupied, and to afford room, as it
were, for the wish to enjoy some other object, but that whatever
else suggests itself to the mind as something worthy of love is
to be borne into the same channel in which the whole current
of our affections flows. Whoever, therefore, loves his neighbour
aright, ought to urge upon him that he too love God with his
whole heart and with his whole soul and with his whole mind.
For in this way, loving his neighbour as himself, a man turns
the whole current of his love both for himself and his neighbour
into the channel of the love of God, which suffers no stream to
be drawn off from itself by whose diversion its own volume
would be diminished.

De doct. christ. I, xxii, 21.

632

The soul which went away from herself is recalled to herself.
As she had gone away from herself, so she went away from her

Lord. For she had respect to herself, and pleased herself, and became enamoured of her own power. She withdrew from Him, and abode not in herself; and from her own self she is repelled, and is shut out from herself, and she falleth away unto things without her. She loves the world, loves temporal things, loves earthly things. And if she loved herself to the neglect of Him by whom she was made, she would at once be less, would at once fail by loving that which is less. For she is less than God, and less by far, by so much less as the thing made is less than the Maker. It was God, therefore, that ought to have been loved, and in such wise loved that, if this be possible, we forget ourselves. What then is this change? The soul forgot herself, but this was by loving the world; let her now forget herself by loving the Creator of the world.

Serm. (de Script. N.T.) CXLII, iii, 3.

633

I am overjoyed to know that your mind, touched by love of eternity and of truth and drawn to that divine and heavenly empire over which Christ reigns and in which alone there can be eternal happiness, if we have lived uprightly and piously on this earth, is yearning for that Kingdom, I see that you are drawing nigh to it and I love you for your ardent desire to possess it. From that Kingdom flows all true friendship, not to be weighed by temporal advantages but esteemed for the love gratuitously given. No one can be truly the friend of a man unless he has been in the first place a friend of truth, and unless this be brought about gratuitously, it can never be done by any common covenant.

Ep. CLV, i, 1.

634

What, should there be no bond of love between men? Truly there should be, so that no surer step towards God may be imagined than the charity between man and man.

De mor. Eccl. I, xxvi, 48.

635

Blessed is the man that loves Thee, and his friend in Thee and his enemy for Thee. For he alone never loseth a friend, to whom all men are dear for His sake who is never lost.

Conf. IV, ix, 14.

636

Because as long as man is in the body he is absent from the Lord, he walks by faith and not by sight (cf. 2 Cor. v, 6 *sqq.*); and therefore he refers all his peace of body, or of soul, or of body and soul together to that peace which mortal man has with immortal God, that he may live in an orderly obedience under His eternal law, by faith. Now God our Master teaches us the two great commandments, namely, love of God and love of our neighbour (Matt. xx, 35 *sqq.*; Mark xii, 30 *sqq.*), and in these man finds three things he should love: God, himself, and his neighbour. And seeing that he who loves God offends not in loving himself, it follows that he ought to counsel his neighbour, whom he is commanded to love as he does himself, to love God, and he should tend him as, if he by chance should be in need, he would wish his neighbour to tend him; and thus he will be settled in peace with all men.

De civ. Dei XIX, xiv.

637

This farness, brethren, you must understand to be of the heart, not of the body. For it often comes to pass that he that is far distant from thee in body, is united to thee, because he loves that which thou lovest. And oft-times it comes to pass that one standing beside thee is far away from thee, because he loves the world, while thou lovest God.

In Ps. LV, 2.

638

Love is a powerful thing, my brethren; love is a powerful thing. Do you wish to see how powerful a thing love is? Whosoever through some necessity cannot fulfil what God commandeth, let him love him who fulfilleth it in him. I pray your attention, beloved. For example, one hath a wife whom he may not divorce; he must obey the Apostle who saith, 'Let the husband render the debt to his wife,' and, 'Art thou bound to a wife? Seek not to be loosed.' It cometh to his mind that

that life is better, whereof the Apostle saith, 'I would that all men were even as myself' (1 Cor. vii, 3, 27, 7). He observeth those who have done this; he loveth them, and fulfilleth in them what he cannot in himself.

In Ps. CXXI, 10.

639

Of all that has been said . . . this is the sum: that we should clearly understand that the fulfilment and the end of the law and of all Holy Scriptures is the love of an object which is to be enjoyed, and the love of an object which can enjoy that other in fellowship with ourselves. For there is no need of a commandment that each man should love himself.

De doct. christ. I, xxv, 39.

640

He alone has a proper love of himself who loves God. . . . Thou lovest thyself wholesomely if thou lovest God more than thyself. That, therefore, which thou aimest at in thyself, thou must aim at in thy neighbour, namely, that he may love God with a love which is perfect.

De mor. Eccl. I, xxvi, 48, 49.

641

The price of the wheat is thy copper, the price of the farm is thy silver, the price of the pearl is thy gold; the price of charity is thyself. Thou seekest how thou mayest get a farm, a precious stone, a beast of burden: thou seekest with what to buy a farm and thou seekest in thy house. But if thou wishest to have charity, seek thyself, and find thyself. What, dost thou fear to give thyself, lest thou spend thyself utterly? Nay, if thou dost not give thyself, thou losest thyself. . . . 'My son, give me thy heart' (Prov. xxiii, 26). . . . It was bad when it was away from thee, when it was thine. . . . Let it be mine, and it is not lost to thee. . . . He demands the whole of thee, Who made thee. . . . With this thou lovest thyself, because thou lovest God with thy whole self. Dost thou think to profit God because thou lovest God? And that something is added to God because thou lovest Him? and that if thou dost not love Him,

He will have less? When thou lovest Him, thou dost profit
thou wilt be there where thou art not lost.

Serm, XXXIV, lv, 7; v, 8.

642

. The love of God comes first in the order of enjoining, but
the love of our neighbour first in the order of doing. . . .
Because thou dost not yet see God, thou dost earn the seeing of
Him by loving thy neighbour. By loving thy neighbour thou
purgest thine eyes for the seeing of God. . . . Love, therefore,
thy neighbour; and behold that in thee whereby thou lovest
thy neighbour; there wilt thou see, as thou mayest, God.

In Joan. Evang. XVII, 8.

643

Let no one say, I know not what I love. Let him love his
brother, and he will love the same love. For he knows the love
by which he loves, more than the brother whom he loves. Lo,
now he already can know God more than he knows his brother,
clearly knows Him more, because He is more present, because
He is more within him, because He is more sure. Embrace
the love of God, and by love embrace God. That is very love
which associates together all good Angels, all the servants of
God by the bond of holiness, and joins us together and them
mutually with us, and makes us all subject to itself. In proportion, therefore, as we are healed from the swelling of pride,
so are we the more filled with love, and with what is he filled
who is full of love, if it be not with God. . . . 'He that loveth
not knoweth not God: for God is charity' (1 John iv, 8). And
this passage declares sufficiently and plainly, that this same
brotherly love (for that is brotherly love by which we love
one another) is preached by so great an authority as being
not only from God, but also as being God. . . . And so a little
later he says, 'He that loveth not his brother whom he seeth,
cannot love God whom he seeth not' (*ibid.*, 20). . . . He sees
his brother with human sight, and with this God cannot be seen.
But if he loved him whom he sees with human sight with a

spiritual love, he would see God, who is charity itself, with the inner sight by which He can be seen.

De Trin. VIII, viii, 12.

644

I dare to say, . . . let us give heed in the lower things to that which we may find in the higher. . . . Some lewd and lascivious fellow, say, loves a beautiful woman. He is, it is true, disturbed by the beauty of her body, but inwardly he wants his love returned. For if he should hear that she disliked him, does not all the fire and violence of his feelings for her beautiful limbs cool off, and does he not now recoil from that which he had before purposed; is he not now estranged and offended, and does he not begin even to hate what before he loved? Is her form then changed? Are not all those things in it which had bound him to her? They are there, and yet he was inflamed by that which he could see, and in his heart demanded what he could not see. But if he knew that his love was returned how much more violently would he be inflamed! She sees him, he sees her, no one sees love; and yet this love itself is loved which is not seen. . . . God thou dost not see; love Him and thou hast Him. . . . Love me, and thou wilt have me; for thou couldst not even love me, unless thou hadst me.

Serm. XXXIV, ii, 4; iii, 5.

645

What dost thou who lovest charity love? And if thou lovest, whence dost thou love? It comes to thee, and thou knowest it, and thou seest it; yet it is not seen as in space, nor is it sought by the eyes of the body, so as to be ardently loved; nor is it heard in speech, and when it comes to thee, it is not perceived by its gait. Hast thou ever perceived the footprints of charity walking in thy heart? What then is it? Whose is this thing, which is already in thee, and is not grasped by thee? Thus learn to love God.

Serm. XXIII, xiii, 13.

646

Upon the love of such friends, I confess, I readily cast myself, especially when chafed and wearied by the scandals of this world, and in this love I rest without any disturbing care; for I perceive that God is there, and on Him I confidently cast myself and in Him confidently rest. Nor in confidence have I to fear that uncertainty as to the morrow which must be present when we lean on human weakness For when I perceive that a man is burning with Christian charity, and feel that thereby he has been made a faithful friend to me, whatever plans or thoughts of mine I entrust to him, I regard as entrusted not to the man, but to Him in whom, as his character shows, He dwells.

Ep. LXXIII, 10.

647

Let us, however, resolve to maintain between ourselves the liberty as well as the charity of friendship, so that in the letters which we exchange, neither of us shall be restrained from frankly stating to the other whatever troubles him, provided always that this be done in the spirit which does not, as inconsistent with brotherly love, displease God. If, however, you do not think that this can be done between us without danger to that brotherly love, let us not do it. For the love which I would see maintained between us is assuredly the greater love which would make this mutual freedom possible; but the smaller measure of it is better than none at all.

Ep. LXXXII, v, 36.

648

'If one strike thee on thy right cheek, turn to him also the other' (Matt. v, 39). . . . . That these precepts pertain rather to the inward disposition of the heart than to the actions which are done in the sight of men, requiring us to cherish patience along with benevolence in the inmost heart, but in the outward action to do that which seems most likely to benefit those whose good we ought to seek, is manifest from the fact that the Lord Jesus Himself, the perfect example of patience, when He was struck in the face, answered: 'If I have spoken evil, give testimony of the evil: but if well, why strikest thou me?' (John xviii, 23). If we look only at the words, He did not in this obey His own precept, for He did not turn another part of

His face to him who had struck Him, but on the contrary prevented him who had done the wrong from adding thereto. And yet He had come prepared not only to be struck on the face but even to be slain for those very men at whose hands He suffered crucifixion, and for whom, when hanging on the cross, He prayed: 'Father, forgive them, for they know not what they do' (Luke xxiii, 34). . . .

These precepts concerning patience ought, therefore, to be always retained in the disciplining of the heart, and the benevolence which prevents the return of evil for evil must be always fully cherished in the will. At the same time, many things must be done in correcting with a certain benevolent severity, even against their own wishes, men whose welfare rather than their wishes it is our duty to consult. . . .

If the Christian teaching condemned wars of every kind, the injunction given in the Gospel to the soldiers seeking counsel as to salvation, would rather be to cast away their arms and withdraw themselves wholly from military service, whereas what was said to them was: 'Do violence to no man, neither calumniate any man; and be content with your pay' (Luke iii, 14). The command to be content with their pay in no way implies prohibition to continue in military service.

Ep. CXXXVIII, ii, 12–15.

XIII. MAN TO GOD

I. MAN-UNTRUTH TO GOD-TRUTH

649

Seek what the property of man is, and you will find sin. Seek what is the property of man, and you will find untruth. Remove sin, and whatsoever you then perceive in man is of God. Let therefore man not love that which is proper to himself. . . . Seek not, then, sin and you will not seek what is your own. Seek not untruth, and you will not seek what is your own. For truth is of God, untruth of yourself.

Serm. XXXV, x, 10.

650

The old man, that is, Adam, is concerned with lying; the new Man, the Son of Man, that is Christ God, with truth. . . . If thou wouldst be a man, thou wilt be a liar. Be not minded to be a man and thou wilt not be a liar. Put on Christ and thou wilt be truthful; that the words which thou shalt speak may not be thine, as if thine own, and originated by thee, but Truth's enlightening and illuminating thee. For if thou be deprived of the light, thou shalt remain in thy own darkness and shalt be able to speak naught but lies. For the Lord himself saith, 'He who speaketh a lie, speaketh of his own' (John viii, 44), for 'every man is a liar' (Ps. cxv, 11). Whoso therefore speaketh the truth, speaketh not of his own but of God's. Not indeed in such sense as that we should say he speaketh what is another's; for they become his own, when he loves what he receives and renders thanks to Him who gave.

Serm. (*de Script. N.T.*) CLXVI, ii, 2; iii, 3.

651

For as far as pertaineth to the man himself, he is a liar, but by the grace of God he is made true. . . . Therefore it is most truly said that, 'Every man is a liar, but God is true' (Rom. iii, 4; Ps. cxv, 11), who said, 'You are gods, and all of you the sons of the most High. But you like all men shall die, and shall fall like one of the princes.' (Ps. lxxxi, 6 *sq.*). . . . For if all men are liars, so far they will not be liars, as they are not men; since they will be gods and the sons of the most High. . . . O man, a liar by thine own sin, true by the gift of God, and therefore no longer a man.

In Ps. CXV, 3, 5.

652

For 'God is true and every man a liar' (Rom. iii, 4); for no man is true, save him in whom God speaketh.

In Ps. CVIII, 2.

653

Men toil in speaking falsehood; for truth they could speak with entire facility. For he toileth who fashioneth what he saith; he who wishes to speak the truth toileth not, for truth herself speaketh without toil. Of this man therefore he said to God, Thine overshadowing shall protect me; their own lie shall overwhelm them (cf. Ps. cxxxix, 8 *sqq.*); and their own lie is the labour of their own lips. 'Behold he hath been in labour with injustice; he hath conceived sorrow, and brought forth iniquity' (Ps. vii, 15). For in every evil work there is toil, and every evil work devised hath a lie for its leader. For there is no truth, save in a good work. And forasmuch as all have toil in lying, what crieth the Truth? 'Come to me, all you that labour and are burdened; and I will refresh you' (Matt. xi, 28).

In Ps. CXXXIX, 13.

654

When I set before the eyes of my heart, such as they be, the intellectual beauty of Him out of whose mouth nothing false proceedeth, though my weak and throbbing senses are driven back where truth in her radiance doth more and more brighten upon me, yet I am so inflamed with love of that surpassing comeliness, that I despise all human considerations which would recall me thence.

Contra mend. xviii, 36.

655

A man living according to man and not according to God is like the devil. For even an angel must live not according to an angel but according to God, that he may stand fast in the truth and speak truth from Him and not lies from himself. For the Apostle in another place speaks thus of man: 'If the truth of God hath more abounded through my lie' (Rom. iii, 7), calling lying ours and the truth God's; when therefore a man lives according to the truth he lives not according to himself but according to God. For God himself said: 'I am the truth' (John xiv, 6). But if a man live according to himself, that is according to man, not according to God, assuredly he lives according to a lie; not that man himself is a lie, for God is his author and creator and He certainly is not the author and creator of a lie, but because man was created upright, that he might live not according to himself but according to Him by whom he was created, that is to say to do God's will rather than his own. For man not to live as he was created to live is a lie.

De civ. Dei XIV, iv, 1.

656

As light and darkness, piety and impiety, justice and iniquity, sin and right-doing, health and feebleness, life and death, are contraries, so too are truth and falsehood.

Contra mend. iii, 4.

657

The martyrs were quickened, lest by loving life they should deny life, and by denying it, should lose it. And thus they who refused to forsake the truth for their lives, lived by dying for the truth.

In Ps. CXVIII, *Serm.* xx, 8.

If there were no other way at all of drawing heretical impiety from its lurking places than by the Catholic tongue deviating from the path of truth; it were more tolerable that the former should be hid than that the latter should be cast down.

Contra mend. vii, 17.

II. MAN'S POVERTY TO GOD'S ABUNDANCE

659

Behold, I say to you, in this regiment of human affairs God thy Father is in some manner saying to thee. . . . O my son, why is it that thou daily risest, and prayest, and pressest the ground with thy knee and strikest it with thy forehead, and sometimes even weepest, and sayest to Me, My Father, my God, give me riches? . . . Because thou didst ask thou didst receive. See that thou do good with them. Before thou hadst them, thou wast humble; thou hast begun to have riches and thou hast despised the poor. . . . I gave thee them and proved thee; thou didst find and wast found. When thou hadst them not, thou didst lie hid. . . . What is the great thing which thou art asking of me? thy God is saying to thee. Dost thou not see to whom I have given these things? Dost thou not see the kind of people to whom I have given these things? If that which thou askest of me is a great good, would a thief have it? Would a treacherous scoundrel have it? Would one who blasphemed Me have it? Would a low play-actor have it? Would a shameless harlot have it? Would these all have gold, if gold were a great good? But thou sayest to Me, Is not gold a good thing? Certainly gold is a good thing; but the wicked work evil with the good gold; the good work good with the good gold. Now that thou seest to whom I have given these things, ask better things of Me, ask greater things of Me, ask spiritual things of Me, ask of Me Myself. . . . Hear me, ye poor. What is it you have not, if you have God? Hear me, ye rich, What have you, if you have not God?

Serm. CCCXI, xiv, 13; xviii, 15.

660

One man is wealthy in money, and is proud on that score; another is wealthy in honours, and is proud on that account; another thinks himself to be wealthy in justice, and hence his pride, which is worse. Those who seem not to be wealthy in money, seem to themselves to be wealthy in justice towards God; and when calamity overtakes them, they justify themselves, accuse God, and say, What wrong have I been guilty of, or, what have I done? And thou repliest, look back, call to mind thy sins, see if thou hast done nothing. He is somewhat touched in conscience, and returneth to himself, and ponders over his evil deeds. But when he hath reflected on his evil deeds, he doth not even then choose to confess that he deserves his sufferings, but saith, Behold, I have clearly done many things; but I see that many have done worse, and suffer no evil. He is just towards God. He also therefore is wealthy; he hath his breast puffed up with justice; since God seemeth to do him ill, and he seemeth to himself to suffer unjustly. And if thou gavest him a vessel to pilot, he would be shipwrecked with it; yet he wishes to deprive God of the piloting of this world, and himself to hold the tiller of creation, and to distribute among all men pains and pleasures, punishments and rewards. Miserable soul! Yet why do you wonder? He is wealthy, but wealthy in iniquity, wealthy in malignity; but he is the more wealthy in iniquity, the more he seemeth to himself to be wealthy in justice.

But a Christian ought not to be wealthy, but ought to acknowledge himself poor; and if he hath riches, he ought to know that they are not true riches, so that he may desire others. For he who desireth false riches, seeketh not the true riches; while he who seeketh the true riches, is as yet poor, and rightly doth he say, 'I am poor and sorrowful' (Ps. lxviii, 30). Again, in what sense is he who is both poor and full of iniquity, said to be rich? Because it displeaseth him to be poor, and in justice itself he seemeth wealthy in his own heart as opposed to the justice of God. And what is the wealth of our justice? However much justice there be in us, it is a sort of dew compared to that fountain; compared to that superabundance it is as a few drops, which may soften our life and dissolve our hard iniquity. Let our only desire be to be filled to overflowing with the full fountain of justice, let us long to be filled with that abounding plenty, of which it is said in the Psalm, 'they shall be inebriated with the plenty of thy house; and thou shalt make them drink of the torrent of thy pleasure' (Ps. xxxv, 9). But while we are here, let us understand ourselves to be destitute and in want, not only in respect of those riches which are not true riches, but of salvation itself. And when we are whole, let us understand that we are weak. For as long as this body hungers and thirsts, as long as this body is weary with watching, weary with standing, weary with walking, weary with eating; whither-soever it turneth for a relief from weariness, there it discovereth another source of fatigue. There is therefore no perfect sound-ness, not even in the body itself. Those riches are then not riches, but beggary; for the more they abound, the more doth destitution and avarice increase. This is not the health of the body, but weakness. We are every day alleviated with medica-ments from God, in that we eat and drink. These things which are set before us are medicaments. Brethren, if you wish to see what sort of disease is upon us, he who fasts for seven days is devoured by hunger. That hunger is therefore there, but thou feelest it not, since every day thou givest it attendance. Not even health, therefore, is to us perfect.

Consider, beloved, in what sense we should understand ourselves to be destitute, that we may rejoice in Him, and may lift up our eyes towards Him who dwelleth in Heaven. They are not true riches; they increase still more the cupidity of those who possess them. This is not true health of the body, because we carry about with us that which faileth every way; wher-ever it turn, it faileth. In the very relief thou wilt not find perman-ence. One is tired with standing; he wishes to sit down; will he ever persist in sitting? What he adopted as a remedy against fatigue, in that he findeth failing. He is tired with watching, he is about to sleep; doth he never grow weary again because he hath slept? He is tired with fasting, he is about to take refreshment; if he exceed in refreshment, he thence becometh weak. This our weakness cannot persevere in anything. What about justice? How much justice is there among so great temptations? We are able to refrain from homicide, from adultery, from thefts, from perjuries, from frauds; but are we able to refrain from iniquitous thoughts? Are we able to refrain from the suggestions of evil desires? What then is our justice? Let us then wholly hunger, wholly thirst, after true riches, and true health, and true justice. What are true riches? That heavenly abode in Jerusalem. For who is called rich on this earth? When a rich man is praised, what is meant? He is very rich; nothing is wanting to him. This surely is the praise of an adulator; for it is not praise, when it is said, he wants nothing. Consider if he really wants nothing. If he desires nothing, he wants nothing; but if he desires more than what he hath, his riches have increased in such wise, that his wants have increased also. But in that City there will be true riches, for there will be nothing wanting to us there; we shall not be in need of anything, and there will be true health. What is true health? When 'death is swallowed up in victory, and when this corruptible hath put on incorruption; and this mortal hath put on immortality' (1 Cor. xv, 53, 54). Then will there be true health, then will there be true and perfect justice, so that we shall not only be incapable of doing, but even of thinking any thing evil. But at present, destitute, poor, in want, in heaviness we sigh, we groan, we pray, we lift up our eyes towards God; since they who are fortunate in this world, scorn us; for they are wealthy; and those who are unfortunate in this world, despise us, for they too are wealthy; and there is a justice in their hearts, but a false one. And the reason why they do not attain to a true justice is that they are filled with a false one. But do thou, that thou mayest attain to true justice, be poor and a beggar of this justice; and mark the words of the Gospel: 'Blessed are they that hunger and thirst after justice: for they shall have their fill' (Matt. v, 6).

In Ps. CXXII, 10–12.

661

If in the stewardship of temporal things we act in a manner that is just and courteous, and with the moderation and sobriety befitting their nature, such conduct merits us the reward of eternal blessings, if we possess these temporal things without being possessed by them, if they are multiplied without entangling us, and if they serve us without bringing us into bondage. . . . Let us therefore disengage ourselves from care about mutable things; let us seek the blessings that are imperishable and sure; let us soar above our earthly possessions. The bee does not the less need its wings when it has gathered an abundant store; for if it sink in the honey it dies.

Ep. XV, 2.

662

Let us be poor, and we shall then have our fill. Many who trust in the world and are proud, are Christians; they worship Christ but have not their fill, for they have been satisfied, and abound in their pride. . . . They worship Christ, they venerate Christ; but they are not satisfied by his wisdom and justice. Wherefore? Because they are not poor. For the poor, that is, the humble of heart, the more they hunger, the more they eat; and the more empty they are of the world, the more hungry they are. He who is full refuseth whatsoever thou wilt give him, because he is full. Give me one who hungereth, give me one of whom it is said, 'Blessed are they that hunger and thirst after justice, for they shall have their fill' (Matt. v, 6), and there will be the poor of whom he hath just said, 'I will satisfy her poor with Bread' (Ps. cxxxi, 15).

In Ps. CXXXI, 24.

663

God's poor one is poor in spirit, not in his purse. Sometimes a man appeareth who hath a full house, rich lands, many estates, much gold and silver; he knoweth that he must not trust in these, he humbleth himself before God, he doth good with them. Thus his heart is raised to God, so that he is aware that not only do riches themselves profit him nothing, but that they even impede his feet, save God rule and direct them. He is counted among the poor who are satisfied with bread (Ps. cxxxi, 15). Thou findest another a beggar and puffed up; he may be not puffed up because he hath nothing, yet seeking whereby he may be puffed up. God doth not heed the means a man hath, but his desire, and judgeth him according to the desire with which he regards temporal blessings, not according to the means which it is not his lot to have. . . . Let them, saith the Apostle, 'lay up in store for themselves a good foundation against the time to come, that they may lay hold on the true life' (1 Tim. vi, 19). When they have laid hold of it, then they will be rich; but since they have it not as yet, they should know that they are poor. Thus it is that God numbereth among His poor all the humble of heart who are established in that twofold commandment of love (v. Matt. xxii, 37, 39), whatever they may have in this world. And these are they whom he satisfieth with bread.

In Ps. CXXXI, 26.

664

There are some who are more ready to give all their goods to the poor than themselves to become the poor of God. . . . For of their own they think they have, and they glory as if they had not received it (cf. 1 Cor. iv, 7), being rich to themselves, not poor to God; abounding to themselves, not needing God.

In Ps. CXXI, 3.

665

I see that thou sayest this, that thou hast first given something to God, that He might give the rest to thee. Thou hast indeed given to Him thy faith and thy prayer. . . . Hast thou then first given to God, and given that which God did not give thee? Hast thou found wherewith to give, O beggar man? Whence hadst thou it? Hadst thou then wherewith to give anything? 'What hast thou that thou hast not received?' (1 Cor. iv, 17). Therefore it is God's that thou givest to God; of that which He hath given He receiveth from thee. For thy beggary, had He not first given, would have remained most unprofitable.

Serm. (de Script. N.T.) CLXVIII, v, 5.

666

A beggar is he who ascribeth nothing to himself, who hopeth all from God's mercy. Before the Lord's gate he crieth every day, knocking, that it may be opened unto him, naked and trembling, that he may be clothed, casting down his eyes to the ground, beating his breast. This beggar, this poor man, this humble man, God hath greatly helped, . . . because 'he will understand the mercies of the Lord' (Ps. cvi, 43); not his own deserts, not his own strength, not his own power, but 'the mercies of the Lord,' Who when he was straying and in want led him back to the path, and fed him; Who, when he was struggling against the difficulties of his sins, and was fettered by the chains of habit, released and freed him; Who, when he loathed the word of God, and was almost dying with a kind of weariness, restored him by sending him the medicine of His word; Who, when he was in danger among the perils of storm and shipwreck, stilled the sea and brought him into port.

In Ps. CVI, 14, 15.

667

If thou dost think to be rich in that kingdom, thou dost but change thy desire, not cut it off. And yet thou wilt be rich, and in no other place but there wilt thou be rich. For here thy want gathers together a multitude of things. Why have the rich much? Because they want much. A greater want heaps together as it were greater means. Then want itself will die. Then thou shalt be truly rich, when thou shall be in want of nothing. For thou art not rich, and an angel, who has not horses and carriages and servants, poor. Why is this? Because he does not want any of these; because in proportion to his greater strength, his want is the less. . . . Figure not to thyself banquets of this earth there. For the banquets of this earth are daily medicaments; they are necessary to a kind of sickness we have, wherewith we are born. . . . Immortality will be health. For this present is but one long sickness. Because thou dost support thy disease by daily medicaments, thou fanciest thyself in health. Take away the medicaments and then see what thou canst do. . . . For from the moment we are born we must needs be dying. . . . Where then is there true health except where there is true immortality? But if it be true immortality—no corruption, no wasting—what need will there be there of nourishment? Therefore when you hear it said, 'They shall sit down with Abraham and Isaac and Jacob' (Matt. viii, 11), get not thy body but thy mind in order.

There thou shalt be filled, and the interior man have its proper food. . . . 'Blessed are they that hunger and thirst after justice for they shall have their fill' (Matt. v, 6). And they shall truly have their fill, so that they shall hunger no more.

Serm. (de Script. N.T.) LXXVII, ix, 13; x, 14.

668

Whosoever wisheth to be the heir of this covenant commanded for ever (Ps. cx, 9), deceive not thyself, think not of a land flowing with milk and honey, nor of pleasant farms, nor of gardens abounding in fruit and shade, plan not how to obtain things of the kind which the eye of avarice is wont to lust after. For since 'the desire of money is the root of all evils' (1 Tim. vi, 10), it must be cut off to be consumed here, not put off, that it may be satisfied there. First escape punishment, avoid hell; before thou longest for a God who promiseth, beware of One who threateneth. For 'holy and terrible is His name' (Ps. cx, 9). But instead of all the delights of this world, which thou hast either experienced, or mayest contrive the means of enhancing and multiplying, long for wisdom, the mother of immortal delights; but 'the fear of the Lord is the beginning of wisdom' (*ibid* 10.). It will delight, and beyond all doubt will ineffably delight, with the chaste and eternal embraces of truth; but thy debts must first be remitted thee, before rewards may be asked for.

In Ps. CX, 8, 9.

669

Let each one . . . look within himself, weigh himself, prove himself in all his actions, in all his good works which he doeth with charity, not looking for temporal recompense but for the promise of God, the face of God. For whatever God promiseth thee availeth nothing without God himself. Most truly God would not satisfy me unless he promised me Himself, the very God. What is the whole earth? What is the whole sea? What is the whole sky? What are all the stars? What the sun? What the moon? What the hosts of Angels? It is for the Creator of them all I hunger, for Him I thirst. To Him I say, 'For with Thee is the fountain of life' (Ps. xxxv, 10), and He saith to me, 'I am the living bread which came down from heaven'

(John vi, 41). Let my pilgrimage hunger and thirst that my presence may be made full. The world smiles with its multitude of objects, beautiful, strong, diversified; but He who made them is more beautiful; stronger and brighter is He who made them; sweeter is He who made them. 'I shall be satisfied when Thy glory shall appear' (Ps. xvi, 15).

Serm. (de Script. N.T.) CLVIII, vii, 7.

670

He sufficeth thee; apart from Him nothing sufficeth thee. . . . When at the end will that come to pass of which the Apostle says, 'That God may be all in all' (1 Cor. xv, 28), so that He himself is to us whatever without Him we here desire, and by the desire for which we too often sin against Him? He will take the place of all things for us, when God is all in all. Thou sinnest against God that thou mayest eat, thou sinnest against God that thou mayest be clothed, thou sinnest against God that thou mayest live, thou sinnest against God that thou mayest receive honour. . . . Dost thou sin against God for food? God will be eternal food to thee. Dost thou sin against God for raiment? God is to clothe thee with immortality. Dost thou sin against God for honours? God will be thine honour. Dost thou sin against God out of love for this temporal life? God will be to thee eternal life.

Serm. CCCXXXIV, 3.

671

God is over all men, and yet somehow or other one does not easily dare to say, My God, except he believes in Him and loves Him; then he says, My God. Thou hast made thine own Him whose thou art; and this He himself loves. Straightway, with all the sweetness of thy affection, and with sure and utterly trustful love, say, My God. Thou sayest it in all confidence, thou sayest it truly. But because He is thine, thou hast not brought it to pass that He is not thy neighbour's also. For thou dost not say, My God, as thou wouldst say, my horse. For the horse is thine, it is not another's horse. God is thine, but He is also his who has said, My God, as thou sayest it. All individually say, My God; He belongs to all, and offers Himself to be enjoyed by all in common, undiminished in all collectively, undiminished in all singly. . . . The rich man Zaccheus gave away the half of his goods that he might attain to God (Luke xix, 8); that he might so attain, Peter left his nets and ship (Matt. iv, 20); that she might attain, the poor widow gave her two mites (Luke xxi, 2 *seq*.); that a still poorer person might attain he held out a cup of cold water (Matt. x, 42); and one utterly poor and needy proffered only good will, that he might attain (Luke xv, 14). These gave diverse things, but they all attained to Him, because they did not love diverse things. . . . Some in honour, others without honour, some with money, others without money, some fair of body, others less fair, some tired with age, others in the vigour of youth, some of them boys, others grown men, others women—God is equally present to all. . . . O happy we, with such a possession, such a Possessor! . . . Behold, we are His possession. . . . Behold, He is our possession; but yet with what a distinction. You are men; I am the Lord thy God, saith the Lord our God.

Serm. XLVII, xvi, 30.

672

Thou shalt both be a possession, and shalt possess. Thou shalt be God's possession, and God shall be thy possession; thou shalt be His possession to be cultivated by Him; He shall be Thy possession for thee to worship Him. . . . God cultivateth thee; that thou mayest be fruitful; and thou worshippest God, that thou mayest be fruitful. It is good for thee that God cultivateth thee; it is good for thee that thou worshippest God. If God the cultivator depart from man, man is abandoned; if man the worshipper depart from God, it is the man himself who is abandoned. God neither increaseth by thy approach to Him, nor decreaseth by thy withdrawal. He then will be our possession, that He may find us; we shall be His possession, that He may rule us.

In Ps. CXLV, 11.

673

To procure any great and precious thing, thou wouldst get ready gold, or silver, or money, or the increase of cattle or fruits which might be produced in thy possessions, so as to buy this I know not how great and excellent thing, whereby to live happily on this earth. Buy [eternal life] too, if thou wilt. Do not look for what thou hast, but for what thou art. The price of this thing is thyself. Give thyself and then thou shalt have it. Why art thou troubled? Why disquieted? Art thou going to seek for thine own self or to buy thyself? Behold, give thyself as thou art, such as thou art, to that thing, and thou shalt have it. 'But I am wicked,' thou wilt say, 'and perhaps it will not accept me.' By giving thyself to it thou wilt be good. The giving of thyself to this faith and promise, that is to be good.

Serm. (de Script. N.T.) CXXVII, iii, 3.

674

Pay therefore to God that which you have vowed to Him (cf. Ps. lxxv, 12), for this is yourselves, and you will be paying yourselves to Him to whom you owe your being. . . . That which you pay to Him will not be thereby diminished but rather conserved and increased. For in collecting what is due to Him He acts in kindness and not from any need; nor does He increase by that which is paid Him, but He makes those who pay to Him to increase in Him. That which is not paid to Him is therefore lost, but what is paid to Him is an added good to him who pays. Indeed in Him to whom the debt is paid the debtor himself finds his surety and preservation. That which is paid and he who pays use one and the same thing, for the debt and the debtor were one. For Man owes his very being to God, and to Him from whom he has received his being he must pay himself if he would be happy.

Ep. CXXVII, 6.

675

What thou holdest, passes away from thee, what thou losest, thou findest in thee.

Serm. CCCXXXI, i, 1.

III. MAN'S LOWLINESS TO GOD'S EXALTEDNESS

676

It is good to have the heart lifted up, yet not unto one's self, for that is pride, but unto the Lord, for that is obedience, and

obedience can only be a property of the humble. There is there
fore something in humility which strange to say lifts up the
heart, and something in pride which casts it down. This seems
curiously contrary that pride should cast down and humility
lift up. But godly humility subjects one to his superior. And
there is nothing superior to God; and therefore humility in
making one God's subject exalts him. But pride, which is a
vice, refuses subjection and falls away from Him who is above
all, and therefore will be inferior. . . . Its very elevation is its
fall. Wherefore in the city of God and to those of the city of
God who are pilgrims in this world, it is humility which is
chiefly commended, and by its King who is Christ the chief
subject of His preaching. . . . And this assuredly is the great
difference which distinguishes the two cities, that of the godly
and of the ungodly, with the angels pertaining to each, that in
one the love of God holds sway, in the other love of self.

De civ. Dei XIV, 13.

677

God could not more perfectly have shewn how great is the
goodness of obedience than when he prohibited that object
which was not evil. There obedience alone beareth the palm,
there disobedience alone doth find punishment. It is a good
thing, I will that thou teachest it not. . . . It is a good thing, but
obedience is better. Did He that withheld this from thee with-
hold other things? Is not Paradise full of fruitful trees? What
is wanting to thee? This thing I will not have thee touch, of
this I will not have thee taste. It is a good thing, but obedience
is better. Moreover, when thou shalt have touched it, will
that thing be an evil thing so that thou shalt die? No,
disobedience hath made thee subject to death, because thou
hast touched forbidden things.

In Ps. LXX, *Serm.* ii, 7.

678

Acknowledge Him that is above thee, that those may acknowledge thee that are beneath thee. . . . But if thou acknowledge
not Him that is above thee . . . thou becomest subject to
thine inferior.

In Epist. Joannis ad Parthos, Tr. viii, 7.

679

If thou settest thy hope in another man, thou art unorderedly humble; if thou settest thy hope in thyself, thou art dangerously proud . . . the unorderedly humble is not raised up, the dangerously proud is cast down.

Serm. XIII, ii, 2.

680

Found not thy hopes on thyself but on thy God. For if thou restest thy hopes on thyself, thy soul is troubled within thyself, for it has not yet found anything about thee that should make it secure. Since then my soul is troubled within myself, what remains for her but humility, but that the soul should not presume on her own merits? What remains but that she should make herself the very meanest of all things, that she should humble herself that she may deserve to be exalted (cf. Luke xiv, 11; xviii, 14), that she give herself credit for nothing, so that what is good for her may be given to her by Him?

In Ps. XLI, 12.

681

Cast thy care upon the Lord, and hope in Him, and He shall support thee (cf. Ps. liv, 23). What canst thou effect for thyself by taking care? What canst thou provide for thyself? Let him who made thee care for thee. He who cared for thee before thou wert, how shall He fail to have a care for thee now that thou art what He would have thee be? . . . By giving He comforteth thee, that thou mayest endure unto the end; by taking away He chastens thee, that thou perish not. The Lord careth for thee, be thou untroubled. He beareth thee who created thee. Do not fall out of the hands of thy Maker; thou wilt be broken if thou fallest out of thy Maker's hands. But it is good will that enables thee to continue in the hand of thy Maker. Say, 'My God hath so willed it; He will sustain me; He will hold me fast.' Cast thyself upon Him; think not that He is an empty space, so that thou wouldest fall headlong. Think not so in thyself. He hath said, 'I fill heaven and earth' (Jer. xxiii, 24). In no place is He wanting

to thee. Be not thou wanting to Him, be not wanting to thyself.
The Lord careth for thee.

In Ps. XXXIX, 27.

682

Believe in God steadfastly, and commit thyself wholly to Him
as much as thou canst. Do not desire to be as it were thine
own and subject only to thyself, but declare thyself to be the
servant of that most merciful and beneficial Lord. For thus He
will not desist from raising thee to Himself, and will suffer nothing
to befall thee save what shall profit thee, even though thou
know it not.

Solil. I, xv, 30.

683

What, art thou committing thyself to thine own self? Better
is He able to preserve thee, Who was able, before thou wert,
to create thee. . . . . He saith to thee, Seek thou My gifts,
forget thine own merits, for if I were to seek for thy merits,
thou wouldst not come to my gifts.

Serm. (de Script. N.T.) CLXXIV, ii, 2.

684

Keep yourselves, therefore, but not by yourselves, for God who
keepeth you is your defence, and He neither slumbers nor sleeps
(Ps. cxx). Once hath He slept for us; but He hath risen again, He
will never again sleep. Let no man place trust in himself. We
are ascending from the valley of lamentation, let us not tarry
in the way. There are stages in the road still to go; we ought
not to dawdle indolently; we ought not to fall through pride.
Let us say unto God, 'Suffer not our feet to be moved.' He
will not slumber that keepeth us (*id.*, 3). By God's gift it is
in our power to make Him, who neither slumbers nor sleeps,
our keeper.

In Ps. CXX, 14.

685

We are little ones, therefore may God protect us under the
shadow of His wings. But what when we shall have become

373

larger? A good thing it is for us that even then He should protect us, so that under Him who is the greater we always be chickens. For He is always the greater, however much we may have grown. Let no one say, let Him protect me while I am a little one, as if at some time he would attain to such magnitude as should be self-sufficient. Without the protection of God thou art nought. Let us desire ever to be protected by Him. Then we shall always have the power to be great in Him, though under Him we be very little.

In Ps. LXII, 16.

686

Whoever thinketh that he is now able to fulfil justice, when he shall have lived well and innocently according to the credibility of human estimation, he hath stopped by the way; he desires no better, because he thinks that he has accomplished it; and more than all, attributing this to himself, he will be proud. But a humble sinner is better than a proud just man.

Serm. (de Script. N.T.) CLXX, vii, 7.

687

Remain thou unarmed, having no help of thine own; and the more weak thou art, having no weapons of thine own, the more He sustaineth thee, of Whom it is written: 'the God of Jacob is our protector' (Ps. xlv, 8). For thou didst prevail as it were through thyself; thou art troubled in thyself. . . . Not thou but I am God. I created, I re create; I formed, I reform; I made, I remake. If thou couldst not make thyself, how canst thou remake thyself?

In Ps. XLV, 13, 14.

688

Away with thee, away with thee, I say, from thyself. Thou dost hinder thyself. If thou buildest thine own self, thou dost build a ruin. 'Unless the Lord build the house, they labour in vain that build it.' (Ps. cxxvi, 1.)

Serm. (de Script. N.T.) CLXIX, ix, 11.

689

Let the proud man lift himself as much he will; certainly God dwelleth on high; God is in heaven. Dost thou wish that he come nigh to thee? Humble thyself. For the more thou liftest thyself up, the higher will He be above thee.

In Ps. CXXXVII, 11.

690

The greatest of all men was sent, a man who was to bear witness to Him who was greater than man. For when he, than whom none greater had risen among them that are born of women (Matt. xi, 11), says, 'I am not the Christ,' and humbles himself before Christ, we must understand something that is more than man. . . . For if thou seekest John as the greatest of all men, Christ is more than man. . . . Therefore if we have rightly understood the mystery, my brethren, John is man, Christ is God, the man is humbled, and God is exalted. . . . Let us grow less in man, let us grow greater in God. Let us be humbled in ourselves, that we may be exalted in Him.

Serm. CCLXXXIX, 5.

691

'I am the voice of one crying in the wilderness' (John i, 23). . . . Thou hast John as the voice. As what hast thou Christ, if not as the Word? The voice is sent out in advance that the Word may afterwards be understood. . . . 'In the beginning was the Word. . . . All things were made by Him.' If all things, then John also. Is it to be wondered at that the Word mades a voice for itself? . . . The word, if it have no means of expression, is not called a word. Now the voice, even though it but sound, makes an irrational noise, such as the sound of one merely crying out, not speaking, can still be called a voice; it cannot be called a word. . . . The word even without a voice can effect much, the voice without the word is an empty thing. . . . In me, in the apex of my heart, in the secret chamber of my mind, the word precedes my voice. The voice has not yet sounded in my ear, but the word is already in my heart. But that that which I have conceived in my heart may

go forth to thee, it requires the ministry of the voice. . . .
In me there is first the word and afterwards the voice. But to
thee, so that thou mayest understand, the voice comes first
to thy ear, in order that the word may find its way into thy
mind. For thou canst not know what had been in me before
thou heard the voice, except by it being in thee after hearing
the voice. Therefore if the voice is John, the Word Christ;
before John, was Christ with God; after John was Christ with
us. Voices die away but the word increases. For 'He must
increase, but I must decrease' (*id.* iii, 30). The Word does
not indeed increase of itself, nor does it decrease in itself. In
us, however, the Word is said to increase as by progressing
to Him we increase; just as the light increases in our eyes when,
owing to our sight getting better, it is better seen, for with
feeble sight it certainly is less well seen. Hence the ministry
of the voice diminishes as the mind makes progress towards
the Word. Thus Christ must increase, but John diminish.
. . . John was diminished, his head cut off. Christ was
lifted up, increased, so to speak, on the cross.

Serm. CCLXXXVIII, 2–5.

692

(John the Baptist) had no wish to increase by the words
of men, seeing that he had comprehended the Word of God.

Serm. (*de Script. N.T.*) LXVI, 1.

693

Admire John as much as thou canst. That thou shouldst
admire profits Christ. Profits Christ, I say, not because thou
art giving anything to Christ, but that thou progressest in
Christ.

Serm. CLXCL, 1.

694

'Learn of me, because I am meek and humble of heart'
(Matt. xi, 29). Wherefore dost thou doubt to bear this burden?
Is this burden, humility and piety, grievous? Is this burden,
faith, hope, charity, grievous? For these make a man humble,
these make him meek. And see how thou wilt not be burdened

if thou wilt hearken unto Him. 'For my yoke is gentle (*lenis*: vlg. *suavis*) and my burden light' (Matt xi, 30). What is 'is light'? What if it have a weight, only a lesser one? Avarice more, justice less? I would not have thee understand it so. This burden is not the weight of one laden, but the wings of one ready to fly. For birds too have the burden of their wings. And what do we say? They bear them and are borne. They bear them on the ground, they are borne by them in the air. If thou shouldst wish to show mercy to a bird, in the summer especially, and say, 'The wings burden this wretched little bird,' and took off this burden, the bird thou didst wish to help will remain on the ground. Bear then the wings of peace, receive the wings of charity.

Serm. (de Script. N.T.) CLXIV, v, 7.

695

For no one ever succeeds in raising another to the height on which he himself stands, unless he stoop somewhat towards the level where that other is.

Ep. XI, 4.

696

We are making our way to great things; let us receive the little things, and we shall be great. Wouldst thou comprehend the majesty of God? Comprehend first the humility of God. Condescend to be humble for thine own sake, seeing that God condescended to be humble for thy very sake; for it was not for His own. . . . When thou hast comprehended His humility, thou risest with him; not as though He should rise himself; . . . but thou rather, that He may be more and more comprehended by thee. At first thou didst understand falteringly and hesitatingly; afterwards thou wilt understand more surely and clearly. He doth not increase, but thou dost progress, and He seemeth as it were to rise with thee.

Serm. (de Script. N.T.) CXVII, x, 17.

697

Let us ascend with Him, and lift up our hearts. . . . For we ought to lift up our hearts, but to the Lord. For a heart lifted up but not to the Lord, is called pride; a heart however that is lifted up to the Lord is called a taking of refuge, thou fallest if thou have lifted up thyself, thou remainest if He has lifted thee up.

Serm. CCLXI, i, 1.

698

Nor doth He stand in need of His own works, as if He had a place in them where to abide; but He endureth in His own eternity, wherein He abideth and hath done whatsoever he listed, both in heaven and earth. For they did not support Him as a condition of their being created by Him; since, unless they had been created, they could not have supported Him. Therefore in whatsoever thing He dwelleth, He contains it as, so to speak, in need of Himself; He is not contained by it as if He needed it.

In Ps. CXIII alterum. Serm. i, 14.

699

Whosoever then so beareth God as to be a temple of God, let him not think that God is so borne of him, that he may make God afraid if he withdrew himself. Woe to him if God withdrew Himself, for it is he who would fall, since God abideth in Himself for ever. The houses in which we live, themselves contain us; those in which God dwelleth are contained by Him Himself.

In Ps. CXXII, 4.

700

Let us continue in Him who continueth in us. As for us, if we continue not in Him, we fall; but He, if He continue not in us, hath not on that account lost an habitation. For He, who never leaveth Himself, is able to continue in Himself. But for man, who hath lost himself, God forbid that he should continue in himself. So then we continue in Him through indigence, but He in us through mercy.

Serm. (*de Script. N.T.*) CXXXIV, i, 1.

701

We also are made partakers of this eternal life, and become in our own measure, immortal. But the eternal life itself, of which we are made partakers is one thing; we ourselves who by partaking of it shall live eternally, are another.

De Trin. I, vi, 10.

702

However much I may draw near, however much I may ascend, however much I leap over, I shall be under God, not against God. Safely therefore I mount above other things when He that is above all things doth hold me under Him.

In Ps. LXI, 2.

703

'In God I will praise my words' (Ps. lv, 5). . . . . For thou wilt have thy words either false, and therefore thine own, because false; or if thy words shall be true and thou shalt deem thyself not to have them from God, but of thyself to be speaking, they will be true, but thou wilt be false. But if thou shalt have known that thou canst say nothing true in the wisdom of God, in the faith of the Truth, save that which thou hast received from Him, of Whom it is said: 'For what hast thou that thou hast not received?' (1 Cor. iv, 7) then in God thou art praising thy words, in order that in God thou mayest be praised by the words of God. For if whatever is in thee that is of God is honoured by thee, thou also having been made by God will be honoured in God. But if whatsoever is in thee that is of God is honoured by thee as thine own and not of God, like as that people was put afar off from holy men, so too wilt thou be put afar off from the Holy One. Therefore 'in God I will praise my words.' If 'in God,' wherefore 'my?' Both in God and mine. In God, because they are from Him; mine, because I have received them. He Himself Who hath given, willed them to be mine, by loving Him of Whom they are; and they have been made mine because they are come to me from Him. . . . By asking of Him thou wilt not be empty; by confessing it to be thine thou wilt not be ungrateful. For if thou say it is not

thine, thou hast not received it. Again, if thou say 'thine' as
if that which thou callest thine were from thyself, thou
losest what thou hast received, because thou art ungrateful
to Him from Whom thou hast received. 'In God, therefore,
'I will praise my words,' because He is there Himself as the
fountain of true words. 'Mine,' because, thirsting, I have drawn
near and drunk.

In Ps. LV, 7.

704

Therefore, in doing such [wonderful] things, the Lord Jesus
Christ Himself, in order to teach the greater things to those
who marvelled at them, and to turn those who were intent
on and in doubt about unusual temporal things to eternal
and interior things, says, 'Come to me, all you that labour and
are burdened: and I will refresh you,' or 'Take up my yoke
upon you.' And He does not say, Learn of me because I bring
to life men who have been dead four days, but He says, 'Learn
of me, because I am meek, and humble of heart.' For the most
solid humility is more powerful and safer than the most puffed-
up bearing. Accordingly He goes on to say, 'And you shall
find rest for your souls' (Matt. xi, 28 *sq.*). For, 'Charity is not
puffed up' (1 Cor. xiii, 4); and 'God is charity' (1 John iv, 8);
and, 'the faithful in love shall rest in him' (Wis. iii, 9), called
back from the crashing din which is without to silent joys.
Behold, 'God is charity.' Why do we go forth and run to the
heights of the heavens and to the deepest recesses of the earth
in search of Him Who is within us, if we wish to be with Him?

De Trin. VIII, vii, 11.

705

What then? When I shall see what I could not see, and
receive what I could not receive, shall I then be untroubled,
shall I then be perfect? No, not as long as you live here. Our
very perfection is humility. You have heard the conclusion
of the reading from the Apostle, if it hath been retained in
your memory; how he who received a buffet, lest he should be
exalted by the revelations (and how great they were!) on account
of the very magnitude of those revelations, because he might
have been exalted, if he had not received the angel of Satan,

and yet, what doth he to whom so great revelations were made, say? 'Brethren, I do not count myself to have apprehended.' Paul saith, 'Brethren, I do not count myself to have apprehended' (Phil. iii, 13). . . . Who dareth to say that he apprehendeth? . . . I so run, he saith, that I may apprehend. Paul is still on the path, and dost thou think thyself at thy home? 'But one thing I do,' he saith, 'forgetting the things that are behind and stretching forth myself to those that are before, I press towards the mark, to the prize of the supernal vocation of God in Christ Jesus' (*id.* 13 *sq.*). I hear the voice of God from above, and I run that I may apprehend. For He hath not left me to abide in the path, since He ceaseth not to address me. God therefore, my brethren, ceaseth not to address us. For if He cease, what are we doing? . . . 'Let us therefore, as many as are perfect, be thus minded' (*id.*, 15). I speak not, he saith, to the imperfect, unto whom as yet I cannot speak wisdom, who still must be nourished with milk, and are not fed with strong meat. They seem already to be perfect, because they understand the equality of the Word with the Father; still as yet they see not, as we must see, face to face, but in part only, in a dark manner (1 Cor. xiii, 12). Let them run therefore, for when our path is ended, we then return to our home.

In Ps. CXXX, 14.

706

This then is the first grace of God's gift, to bring us to the confession of our infirmity, that whatever good we can do, whatever ability we have, we may be that in Him; that 'he that glorieth may glory in the Lord' (1 Cor. i, 31).

In Ps. XXXVIII, 18.

707

This then is the sum of great knowledge for a man to know that by himself he is nothing, and that whatever he is, he is from God and is for God. . . . It is however not enough that thou acknowledge that which in thee is good to be from God, unless also on that account thou exalt not thyself above him that hath not yet, who perchance will outstrip thee when he shall have received.

In Ps. LXX, *Serm.* I, l, 4.

708

Though Thou callest me friend, I confess myself a servant.

In Ps. CXLII, 6.

709

For that we shall be just from being unjust, whole from being frail, alive from being dead, immortal from being mortal, happy from being wretched, is of His mercy.

In Ps. CXXXV, 1.

710

Humility raised to the heights, drunkenness sober! . . . 'We love' . . . we men, God; mortals, the Immortal; sinners, the Just One; fragile, the Immovable; the thing fashioned, the Artificer; . . . 'because He hath first loved us' (1 John iv, 10). . . . He Whom we have loved has given Himself, has given whence we might love. . . . Let us love God through God (cf. Rom. v. 5).

Serm. XXXIV, i, 1; ii, 2.

IV. MAN-BEGGAR TO GOD-GOODNESS

711

Seek thy own good, O soul, for one thing is good to one creature, another to another; and all creatures have a certain good of their own, to make up their completeness and the perfection of their nature. There is a difference in what is essential to each imperfect thing, in order that it may be made perfect. Seek thy own good. . . . The supreme good is thy good. . . . What, brethren, is good for cattle, save to fill the belly, to avoid want, to sleep, to have their desires, to live, to be in health, to propagate? . . . Dost thou seek such good as this? God giveth this also; but do not make it the sole object of thy search. . . . Set thy hope high, to the good of all goods. He will be thy good, by Whom thou in thy kind hast been made good, and by Whom all things in their kind were made good.

In Ps. CII, 8.

712

He gave us a nature, that we might be; He gave us a soul, that we might live; He gave us a mind that we might understand; He gave us foods, that we might sustain mortal life; He gave us light from the sky, waters from the earth. But all these things are gifts common to the good and the wicked. If he has given all these things also to the wicked, does He reserve nothing special for the good? Assuredly He does. And what is it that He reserves for the good? 'Eye hath not seen, nor ear heard: neither hath it risen up into the heart of man' (I Cor. ii, 9). Now that which rises up into the heart of man was below the heart of man, and therefore it rises up into the heart, since above it is the heart to which it is rising. The heart rises to that which He reserves for the good. Not that which rises up into thy heart, but that to which thy heart rises: this is what God reserves for thee. . . . Look what it is that God reserves for the good alone, whom nevertheless He Himself has made good. Look what it is. Our reward is concisely defined through the Prophet: 'I will be their God: and they shall be my people' (Lev. xxvi, 12; 2 Cor. vi, 16). . . . For a reward He promises Himself to us. . . . He gives Himself to us, and it is enough for us. May He give Himself to us and satisfy us! (cf. John. xiv, 8).

Serm. CCCXXXI, iv, 3.

713

He Who knows how to give good gifts to His children urges us to ask and seek and knock (cf. Luke xi, 9). . . . Why this should be done by Him Who 'knoweth what is needful for us before we ask Him' (Matt. vi, 8), might perplex our minds, if we did not understand that the Lord our God requires us to ask not that thereby our wish may be made known to Him for to Him it cannot be unknown, but in order that by prayer there may be exercised in us that desire by which we may receive what He prepares to bestow. For that gift is very great, but we are small and straitened in our capacity of receiving. Wherefore it is said to us: 'Be you also enlarged. Bear not the yoke with unbelievers' (2 Cor. vi, 13 *sq.*). For in proportion to the simplicity of our faith, the firmness of our hope, and the ardour of our desire, shall we more largely receive of that which is immensely great, 'that eye hath not seen,' for it is not colour, 'nor ear heard,' for it is not sound, 'neither hath it entered into the heart of man,' for the heart of man must ascend to it (1 Cor. ii, 9).

When we cherish uninterrupted desire in the exercise of faith, hope and charity, we pray continually. But at certain stated hours and seasons we also use words in prayer to God, that by these signs of things we may admonish ourselves, and may acquaint ourselves with the measure of progress which we have made in this desire, and may the more warmly excite ourselves to obtain an increase of its strength. For the effect following upon prayer will be excellent in proportion to the fervour of the desire which precedes its utterance. And therefore what else is intended by the words of the Apostle: 'Pray without ceasing' (1 Thess. v, 17) than to desire 'without ceasing, from Him Who alone can give it, a happy life, which no life can be but that which is eternal?' This therefore let us desire continually from the Lord our God, and thus let us pray continually. But at certain hours we recall our minds from other cares and business, in which desire itself somehow is cooled down, to the business of prayer, admonishing ourselves by the words of our prayer to fix attention upon that which we desire, lest what had begun to lose heat become altogether cold, and be finally extinguished, if the flame be not more frequently fanned. Whence, also, when the same Apostle says, 'Let your petitions be made known to God' (Phil. iv, 6), this is not to be understood as if thereby they become known to God, Who certainly knew them before they were uttered, but in this sense, that they are to be made known to ourselves in the presence of God by patient waiting upon Him, not ostentatiously in the presence of men. . . .

Far be it from us either to use 'much speaking' in prayer (cf. Matt. vi, 7), or to refrain from much prayer, if fervent attention of the soul continue. To use much speaking in prayer is to employ a superfluity of words in asking a necessary thing; but to pray much is to have the heart throbbing with continued pious emotion towards Him to whom we pray. For in most cases prayer consists more in groaning than in speaking, in tears rather than in an outpouring of words. But He setteth our tears in His sight, and our groaning is not hid from Him Who made all things by the Word, and does not need human words.

Ep. CXXX, viii, 16 – x, 20.

714

Seeing that our Father knoweth already what is needful for us, why do we ask? Why seek? Why knock? Why weary ourselves in asking, and seeking, and knocking, to instruct Him Who knoweth already? . . .Other hope have we none amid the manifold ills of this present world, than to knock in prayer, to believe, and to maintain the belief firm in the heart that thy Father only doth not give thee what He knoweth is not expedient for thee. For thou knowest what thou dost desire; He knoweth what is good for thee. Imagine thyself under a physician, and in weak health, as is the very truth; for all this life of ours is an infirmity, and a long life is nothing but a prolonged infirmity. Imagine thyself, then, to be sick and under a physician's care. Thou hast a desire to ask thy physician leave to drink a draught of fresh wine. Thou art not prohibited from asking, for it may chance to do thee no harm, and may even do thee good to receive it. Do not then hesitate to ask; ask, do not hesitate, but if thou dost not receive it, be not cast down. If this be the case when under the care of a man, a physician of the body, how much more when in the hands of God, who is the Physician, the Creator, and the Restorer both of thy body and thy soul.

Serm. (*de Script. N.T.*) LXXX, 2.

715

For such as thy son who knows not the ways of men in regard to thee, such in regard to the Lord art thou thyself, who knowest not the ways of God. Lo, thy son cries a whole day before thee, that thou give him a knife, or a sword. Thou dost refuse to give it him, thou dost not give it, thou disregardest his tears, lest thou shouldst have to bewail his death. Let him cry, dash himself about, throw himself upon the ground, that thou mayest set him on horseback; thou dost not do it for he cannot manage a horse; he may throw him and kill him. For him to whom thou art refusing a part thou art reserving the whole. But, that he may grow up and possess the whole in safety, thou givest not him that little part which is full of peril to him.

Serm. (de Script. N.T.) LXXX, 7.

716

For a sick man too asketh many things of the physician; but the physician giveth them not. His concern is not with the patient's desires but with his cure. Make God therefore thy Physician. Seek health of Him, and He Himself will be thy health. Seek not as if thou wouldst find salvation from any other source, but so that He Himself may be salvation unto thee; lest thou shouldst again love any salvation save Him. . . . What is it to thee what He saith to thee, if He do but give Himself to thee? Dost thou wish that He give Himself to thee? What if He wills that thou shouldst not have what thou desirest, in order that He may give Himself to thee? He removes impediments, that He may enter into thee.

In Ps. LXXXV, 9.

717

God, who giveth to thee, giveth thee nothing better than Himself. O thou greedy one, what else wast thou seeking for? Or if thou seek for aught else, what will suffice thee whom God doth not suffice?

Serm. (de Script. N.T.) CV, iii, 4.

718

'I sought the Lord, and He heard me' (Ps. xxxiii, 5). . . . He did not say, I sought gold from the Lord, and He heard me; I sought from the Lord long life, and He heard me; I sought from the Lord this or that, and He heard me. It is one thing to seek anything from the Lord, another to seek the Lord Himself. 'I sought,' saith he, 'the Lord, and He heard me.' . . . Therefore seek not from the Lord anything without, but seek the Lord Himself, and He will hear thee, and while thou yet speakest, He will say, Behold, I am here (cf. Is. lxv, 24). What is, 'Behold, I am here?' Behold, I am present: what wouldest thou? What seekest thou of Me? Whatever I should give thee is of less value than I. Take thou Myself; enjoy Me; embrace Me. This thou canst not yet do wholly. Touch Me by faith, and thou shalt cleave to Me (this God saith to thee), and thy other burdens will I take from off thee, when I have changed thy mortality to immortality (1 Cor. xv, 54), that thou mayest be equal to My angels (cf. Matt. xxii, 30) and ever see My face, and mayest rejoice; and 'thy joy no man shall take from thee' (John xvi, 22); because thou didst seek the Lord, and He heard thee, and delivered thee out of all thy troubles.

In Ps. 33, *Serm.* II, 9.

719

Do not think God to be in places. As thou hast been, so is He with thee, . . . good if thou hast been good, and if thou hast been evil, He will seem evil to thee. He will be a succourer if thou hast been good, an avenger if thou hast been evil. There in thy secret place thou hast a Judge. Wishing to do something evil thou retirest into thy house where no enemy may see thee; from those places in thy house which are open and visible to men thou withdrawest into a chamber; thou fearest even in thy chamber some witness from some other quarter; thou retirest into thy heart, there thou dost meditate. God is more inward than thy heart. Whithersoever therefore thou hast fled, there He is. Whither shalt thou flee from thyself? Wilt not thou follow thyself whithersoever thou fleest? But since there is One more inward even than thyself, there is no place whither thou mayest flee from an angered God save to a reconciled God. There is no place of any kind to which thou mayest flee. Wilt thou flee from Him? Flee to Him.

In Ps. LXXIV, 9.

720

Be Thou a house of refuge unto me, a protecting God, a house of refuge. For sometimes I am in peril and would fly. Whither do I fly? . . . Whithersoever I go I accompany myself. . . . Enter into thy house, rest on thy bed, enter the inner chambers;

thou canst have no place within, whither thou mayest fly from thy conscience, if thy sins torment thee. . . . Thou shalt be to me a house of refuge, to Thee do I fly. For whither shall I fly from Thee? . . . Whithersoever I go, there I find Thee. And if thou art angry, I find Thee an avenger; if reconciled a helper. Nothing then remains for me but to fly unto Thee, not from Thee. If thou art a servant and wouldest escape a human master thou fleest to plains where thy master is not. To escape God flee to the Lord.

In Ps. **XXX,** *En.* **II,** *Serm.* **I, 8.**

721

He whom we desire to receive Himself causeth us to ask; He whom we wish to find causeth us to seek; He to whom we strive to attain causeth us to knock. . . . And when He is received, He brings it about that He is besought by asking. by seeking, by knocking, to be more fully received.

In Ps. **CXVIII,** *Serm.* **XIV, 2.**

722

Great is the secrecy of a judge; . . . great is the fear of those whose cause is before him. What he is thinking, and what he is writing, is not known. And he is a man, and those on whom he is passing judgment are certainly men. But our judge is our God, 'and we are the people of His pasture and the sheep of His hand' (Ps. xciv, 7). And since He is the Creator, we the creature; He immortal, we mortal; He invisible, we visible; He did not will that in this life we should remain ignorant of the fact that at the last day He would pronounce the final sentence. No one says beforehand, I condemn, when he intends to condemn; no one says beforehand I am hitting when he intends to hit. Great tenderness, therefore, great mercy, great gentleness, but only if we do not misuse His patience to our own evil ends, and do not add to our sins by further sins, to make them as it were a burden to Him Who bears our sins, as if He should bear more, to Whom it is no labour to bear them: our sins, which He as yet forbears to punish, because as yet He is bearing them, show forth His patience, and pile up our burden.

Serm. XLVII, iii, 4–iv, 5.

723

'Hear with thine ears, O Lord, the voice of my supplication' (Ps. cxxxix, 7). This is a simple sentence and easy to understand; yet it is pleasant perhaps to consider why he did not say, 'Hear with thine ears my supplication.'; but, as though expressing more plainly the affection of his heart, the *voice* of my supplication, the life of my supplication, the soul of my supplication; not that which soundeth in my words, but that which giveth life to my words. For all other noises without a soul may be called sounds; they cannot be called voices. The voice belongs to those who have souls, to the living. But how many supplicate God, who have neither perception of God, nor right thoughts concerning Him. These may have the sound of supplication, the voice they cannot have, for there is no life in them. This was the voice of the supplication of one who was alive, forasmuch as he understood that God was his God, and saw by whom he was liberated, and perceived from what men he was freed.

In Ps. CXXXIX, 10.

724

Now the wholesomeness of faith is this, that it makes us seek, that we may find; ask, that it may be given to us; knock, that it may be opened to us (Luke xi, 9).

De perf. just. hominis, XIX, 40.

725

However much a man progress, however much he stretch forth himself to the things that are before and forget those that are behind (Phil. iii, 13), if once he say to himself, 'It is well,' there cometh forth a rule from God's treasury; it examineth him in no uncertain way; and who shall boast that he hath a clean heart, who shall boast that he is pure from sin? (Prov. xx, 9). . . . However much thou progress, thou must set thy hope on mercy.

In Ps. CXLVII, 12.

V. MAN STRAIGHTWAY TO GOD

726

We ascend into heaven if we think of God, who hath made modes of ascent in the heart. What is to ascend in heart? To advance towards God. As every one who faileth, doth not descend but falleth; so every one who progresseth, doth ascend, provided he so progress as to avoid pride; but if while he is progressing he become proud, in ascending he again falleth. But what ought he to do to avoid becoming proud? Let him not heed himself, but let him lift up his eyes to Him Who dwelleth in heaven. For every proud man heedeth himself, and he who pleaseth himself seemeth to himself to be great. But he who pleaseth himself, pleaseth a fool; for he is himself a fool when he pleaseth himself. He alone safely pleaseth, who pleaseth God. And who is he who pleaseth God? He whom God hath pleased. God cannot displease Himself. May He please thee also, that thou mayest please Him. But He cannot please thee, except thou hast displeased thyself. But if thou displeasest thyself, remove thine eyes from thyself. For why dost thou regard thyself? For if thou truly regard thyself, thou findest in thee what will displease thee; and thou sayest to God, 'My sin is always before me' (Ps. l, 5). Let thy sin be before thee, that it may not be before God; and refuse to be before thyself, that thou mayest be before God. For as we wish that God may not turn away His face from us, so do we wish that He may turn His face from our sins. . . . He who saith, 'Turn not away thy face from me,' saith in another place, 'Turn away thy face from my sins' (Ps. xxvi, 9; l, 11). If thou wouldst have Him turn away His face from thy sins, do thou turn away thy face from thyself, and do thou not turn away thy face from thy sins. For if thou turn not away thy face from them, thou art thyself angry with thy sins, and if thou turn not away thy face from thy sins, thou dost confess them and God will pardon them.

In Ps. CXXII, 3.

727

Those who wish to follow God, allow Him to go before, and they follow; they do not make Him follow, while they go before.

And in all things they find Him good, whether chastening, or consoling, or exercising, or crowning, or cleansing, or enlightening; for as the Apostle saith, 'We know that to them that love God, all things work together unto good' (Rom. viii, 28).

In Ps. CXXIV, 9.

728

Look to Him Who doth guide thee, and thou wilt not look back to the place whence He is leading thee. He that guideth thee is walking before thee; the place whence He is leading thee is behind thee. Love Him guiding, and He doth not condemn thee looking back.

In Ps. LXXV, 16.

729

Let what thou art be ever displeasing to thee, if thou wouldst attain to what thou art not yet. For where thou hast pleased thyself, there thou hast remained. But if thou hast said, 'It is enough,' then art thou lost. Be ever adding, be ever walking, ever making progress. Stand not still in the way, turn not back, go not out of the way. He standeth still who doth not advance; he returneth back who relapses into the state whence he had once departed; he goeth out of the way who apostasizes. The lame man gets on better in the way than the swift of foot out of the way.

Serm. (de Script N.T.) CLXIX, xv, 18.

730

Thou wilt then truly possess the earth when thou dost cleave to Him who made heaven and earth. For to be meek is this: not to resist thy God; so that in that thou doest well He may be well-pleasing to thee, not thou to thyself; and in that thou sufferest justly, He may not be displeasing to thee, but thou to thyself. For it is no small matter that thou shalt be well-pleasing to Him, when thou art displeased with thyself; whereas if thou art well-pleased with thyself thou wilt be displeasing to Him.

Serm. (de Script. N.T.) LIII, ii, 2.

731

For God is right, and therefore by adhering to the right as to an immutable rule, the heart of man, which while in itself was crooked, can be made right. But in order that the heart may be with Him and thereby may become right, we draw near to Him and thereby may become right, we draw near to Him not with our feet but with faith. . . . The will, therefore, which is in a right heart, is prepared by the Lord, faith preceding; thereby it draweth near to God, Who is right, in order that the heart may be made right. The which faith, the mercy of God preventing and inviting, is raised up by obedience; and doth begin to apply the heart to God, in order that it may be directed. And the more and more it is directed, so much the more it seeth what it saw not, and is able to do what it could not.

In Ps. LXXVII, 10.

732

Thou wast seeking what thou shouldst offer in thy behalf; offer thyself. For what doth God ask of thee, except thyself? Since in the whole earthly creation He made nothing better than thee. He asks thyself of thee, because thou hadst lost thyself. But if thou do what He commands, he finds in thee judgment and justice, judgment first in thyself, justice towards thy neighbour. How judgment in thyself? So that thou art displeased with thyself for what thou wast, and art able to be what thou wast not. . . . In thy good things thou wast wont to praise thyself; in thy bad, to blaspheme God. This is perverse judgment. . . . Praise God in thy good things, reproach thyself in thy bad. . . . As an upright man thou wilt be observing justice. . . . As an upright man thou wilt be in accord with rectitude, and without any doubt God will be pleasing to thee.

Serm. XLVIII, ii, 2.

733

Because his heart was fixed in God, therefore was it right; for because God is right, when thou dost fix thine heart in Him, He becometh thy model, that thine heart may be right.

In Ps. XCIII, 19.

734

Nothing, indeed, in thee pleases God, save that which thou hast from God. . . . In thyself thou canst do nothing except lose thyself; nor dost thou know how to find thyself, unless He who made thee seeks thee.

Serm. XIV, iii, 3.

735

The heart of a man is called right if he wisheth all things that God wills, not what he himself wisheth. . . . Some one prayeth that something or other may not happen; he prayeth, and it is not averted. Let him ask as much as he can; but something happeneth against his own will; let him submit himself to the will of God, let him not resist the great Will.

In Ps. C, 6.

736

'Good is God to Israel,' but to whom? 'to them that are of a right heart' (Ps. lxxii, 1). Who are of a right heart? Those who do not find fault with God. Who are of a right heart? Those who direct their own will by the will of God, and do not attempt to bend the will of God to their will. It is a short commandment, that man make right his heart. Dost thou wish to have thy heart right? Do that which God willeth, do not wish God to do that which thou willest. They therefore are depraved of heart, that is, they have not a right heart, who sit and discuss how God ought to have acted; not praising what He hath done, but censuring it. They wish to correct Him; it is not enough that they refuse to be corrected by Him. . . . And all the things which God did, he did rightly. And if we cannot see His counsel, why He did this thing so and that thing so, it is good for us that we should be subject to His wisdom and to believe that He did well, although we know not yet why He did it. We shall then have a right heart, so that we may trust and confide in the Lord, and our feet shall not be moved.

In Ps. CXXIV, 2.

737

Thou wilt be right when in all the good which He doth, God pleaseth thee; and in all the evils which thou dost suffer, He displeaseth thee not. This it is to 'call upon God in truth' (Ps. cxliv, 18). Those who thus call upon God, He heareth, 'He is nigh unto them'; that is to say, though He has not yet given thee what thou wisheth, He is there nevertheless. . . . He is nigh, yet He doeth it not; yea, all the more He doeth it not because He is nigh. For in healing a patient a physician imposes what he imposes, and in healing him doth not do what he is asked. God heareth thee not in regard to thy present wish but in regard to thy future healing; and this assuredly according to His will. For surely the patient wisheth to be made whole, even if he doth not wish to be burnt.

In Ps. CXLIV, 22.

738

When art thou right? Wilt thou hear? When in that good which thou doest, God is pleasing to thee; but in that evil which thou sufferest, God is not displeasing to thee.

In Ps. LXX, *Serm.* I, 14.

739

Let God please thee as He is, not as thou wouldst like Him to be. Thou art indeed perverse and wishest God to be such as thou art, not as He is. . . . Be in accord with Him, and first of all begin to will rightly, and to hate thyself as thou art. . . . When too thou hast begun to hate thyself for being such as thou art, and such as God hates in thee, thou beginnest thyself to love God as He is.

Serm. IX, viii, 9.

740

We had prepared us a short Psalm, which we had charged the reader to recite; but he, through confusion at the time, it seems, read another in its place. We have chosen to follow the will of God in the reader's mistake, rather than our own will by keeping to our purpose. If then through its length we detain you somewhat long, impute it not to us, but believe that God hath willed that we should not labour fruitlessly.

In Ps. CXXXVIII, 1.

741

There is a short precept: He pleaseth God whom God pleaseth.

In Ps. XXXII, *En.* II, *Serm.* i, 1.

VI. . . . GIVING PRAISE

742

If thou wilt be brought from the road of faith to the possession of the reality, 'begin in confession' (Ps. cxlvi, 7). First accuse thyself, and, having accused thyself, praise God. Call on Him whom as yet thou knowest not, that He come and be known; not that He come to thee himself, but that He lead thee to Him.

In Ps. CXLVI, 14.

743

Whoso praiseth himself doth not praise God; as when a man chooses to withdraw from a fire, the fire continues warm, but he grows cold; as when a man chooses to withdraw from the light, if he withdraws, the light continues bright in itself, but he is in darkness. .

Serm. (*de Script. N.T.*) CLXX, xi, 11.

744

The soul itself giveth itself counsel from the light of God through the rational mind, whereby it conceiveth the counsel fixed in the eternity of its Author. It readeth there of something to be feared, to be praised, to be loved, to be descried and sought after. As yet it graspeth it not, it comprehendeth it not; it is as it were dazzled by the brightness; it has not the strength to abide there. Therefore it collects itself into a sound state and saith, 'Praise the Lord, O my soul' (Ps. cxlv, 1).

In Ps. CXLV, 5.

745

'Give praise to the Lord, for He is good' (Ps. cxvii, 1). . . . Confess Him either with praise or with repentance. . . . If thou wouldst confess Him with praise, what canst thou praise more surely than the Good? If thou wouldst confess thy sins, to whom more safely than to the Good? . . . If thou art good, praise that whence thou art good; if thou art evil, praise that whence thou mayest be good. Flee thyself, and come to Him who made thee. For by fleeing thyself thou followest thy true self, and by following thy true self thou cleavest to Him who made thee.

Serm. XXIX, i, 1; ii, 2; iii, 3; iv, 4.

746

Even when one confesses his sins, he ought to do so with praise of God; nor is a confession of sins a pious one unless it be made without despair, and with a prayer for God's mercy.

In Ps. CV, 2.

747

In either case it is a godly confession, either when thou blamest thyself who art not without sin, or when thou praisest Him who can have no sin. But properly considered, thine own blame is His praise. For why is it that thou dost now make confession in accusing thyself of sin, . . . but because thou art become alive from the dead?

Serm. (*de Script. N.T.*) LXVII, i, 1–2.

748

Behold, there is a way whereby thou mayest praise thyself also, and yet not be arrogant. Praise God in thee, not thyself: not because thou art what thou art, but because He made thee so; not because thou canst do anything, but because He can do it in thee and through thee. And by this means shall men praise Thee, 'and shall tell of Thy power' (Ps. cxliv, 11), not theirs but *Thine.*

In Ps. CXLIV, 7.

749

This indeed is the very wisdom which is called piety, in which is worshipped 'the Father of lights,' from whom is 'every best gift and every perfect gift' (Jas. i, 17). This worship, however, consists in the sacrifice of praise and thanksgiving, so that the worshipper glories not in himself but in God. Accordingly by the law of works God says to us, Do what I command thee; but by the law of faith we say to God, Give me what Thou commandest. Now to the end the law commands, that it may admonish us what faith should do; that is, that he to whom the command is given, if as yet he is unable to perform it, may know what to ask for. But if he has at once the ability, and is obedient to the command, he ought also to know from whose gift the ability comes.

De spir. et litt. xiii, 22.

750

Our meditation in this present life should be in the praise of God; for the eternal exultation of our life hereafter will be the praise of God; and none can become fit for the future life, who hath not practiced himself for it now.

In Ps. CXLVIII, 1.

751

Now, when we are gathered together in the church, we praise God; but when we depart each to his own business, it is as if we cease to praise Him. Let a man not cease from right living, and then he is ever praising God. Thou dost cease from praising God when thou turnest aside from justice and from all that pleaseth Him. For, if thou never turn aside from a good life, though thy tongue be silent, yet thy life crieth out, and the ear of God is open to thy heart.

In Ps. CXLVIII, 2.

752

On the timbrel leather is stretched, on the psaltery strings of cat gut, on either instrument the flesh is crucified (*v.* Ps. cxlix, 3). . . . The more the strings are stretched the higher in the scale they sound. . . . Christ touched them, and the sweetness of truth rang out.

In Ps. CXLIX, 8.

753

Begin then to praise now, if thou intendest to praise for ever. He who will not praise in this transitory world, will be silent when the world without end has come. . . . Therefore praise and bless the Lord thy God every single day, so that when the time of single days has passed, and there has come one day without end, thou mayest go from praise to praise, as 'from virtue to virtue' (Ps. lxxxiii, 8).

In Ps. CXLIV, 2, 3.

754

It is a short lesson, that thou ever praise God, and with a true, not false heart say, 'I will bless the Lord at all times: his praise shall be always in my mouth.' It is a short lesson: it is, namely, that thou know that He giveth of His mercy, when He giveth; that He taketh away of His mercy, when He taketh away; and that thou must not believe that thou art abandoned by the mercy of Him who either comforteth thee by giving, lest thou fail, or punisheth thee when thou art uplifted, lest thou perish. Praise Him therefore, whether in His gifts or in His scourges. The praise of the scourges is the medicine for the wound.

In Ps. CXLIV, 4.

755

Man's chief work is but to praise God. To Him it belongs to satisfy thee by His beauty, to thee to praise Him in acts of thanksgiving. If thy works be not the praise of God, thou art beginning to love thyself. . . . Be dissatisfied with thyself; find satisfaction in Him Who made thee, in that thou art dissatisfied with that in thee which thou thyself hast made. Let therefore thy work be the praise of God.

In Ps. XLIV, 9.

756

For if we dispute concerning the works of God; wherefore this, wherefore that; and He ought not to have done this,

He has done this ill; where is then praise of God? Thou hast lost the Alleluia. View all things in such manner how thou mayest please God and praise the artificer.

In Ps. CXLVIII, 12.

757

Since 'of His greatness there is no end' (Ps. cxliv, 3), and since we cannot contain Him, we ought to praise Him. . . . Let us, as we are deficient in His greatness, look to His works, that we may be refreshed by His goodness, and by His works praise the worker; by what He hath made, the Maker; by His creation the Creator.

In Ps. CXLIV, 6.

758

Will God's glory be greater because thou glorifiest Him? Or do we add anything to God's glory when we say to Him, 'I glorify Thee, O my God'; or make Him more holy when we say, 'I bless Thee, O my God?' . . . 'There is the way,' saith He, 'by which I will shew him my salvation' (Ps. xlix, 23). Thou seest that it is thyself, not God, that it will profit; if thou praisest God. Dost thou praise God? Thou art walking in the right way. Dost thou reprehend God? Then thou hast lost the way.

In Ps. XXXIX, 4.

759

For it is not He that increaseth by our praises, but we. God is neither the better if thou praise Him, nor worse if thou disparage Him; but thou, by praising Him that is good, art the better; by disparaging thou art the worse, for He remaineth good, as He is.

In Ps. CXXXIV, 1.

760

Think not therefore that He, 'of whose greatness there is no end' (Ps. cxliv, 3), can never be enough praised by thee. Is it not then better that as He has no end, so too thy praise should have no end? . . . For if thou shalt be never ought but His, thou shalt never be silent from His praise.

In Ps. CXLIV, 5.

761

'I will praise thee, O Lord, with my whole heart' (Ps. cxxxvii, 1). My whole heart I lay upon the altar of thy praise, a holocaust of praise I offer to Thee. . . . Let the flame of Thy love set on fire my whole heart; let nought in me be left to me, nought wherein I may look to myself, but may I wholly burn towards Thee, wholly be on fire towards Thee, wholly love Thee, as though set aflame by Thee.

In Ps. CXXXVII, 2.

762

He must increase but I must decrease (John iii, 30): that is, He must give, but I must receive; He must be glorified, but I must confess. . . . Let man, then, understand that he has received, man who wanted to call that his own which is not his. Let him be decreased in himself that he may be increased in God. . . . Let therefore the glory of God increase in us and our own glory be diminished, that in God even ours may increase. For this is what the Apostle says, this is what Holy Scripture says: 'He that glorieth, let him glory in the Lord' (1 Cor. i, 31; *v.* Jer. ix, 23, 24). Wouldst thou glory in thyself? Thou wouldst increase, but with an increase for the worse, to thy evil; for he whose increase is for the worse is justly decreased. Let God, then, the ever perfect, increase. . . . Thus is it also with the interior man. He makes progress indeed in God, and God seems to be increasing in him, yet the man himself is decreasing, that he may fall from his own glory, and rise into the glory of God.

In Joan. Evang. XIV, 5.

763

But as for me, when I am praised by one who is very kind and dear to my soul, it is as if I were praising myself. And you must see how irksome that must be even when what is said is only the truth. It is precisely because you are my other self and that we form together but one soul, that you deceive yourself in thinking that you see in me things which are not there, as a man deceives himself about himself. And I would that you did not have this idea both because I do not want you, whom I love, to be in error and also because I fear that you will in your prayers ask less fervently that I may really be what you believe me to be. Nor am I your debtor in that through benevolence I should believe and ascribe to you all the good qualities which you yourself know to be still wanting in you, but that with a heart equally kindly I should ascribe to you only those good qualities which I am certain of in you, and which are the gifts of God. And I do not do this, not from fear lest I should be deceived, but because if I praised you, you would seem to have been praising yourself, and because according to this rule of justice, I would not have it done to me. If it should be thought that I ought to do it, I prefer to remain your debtor, so long as I think it ought not to be done. If however it ought not to be done, then am I not your debtor.

Ep. CX, 4.

764

Let us exclaim with faithful heart and devoted voice, 'Glory to God in the highest; and on earth peace to men of good will' (Luke ii, 14). And, in faith and hope and charity, let us meditate on these divine words, this praise of God, this rejoicing of the Angels, so far as we are able by thought to explore them. As indeed we believe and hope and desire, we too shall be 'Glory to God in the highest,' when, caught up in the spiritual body, we shall meet Christ in the clouds of heaven; if only while we are on earth, we pursue peace with good will. Life there is 'in the highest,' for there is the land of the living, and there are the good days, where is the selfsame Lord, and His years do not fail (cf. Ps. ci, 28).

Serm. CXCIII, 1.

765

That He might be properly praised by man, God hath praised Himself; and because He hath deigned to praise Himself, therefore hath man found how to praise Him. . . . For that man should praise himself is arrogance; but for God to praise Himself is mercy. It is good for us to love one whom we praise; by praising one that is good, we are ourselves made better. Hence, since He knoweth that it is for our good that we should love Him, by praising Himself, He maketh Himself lovable. And herein he consulteth our good, in that He maketh Himself lovable. He exhorteth then our heart to praise Him, and He hath filled His servants with His Spirit, that they may praise Him. And since His Spirit in His servants praiseth Him, what doth He but praise Himself?

In Ps. CXLIV, 1.

VII. . . . IN THE CULT OF CHASTE LOVE

766

When by God's gift we live by the true faith, God himself is present, to enlighten the mind, to overcome concupiscence, to bear affliction. For all this is rightly done when it is done for His sake, that is, when He is loved for no reward; but love such as this cannot be ours, except it be from Him. For the rest, when a man is much pleased with himself, and puts his trust in his own powers, if he surrenders to the desires of his pride, this evil will be increased the more in proportion as the other lusts have abated in him, and pandering to that one, he restrains them as if he were laudable in so doing.

Contra Julianum, V, iii, 9.

767

If thou dost love to see thy God, if in this exile thou sighest with that love; behold the Lord thy God maketh trial of thee, as if He were saying to thee, 'See, do what thou wilt, fulfil thy desires, prolong wickedness, enlarge luxuriousness, think whatever pleaseth lawful. I will not punish thee for this, I will not send thee to hell, I will only deny thee My face.' If thou hast been horrorstruck, thou hast loved. If at this that was said, 'Thy God will deny thee His face,' thy whole heart hath trembled, if in the not seeing thy God thou hast imagined a great punishment, thou hast loved gratis.

Serm. (de Script. N.T.) CLXXVIII, x, 11.

768

The cause of all things which He made was His will. Thou makest a house because, if thou didst not will to make it, thou wouldst be left without a dwelling. Necessity compels thee to make a house, not free-will. Thou makest a garment because, if thou didst not make it, thou wouldst walk about naked, thou art therefore led to making a garment by necessity, not by free-will. Thou plantest a mountain with vines, thou sowest seed, because if thou didst not do so, thou wouldst not have food. All such things thou doest of necessity. God has made things of His goodness. He needed nothing that He made; and therefore, 'whatsoever the Lord pleased He hath done' (Ps. cxxxiv, 6).

Dost thou think that we too have what we do of free-will? The things we have spoken of, we do of necessity, because if we did not do them, we should be needy and destitute. Do we find any thing which we do of free-will? We do indeed, when we praise God out of love of Him. This indeed thou doest of free-will, when thou lovest that which thou praisest; for this is not of necessity, but because it pleaseth thee. Therefore God pleaseth the just and the saints even when He scourgeth them. These He pleaseth, when He displeaseth all the unjust; and though they be subject to His rod, though they be in toils, in labours, in wounds, in want, they yet praise God. Even though He torment them, He displeases them not. This it is to love freely, not for the receipt of specified pay, because God Himself will be thy supreme reward, whom thou lovest freely, and so oughtest to love, as not to cease to desire Him for thy reward, who alone can satisfy thee; as Philip desired, when he said, 'Shew us the Father; and it is enough for us' (John xiv, 8). Rightly, because we do this of free-will, and we ought to do this of free-will, because we do so of our pleasure; we do so of our love, because though we are chastened by Him, He never ought to displease us, for He is ever just.

In Ps. CXXXIV, 10–11.

769

Behold and see in what manner he hath loved him. He hath made his heart chaste: 'the God of my heart, and the God that is my portion for ever' (Ps. lxxii, 26). His heart is become chaste, his love for God is now gratuitous, and he seeks no other reward from Him. He that seeks any other reward from God, and is willing to serve God for it, makes that which he wishes to receive more precious than Him from whom he wishes to receive it. What is this? Has God no reward? None except Himself. The reward belonging to God is God Himself. This he loveth, this he esteemeth, if he shall have loved anything else, the love will not be chaste. Thou art receding from the immortal fire, thou wilt grow cold, wilt be corrupted. Do not recede. It will be thy corruption, it will be thy fornication. . . . To this fornication is opposed chaste love. . . . Now the soul doth love her Bridegroom: what doth she require of Him, from her Bridegroom whom she loveth? . . . She doth love Him alone, she doth love Him asking no reward, because in Him she hath all things, for 'all things were made by Him' (John i, 3). . . . Dissolute men are loved gratuitously, and is a reward to be required of God in order that He may be loved? Love God for no reward; grudge God to no one. Seize Him as many of you as are able, as many as shall possess Him. He is not contained by any bounds; you will find no limits in Him; each of you will possess Him in whole, you all will have Him wholly.

In Ps. LXXII, 32–34.

770

Let God be praised with the will, loved with charity; let it be gratuitous that He is loved and praised. What is 'gratuitous'? Himself for the sake of Himself, not for the sake of something else. For if thou praisest God in order that He may give you something else, thou dost no longer love God gratuitously. Thou wouldest blush if thy wife were to love thee for thy wealth, and perchance if poverty should befall thee should begin to think of adultery. Seeing then that thou wouldest be loved gratuitously, wilt thou for anything else love God? What reward art thou to receive of God, O covetous man? It is not the earth that He reserves for thee but Himself, who created heaven and earth. 'I will freely sacrifice to Thee' (Ps. liii, 8): do not do this of necessity. For if thou praisest God for the sake of anything else, thou praisest out of necessity. If there were present to thee that which thou lovest, thou wouldst not praise God. Mark what I am going to say: thou praisest God, for example, in order that He may give thee abundant money. If thou wert to get abundant money from any other quarter, not from God, wouldest thou praise God? If, therefore, thou praisest God for the sake of money, thou sacrificest not freely to God but of necessity; because beside Him something else has thy love. For this reason was it said 'I will freely sacrifice to Thee.' Despise all things, give heed to Him. Those things also which He hath given are good because of the Giver. For He giveth absolutely. He giveth then temporal things, to some men to their good, to others to their harm, according to the height and depth of His judgments. . . . He knoweth, when He giveth, to whom He giveth; when He taketh away, from whom He taketh away. Ask thou in this present time for that which may help thee in eternity. But Him love gratuitously; for from Him thou findest not anything that He may give better than Himself; or if thou findest a better thing, this ask for.

In Ps. LIII, 10.

771

What is it that Scripture saith in many places: 'they shall call, and I will not hear them'? (Prov. i, 28) Yet surely thou art 'plenteous in mercy to all that call upon Thee' (Ps. lxxxv, 5) —but that some call, yet call not on Him, of whom it is said, 'they have not called upon God' (Ps. lii, 6). They call, but not upon God. Thou callest upon whatever thou lovest, thou callest upon whatever thou wishest should come to thee. Therefore if thy reason for calling upon God is that money may come to thee, that an inheritance may fall to thee, that worldly rank may come to thee, thou callest upon those things which thou desirest may come to thee; but thou then makest God the promoter of thy desires, not the listener to thy needs. . . . What then, thou sayest, am I to do? What am I to pray for? What art thou to pray for? What the Lord hath taught thee, what the heavenly Master hath taught thee. Call upon God as God, love God as God; there is nothing better than He is: long for Him, desire Him. . . . If thou wouldst be a lover of God, love Him from the very bottom of thy heart. Sigh for Him, love Him, burn with love for Him, yearn for Him, than Whom thou shalt find nothing more pleasing, nothing better, nothing more joyful, nothing more lasting. For what is so lasting as that which is everlasting? Thou needest not fear lest He should ever be lost to thee, Who causes that thou be not lost thyself. If therefore thou callest on God as God, be confident that thou wilt be heard. Thou hast part in that verse: 'And plenteous in mercy to all that call upon thee.'

In Ps. LXXXV, 8.

772

Many cry unto the Lord for the sake of getting riches and avoiding losses, for the safety of their friends, for the security of their house, for temporal happiness, for secular dignity, lastly, even for mere soundness of body, which is the poor man's patrimony. For these and such like things many cry unto the Lord; scarce one for the sake of the Lord Himself. For it is an easy thing for a man to desire anything of the Lord and not to desire the Lord Himself; as if forsooth that which He giveth could be sweeter than Himself the Giver. . . . But the man who loved God gratuitously, who sacrificed to God freely, who had leaped over whatever is below, and had seen no other thing above himself to which he might pour forth his soul, save Him of whom and through whom and in whom he had been created, and he had cried out to Him with his voice; this man made this same voice of his to be to Him that voice of which it is said, 'To God is my voice' (*v.* Ps. lxxvi, 2). . . . 'And he gave ear to me' (*ibid.*). He doth indeed give ear to thee when thou doest seek Himself, not when through Him thou seekest any other thing.

In Ps. LXXVI, 2.

773

God would have Himself gratuitously worshipped, would have Himself gratuitously loved, that is chastely loved; not to be loved for the reason that He giveth anything besides Himself, but because He giveth Himself. He therefore that calleth upon God in order that he may be made rich, doth not

call on God, for he calleth upon that which he wisheth to come
to him. For what is to 'call upon' but to call to oneself? To
call to oneself, therefore, means to call upon. For when thou
sayest, O God, give me riches; thou dost not wish that God Himself should come to thee, but that riches should come to thee.
That which thou wishest should come to thee, upon that thou
callest. But if thou wert to call upon God, He would Himself
come to thee, He would be thy riches. But now thou wouldest
have thy coffer filled and thy conscience void. God filleth not
coffer but heart. What do outward riches profit thee if inward
need presseth thee?

In Ps. LII, 8.

774

For we cultivate God, and God cultivateth us. But we do
not so cultivate God as to make Him any better thereby. For
our cultivation is the labour of an adoring heart, not of the
hands. He cultivateth us as the husbandman tilleth his field.
In then that He cultivateth us, He maketh us better, just as
the husbandman by tilling his field maketh it better. And the
fruit He seeketh in us is that we may cultivate Him. The
tillage He practises on us is that He ceaseth not to root out
by His word the evil seeds from our hearts, to open, as it were,
our heart by the plough of His word, to plant the seed of His
precepts, to wait for the fruit of piety. For when we have so
received that tillage in our heart as to cultivate Him well, we
are not ungrateful to our Husbandman, but yield the fruit
wherein He rejoiceth. And our fruit doth not make Him the
richer but us the happier.

Serm. (*de Script. N.T.*) LXXXVII, i, 1.

775

There was lavished upon them even temporal blessings by
His mercy. . . . Not that they should worship Him on account
of these blessings, but that they should refer and convert these
also to everlasting good. . . . If prosperity in temporal matters
attend you, use not God on account of it, but use it on account
of God; nor think that He is worshipped by His worshippers

for the sake of the necessaries of this life, which He giveth even to those who blaspheme Him, but 'seek ye first the kingdom of God and His justice: and all these things shall be added unto you' (Matt. vi, 33).

In Ps. CIV, 40.

776

Thou wast not, and thou wast created. What has thou given to God? Thou wast evil, and thou wast redeemed. What hast thou given to God? What is there that thou hast not received from Him gratuitously? With reason it is called 'grace' because it is bestowed 'gratis.' What is required of thee, therefore, is this, that those too should worship Him 'gratis'; not because He gives things temporal, but because He offers thee things eternal.

Beware, however, lest thou think of those eternal things otherwise than as they are, and lest, understanding those eternal things in a carnal sense, thou shouldst nevertheless not be worshipping God 'gratis.' For if thou worshippest God because He gives thee an estate, wilt thou abstain from worshipping Him because He takes thy estate from thee? But perhaps thou sayest, 'I will serve God because He will give me an estate, though not a temporal one'? Nevertheless, thou dost still bear a corrupt mind; for thou dost not yet worship Him with a chaste love; thou art still seeking a reward. For thou wouldst fain possess, in the world to come, the things which thou must of necessity leave behind thee here; thou wouldst change thy carnal pleasure, not cut it off entirely. We do not commend the fasting of the man who is storing up his appetite for a luxurious dinner. . . . Do not therefore hope to have such things given thee by God, as He calls upon thee to despise here below. . . . Woe to that love of thine, if thou canst conceive anything more beautiful than Him, from Whom is all beauty, to keep thee back from deserving to think of Him. The Lord was incarnate, and appeared unto men as a Man. . . . It is as if He had said, you see 'the form of a servant,' the 'form of God' is hidden. I employ the former to win you, the latter I reserve for you; with the former I nourish you while yet babes, with the latter I feed you when full grown. . . . In order that this faith of ours, whereby we are made clean, may be prepared for things invisible; . . . in order that men may not worship the Everlasting Himself with a view to those self-same temporal things but out of a chaste love of Him all these things that they are suffering for a time, all these things have been done 'for the sons of love to give understanding' (Ps. xliii, 1).

In Ps. XLIII, 15, 16.

777

They that sought God for the sake of temporal blessings, certainly did not seek God but those things. God is then worshipped only with servile fear, not with freely given love. Thus God is not worshipped, for that thing is worshipped which is loved. Whence because God is found to be greater and better than all things, He must be loved more than all things, in order that He may be worshipped. . . . Therefore the heart is right with God when it doth seek God for the sake of God. . . . Of such sort was the generation, 'perverse and exasperating,' (Ps. lxxvii, 8) even when they were seeming to seek God. They were loving with their lips and lying with their tongue; but in heart they were not right with God, while they loved rather those things for the sake of which they required the help of God.

In Ps. LXXVII, 20, 21.

778

Let the Lord thy God be thy hope. Hope for nothing else from the Lord thy God, but let the Lord thy God Himself be thy hope. For many persons hope to obtain from God riches, and many hope for perishable and transitory honours; in short, they hope to get at God's hands anything else, except only God Himself. But do thou seek after thy God Himself, nay, indeed, despising all other things, make thy way to Him. Forget other things, remember Him. Leave other things behind and stretch forth to Him. It was He assuredly that set thee right when turned away from the right path. He it is who is leading thee to thy goal. Therefore, let Him be thy hope who is guiding thee and is leading thee to thy destination. Whither at the end does worldly covetousness lead thee? Thou didst desire a farm; then thou wouldest possess an estate; then thou didst shut out thy neighbours, and having shut them out thou didst set thy heart on the possessions of other neighbours; and thou didst extend thy covetous desires till thou hadst reached the shore; arrived at the shore, thou didst covet the islands; having made the earth thine own, thou desirest haply to seize upon heaven. O leave all then thy desires. He who made heaven and earth is more beautiful than all. . . . He who made all things is better than all. He who made the beautiful things is more beautiful than them all. He who made the mighty things is Himself mightier. He who made the great things is Himself greater. He will be to thee everything that thou lovest. Learn in the creature to love the Creator, and in the work Him who made it. Let not that which was made by Him take hold of thee, so that thou lose Him by Whom thou also wert thyself made.

In Ps. XXXIX, 7 8.

779

God indeed enjoins us by His testimonies to worship Him for nought; and this avarice, the root of all evils, hindereth. . . . For the first human beings would not have been deceived and overthrown by the serpent, if they had not desired to have more than they had received, and to be more than they had been made. . . . But all avarice is cut away from about us, if God be worshipped for nought. This is the challenge given by the tempter to the holy man Job in his temptation, when he asks respecting him, 'Doth Job worship God for nought?' (Job i, 9). For the devil thought that in worshipping God this just man's heart was inclined to avarice, and that he served Him like a hireling for his wage, in the hope of profit or the advantage of his temporal fortunes wherewith God had enriched him. But when he was tempted, it appeared that he worshipped God, looking for nought in return. If therefore our heart be not inclined to avarice, we worship God only for God's sake, so that He is the only reward of our worshipping Him. Let us love Him in Himself; let us love Him in ourselves; let us love Him in our neighbour, whom we love as ourselves, whether they have Him, or in order that they may have Him.

In Ps. CXVIII, *Serm.* xi, 6.

780

Aforetime we did love the earth, not Thee; but Thou hast mortified our members which are upon the earth (cf. Cor. iii, 5). For the Old Testament, holding earthly promises, seemeth to exhort that God should be worshipped not for nought but that He should be loved because He giveth something on the earth. What dost thou love so as not to love God? Tell me. Love, if thou canst, anything which He hath not made. Look round upon the whole of creation; see whether in any place thou art held by the birdlime of desire and hindered from loving the Creator, except it be by that very thing which He Whom thou disregardest hath Himself created. But why dost thou love those things, except because they are beautiful? Can they be as beautiful as He by Whom they are made? Thou admirest these things because thou seest not Him; but through those things which thou admirest love Him whom thou seest not. Examine creation; if it is of itself, remain in it; but if it is of Him, for no other reason is it baleful to a lover, than because it is preferred to the Creator. . . . They were dead that did worship God that it might be well with them after the flesh; 'because the wisdom of the flesh is death' (Rom. viii, 6). And they are dead who do not worship God gratis, that is, because He Himself is the good, not because He giveth such and such good things, which He giveth even to those who are not good. . . . All these things He giveth even to evil men, He reserveth Himself alone for good men.

In Ps. LXXIX, 14.

781

Let us therefore love God, brethren, purely and chastely. It is not a chaste heart, if it worshippeth God for a reward. How is this? Shall we not have a reward from the worship of God? Certainly we shall have; but it will be God Himself, Whom we worship. He Himself shall be our reward, 'because we shall see Him as He is' (1 John iii, 2). . . . A man doth not love his wife, that loveth her because of her dowry, a woman doth not love her husband chastely, who loves him for the reason that he hath given her something or hath given much.

. . . If therefore a husband in the flesh is loved gratis, if he is chastely loved; and if a wife in the flesh is loved gratis and chastely loved; in what manner must God be loved, the true and truth-speaking spouse of the soul, who maketh fruitful unto the offspring of eternal life, and who doth not suffer us to be barren? Let us then love Him in such wise that beside Him no other thing is loved. . . . Great riches of the heart, great light of the interior eye, great confidence of security! 'Behold I know thou art my God' (Ps. lv, 10).

In Ps. LV, 17.

VIII. . . . IN CHASTE FEAR

782

The Apostle saith, 'with fear and trembling work out your own salvation. With fear and trembling, for it is God who worketh in you' (Phil. ii, 12 *sq.*). Thou sayest, O Paul, work; thou tellest us to work; wherefore 'with trembling'? 'For it is God,' he saith, 'who worketh in you.' The reason why it is 'with trembling' is that 'God worketh.' Because He gave, because what thou hast cometh not from thee, thou shalt work with fear and trembling, for if thou fearest Him not, He will take away what He gave.

In Ps. CIII, *Serm.* iv, 16.

783

'With fear and trembling,' saith the Apostle, 'work out your own salvation.' If we do work out our own salvation, why with fear, why with trembling, when what we work out is in our own power? Hear why it is with fear and trembling: 'For it is God who worketh in you, both to will and to accomplish, according to His good will' (Phil. ii, 12 *sq.*). Therefore with fear and trembling, that it may delight our Maker to work in the lowly valley.

In Ps. CXLII, 10.

784

'Perfect charity casteth out' this 'fear,' with which punishment is feared (1 John iv, 18); and this charity freeth us not by fear of punishment, but by delight in justice. For that fear with which justice is not loved, but punishment dreaded, is servile, because it is carnal, and therefore doth not crucify the flesh. For the inclination to sin liveth, and, when impunity may be looked for, it then appeareth in act. But when punishment is considered sure to follow, it liveth latent; nevertheless it liveth. For it would rather it were lawful to sin, and it grieveth that what the law forbideth is not lawful, because it is not spiritually delighted with the good of the law, but carnally feareth the evil which it threateneth. But that charity which casteth out this fear, feareth to sin with a chaste fear, though no punishment follow; because it doth not even consider that impunity will follow, since from love of justice it judgeth the very sin itself a punishment. With such a fear the flesh is crucified, since carnal delights, which are forbidden rather than evaded by the letter of the law, are overcome by the delight in spiritual blessings, and when the victory is perfected are destroyed.

In Ps. CXVIII, *Serm.* xxv, 7

785

For it is another fear which charity excludeth, as St. John saith: 'Fear is not in charity; but perfect charity casteth out fear' (1 John iv, 18). It is not every fear which he saith is cast out by charity, for thou findest the Psalm saying, 'the fear of the Lord is chaste, enduring for ever and ever' (Ps. xviii, 10). One fear therefore endureth, the other is cast out. The fear which is cast out is not chaste, but that which endureth is chaste. What is the fear that is cast out? Pray consider. Some fear only for this reason, lest they suffer some evil on earth,— lest sickness befall them, or loss, or bereavement of children, or the loss of someone who is dear, or exile, or condemnation, or prison, or any tribulation. For these reasons they fear and tremble; yet this fear is not chaste fear. Consider again. Another feareth not to suffer on this earth, but feareth hell, with which the Lord also frightened men. You have heard, when the Gospel was being read, the words, 'Where their worm dieth not, and the fire is not extinguished' (Mark ix, 43). Men hear these words;

and because these things will really happen to the ungodly, they fear, and restrain themselves from sin. They have fear, and through fear restrain themselves from sin. They fear indeed, but they love not justice. But when through fear they refrain from sin, justice becometh a habit, and what was hard beginneth to be loved, and good becometh sweet; and the man now beginneth to live justly, not because he feareth punishments, but because he loveth eternity. Fear therefore is cast out by charity, but a pure fear hath succeeded.

In Ps. CXXVII, 7.

786

'Fear is not in charity: but perfect charity casteth out fear' (1 John iv, 18). It is that servile fear, which keeps man from sin by his terror of punishment and not by his love of justice, that charity casteth out when iniquity no longer pleases even though it can be done with impunity. As for the fear with which the soul fears it may lose that grace by which it is brought about that it takes no pleasure in sin, and the dread lest God may abandon it even though there be no torments to punish it at the end, this fear is holy, and charity does not cast it out but furthers it; for as the Scripture says: 'the fear of the Lord is holy, enduring for ever and ever' (Ps. xviii, 10). The Psalmist would never have said that this would thus endure if he had not known another fear which would not endure. And well is it called 'holy,' for the love by which the soul clings to God is a part of it, as is said in another psalm: 'Thou hast destroyed all those that are disloyal to Thee. But it is good for me to adhere to my God' (Ps. lxxii, 27 *sq.*). The spouse whose heart is adulterous, though she may not commit adultery out of fear of her husband, sins in her will though she may not do so by any act. But the chaste wife's fear is of another kind, for though she fear her husband it is with a chaste fear. In short the former fears lest a troublesome husband come upon the scene, the latter lest an offended husband absent himself. To the loving spouse it is the absence, to the unloving the presence of the husband that is troubling.

Ep. CXL, xxi, 53.

787

What is chaste fear? By which we ought, my brethren, to understand what is said: 'Blessed are all they that fear the Lord; that walk in His ways' (Ps. cxxvii, 1). If I shall be enabled to speak worthily of this chaste fear, the Lord our God helping me, many will perchance be inflamed by this chaste fear to a chaste love. Nor can I perhaps explain, except by putting forward some similitude. Suppose some chaste woman, fearing her husband; suppose another, an adulterous woman, and she also feareth her husband; the chaste woman feareth lest her husband depart; the adulterous wife feareth lest hers come. What if both be absent? The one feareth lest he come, the other lest he tarry in coming. He to Whom we have been betrothed is in a certain sense absent. He is absent, Who gave us as a pledge the Holy Ghost; He is absent, Who redeemed us with His blood; He is that Bridegroom than whom there is nothing more beautiful. . . . He is beautiful, and is absent. Let the spouse ask herself if she be chaste. We are all among His members, my brethren; we are among His members, and for this reason we are one man. Let each man see what sort of fear he hath, whether that which charity casteth out, or that chaste fear which endureth for ever and ever. . . . Our Bridegroom is absent; ask thy conscience; dost thou wish that He come, or dost thou still wish that He tarry? . . . What the consciences of each one of you may have answered, . . . He who is absent in respect of bodily presence, but is present in the power of His majesty, hath heard. How many, if it be said to them, Lo, here is Christ, to-morrow is the day of judgment, do not say, would that He may come! Those who speak thus, love much; and if they are told, He will delay, they fear lest He delay, for their fear is chaste. And as His tarrying is now feared, so after His coming, His leaving will be feared. That will be a chaste fear, for it is tranquil and secure. For we shall not be forsaken by Him when He hath found us, since He sought us before we sought Him. A chaste fear therefore, my brethren, hath this quality, that it cometh from love. But that fear which is not yet chaste, feareth His presence and punishment. From fear the man doeth whatever of good he doeth: not from fear of losing that good, but from fear of suffering that evil. He feareth not lest he lose the embraces of his most beautiful spouse, but lest he be cast into hell. This fear is good and useful; it will not indeed endure for ever; it is not yet that chaste fear which endureth for ever and ever.

In Ps. CXXVII, 8.

788

In whom is it chaste? I will now put a question for the second time, which you may be asking yourselves. If God should come and speak to us with His own voice (although he ceaseth not to speak through His Scriptures), and should say to man, thou wishest to sin, sin; do whatsoever pleaseth thee; whatever thou lovest on earth, let it be thine; if thou art angry with anyone, let him perish; if thou wouldst seize anyone, let him be seized; or kill anyone, let him be killed, or condemn anyone, let him be condemned; whomsoever thou wishest to possess, possess him; let no man resist thee, no man say to thee, What art thou doing, or Do it not, or, Why hast thou done it? Let all these earthly things which thou hast desired abound unto thee, and live in them, not for a season, but for ever; but My face thou shalt never see. My brethren, wherefore did you groan, save because a chaste fear enduring for ever and ever hath been born in you? Why is your heart stricken? If God should say, Thou shalt never see My face, what of it? Thou wilt abound in all that earthly felicity; temporal goods will surround thee; thou wilt not lose them, nor forsake them; what more dost thou want? Chaste fear would weep indeed and groan, and would say, Nay, let all be taken away, and let me see Thy face. Chaste fear would cry out in the words of the psalm, 'O God of hosts, convert us, and shew Thy face: and we shall be saved' (Ps. lxxix, 8). Chaste fear would cry out in the words of the psalm, 'one thing I have asked of the Lord.' See how burning is that chaste fear, that true, unmixed love. 'One thing I have asked of the Lord, this will I seek after.' What is this? 'That I may dwell in the house of the Lord all the days of my life.' What if he desire this for the sake of earthly felicity? Hear what followeth: 'that I may see the delight of the Lord,' and as His temple be protected (Ps. xxvi, 4 *sq.*);

that is, the one thing I asked of the Lord is to be His temple and to be protected by Him. If you ask this one thing, if you train your hearts to this one thing, and fear to lose this one thing only, you will not envy earthly delights, and you will look for that true happiness, and you will be in His body to Whom it is sung: 'Blessed are all they that fear the Lord: that walk in His ways' (Ps. cxxvii, 1).

In Ps. CXXXVII, 9.

789

God establisheth His word in His fear to those to whom He giveth the spirit of the fear of Him (cf. Ps. cxviii, 38); not that fear of which the Apostle saith, 'You have not received the spirit of bondage again in fear' (Rom. viii, 15), for 'perfect charity casteth out' this 'fear' (1 John iv, 18), but that fear which the Prophet calleth 'the spirit of the fear of the Lord' (Is. xi, 3), that fear which is chaste, enduring for ever and ever (Ps. xviii, 10), that fear which feareth to offend Him whom it loveth.' For the adulteress hath a different fear of her husband from that of the chaste wife: the adulteress feareth lest he come, the chaste feareth lest he forsake her.

In Ps. CXVIII, *Serm.* xii, 3.

790

And let us fear Him, not with the servile fear wherewith bodily evils are feared, but with a chaste fear abiding for all eternity, which fear doth deem it great punishment to be deprived of the light of justice.

In Ps. LXXVII, 12.

791

Far be it therefore that love should perish through fear, where fear is chaste. Thus fathers are at once feared and loved by dutiful sons; thus doth a chaste wife at once fear her husband, lest she be forsaken by him, and loveth him, that she may enjoy his love. If then the human father and the human husband desire to be at once feared and loved, much more doth our Father who is in heaven, and that Bridegroom who is 'beautiful above the sons of men' (Ps. xliv, 3), not in the flesh but in goodness.

In Ps. CXVIII, *Serm.* xxxi, 3.

792

As spiritual grace descending upon us starts from wisdom and ends at fear, we in ascending, struggling from the lowest to the highest, must start from fear and end at wisdom. 'The fear of the Lord is the beginning of wisdom' (Ps. cx, 10).

Serm. CCLXX, 5.

793

The divine utterances . . . teach us in fearing not to fear, and in not fearing to fear, . . . by admonishing us not to fear, and withal to fear. For He saith, 'Fear ye not them that kill the body and are not able to kill the soul,' . . . 'but rather,' He saith, 'fear him that can destroy both soul and body in hell' (Matt. x, 28). Let us therefore fear that we may not fear.

Serm. (de Script. N.T.) LXV, i, 1.

794

Love the goodness of God; fear His severity. Neither suffers thee to be proud. For by loving thou fearest lest thou grievously offend Him who is loved and loves. . . . That other fear is not in charity, but this chaste fear doth not depart from charity. If thou lovest not, fear lest thou perish; if thou lovest, fear lest thou displease. Charity casteth out the former fear, it accompanieth the latter.

De scta. virg. xxxviii, 39.

IX. . . . IN LOVING FEAR AND FEARING LOVE

795

Thou who art more inward than my most inmost self, hast set a law within my heart by Thy Spirit, as it were by Thy fingers, that I might not fear it as a slave without love, but might love it with a chaste fear as a son, and fear it with a chaste love.

In Ps. CXVIII, *Serm.* xxii, 6.

796

Love and fear lead to every right deed; to every sin love and fear lead. In order that thou mayest do well, thou lovest God and thou fearest God; but to do evil thou lovest the world and thou fearest the world. Let these two things be turned into good: thou didst love the earth, love life eternal; thou didst fear death, fear hell. Whatever the world hath promised to thee as an iniquitous man, will it be able to give as much as God will give to the just man? Whatever the world has threatened thee as a just man, will it be able to do what God doeth to the iniquitous man? . . . It is well that thou shouldst wish for nothing else than that it should be well with thee. For in that which thou lovest, thou dost wish that it may be well with thee, and in that which thou fearest, thou dost wish that it may not be ill with thee; but thou dost not seek it in that region where it ought to be sought. Thou art in haste; for thou wishest to be without indigence and without trouble. It is a good thing which thou wouldst have, but suffer that which thou wouldest not have, that thou mayest attain to that which thou wishest.

In Ps. LXXIX, 13.

797

As men must keep the way carefully in walking between fire and water, so as to be neither burned nor drowned, so must we order our steps between the pinnacle of pride and the chasm of sloth, as it is written: 'neither declining to the right hand nor to the left hand' (Deut. xvii, 11). For some, while guarding too anxiously against being lifted up and raised, as it were, to the heights on the right hand, have fallen and been engulfed in the depths on the left. Again, others, while turning too eagerly from the danger on the left hand of being immersed in the torpid effeminacy of inaction, are, on the other hand, so destroyed and consumed by the extravagance of self-conceit, that they vanish into smoke and ashes.

Ep. XLVIII, 2.

798

There is fear in gladness. . . . There will hereafter be gladness without fear, whilst now there is gladness with fear; for
there is not yet full security, nor perfect gladness. If there
is no gladness, we faint; if there is full security we rejoice wrongly.
Therefore may He sprinkle gladness on us, and strike fear into
us, that by the sweetness of. gladness He may lead us to the
abode of security.

In Ps. LXXXV, 16.

799

Fear God that ye may not retrogress; love Him that ye may
progress.

Ep. CXLIV, 2.

XIV. MAN IN GOD

I. MAN-ABYSS

800

Thou seekest the depth of the sea, what is deeper than the human conscience?

In Ps. LXXVI, 18.

801

All the miracles done in this world are less wonderful than the world itself. . . . Yet God who made it all made it after a manner that man cannot conceive nor comprehend. For though these visible miracles of nature become commonplace from being seen so frequently, yet if they be wisely pondered, they are greater than the rarest and most extraordinary. For of all miracles which He works through man, man is the greatest miracle.

De civ. Dei X, xii.

802

If by 'abyss' we understand a great depth, is not man's heart an abyss? For what is there more profound than that abyss? Men may speak, may be seen by the operations of their members, may be heard speaking; but whose thought is penetrated, whose heart is seen into? What he is inwardly engaged on, what he is inwardly capable of, what he is inwardly doing, or what purposing, what he is inwardly wishing to happen or not to happen, who shall comprehend? . . . Do not you believe that there is in man a deep so profound as to be hidden even to him in whom it is?

In Ps. XLI, 13.

803

Man is a great deep, the very hairs of whose head are numbered by Thee, O Lord, so that not one escapes Thee (cf. Matt. x,

30); yet are those hairs more easily to be numbered than are the affections and the motions of his heart.

Conf. IV, xiv, 22.

804

For now, since thou seest not my heart, and I do not see thine, it is night. Thou hast asked something of a man; thou hast not received it; thou thinkest thyself despised; and perhaps thou art not despised; for thou seest not the heart, and thou dost at once blaspheme: pardon must be given thee for thou art wandering in the night. Some man perhaps loveth thee, and thou thinkest that he hateth thee; or he hateth thee, and thou thinkest that he loveth thee. But, be that as it may, it is night. Fear not, trust in Christ, in Him find the day. Thou canst not think anything evil of Him, since we are securely certain that He cannot be deceived. He loveth us; but we cannot as yet be sure of one another. For God knoweth our love for one another; but, though we love one another, which of us knoweth with what disposition our intercourse is carried on?

In Ps. C, 12.

805

Every man is a stranger in this life, in which you see that we are girt round with flesh, through which flesh the heart cannot be seen. . . . In the sojourning of this carnal life each one carrieth his own heart, and every heart is closed to every other heart.

In Ps. LV, 9.

806

The good heart lies hid, the evil heart lies hid, there is an abyss in the good heart and in the bad. But these things are bare to God's sight, from whom nothing is hid.

In Ps. CXXXIV, 16.

807

Within in the consciousness. A great solitude which is not only not passed through by any one, but also not seen. There let us dwell in hope, since we do not yet in reality. For all that is without us is driven hither and thither by the storms and trials of the world. It is an interior hermitage, there let us examine our faith. . . . There where no man can see is this hermitage, where we rest in hope, for all this trouble passes it by; and what was hope will become reality, and will be our all in repose. We shall already be visible to ourselves; . . . and the consciousness will not be a hermitage, since all will be known to themselves, and this very thought will not remain unknown, since the Lord will have come, and will have brought to light the hidden things of darkness, and will make manifest the counsels of the hearts. And then shall every man have praise from God (1 Cor. iv, 5).

Serm. XLVII, xiv, 23.

II. NIGHT OF THE HEART

808

Certain it doubtless is, brethren, that either thou killest iniquity or art killed by iniquity. But do not seek to kill iniquity as if it were something outside thyself. Look to thyself, mark what fighteth with thee in thee, and take heed lest thy iniquity, thine enemy, defeat thee, if it have not been killed. For it is from out thee, and thy soul rebelleth against thyself, not any other thing. With some part of thyself thou cleavest to God, with some part thou art allured by the world. That wherewith thou delightest in the world fighteth against the mind which cleaveth to God. Let it cleave, let it adhere, let it not weaken, let it not give way; it hath great help. It conquereth that in itself which is in rebellion against itself, if it but persevere in fighting.

In Ps. LXIII, 9.

809

But now, however firm be our path, which is Christ, yet since we are bringing the flesh, which we are enjoined to subdue, into subjection; in the very work of chastening and subduing it, it is a great thing not to fall. And who is able to say that he doth not slip in the flesh?

In Ps. CXIV, 7.

810

Do we not carry our destruction about with us in this flesh? Are not we more brittle than if we were made of glass? Yet even though glass is brittle it lasts a long time if looked after; and thou findest cups which had belonged to grandfathers and great-grandfathers out of which their grandchildren and great-grandchildren are drinking. Such brittleness as this has been kept safe for many years. But we men, brittle as we are, go about subject to such great accidents, that, even if the immediate mischance does not strike us, we cannot live for very long.

Serm. XVII, vii, 7.

811

If nothing in thee is in opposition to thy neighbour, look where the whole may be. If thy spirit does not dissent from the flesh coveting things opposed to it, look and see whether thy whole mind does not perhaps agree with the flesh; see whether there be not perhaps war, for the reason that the peace is a wrong one. Perhaps thou agreest wholly with the flesh, and there is no conflict. What hope hast thou of ever being able to conquer if thou hast not yet begun to fight? But if thou art 'delighted with the law of God, according to the inward man: but seest another law in thy members, fighting against the law of thy mind' (Rom. vii, 22, 23); if thou art delighted by this latter, if thou art fettered by it, thou art free in the mind but a servant in the flesh. . . . For it is not that that very thing which the flesh covets as opposed to the spirit is not mine. Or is it that I am composed of contradictory natures? And both that is mine, and that which I do not agree with it about is mine. A part of me which is in some measure free opposed the other parts which are in bondage. I wish the whole to be healthy, since I am the whole. . . . God when He created man, made both soul and body, and joined the two together; and made the flesh subject to the soul, and the soul to Himself. If the latter were always subject to her Lord, the former would always be obedient to its mistress.

Serm. XXX, iii, 4.

812

Suppose a man to be at first seeking nothing, living after the old life in a seductive sense of security; not thinking there is anything else after this life, when it shall sometime end; one negligent and thoughtless, with his heart absorbed in the allurements of the world, and lulled to sleep with deadly delights: if such a man is to be roused to seek the grace of God, and to become anxious, and to wake as it were from sleep; is it not the hand of God that arouses him? But yet he knoweth not by whom he was aroused; however, he begins to belong to God now that he has come to know the belief of the Truth. But before he knoweth, he grieveth for his error. For he findeth himself in error, wisheth to know the Truth, knocketh where he can, trieth what he can, wandereth which way he can, feeleth even a hunger for the Truth itself. So then the first trial is one of wandering and hunger. When he hath grown weary in this trial and hath cried unto God, he is led to the way of faith, on which he may begin to journey towards the City of Peace. He is led therefore to Christ, who said, 'I am the way' (John xiv, 6).

When therefore he is come there, knowing now what he ought to observe, it happens sometimes that through attributing too much to himself, and as it were presuming on his own powers, he beginneth to think of striving against sins, and to be worsted because of his pride. He then findeth himself fettered by the difficulties of his desires, and because of his shackles unable to walk on the way. He feeleth himself imprisoned by the difficulty of his vices, with a wall, as it were, of impossibility built up, and the gates shut upon him, and how to get out and live aright he cannot discover. He already knoweth how he ought to live, for before he was wandering and suffered hunger for the Truth, but he hath now received the food of truth, and is set in the way. He heareth, Live rightly, according to that which thou knowest; for before, thou knewest not how thou shouldst live. Now thou hast received the truth and knowest. He tries; he cannot. He feels himself in fetters; he cries unto the Lord. The second trial therefore is that of the difficulty of working well, as the first was that of wandering and hunger. In this also he crieth to the Lord, and the Lord delivereth him from his necessities, breaketh the chains of difficulty, and establisheth him in the working of righteousness. That which had been difficult now begins to be easy to him. To abstain from evil things, not to commit adultery, not to steal, to do no murder, to commit no sacrilege, not to covet what is another's.

That which was before hard is become easy. God could grant this without the difficulty, but if we had it without the difficulty, we should not acknowledge the Giver of this good gift. For if man at first, when he wished, were able, and if he did not feel his desires striving against him, and if his soul were not bruised by the weight of its chains, he would attribute to his own strength what he felt himself able to do, and would not confess to the Lord His mercies.

After those trials, the first of wandering and of wanting the truth, the second of difficulty in acting rightly, a third trial overtakes a man—a man, I mean, who has already passed through the first two; for these, I admit, are known to many. For who doth not know that he came out of ignorance into truth, out of wandering into the way, out of a hunger for wisdom to the word of faith. Then there are many who are struggling with difficulties due to their own bad dispositions, and who, still bound by habit, are groaning as if shackled in a prison. They recognize this trial, and indeed perhaps may be saying, 'Unhappy man that I am, who shall deliver me from the body of this death?' (Rom. vii, 24). For note the most cramping chains: 'the flesh,' he saith, 'lusteth against the spirit; and the spirit against the flesh, so that you do not the things that you would' (Gal. v, 17). Accordingly, let him who has already been helped by the Spirit, so that wishing not to be an adulterer, he is not; and wishing not to be a thief, he is not; and all those other things which men desire to conquer, and often are bent and overcome by them, so that they cry out to God that He deliver them from their necessities, and being freed from them, confess to the Lord His mercies. Whoever, I say, is such an one, and hath conquered those difficulties, and now liveth commendably among men, without any complaint of evil living, is met by a third trial, that of a kind of weariness in the length of this life, so that it is sometimes no pleasure to him either to read or to pray. The third trial is contrary to the first, for then he was in danger through hunger, but now through distaste for his food. And what is the origin of this, but a certain apathy of the soul? Adultery no longer now allures thee, yet neither doth the word of God delight thee. Now, after the danger of ignorance and concupiscence, from which thou rejoicest to have escaped, see that weariness and satiety stay thee not. This too is no slight trial; recognize that thou art in it, and cry unto the Lord, that here also He may free thee from thy necessities, and, when thou art free from this trial, let His mercies confess unto Him. . . . So that even when the word of God delighteth thee, thou attribute that not to thyself; nor be puffed up with any sort of arrogance on this account, nor because thou hast an appetite for food, spurn in thy pride those who are in danger from distaste for food.

In Ps. CVI, 4-6; 11.

813

Do not darken thy darkness; God doth not darken it, but rather enlighteneth it. . . . God darkeneth not our darkness, because He mingleth scourging with our sins, and bitterness with our evil delights. Let us not darken our darkness by defending our sins, and night will be an enlightening in our delights.

In Ps. CXXXVIII, 15.

814

He prayeth not that he may be released from the body of this death by the intervention of the death of this body, for this the last day of his life, which on account of its brevity cannot last long, will at some time bring about, but that the lust whereby we lust against the spirit may be more and more diminished, and that the lust whereby we lust against the flesh may more and more increase, until this is consummated in us, and that this lust of the spirit may be consummated through the Holy Spirit which is given us.

In Ps. CXVIII, *Serm.* X, 2.

815

Let us not relapse to the point whence we have already made a start, nor remain stationary in the place to which we have already arrived. . . . Be not so confident in consequence of what thou hast already passed by, as anxious for that to which thou hast not as yet attained. . . . It is this that this suppliant would fain have made known to him, while he was here, that he might know what was yet wanting to him, and so much rejoice in what he had already attained to, as long for that to which he had not yet attained; and having passed through some stages, should not linger on the road, but should be carried away by desire for things above, till he who had already passed some stages should have passed them all, and from the sprinkling of the rain-drops of the Lord, which come from the clouds of the Scriptures, he should come, like the hart, to the fountain of life (Ps. xli, 2), and in that light should see light (Ps. xxxv, 10), and be hidden in the face of God from the disturbance of men (Ps. xxx, 21), when he might say, It is well, I wish for nothing further; here I love all men, I fear none.

In Ps. XXXVIII, 6.

816

Let man will to be prudent, will to be steadfast, will to be temperate, will to be just; and that he may be able truly to be these, let him certainly desire power, and seek to be powerful in himself, and, strange though it be, against himself for the sake of himself. . . . But as to all the other things which he rightly wills to have, such, for instance, as immortality and true and full felicity, let him not cease to long for them, and let him patiently wait for them.

De Trin. XIII, xiii, 17.

817

There are two things prescribed for us in this life as burdensome, namely to contain ourselves and to endure. For we are ordered to contain ourselves from those things which are called good in this world, and to endure those ills which abound in this world. The former is called continence, the latter endurance; two virtues which cleanse the soul and make it capable of divine qualities. In reining our passions and in keeping our pleasures within limits, so that that which flatters us evilly may not seduce us, and that which is called prosperity may not enervate us, we have need of continence: that is, not to put our trust in earthly felicity and to the very end to seek that felicity which has no end. Now as it is the part of continence not to put trust in the felicity of the world, so it is that of endurance not to give way under the misfortunes of the world. Therefore whether we are in affluent circumstances or in needy, we must wait for the Lord, who may both give us what is truly good and sweet and avert from us what is truly evil.

Serm. XXXVIII, i, 1.

818

Because a man for the most part is unknown even to his own self, he knoweth not what he may bear or what he may not bear. And he sometimes presumeth that he may bear that which he cannot, and sometimes despaireth of himself to be able to bear that of which he is capable. Temptation cometh up like a sort of inquisition, and a man is found out by himself; because he was hidden from himself, but from his Maker he was not hidden. Furthermore, Peter presumed of something which was not yet in him, that he would persevere with the Lord Jesus Christ even unto death. Peter knew not his own powers but the Lord knew. He who had fashioned him replied to him that he was not fitted to do so; and He knew that He would give to him that was the work of His hands meet powers, though then He had not yet given them to him. But he who had not yet received them knew this not. Temptation came; he denied Him, he wept, he received the powers (Luke xxii, 33–62). Since therefore we know not what we should ask, as though not having, and for what we should give thanks, as of receiving, there is always need that we be educated in this world by temptations and tribulations.

In Ps. LV, 2.

819

'Lest I should be exalted by the greatness of my revelations' (2 Cor. xii, 7). Who says, 'Lest I should be exalted'? O fear, O terror! Who says, 'Lest I should be exalted'? When so many words of his are beating down elation, repressing swollen pride, doth he yet say, 'Lest I should be exalted'? It is but little that he saith, 'Lest I should be exalted'; mark the remedy which he says was applied to him. 'Lest I should be exalted,' he says, 'there was given me a sting of my flesh, an angel of Satan.' O poison, which is not cured save by poison! 'There was given me a sting of my flesh, and angel of Satan, to buffet me! The head was beaten lest the head should be exalted. O antidote, which is made, as it were, from a serpent and therefore is called *theriaca!* For that serpent persuaded to pride. 'Eat, and you shall be as gods' (Gen. iii, 5). This is the persuasion of pride; whereby the devil fell, thereby he cast down. Justly therefore the serpent's poison is healed by the serpent.

Serm. (de Script. N.T.) CLXIII, viii, 8.

820

For our cross which the Lord bids us carry to the end that we may follow Him with least impediment, what is it but the mortality of our flesh? And it will crucify us until 'death is swallowed in victory' (1 Cor. xv, 54). This cross itself must therefore be crucified and be pierced by the nails which are the fear of God, lest if its members were unfettered and free it would resist and we could not carry it. You cannot possibly follow the Lord except you carry this cross. For how can you follow Him unless you are His? For, as the Apostle says, 'they that are Christ's, have crucified their flesh, with the vices and con-cupiscences' (Gal. v, 24).

Ep. CCXLIII, 11.

821

When it is well with a man, the Christian is left to himself.

In Ps. XXI, *En.* II, 5.

III. NIGHT IN LOVE

822

When a Christian hath begun to think of spiritual progress, he beginneth to suffer from the tongues of adversaries. Whoever hath not yet suffered from these, hath not yet made progress; and whoever suffereth them not, doth not even endeavour to progress. Doth he wish to know what we mean? Let him experience at the same time what we have to listen to. Let him begin to progress, let him begin to wish to ascend, to wish to despise earthly, perishable, temporal things, to hold the happiness of this world as nothing, to think of God alone, not to rejoice in gain, not to pine at losses, to wish to sell all his goods and to give them to the poor, and to follow Christ; let us see how he suffereth the tongues of detractors and many things from opponents, and—a still graver thing—the efforts of pretended counsellors who lead him away from salvation.

In Ps. CXIX, 3.

823

You have said with perfect truth, that before we meet the dissolution of this mortal body, we must die, in the sense of the Gospel, by a voluntary departure, withdrawing ourselves not by death but by an act of will from the life of this world. This course is a simple one and beset with no waves of uncertainty, because we believe that we ought so to live in this mortal life that we may be in some measure fitted for immortality. The whole question, however, which, when discussed and investigated, perplexes men like myself, is this: how we ought to live among or for the welfare of those who have not yet learned to live by dying, not in the dissolution of the body, but by turning themselves by a certain act of volition from the allurements of bodily things. For in most cases, it seems to us that unless we in some small degree conform to them in regard to those very things from which we desire to see them delivered, we shall not succeed in doing them any good. And when we do thus conform, a pleasure in such things steals upon ourselves, we are often pleased to say and to lend our ear to frivolous things, and not only to smile at them but even to be completely overcome with laughter. And by thus burdening our souls with feelings which are of the dust and even of the mire of the world, we experience greater difficulty and reluctance in raising ourselves to God, so that by dying a Gospel-death we may live a Gospel-life. But once we have succeeded in this, there will immediately follow the commendation, 'well done! well done!' not from men—for no man perceives in another the mental act by which divine things are apprehended—but in a certain inward silence there sounds I know not whence the words, 'well done! well done!' Because of this kind of temptation the great Apostle

431

confesses that he 'was given an angel of Satan to buffet him' (2 Cor. xii, 7). Behold whence it comes that our whole life on earth is a temptation; for man is tempted even in that thing in which he is being conformed, so far as he can be, to the likeness of the celestial life.

What shall I say as to the infliction or remission of punishment in cases in which we have no other desire than to forward the spiritual welfare of those in whose case we have to judge whether they ought or ought not to be punished? Again, if we consider not only the nature and magnitude of faults but also what each is able or unable to bear according to his strength of mind, how deep and dark a question it is to adjust the amount of punishment so as to prevent him who receives it not only from getting no good but also from suffering loss thereby! Besides, I know not whether a greater number have been improved or made worse when alarmed by the threats of such punishment at the hands of men as is an object of fear. What, then, is the path of duty, seeing that it often happens that if you inflict punishment on one he goes to destruction, whereas if you leave him unpunished another is destroyed? . . .

Moreover, as to the pronouncements of God, is it not true that they are lightly touched rather than grasped and handled by us, seeing that in by far the greater part of them we do not already possess opinions definite and ascertained, but are rather inquiring what our opinion ought to be? And this caution, though attended by abundant disquietude, is much better than the rashness of dogmatic assertion. Also, if a man is not wise with 'the wisdom of the flesh,' which the Apostle says 'is death' (Rom. viii, 6), will he not be a great cause of offence to those who are still wise according to the flesh in the many things on which it is most perilous to say what you believe, and to refrain from saying this is most harassing, and to say something other than you believe is most pernicious? Nay more, when in the discourses or writings of those who are within the Church we find things which we do not approve, and, supposing it be in accord with brotherly love, we do not conceal our judgment on them, how great a sin is committed against us when we are suspected of being actuated in this by envy and not by good will! and how much do we sin against others, when in like manner we impute to those who find fault with our opinions a desire rather to wound than to correct us! Truly, there arise from this cause bitter enmities even between persons bound to each other by the greatest affection and intimacy; and when one is 'puffed up against the other for another, above that which is written' (1 Cor. iv, 6), and when they 'bite and devour one another,' let them 'take heed they be not consumed one of another' (Gal. v, 15). Therefore, 'who will give me wings like a dove, and I will fly and be at rest?' (Ps. liv, 7), for whether it be that the dangers by which one is beset seem to him greater than those of which he has no experience, or that in very truth this is the case, I cannot help thinking that any amount of weakness and of tempest in the wilderness would be more easily borne than the things we suffer or fear in the busy world.

Ep. XCV, 112-4.

824

He now ascendeth a step, he beginneth to progress; but he is still living among the wicked, unrighteous men. The floor hath not yet been winnowed, suppose he hath become wheat, is he then already in the barn? It has been necessary so far that he be crowded with much chaff; and the more he progresseth, the greater scandals doth he see in the people. For if he were not a true Christian, he would not see the hypocrites. The Lord, my brethren, teaches us this lesson also from that parable of the wheat and the cockle. 'When the blade was sprung up and had brought forth fruit, then appeared also the cockle' (Matt. xiii, 26); that is to say, the wicked appear unto no man, save he himself is become good; for 'when the blade was sprung up and had brought forth fruit, then appeared the cockle.'

In Ps. XIX, 6.

825

Evils abound, and God hath willed that evils should abound. Would that evil men did not abound, and the evils would not abound. Bad times, troublesome times, this is what men say. Let us live a good life, and the times are good. We are the times; such as we are so are the times. But what are we to do? We cannot, it may be, convert the mass of mankind to a good life.

But let the few who do give ear live a good life; let the few who live a good life endure the many who live ill. They are grains of corn; they are on the threshing-floor; on the threshing-floor they can have the chaff with them; in the barn they will not have them. Let them endure what they would not that they may attain to what they would have. Why are we sad and blame God? Evils abound in the world in order that the world may not engage our love. Those who have despised the world with all its superficial attractions were great men, faithful saints; we are not able to despise it foul as it is. The world is evil, yea, it is evil, and yet it is loved as though it were good. But what is this evil world? For the sky and the earth and the waters and the things that are in them, the fishes and the birds and the trees are not evil. All these are good; it is evil men who make this evil world. Yet as we cannot be without evil men, let us, as I have said, whilst we live pour out our groans before the Lord our God, and endure the evils that we may attain to the things that are good. Let us not find fault with the Master of the household, for He is loving to us. He beareth us and not we Him. He knoweth how to govern what He made. Do what He hath commanded, and hope for what He hath promised.

Serm. (de Script. N.T.) LXXX, 8

826

And you say, the times are troublesome, the times are burdensome, the times are miserable. Live rightly and by living rightly you change the times; you change the times, and you have not whereat to grumble. For what are the times, my brethren? The periods and cycles of the ages. The sun is risen; after twelve hours are accomplished it sets onto another part of the world; rising in the morning on another day, it again sets. Count how many times this happens. These are the times. Whom has the rising of the sun hurt? Whom has the setting of the sun hurt? Therefore the time has hurt nobody. Those who are hurt are men; those by whom they are hurt are men. What an affliction! Men are hurt, men are despoiled, men are oppressed, and by whom? Not by lions, not by serpents, not by scorpions, but by men. Those who are hurt suffer pain. If they can, do not they themselves do that which they reprehend? Then we und

434

a man grumbling when he could do that whereat he was grumbling. I give praise, I give praise, if he did not do that which he blamed.

Serm. CCCXI, viii, 8.

827

So long, he saith, as this is the work with me, as this command is given me that I should love enemies, the revilings of these men, growing in strength and casting their shadow on me, do derange mine eye, perturb my sight, penetrate my heart, slay my soul. I could wish to depart, for I am weak, lest by abiding I should add sins to sins. Or at least may I be separated for a little space from mankind, lest my wound suffer from frequent blows, in order that when it hath been made whole it may be brought back to the exercise. This is what takes place, brethren and there ariseth oft-times in the mind of the servant of God a longing for solitude, for no other reason than because of the multitude of tribulations and scandals. . . . For the Apostle himself too, although strong, although great, although most stout of heart, although an invincible soldier in Christ, was troubled, as we read, in his exercise, and he saith: 'From henceforth let no man be troublesome to me' (Gal. vi, 17). . . . A man often endeavoureth to amend perverted and depraved men, who belong indeed to his care but in whom there is but failure for all human pains and vigilance. . . . I have done everything; whatever powers I had I have expended and have drained. I see that I have prevailed nothing. All my labour hath been spent, sorrow hath remained. . . . The revilings of men I cannot bear; they roar, they are carried away with frenzy, they are inflamed with indignation, their anger casts its shadow on me; to do good to them I am unable, O that I might rest somewhere, separated from them in body, not in love; lest love itself should be confounded in me. With my words and my struggling I can do no good to them; by praying for them I shall perchance do good. . . . Behold they go afar off flying away, they abide in the wilderness; but do they singly? Charity holdeth them, so that they abide with many; and from these same many there emerge some to direct them. For in any gathering of a multitude there must needs be found evil men.

. . . Wherever thou shalt be, other men will gather there together; they will seek the desert with thee. They will attach themselves to thy life, thou canst not thrust away the society of brethren. There are mingled with thee evil men, thy portion is still exercise. 'Lo, I have gone far off . . . and I abode in the wilderness' (Ps. liv, 8). In what wilderness? Perchance in the conscience whither no man entereth, where no one is with thee, where thou art and God. For if in the wilderness, in any place, what wilt thou do with men gathering themselves together? For thou wilt not be able to be separated from mankind so long as thou livest among men. Observe rather that Comforter, our Lord and King, our Ruler and Creator, created also among us: observe that with His Twelve He included one man whom He was to suffer.

The Psalmist saith, 'I have gone far off, flying away; and I abode in the wilderness' (*ibid.*). Perchance that man, as I have said, hath fled unto his conscience, there he will have found some little wilderness wherein to rest. But that love doth trouble him; he was alone in his conscience, but not alone in charity. Within, he was comforted in conscience; but without, tribulations left him not. Therefore though at peace in himself when, depending on others, he was still being troubled, what doth he say? 'I waited for him that should save me from pusillanimity of spirit and a storm' (*id.* 9; Aug. *faceret*, vlg. *fecit*). There is a sea, there is a storm. Nothing remaineth for thee but to cry out, 'Lord I perish' (cf. Matt. viii, 25; xiv, 30). Let Him who doth tread the waves fearlessly stretch forth His hand, let Him relieve thy dread; let Him confirm in Himself thy security; let Him speak to thee within and say to thee, 'Give heed to me, what have I not suffered? Perchance thou art suffering an evil brother, or thou art suffering an enemy without. Which of these have I not suffered?' Without, the Jews were roaring; within, a disciple was a traitor. The storm is therefore raging, but He saveth men 'from pusillanimity of spirit and a storm.' Perchance thy ship is being tossed because in thee He is asleep. The sea was raging, the boat wherein the disciples were sailing was being tossed; but Christ was asleep. At length it was seen by them that the Ruler and Creator of the winds was asleep. They came to Christ and awaked Him; He commanded the winds, and there came a great calm (Matt. viii, 23 *sqq.*). Perchance thy heart is rightly troubled, because thou hast been unmindful of Him in whom thou hast believed. Thou art suffering beyond endurance because it hath not come into thy mind what Christ hath borne for thee. If Christ cometh not into thy mind, He is asleep. Awake Christ, renew thy faith. If thou hast forgotten the sufferings of Christ, then is Christ asleep in thee. If thou hast remembered the sufferings of Christ, then is Christ watching in thee. But when with a full heart thou hast contemplated what He hath suffered, wilt not thou also endure thy sufferings with a calm mind, perchance too rejoicing because thou hast been found to be in some similitude of the sufferings of thy King?

In Ps. LIV, 8–10.

828

There is no sea so deep as these thoughts of God, Who maketh the wicked to flourish, and the good to be afflicted—nothing so profound, nothing so deep; and in that deep, in that profundity, every unbelieving soul is wrecked. Dost thou wish to cross this deep? Move not away from the wood of Christ's cross. Thou shalt not sink; hold thyself fast to Christ.

In Ps. XCI, 8.

829

Whether anyone is to persevere unto the end in that wherein he is evil, we do not know; and oft-times when thou seemest to thyself to have been hating an enemy, thou hast been hating a brother, and knowest it not. The devil and his angels have been manifested to us in the Holy Scriptures as being destined for everlasting fire. Of them only must amendment be despaired of; and against them we have a secret wrestling. . . . 'Our wrestling is not against flesh and blood'; that is, against men whom you see, ' but against principalities and powers, against the rulers of the world of this darkness' (Eph. vi, 12). . . . Concerning these same rulers therefore we have a definite sentence of Scripture, that there is for any one of them no hope of any return thence. But of the darknesses themselves of whom these are the rulers we truly are not sure, whether haply they that were darkness may not be made light. Indeed, to them that were lately made believers the Apostle saith: 'You were heretofore darkness, but now light in the Lord' (Eph. v, 8): Darkness in yourselves, light in the Lord. . . . Before thee this rule of goodness hath been set, that thou mayest imitate the goodness of the Father, 'who maketh His sun to rise upon the good, and bad, and raineth upon the just and the unjust' (Matt. v, 45). . . . Thou indeed hast for an enemy him that in common with thee was created, but God him that he hath created. . . . And He spareth them, He who hath nothing that an enemy may lay to His charge, to Whom every enemy is ungrateful; for from Him he hath whatever of good he hath. . . . As to thyself, what hast thou bestowed on thy enemy whom thou findest so intolerable to endure? If He hath him for an enemy, He Who hath bestowed so great things on him and 'maketh His sun to rise upon the good, and bad, and raineth upon the just and the unjust', thou that neither canst make the sun rise nor cause rain to fall upon the lands, canst thou not keep one thing for thine enemy, so that there may be to thee on earth peace to a man of good will? (cf. Luke ii, 14). Since therefore this rule of love is fixed for thee, that, imitating the Father, thou shouldst love an enemy; for He saith, 'Love your enemies' (Luke vi, 27, 35); how wouldst thou be exercised in this precept, if thou hadst no enemy to suffer? Thou seest then that he profiteth thee somewhat; and let the fact that God spareth evil men profit thee, so that thou show mercy; since thou too, if thou art a good man, hast perchance been made a good man out of an evil man. And if God spared not evil men, thou wouldst not even be found to return thanks. May He therefore that hath spared thee spare others also. For it were not right, when thou hadst passed through, to close up the way of godliness.

In Ps. LIV, 4.

830

We need not despair of any man, so long as he lives.

In Ps. XXXVI, *Serm.* II, 11.

831

As long as a man doth not turn away his eyes lest they behold vanity, he suspecteth in others what is going on in himself; so that he believeth another to worship God, or do good works, from the same motive as himself. For men can see what we do, but our purpose for so acting is hidden; and there is thus room allowed for suspicions, so that one man dareth to judge of the hidden secrets of another, and in general falsely; and to suspect at random things that are unknown to him, even if they be true. . . . A lover of truth declares that to be sweet which is true. But the judgments of men concerning the hidden secrets of men are not sweet, but reckless. . . .

But since nothing save envy willingly suspecteth another's reproach, while a good work cannot be censured because that which is open speaketh for itself, it is censured on the score of the end for which it was done, because what is hidden doth not reveal itself. And thus any man who pleaseth may suspect the doer of evil, because he seeth not what is hidden, and envieth that which is eminent. Against this fault truly, which leads one willingly to suspect in a man evil, though he see it not, charity which 'envieth not' (1 Cor. xiii, 4) must be held fast.

In Ps. CXVIII, *Serm.* xii, 4, 5.

832

But nevertheless, he saith, men add to their sins under the hope of pardon. On the contrary, they would add to them if they despaired of pardon. . . . Wouldst thou not also say to thyself: I am already a sinner, already an unjust man, one already doomed to damnation; hope of pardon there is none, why should I not do whatever pleaseth me, though it be not lawful? Why not satisfy, so far as I can, any desires I may have, if, after these, there are only torments in store for me? Wouldst thou not speak thus to thyself, and from this very despair become still worse? Rather than this, He who promiseth forgiveness correcteth thee. . . . In order that men might not live the worse from despair, He promised a harbour of forgiveness; further, that they might not live the worse from hope of pardon, He made the day of death uncertain—establishing both most providentially, as a refuge for the returning and a terror to the loitering.

In Ps. CI, *Serm.* I, 10.

833

'I have hated them with a perfect hatred' (Ps. cxxxviii, 22). . . . I hated in them their iniquities, I loved the work of Thy

439

hand. This it is to hate with a perfect hatred, that thou neither hate the man on account of the vices, nor love the vices on account of the man. . . . How will [the Psalmist] fulfil in them both his own words, 'Have I not hated them, O Lord, that hated thee' (*id.*, 21), and the Lord's command, 'Love your enemies'? (Matt. v, 44). How will he fulfil this save with that 'perfect hatred,' so that what he hates in them is that they are wicked, what he loves in them is that they are men? For even in the time of the Old Testament, when the carnal people was kept in restraint by visible punishments, how did Moses, the servant of God, who by understanding belonged to the New Testament, hate sinners, when he prayed for them? Or how did he not hate them when he slew them, save that he 'hated them with a perfect hatred'? For with such perfection did he hate the iniquity which he punished, as to love the manhood for which he prayed.

In Ps. CXXXVIII, 28.

834

For living in things human, we cannot withdraw from things human. Among evil men we must live with forbearance, for when we were evil good men have lived with forbearance among us. If we do not forget what we have been, we shall not despair of those that now are what we once were.

In Ps. L, 24.

835

Now it seemed to the servants a grave matter that there was cockle among the wheat; and indeed it was a grave matter. But the working of the field is one thing, another the quiet of the barn. Endure, for to this thou wert born; endure, for perchance thou art endured. If thou hast always been good, have mercy. If thou hast at any time been evil, do not be forgetful of it. And who is always good? If God should sift thee carefully, He will more easily find thee even now evil, than thou wilt find thyself always good. . . . The gathering of the crop in the field will come to an end, the separation of the harvest will follow. The Lord only demands patience of us, which He displays in Himself, saying to thee: If I willed to judge now, should

I judge unfairly? If I willed to judge now, could I be deceived? If I who always judge rightly and who cannot be deceived, defer my judgment, dost thou, ignorant as thou art how thou art to be judged, dare to judge so very hastily? Mark, brethren, how He did not grant to those servants who wanted to pull up the cockle before the proper time, this task even at the harvest; for He said to them, 'In the time of the harvest I will say to the reapers.' He does not say, I will say to you; . . . for He tells that 'the reapers are the angels' (Matt. xiii, 24–30, 37–43). Man, fettered as thou art by the flesh, bearing the flesh, or perchance all flesh, that is flesh in the body, fleshly in the mind, dost thou dare to usurp beforehand the office of another, an office which will not be yours even at the harvest?

Serm. XLVII, v, 6.

836

What is so much to be feared as when a man sees many living evilly, and those of whom good was hoped found in many evil practices? He fears lest all whom he thought good be such, and almost all the good come under evil suspicion. What kind of man is he? How has he fallen? How has he been found in that disgraceful business, in that wickedness, in that evil deed? Think you not all are the same? This is 'a fear to my acquaintance' (Ps. xxx, 12), that even with those to whom we are known we very often come under suspicion. And, if thou art anything, unless what thou art thyself console thee, thou dost not believe there is another like thee. A good conscience, whatever it be, consoleth a man, so that a man whose life is good may say to himself, 'O thou who art now fearing lest all be such, art thou such?' Conscience makes answer, 'I am not.' Then if thou art not such, art thou alone? Beware lest this pride be worse than that wickedness. Say not that thou art alone. For so Elias once for weariness of the multitude of the ungodly said, 'Lord, they have slain thy prophets, they have dug down thy altars. And I am left alone: and they seek my life.' But what saith the divine answer to him? 'I have left me seven thousand men that have not bowed their knees to Baal' (Rom. xi, 3, 4; cf. III Kings xix, 10, 18). Therefore, brethren, amid these offences there is one remedy—that thou think not badly of thy brother.

Be thou humble, as thou wouldst have him be, and thou wilt not think to be what thou art not.

In Ps. XXX, *En.* II, *Serm.* II, 7.

837

'Who is he, and we will praise him?' (Ecclus. xxxi, 9). Who is he? or who is there here? God forbid that I should despair of there being some one here; no, not some one but some. God forbid that I should despair of the threshing-floor of so great a master of the house. He who sees a threshing-floor from afar, thinks there is only chaff in it; but he who knows how to look, finds the grain. There where the chaff displeases thee, lies the mass of grain. There where that which is being beaten in the threshing displeases thee, is what is purged by the threshing; it is there, be sure of that, it is there. Lastly, he is sure, who sowed the crop that that is there with which his barn will be filled when it has been winnowed.

Serm. CCCXI, x, 10.

838

For to separate them now is not safe for every one. Separation will belong to Him who knows not how to err. What is the meaning of, 'Who knows not how to err'? That He neither transfer the evil to the right hand nor the good to the left. But we in this life find it difficult to know ourselves; how much less ought we to pass a hasty sentence on any one. For even if to-day we know him to be evil, we know not what he will be to-morrow; and perhaps he whom we violently hate is our brother, and we know it not. It is therefore safe for us to hate in the wicked their wickedness, and to love the creature, so that we love what God made in him, but hate what man has made in himself. For God made man himself, man made sin. Love what God has made, hate what man has made; for thus thou wilt persecute what man has made, that what God has made may be set free.

In Ps. CXXXIX, 2.

839

If thou wouldst obtain the mercy of God, be thou thyself merciful. If thou deniest humanity to man, though thou thyself art a man, God also will deny thee divinity, that is, the incortuption of immortality, by which He makes us gods. For God has no need of anything from thee, but thou hast need from God. He seeks nothing from thee that He may be blessed, but thou, unless thou receive from Him, canst not be blessed. . . . But He will give thee not anything of those things which He has created, but Himself that you may enjoy Him, Him the very Creator of all things. . . . And how will He give to thee? Dost thou suppose as it were for thy merits? If thou seekest what thou hast merited, give heed to thy sins. If thou seekest a recompense for thy sins, what can befall thee but the penalty of death? . . . Have pity on man, O man, and God will have pity on thee. Thou a man and thy neighbour a man, are two pitiable creatures. But God is not pitiable but has a pitying heart [*non est miser, sed misericors*]. If then the pitiable creature has not pity on his pitiable fellow creature, how can he demand a pitying heart of Him who never will be pitiable? . . . Whoever, for example, is cruel to a shipwrecked person, is cruel for so long until a shipwreck happen to him. But let a shipwreck once befall him, and when he sees a shipwrecked person, thinking back into his past life, he is affected by a misery similar to that he once felt; and he whom the common bond of humanity could not move to pity, is so moved by a fellowship in misfortune. How quickly one who has once been a slave has pity on a slave. How quickly one who has himself been a hireling grieves for the hireling who has been defrauded of his hire. And one will bitterly sympathize with a man who has something serious to complain of in his son, if he himself has had to complain of some similar thing. Similarity of misery, therefore, softens the hardness of the human heart, however hard it be. If then thou, who either hast been miserable or fearest that thou mayest be miserable—and as long as thou art living here thou must fear what thou hast not been, and remember what thou mayest have been, and contemplate what thou art—living as thou art, then, in the memory of past miseries, in the fear of future miseries, and under the affliction of present miseries, hast no pity for a man in serious trouble who needs thy help, how canst thou expect Him whom misery has never touched, to have pity on thee? For thou art not giving that which thou hast received from God and yet thou wishest God to give thee of that which He has not received from thee.

Serm. CCLIX, 3.

840

Let us remember therefore, most dearly beloved brethren, we pray you: Let whosoever shall have been delivered from sin, remember what he was. . . . For then he beareth another man to be healed, if he shall remember that he himself was healed. Therefore let each call to mind what he was, and whether he be not still so; and then he will succour him that still is what he is no longer.

In Ps. XXV, 15.

841

What man can pass judgment on man? The world is full of rash judgments. He of whom we had despaired, is suddenly converted, and becomes eminently good; another of whom we had expected much, suddenly lapses, and becomes exceedingly bad. Nor is our fear any more certain, nor our love either. What any man may be to-day, the man himself scarcely knows; and if after some fashion he knows what he is to-day, yet what he will be to-morrow not even himself knows.

Serm. XLVI, xii, 27.

842

This psalm (cvi) commendeth unto us the mercies of God, proved in us, and is therefore the sweeter to those who have experienced them. Indeed it is wonderful that it can be pleasing to anyone except to him who has learnt in his own case what he hears in this psalm. . . . What I am about to say may, if this be possible, occur to every man in his own case. But I am speaking to men who walk the way of God, and stand in some sort of spiritual advancement. Wherefore if perchance there are any near this state who do not fully understand me, let them find out where they are, and by advancement hasten to an understanding of it. . . . But whatsoever, while I am speaking, thou mayest recognise in thyself, whoever thou art who hast experienced it, do not in thy thought stay, as it were, at thyself, and think that it taketh place in thee alone, but believe that these things take place in all, or almost in all.

In Ps. CVI, 1, 3.

843

The Psalmist was complaining (Ps. cxxxix) of the stumbling-blocks and snares of sinners, of the evil men, vessels of the devil, that raged around him and laid traps around him, of the proud that envy the just, among the like of whom he has to pass his life, while we live here in this pilgrimage of ours. But that such iniquities should abound the Lord foretold, and said, 'Iniquity shall abound; and because iniquity shall abound, the charity of many shall grow cold.' But He at once added the comforting words, 'He that shall persevere to the end, he shall be saved' (Matt. xxiv, 12 *sq.*). This he observed and feared, and distressed at the abundance of iniquities, he turned himself to hope, for 'he that shall persevere to the end, he shall be saved.' He braced himself to persevere, and saw that the way was long; and, because to persevere is a great and difficult thing, he prayed Him, by whom the command to persevere was given to him, to perfect his perseverance. I shall surely be saved if I persevere to the end; but perseverance, so that I may merit salvation, pertaineth unto strength. Thou art 'the strength of my salvation'; thou makest me to persevere, so that I may attain salvation. 'O Lord, Lord, the strength of my salvation.' And whence cometh my hope that Thou art 'the strength of my salvation?' 'Thou hast overshadowed my head in the day of battle' (Ps. cxxxix, 8). Lo I am still fighting: I fight without against those who falsely pretend to be good, I fight within against my own lusts. For 'I see another law in my members, fighting against the law of my mind and captivating me in the law of sin that is in my members. Unhappy man that I am, who shall deliver me from the body of this death? The grace of God, by Jesus Christ our Lord' (Rom. vii, 23 *sqq.*). Labouring then in this battle, he turned to the grace of God; and because he had already begun to be heated and parched, he found as it were a shade, under which to live. 'Thou hast overshadowed my head in the day of battle'; that is, in the heat, lest I be wearied, lest I be parched.

In Ps. CXXXIX, 11.

844

'For thou, O Lord art sweet and mild' (Ps. lxxxv, 5). . . .
As though wearied with the bitterness of earthly things [the
Psalmist] wished to be sweetened, and sought the fountain of
sweetness, but found it not on earth. For wherever he turned
he found scandals, fears, tribulations, temptations. In what man
was there safety? In whom could he surely rejoice? Certainly
not in himself; could he any more in others? Either men are
bad and we must suffer them, and hope that they can be changed;
or they are good, when we ought to love them in such wise that
we fear—since they are capable of change—lest they become
bad. In one case their wickedness causes bitterness of soul, in the
other this is caused by anxiety and fear, lest he who is walking
well should slip. Wherever therefore he turns he finds bitterness
in earthly things; he has not whereby he may be sweetened,
except he lift himself up to God. . . . Now I will speak, my
brethren, as a man among men, and sprung from men. Let
each one take his own heart and examine himself without
flattery and without false soothing. For nothing is more foolish
than for a man vainly to soothe and seduce himself. Let him
take notice, then, and see what things pass in the human heart;
how even prayers are often hindered by vain thoughts, so that
the heart scarcely remains fixed on God for any time; and it
wishes to hold itself so as to stay set on Him, sometimes flees
from itself, but finds no bars in which it can enclose itself, no
barriers by which it may restrain its flights and wanderings,
and stand still to be made glad by God. . . . And God bears
with these failings of ours, and yet expects prayer from us, in
order to make us perfect; and when we have given it to Him,
He receives it gratefully, and hearkens to it, and remembers
not those prayers which we pour out unthinkingly, and accepts
the one which we can scarcely find. . . . What then? Must
we despair of mankind, and say that every man is already
condemned into whose prayers any wandering thoughts have
crept and interrupted? If we say this, my brethren, I know not
what hope remains. Therefore, because there is some hope before
God, since His mercy is great, let us say to Him, 'Give joy to
the soul of thy servant, for to Thee, O Lord, I have lifted up

my soul' (*ibid.*, 4). And how have I lifted it up? As I could, as Thou gavest me strength, as I could catch it as it was fleeing away. And hast thou forgotten (imagine God to say) that as often as thou didst stand before Me, thou didst think of so many vain and useless things, and didst scarcely pour out to Me an earnest and steady prayer? 'For Thou, O Lord, art sweet and mild'; gracious art Thou to suffer me. From infirmity I sink; heal Thou me, and I shall stand; strengthen Thou me and I shall be strong. But until Thou do this, Thou sufferest me; 'For Thou, O Lord, art sweet and mild: and plenteous in mercy'; that is, not only of mercy but plenteous in mercy; for as our iniquity abounds, so also aboundeth Thy mercy.

In Ps. LXXXV, 7–8.

845

For whither should he turn for comfort, whom weariness had possessed because of sinners forsaking the law of God? Whither should he turn him? To any man of God? Already perchance he had found great tribulation in many men the more he had relied on any delight from them. For sometimes men seem to be just, and we rejoice because of them, and we must needs rejoice, inasmuch as charity cannot be without joy at such an one. But in these things wherein man hath rejoiced, if perchance anything perverse shall have happened, as is often the case, in proportion as the joy was great therein before, so the sorrow which ariseth is great, so that henceforth man feareth to give rein to his joys, feareth to trust himself to gladness, lest it may be that the more he hath joyed, the more he may pine, if any mischance shall have arisen. Smitten therefore with abundant scandals, like as it were with many wounds, he hath closed his door against human comfort, and his soul hath refused to be comforted. And whence is he to draw life? Whence a respite? 'I remembered God, and was delighted' (Ps. lxxvi, 4).

In Ps. LXXVI, 6.

846

Dost thou wish to be long-suffering? Consider the eternity of God. For thou regardest thy few days, and in thy few days thou dost wish all things to be fulfilled. . . . The condemnation of all the ungodly, and the crowning of all the good: dost thou wish these things to be fulfilled in these thy days? God fulfilleth them in His own time. Why dost thou suffer weariness? He is eternal; He waiteth; He is long-suffering. But thou sayest, I am not long-suffering, because I am mortal. But thou hast it in thy power to become so; join thy heart to the eternity of God, and with Him thou shalt be eternal. . . . Join thyself to the eternity of God; together with Him wait for those things which are beneath thee. For when thy heart shall have cleaved to the Most High, all mortal things will be beneath thee.

In Ps. XCI, 8, 10.

847

For iniquity is not yet passed away, iniquity is still rife. . . . Thou passest away, and behold passed are thy temptations; and thou goest into another life whither the saints have gone, if thou hast been saintly. . . . Because thou hast passed away hence, hath on this account iniquity now passed away? Other unrighteous men are born, as other unrighteous men die. In like manner therefore just as some unrighteous men die and others are born, so some just men pass away and others are born. Even unto the end of the world there will never be wanting iniquity to oppress or justice to suffer.

In Ps. LVI, 6.

848

In the minds of men there are such lurking places and such depths that, although all suspicious persons deserve to be blamed, they think themselves that they actually deserve praise for their prudence.

Ep. CLI, 4.

849

Nothing conquers except truth: the victory of truth is charity.

Serm. CCCLVIII, 1.

850

Thou dost wish to be satisfied with the good things of God; let mercy be satisfied within thee.

In Ps. CII, 11.

IV. NIGHT OF LIFE

851

For trouble and profitable sorrow were hidden things to me, tribulation by which He giveth aid, to whom it is said, 'Give us help from trouble: for vain is the salvation of man' (Ps. lix, 13). For I thought I might rejoice and exult in the vain salvation of man; but when I had heard from my Lord, 'Blessed are they that mourn; for they shall be comforted' (Matt. v, 5), I did not wait until I should lose those temporal blessings I had, and then mourn, but I gave heed to that very misery of mine, whereby I rejoiced in things such as I both feared to lose and yet could not retain. I gave heed to this earnestly and steadfastly, and I saw that I was not only agonized by the adversities of this world, but even impeded by its prosperities. And thus 'I met with the trouble and sorrow' which had been hidden from me, 'and I called upon the name of the Lord. O Lord, deliver my soul' (Ps. cxiv, 3 *sq.*). . . . We do not enjoin them to seek for a misery for which they have no cause, but to discover that which they harbour without knowing it. Nor is it our desire concerning them, that those earthly necessaries, which they require while they live in this mortal state, should be wanting to them; but that they mourn for this, that having lost that abundance that cometh from heaven, they have deserved to be in want of those earthly blessings which are not permanently to be enjoyed, but which are needful for sustenance. Let them acknowledge and mourn for this misery; and He who willed not that they should be miserable for ever, will make them blessed in their mourning.

In Ps. CXIV, 4

852

For our depths (Ps. cxxix) is this mortal life. Whoever hath understood himself to be in the depths crieth out, groaneth, sigheth, until he be delivered from the depths, and come unto Him whose seat is above all depths and above the Cherubim' above all things He hath created not only bodily but also spiritual things; until the soul come to Him; until His own image, that image which is man, and which in these depths hath been tossed about by constant waves and worn away by them, be liberated by Him. And except it be renewed and repaired by God, Who impressed it on man when He formed man, he is always in the depths; for though man could be equal to his own fall, he is not equal to his own rising again; and, as I have said, unless he be freed, he is ever in the depths. But when he crieth from the depths, he riseth from the depths; and his very cry suffereth him not to be long at the bottom. . . .

'If thou, O Lord, wilt mark iniquities; Lord who shall stand it?' (*ibid.*, 2) Thus he hath disclosed from what depths he was crying out; for he crieth from under the weight and turbulence of his iniquities. He looked upon himself; he pondered upon his own life; he saw it everywhere buried in excesses and crimes. Wherever he looked, he found nothing good in himself, nothing of the serenity of justice could he meet. And when he saw so many and so great sins and such troops of his own crimes, he cried out as if terror-struck, 'If thou, O Lord, wilt mark iniquities; Lord, who will stand it?' He did not say, I shall not stand it, but 'who shall stand it?' For he saw that nigh the whole of human life is ever bayed at by its sins, that all consciences are accused by their thoughts, that a chaste heart trusting in its own justice could not be found. If therefore a chaste heart that can trust in its own justice cannot be found, let the hearts of all trust in the mercy of God, and say, 'If thou O Lord, wilt mark iniquities, Lord, who shall stand it?'

In Ps. CXXIX, 1, 2.

853

For here though the life of believers be day, 'the life of man upon earth is a warfare' (Job vii, 1). Night and day—day in comparison with unbelievers, night in comparison with the Angels. For the Angels have a day, which we have not yet. . . . In this then which is now day, but yet night, night in comparison with the future day for which we yearn, day in comparison with the past night which we have renounced; in this night, I say, let us therefore seek God with our hands. Let not works cease; let us seek God; let there be no idle yearning.

In Ps. LXXVI, 4.

854

For, my brethren, do all of us who now labour in Christ, all of us who tremble at His words, who in any way strive to do His will, and groan while we pray Him to help us fulfil what He hath commanded, already sit in those thrones of bliss which are promised us? No, but in keeping His commandments we hope that this will come to pass. . . . At present they are as fathers, men of hope for the future; but when they have obtained what they hope for, they are children; because they have brought forth and produced in their works that which they gain. And this is preserved unto them for the future, since futurity itself commonly signifieth children.

In Ps. CXXXI, 19.

855

'For the whole life of man upon earth,' as it is written, 'is a warfare' (Job vii, 1). Nor is prosperity as it were to be chosen and adversity alone to be shunned; but we must beware of both of them, of the former lest it corrupt, of the latter lest it crush; so that for every man, in whatever state of affairs he shall have lived in this life, there may be no refuge but God, nor any joy but in His promises.

In Ps. LXXIV, 1.

856

God hath willed that these temporal gifts be promiscuous; for if He were to give them to good men alone, evil men would think that God must be worshipped for the sake of them. On the other hand, if He were to give these gifts to evil men only, good men who were weak would fear to be converted, lest these gifts should perhaps be wanting to them. For a soul being as yet weak is less able to receive the Kingdom of God. God our Husbandman must feed her. . . . Again, if they should be taken away from good men alone, there would be that same fear among weak men preventing them from being converted to God. On the other hand, if they should be taken away from evil men alone, the punishment wherewith evil men are smitten would be thought to be the only one they must suffer. By giving them to good men He comforteth them on their journey;

by giving them to evil men He warneth good men to set their desire on other things which they have not in common with evil men. Again, He taketh them away from good men whenever He willeth, in order that they may question themselves as to their own powers and may find out as to themselves, what perchance was hidden from them, whether now they be able to say, 'the Lord gave, and the Lord hath taken away. As it hath pleased the Lord so is it done. Blessed be the name of the Lord' (Job i, 21). For that soul both blessed the Lord and, being rained upon with the fatness of blessing, rendered back her fruits. 'The Lord gave and the Lord hath taken away.' He hath withdrawn the gifts but hath not withdrawn the Giver. Every soul that is blessed is simple, not cleaving to earthly things, not grovelling with wings entangled by birdlime, but beaming with the brightness of the virtues; in the twin wings of a twin love she doth spring into the free air; and seeing there is withdrawn from her that whereon she was treading, not that whereon she was resting, she saith securely, 'the Lord gave, and the Lord hath taken away. As it hath pleased the Lord so is it done. Blessed be the name of the Lord.' He gave and He hath taken away; there remaineth He that gave, and He hath taken away that which He gave. Blessed be His name. To this end therefore are these gifts taken away from good men. But lest any weak man should perchance say, 'When shall I be of so great virtue as was holy Job?' . . . Mark that they are taken away from evil men also. Why then dost thou delay thy conversion? That which thou fearest to lose when good, if thou art evil thou wilt still perhaps lose. If thou, a good man, hast lost them, there is by thee the Comforter who hath taken them away. The coffer is emptied of gold, the heart is full of faith; outwardly thou art poor, but inwardly thou art rich. Thou carriest thy riches with thee, and these thou wouldst not lose even if thou shouldst escape naked from shipwreck. . . . He hath given to thee, be not lifted up. He hath taken away from thee, be not crushed. Thou fearest lest He take away, He can take away from the evil man as well as the good. It is better as a good man to lose that which is from God and to keep God.

In Ps. LXVI, 3.

857

Thou wishest many things, and even in thine own house thou canst not do all thou wishest. Perchance thy wife gainsays thee, thy children gainsay thee, sometimes even thy servant insolently gainsays thee, and thou doest not what thou wishest. Sometimes thou wouldst punish and canst not; sometimes thou threatenest, and diest before thou doest what thou didst threaten. Do we suppose thou doest in thyself what thou wishest? Dost thou bridle all thy desires? Perhaps; but dost thou even bring about, that the desires thou bridlest do not rise up? Truly thou wishest not to be irritated by the importunity of thy desires, and yet, 'the flesh lusteth against the spirit: and the spirit against the flesh; so that you do not the things that you would' (Gal. v, 17). Thou doest not in thyself the things thou wouldest; but 'whatsoever our God pleased He hath done in heaven and in earth' (Ps. cxxxiv, 6). . . . Love therefore this sweetness, praise this sweetness. Understand that God, who hath done whatsoever He pleased in heaven and in earth, will do in you also what you will; by His help you will fulfil your will.

In Ps. CXXXIV, 12.

858

Every soul that is infirm in this life seeketh for itself something whereon it may rest; since it can with difficulty endure perpetually the tension of labour and of the soul as it reacheth out to God. It seeketh something on earth whereon to rest, a kind of halting place whereon to recline, as are such things which the innocent also love. . . . Nevertheless God, in His will that we should have love only for the eternal life, mixeth bitterness even with those innocent pleasures, so that even in these we may suffer tribulations; and thus He turneth all our couch in our sickness. 'Thou hast turned all his couch in his sickness,' (Ps. xl, 4). Let him not therefore bewail when he suffereth some tribulations in those things which he hath innocently. He is taught to love the better things by the bitterness of the worse; lest going as a traveller to his own country he choose the inn instead of his own home. 'Thou hast turned all his couch in his sickness.'

In Ps. XL, 5.

859

In these temporal things therefore, brethren, we admonish and exhort you in the Lord not to ask for anything as it were settled, but for that which God knoweth to be expedient for you. For what is expedient for you you know not at all. Sometimes that which you think profitable to you is the reverse, and that which you think unprofitable is profitable. For ye are sick; do not dictate to the physician the medicine he may choose to set before you. . . . Let not a sick man draw back from the hands of the physician, let him not give advice to the physician. So it is with all things temporal. There are tribulations: if thou dost worship God well, thou wilt know that He knoweth what is expedient for each man. There are prosperities: take the more heed lest these same corrupt thy soul, so that it withdraw from Him who hath given these things.

In Ps. LIII, 5.

860

If it is night, how is there light there? It is night because here the human race is wandering; it is night because we have not yet reached that true day, the day not cramped by a yesterday and a to-morrow, the eternal day which neither dawns nor sets. Here therefore it is night, but this night has a certain light and darkness of its own. We have said why it is in general night; but what is the light of this night? Prosperity and worldly happiness, temporal joy, temporal honour, these are, as it were, the light of this night. But adversity and the bitterness of tribulations and lowness of station, these are, as it were, the darkness of this night. In this night, in this mortal state of human life, men have light, men have darkness; their light is prosperity, adversity is their darkness. But when Christ Our Lord has come, and has dwelt in the soul by faith, and has promised another light, and has inspired and given patience, and has warned a man not to delight in prosperity or be crushed by adversity, the man, being full of faith, begins to treat this world with indifference; begins not to be lifted up when prosperity befalls him, nor crushed when adversity comes, but to praise God in all things, not only when he is rich, but also when he has losses, not only when in health, but also in sickness; so that in him that song is true, 'I will bless the Lord at all times; His praise shall be always in my mouth' (Ps. xxxiii, 2). If then 'always,' both when this night is bright, and when it is dark; when prosperity smiles, and when adversity is sad; if His praise be in thy mouth 'always,' then shall it be to thee in accordance with what next follows, 'The darkness thereof, and the light thereof are alike' (Ps. cxxxviii, 12). The darkness thereof overwhelms me not, because the light thereof does not lift me up.

In Ps. CXXXVIII, 16.

861

'For thou, O Lord, hast possessed my reins' (Ps. cxxxviii, 13). Not without reason, 'the darkness thereof, and the light thereof are alike' (*ibid.*, 12). The Possessor is within; He occupieth not only the heart, but also the reins; not only the thoughts, but also the delights. He therefore possesses that whereby I might have joy at any light in this 'night.' He occupieth my reins; I know not delight, save from the inward light of His wisdom. What is this? Dost thou not rejoice that thy affairs prosper, that the times are propitious? Dost thou not delight in honours, in riches, in thy family? I do not, saith he. But why not? Because 'the darkness thereof, and the light thereof are alike.' Whence cometh this indifference, so that 'the darkness thereof, and the light thereof are alike to thee'? Whence? Because 'Thou hast possessed my reins: Thou hast protected me from my mother's womb.' While I was in my mother's womb, I was not indifferent to the darkness and the light of that night. For my mother's womb was the custom of my city. What city is that? That which first gave us birth in captivity. We know that Babylon, . . . whence all go forth who believe in and yearn for the true light, the heavenly Jerusalem. . . . Being then protected from that womb, let us now begin to hold other hopes. He hath promised, brethren, that in which you may rejoice. Bring forth fruit now that you are set in other hopes. For now we know no ill, save to offend God, and not to be brought to those things which He promiseth; nor do we know any good, save to be deserving of God, and to be brought to those things which He promiseth. But what of the good things of this world, and the bad things of this world? Let us be indifferent to them; for now, having been protected from the womb of that mother of ours, we hold them in indifference, and say, 'the darkness thereof, and the light thereof are alike.' Neither doth worldly good fortune make us happy, nor adversity wretched. We must maintain justice, love faith, hope in God, love God, and love our neighbour also. After these toils we shall have a light which never wearies, a day which never sets. Fleeting is all the light and darkness of this night. 'For thou, O Lord, hast possessed my reins: thou hast protected me from my mother's womb.'

In Ps. CXXXVIII, 18.

862

He who, if he have any sorrow in matters of this world, so weepeth as inwardly to rejoice in hope, if he have any joy in matters of this world, so rejoices as inwardly to fear in spirit; who yieldeth himself neither to prosperity to corrupt, nor to adversity to crush (and this is to weep as though he wept not, and to rejoice as if he rejoiced not—1 Cor. vii, 30);—he who is such as this awaiteth untroubled the last day, because he is not outside the ark; he is already reckoned among the incorruptible timbers of which the ark is made (Gen. vi, 14). Let him then not fear the coming of the Lord, but hope and long for it.

In Ps. CXLVII, 4.

863

[Job] knew that whether it were darkness or light, it was night wherein he was sojourning in a far country away from his God. But he had as an interior light his God himself, and that interior light made him indifferent, whether it were darkness in this night, or light. And so, as in the light of this night, that is, in the midst of abundance, he worshipped God; when all was taken from him, when his night was made darkness, what did he say? 'The Lord gave, and the Lord hath taken away. As it hath pleased the Lord so is it done. Blessed be the name of the Lord' (Job i, 21). I am not sad in this night, for 'the darkness thereof, and the light thereof are alike' (Ps. cxxxviii, 12); both pass away; so that they that rejoice are as though they rejoiced not, and they that weep as though they wept not (1 Cor. vii, 30); for the darkness thereof, and the light thereof are alike.

In Ps. CXXXVIII, 17.

864

Let my enemies rage. What can they do? They can take my money, strip, proscribe, banish me; they can rack me with sorrows and tortures; and at last, if they be allowed, even kill me. Can they do aught more? But Thou, O Lord, 'hast stretched forth Thy hand against the wrath of my enemies' (Ps. cxxxvii, 7), against what my enemies can do, Thou hast stretched forth Thy hand. For my enemies cannot separate me from Thee; but Thou repayest me the more, because Thou dost still delay: 'Thou hast stretched forth Thy hand against the wrath of my enemies.'

Let my enemy rage as much as he can, he cannot separate me from God. But Thou, O Lord, hast not as yet received me; and still thou weariest me in wandering; as yet thou dost not give me Thy joy and sweetness; as yet thou hast not 'inebriated me with the plenty of Thy house,' as yet thou hast not made me 'drink of the torrent of Thy pleasure. For with Thee is the fountain of life: and in Thy light we shall see light' (Ps. xxxv, 9, 10). But behold! I have given Thee the first-fruits of my spirit, and have believed in Thee, and 'with the mind serve the law of God' (Rom. vii, 25); yet still 'we ourselves groan within ourselves waiting for the adoption, the redemption of our body' (*id.*, viii, 23). This life hath God given to us sinners, wherein also it is needful that Adam be wearied in the sweat and toil of his face, since the earth brought forth to him thorns and thistles (Gen. iii, 18 *sq.*). Can any enemy lay more on him? 'Thou hast stretched forth Thy hand against the wrath

of my enemies'; yet not to make me despair, for there follow
the words, 'and Thy right hand hath saved me.'

In Ps. CXXXVII, 13.

865

There is . . . a certain bone of mine within and hidden.
Thou hast made a bone within me in secret, and it is not hidden
from Thee (Ps. cxxxviii, 15). Thou hast made it in secret,
but hast Thou therefore hidden it from Thyself? This my bone
made by Thee in secret men see not, men know not; but
Thou knowest, who hast made it. This 'bone' is a sort of inward
strength; for strength and fortitude are understood to be in
the bones. There is therefore a certain inward strength of the
soul, which doth not break therein. Whatever tortures, whatever tribulations, whatever adversities of this world rage around
us, that which God hath made strong in secret within us cannot
be broken, or made to yield. For by God is made a certain
strength of patience, of which another psalm saith, 'My
soul is subject to God: for from Him is my patience' (Ps.
lxi, 6). Observe, too, that the Apostle Paul hath within him
this kind of strength, for he saith, 'As sorrowful, yet always
rejoicing' (2 Cor. vi, 10). From what cause, 'as sorrowful'?
From insults, reproaches, persecutions, scourgings, stripes,
-stonings, imprisonments, chains. Who would not think them
wretched who suffered these? Nay, their very persecutors
would not thus rage against them, did they not think that they
were made wretched by their persecutions. For they inferred
this of them from their own weakness, since they had not themselves a bone hidden within; but those who had, seemed
outwardly sorrowful, yet within they rejoiced to God, from
whom their bone was not hidden, which He had made in secret.
And the same Apostle Paul discloseth this bone made in secret
by God in the words: 'Not only so: but we glory also in tribulations.' Is it too small a thing that thou art not sorrowful; must
thou glory also? Let it suffice thee to be not sorrowful. To
Christians, he saith, it is too small a thing; such a bone hath
He made for me in secret, that it is not enough for me not to be
crushed, if I do not glory also. Wherein dost thou glory? 'In
tribulations, knowing that tribulation worketh patience.' Note

how that inward strength is fashioned in the heart: 'knowing that tribulation worketh patience; and patience trial; and trial hope; and hope confoundeth not: because the charity of God is poured forth in our hearts, by the Holy Ghost who is given to us' (Rom. v, 3 *sqq*.). In such a way is that hidden bone fashioned and made strong, that it makes us glory in tribulations. But to men we seem wretched, because that which we have within is hidden from them. 'My bone is not hidden from Thee, which Thou hast made in secret: and my substance in the lower parts of the earth.' Behold, in flesh is my substance, in the lower parts of the earth is my substance; yet have I a bone within, which Thou hast fashioned, such as to make me not yield to any persecutions of this lower region, where still my substance is. For what great matter is it if an Angel be strong; but it is a great matter if flesh is strong. And whence is flesh strong, whence is an earthen vessel strong; except that it is made a bone in secret. 'And my substance is in the lower parts of the earth.'

In Ps. CXXXVIII, 20.

866

For is it a great thing for tribulation to find thee out? Do thou, if thou hast it in thee, find tribulation (cf. Ps. cxiv, 3). And who is there, thou wilt say, who findeth tribulation, or so much as seeks for it? Art thou in the midst of tribulation and knowest it not? Is this life a small tribulation? If it is not tribulation, it is not an exile; but if it is an exile, either thou lovest thy country too little, or else without doubt thou art in tribulation. For who doth not feel tribulation if he is not with that for which he longs? Why therefore seemeth it not to be tribulation to thee? Because thou lovest not. Love the other life, and thou shalt see that this life is tribulation, whatever the prosperity with which it shines, whatever the delights with which it abounds and overflows. Since we have not yet that safe joy free from all trial and struggle, which God reserveth for us at the end, it is without any doubt tribulation.

In Ps. CXXXVII, 12.

867

The reason why I do not now seek earthly happiness is that I have learnt holy desire from the New Testament. I seek not land, nor earthly abundance, nor riches, nor rank, nor the overthrow of my enemies; nought of these do I seek; therefore 'quickly hear me' (Ps. cxxxvii, 3). . . . There are the only good things, not good mixed with evil, safe things, in which thou mayest joy as much as thou wilt, and none to say to thee, Restrain thyself here from joying in earthly goods full of vexation and peril, lest thou joy in them so as to cling to them, and by joying amiss, perish. For why doth God mingle tribulations with earthly joys, except to the end that, feeling tribulation and bitterness, we may learn to long for eternal sweetness?

In Ps. CXXXVII, 7.

868

Let us redeem the time, because the days are evil (cf. Eph. v. 16). . . . 'Redeem the time,' that is to say, when any one brings a suit against thee, lose something, that thou mayest give thy time to God, not to litigation. Lose therefore; the price of time comes out of that thou losest. . . . But when thou losest something that thou mayest have something, thou art then buying. Of what thou hast bought, what thou losest is the price. As then thou losest money to buy thee something, so lose money to buy thee rest. . . .' If a man will contend with thee in judgment and take away thy coat, let go thy cloak also unto him' (Matt. v, 40). He wishes to contend with thee in judgment and take thy coat, wishes to call thee away from thy God by litigation. Thou wilt have no quiet of heart, no tranquillity of mind, thou wilt be agitated in thy thoughts, thou wilt be irritated against this thine adversary. How much better then it is to lose money and redeem the time.

Serm. (*de Script. N.T.*) CLXVII, ii, 3; iii, 4.

869

Behold, when thou art in trouble, that which thou seekest is not before thee, but He whom thou seekest is near thee.

Seek thou Him who never can be wanting. Suppose those things which He gave withdrawn; is He who gave them therefore withdrawn? Let those things which He gave be restored; is it true wealth when these things are restored; is this not He who withdrew them to prove thee and restored them to console thee? For he consoleth us when those things are not wanting to us. He consoleth us in the way, but only if we understand the way. For the whole of this life, and all things which thou usest in this life, ought to be to thee as an inn to a traveller, not as a house to dwell in. Remember though thou hast accomplished somewhat, that somewhat remaineth, that thou hast been tarrying for refection not for defection.

In Ps. **XXXIV**, *Serm.* i, 6.

870

We can . . . rightly call vision the end and rest of the will . . . just as if anyone wish to see a scar, that thence he may learn that there had been a wound, or if he wish to see a window, that he may see the passers-by through the window; all these and suchlike acts of will have their own particular ends, which are referred to the end of that act of will by which we will to live blessedly, and to attain to that life which is not referred to anything else, but of itself suffices him who loves it. The will therefore to see has for its end vision, and the will to see a particular thing has for its end the vision of that thing. Thus the will to see a scar seeks after its own end, that is the vision of the scar, and does not reach beyond it; for the will to prove that there had been a wound is a separate will, though dependent on the former; and its end is again the proving of the wound. But the will to see a window has as its end the vision of the window; for it is another act of will, connected with the former, to see the passers-by through the window; and its end is the vision of the passers-by. Now all the several acts of will that are connected with one another are at once right, if that one is good to which all are referred; but if that is evil, all are evil. And thus the ordered sequence of right acts of will is a sort of road, forming as it were certain steps, for men to ascend to blessedness. But the entanglement of evil and distorted acts of will is a fetter by which he is bound who thus acts, so that he is cast into the exterior darkness (Matt. xxii, 13). Happy therefore are those who by their acts and character chant the gradual canticles, and woe to them that draw sin, as it were a long rope (cf. Isa. v, 18). For it is the same thing to speak of the repose of the will, which we call its end, if this is still referred to something further, as it is to say that a foot is at rest in walking, when it is placed at a spot whence another foot may be planted in the direction of the man's steps. But if something so satisfies that the will reposes in it with a certain pleasure, it is nevertheless not that to which the man ultimately tends; for this too refers to something further, so that it may be considered not as the citizen's native land, but as a place of refection, or even sojourning, for the traveller.

De Trin. XI, vi, 10.

871

In the first and second generations thou art become our refuge. Thou wast our refuge that we, who were not, might be born. Thou wast our refuge that we, who were evil, might be born anew. Thou wast a refuge to feed those that forsake Thee. Thou art a refuge to raise up and direct Thy children. Thou art become our refuge. We will not withdraw from Thee when Thou hast delivered us from all our evils and filled us with Thine own good things. Thou givest good things; Thou art gentle with us that we be not wearied in the way. Thou dost correct and chastise and smite and direct us, that we wander not from the way. Whether therefore thou dealest gently with us, that we be not wearied in the way, or chastisest us, that we wander not out of the way, Thou hast been our refuge (Ps. lxxxix, 1).

Serm. (*de Script. N.T.*) LV, vi, 6.

V. NIGHT BETWEEN NIGHTS

872

If each one begin to die, that is to be in death, the moment death, that is to say a shortening of his life, begins to take effect in him, . . . then he is assuredly in death the moment he begins to exist in the body. For what else do all his days, hours and moments declare, but that they being done, the death wherein he lived is now at an end, and that his time is now no more in death but after death? Therefore if man cannot be in life and in death both at once, he is never in life so long as he is in that dying rather than living body.

De civ. Dei **XII**, 10.

873

All else we have, both good and evil, is uncertain; death alone is certain. . . . A boy is conceived, perhaps he will be born, perhaps there will be a miscarriage. So it is uncertain. Perhaps he will grow up, perhaps he will not grow up; perhaps he will grow old, perhaps he will not grow old; perhaps he will be rich, perhaps poor; perhaps he will be honoured, perhaps abased, perhaps he will have children, perhaps he will not; perhaps he will marry; perhaps not; and so on, whatever good things you name. Now look also at the evil things. Perhaps he will have ill-health, perhaps he will not; perhaps he will be stung by a serpent, perhaps not; perhaps he will be devoured by a wild beast, perhaps he will not. And so look at all evils; everywhere there is a 'perhaps it will be' and 'perhaps it will not be.' But canst thou say, 'Perhaps he will die,' and 'perhaps he will not die'? As when physicians examine a disease and ascertain that it is fatal, they pronounce, 'He is dying, he will not get over this,' so from the moment a man is born it may be said, 'He will not get over this.' When he is born he begins to ail. When he dies, he is finished indeed with this ailment, but he knows not whether he may not fall into a worse. The rich man in the Gospel had done with his voluptuous ailment; he came to a tormenting one. But the poor man ended his ailment and arrived at perfect health (*v*. Luke xvi, 22). But he made choice in this life of what he was to have hereafter, and what he reaped there, he sowed here.

Serm. (de Script. N.T.) XCVII, iii, 3.

874

For who is not sick in this life? Who hath not to support tedious lassitude? For to be born here in a mortal body, is to begin to be sick. Our wants are supported by daily medicaments.

Daily remedies are the restorations in the case of all our wants. Would not hunger cause thy death, unless thou didst apply what would cure it? Would not thirst destroy thee, unless thou didst by drinking satisfy it, not indeed for ever, but for a space? For thirst will return after a short time, though now tempered. We therefore by these means of healing temper the distress of our sickness. Thou wast wearied by standing, by sitting down thou art refreshed; the very act of sitting is the cure of the fatigue. But by this very remedy thou art in turn fatigued; for thou canst not sit for long. Whatever it is that relieves one fatigue, the foundation of another fatigue is laid.

In Ps. CII, 6.

875

For now because of the corruption of frailty, if we eat not, we grow weak and are hungry; if we drink not, we grow weak and are thirsty; if we keep vigil for a long time, we grow weak and sleep; if we sleep a long time we grow weak, and therefore we watch. If we eat and drink for a long time, though we eat and drink for refreshment, the very refreshment thus prolonged is a weakening. If we stand for a long time, we grow weary and therefore we sit; if we sit for a long time, there too do we grow weary, and therefore we rise up. Then again, mark how our flesh is without any permanent state; for infancy passeth quickly into boyhood, and thou seekest infancy, and infancy is not, for now instead of infancy there is boyhood; again, this same passeth into youth, thou seekest boyhood and findest it not; the youth becometh a full grown man, thou seekest the youth, and he is not; the mature man becometh an old man, the old man dieth, thou seekest an old man and findest him not. Our age therefore doth not stand still; everywhere there is weariness, everywhere a heaviness, everywhere corruption. Observing what a hope of resurrection God promiseth to us, in all these our manifold wearinesses we thirst for that incorruption, and thus our flesh doth manifoldly thirst for God. . . . In this desert as it toileth in manifold ways, so in as many ways doth it thirst; as it is wearied in manifold ways, so in as many ways doth it thirst for that unwearying incorruption.

In Ps. LXV, 6.

876

All this life is indeed a tribulation to the understanding. For there are two tormentors of the soul, tormenting it not at once, but alternating their tortures. The names of these two tormentors are Fear and Sorrow. When it is well with thee thou fearest, when it is ill thou dost sorrow. He who is not deceived by the prosperity of this world is not broken by its adversity.

Serm. (de Script. N.T.) CXXIV, ii, 2.

877

Who does not weep on this rough road of ours here, when the very babe begins it with weeping? Certainly the babe, when it is born, is brought forth from the narrow chamber of the womb into the wide spaces of this world, it proceeds from darkness to light; and yet, coming from the darkness into the light, it can weep, but it cannot see. . . . And men laugh and men weep; and what we men laugh at is to be wept at. . . . The tears of the just man for those who are weeping fruitlessly are true tears. He weeps for the weepers, he weeps for the laughers; for those who weep over vain things, weep idly; and those who laugh over vain things, laugh to their own hurt. He weeps over both, and therefore weeps more than they.

Serm. XXXI, iii, 4.

878

We would keep vigil, and we fall asleep; we would fast, and we hunger and thirst; we would stand, and we get exhausted and wish to sit, yet if we do this for long, we get weary. Whatever we provide for our refection, there again we find defection. . . . What then is the peace which men have here who have to make head against so many troubles, desires, wants, wearinesses? . . . What will be perfect peace? 'This corruptible must put on incorruption: and this mortal must put on immortality' (1 Cor. xv, 53). . . . For where there is yet mortality, how can there be full peace? It is from death that that weariness comes, which we find in all our means of refreshment. . . . When therefore death is swallowed up in victory, these things shall no longer be. . . . There shall be peace made pure in the sons of God, all loving one another, seeing one another full of God, since God shall be all in all (*ibid.*, 28). We shall have God as our common object of vision, God as our common possession, God as our common peace. For whatever there is which He now giveth us, He himself shall be unto us in place of His gifts; He will be our full and perfect peace. . . . Our joy, our peace, our rest, the end of all our troubles, is none but God.

In Ps. LXXXV, 10.

879

If a prison be the cause of thy trouble, thou seekest to get out of prison; if fever be the cause of thy trouble, thou seekest health; if hunger be the cause of thy trouble, thou seekest repletion; if losses be the cause of thy trouble, thou seekest gain; if sojourning abroad be the cause of thy trouble, thou seekest the home of thy flesh. . . . Dost thou wish to overleap? In the day of thy trouble seek God (cf. Ps. lxxvi, 3), not some other thing through God, but God from within thy trouble; that God may take away the trouble to the end that thou mayest without anxiety cleave to God. . . . Trouble must not be thought to be this or that thing in particular. For every individual who is not yet overleaping, thinketh that to be as yet no tribulation unless it be something which may have befallen him in this life on some sad occasion; but the man who is truly overleaping doth count this whole life to be tribulation. For he loveth his supernal country so much that the earthly pilgrimage is of itself the greatest tribulation.

In Ps. LXXVII, 3, 4.

880

God also made for thee the world which is one day to perish, and therefore He made thee as one who is one day to die. Man himself, the ornament of the city, man himself, the city's inhabitant, ruler, governor, comes on this condition, that he go, is born that he may die, entered the world that he may pass away. 'Heaven and earth shall pass' (Matt. xxiv, 35); what wonder then if at some time or another the city [of Rome] come to an end?

Serm. (de Script. N.T.) LXXXI, 9.

466

881

Dost thou wonder that the world is failing? Wonder that the world is grown old. It is as a man, who is born, grows up, and waxes old. Many are the complaints in old age: the cough, the rheum, the bleary eyes, fretfulness and lassitude are its lot. As then a man when he is old is full of complaints, so the world when it is old is full of troubles. Is it a little thing that God hath done for thee, in that in the world's old age He hath sent Christ to thee that He may restore thee when all else is failing? . . . The seed of Abraham, saith the Apostle, 'which is Christ' (Gal. iii, 16). . . . Therefore there was born to Abraham in his old age a son, because in the old age of this world Christ was to come. He came when all things were growing old, and made them new. As a made, created, perishable thing, the world was now declining to its fall. It was inevitable that it should abound in troubles. He came both to console thee in thy present troubles and to promise thee everlasting rest. Choose not to cleave to this aged world and to be unwilling to grow young in Christ, who saith to thee: The world is perishing, the world is growing old, the world is failing, has the laboured breathing of old age. Fear not, 'thy youth shall be renewed like an eagle's' (Ps. cii, 5).

Serm. (de Script. N.T.) LXXXI, 8.

882

Hope exhorts us to this, to despise things present and to look for the things to come; 'forgetting the things that are behind,' let us with the Apostle 'stretch forth to those that are before' (Phil. iii, 13). . . . Nothing therefore is so hostile to hope as to look back, to place hope, that is, in those things which flit by and pass away. But we should place it in those things which are not yet given, which at some time will be given, and will never pass away. . . . How loudly does the world talk to thee, what an uproar it makes behind thy back, that thou mayest look back! that is to say, that you mayest place thy hope in things present (and yet not even present, for they cannot be called present which have no fixedness), and mayest turn thy mind away from what Christ hath promised, but not yet given; yet who, because He is faithful, will give it, and that thou mayest be content to look for rest in a perishing world. For for this cause doth God mingle bitternesses with the felicities of the world that another felicity may be sought, in whose sweetness there is no deceit. Yet by those very bitternesses does the world try to turn thee away from the things that are before to which thou art stretching forth, and to turn thee back. Over those bitternesses and those tribulations thou dost murmur and say, 'See all things are perishing in Christian times.' . . . The city which has given us birth according to the flesh still abideth, God be thanked. O that it may receive a spiritual birth, and together with us pass over into eternity. If the city which gave us birth according to the flesh abide not, that which gave us birth according to the spirit abides for ever. 'The Lord buildeth up Jerusalem' (Ps. cxlvi, 2) . . . the holy city, the faithful city, the city a sojourner on earth, hath its foundations in heaven.

Serm. (de Script. N.T.) CV, v, 7; vii, 9.

883

For I say to you, brethren, thou hast the foundation: cleave to heaven, tread the earth under foot. If such thou art, thou buildest not save 'gold, silver, and precious stones' (1 Cor. iii, 12). But when thou sayest, I love that possession, I fear lest it be lost; and the loss approaches, and thou growest sad; thou dost not indeed place it before Christ; for thou lovest that possession in such wise, that if it be said to thee, wilt thou have it or Christ? though thou art sad at losing it, yet dost thou rather embrace Christ, whom thou hast laid for thy foundation; and thou wilt be saved as through fire. . . . Therefore if thou lovest thy possession, yet dost not for its sake commit robbery, dost not for its sake bear false witness, dost not for its sake commit murder, dost not for its sake swear falsely, dost not for its sake deny Christ;—in that thou doest not these things for its sake, thou hast Christ for a foundation. Nevertheless, because thou lovest it, and art saddened if thou losest it, thou hast built upon the foundation not gold, or silver or precious stones, but 'wood, hay, stubble.' Saved therefore thou shalt be when that which thou hast built begins to burn, 'yet so as by fire' (*ibid.*, 12 *sqq.*). For let no one who on this foundation buildeth adulteries, blasphemies, sacrileges, idolatries, perjuries, think he shall be

'saved by fire,' as though they were the 'wood, hay, stubble';
but as to him that buildeth the love of earthly things upon the
foundation of the kingdom of heaven, that is, upon Christ, his
love of temporal things shall be burned, and he himself shall
be saved by the valency of his foundation.

In Ps. LXXX, 21.

884

My pain cometh, there will come my rest also; my trouble
cometh, there will come my purgation also. For doth gold
glitter in the refiner's furnace? In a necklace it will glitter,
in an ornament it will glitter; let it however suffer the furnace
that being purged of impurities it may come into light. This
is the furnace, here is the chaff, there the gold, there the fire.
The refiner bloweth into this; in the furnace the chaff is burned,
and the gold is purified; the former is turned into ashes, the
latter is purified of its dross. The furnace is the world, the chaff
unrighteous men, the gold just men. The fire is tribulation, the
refiner God. That therefore which the Refiner willeth, I do;
wherever the Artificer placeth me, I endure it. I am bidden
to endure, He knoweth how to purify. Though the chaff to set
me on fire burns as if to consume me, it is burned to ashes, I
am purified of dross.

In Ps. LXI, 11.

885

For the very fact that we are not yet with God, the very fact
that we are living amid trials and difficulties, that we cannot
be without fear, is tribulation, since there is not that peace which
is promised us. He that hath not found this tribulation in his
pilgrimage, doth not think of going home to his fatherland.
This, brethren, is tribulation. Surely now we do good works
when we dispense bread to the hungry, a home to the stranger,
and so forth. This too is tribulation. For we find pitiful objects
upon whom we show pity; and the misery of these pitiful
objects makes us compassionate. How much better it would
be for thee to be where thou findest no hungry man to feed,
no stranger to take in, no naked man to clothe, no sick man to
visit, no litigant to reconcile! For in that place all things are of

the highest degree, are true, are holy, are eternal. Our bread there is justice, our drink wisdom, our garment immortality, our house everlasting in the heavens, our strength immortality. Doth sickness steal upon us? Doth weariness force us to sleep? There is no death there, no strife, but in their place, peace, repose, joy, justice. No enemy hath entrance, no friend falleth away. What peace there is there! If we think and observe where we are and where He who cannot lie hath promised that we are to be, from this very promise of His we learn in what tribulation we are. This tribulation none findeth but he who shall have sought it. Thou art in good health, observe whether thou art miserable, for it is easy for one who is sick to feel himself to be miserable. When thou art well, see if thou art miserable because thou art not yet with God.

In Ps. XLIX, 22.

886

Having desired the vanities of this life when you have not tried them, now, after trying them, you despise them, since in them the pleasure is deceitful, the labour fruitless, the anxiety perpetual, and the elevation dangerous. Their beginning is without forethought, their end is penance. This is true of all the things which in the cares of this mortal life are coveted with more eagerness than prudence. Quite other is, however, the hope of the pious, very different is the fruit of their labours, very different the reward of their dangers. For in this world fear and grief, labour and danger are unavoidable; and the great question is, for what cause, with what expectation, with what aim a man suffers these things.

Ep. CCIII.

887

We are not in good case while we are in this world. For when we shall please the Lord in the land of the living, then our tears will be wiped away; and we shall give praise to Him who has delivered us from the chains of death, our feet from falling, our eyes from tears, so that we may please the Lord in the land of the living (Ps. cxiv, 8 *sq.*); since it is difficult to please Him in the land of the dead. There is however even here something by which we may please Him, namely, by praying that He show mercy towards us, by abstaining from sins, so far as we are able, and in so far as we are not able, by confessing them with contrition. And so in this life we are hoping for another life, weeping in hope, nay rather, weeping in reality, rejoicing in hope.

Serm. XLVII, i, 1.

888

Let us not love the world. It overwhelms its lovers, it leads them to no good. We must rather labour in it that it seduce us not than fear it lest it perish. Lo, the world falleth, but the Christian standeth fast since Christ doth not fall. . . . 'Rejoice, I have overcome the world' (Jer. xvi, 33). . . . He hath overcome for us, to whom He hath shown the assurance of resurrection. . . . And thou criest, 'Have mercy on me, O God, for man hath trodden me under foot' (Ps. lv, 2). If thou say the truth and mark thyself well, because thou art afraid of the threats of man, one dead treads thee under foot, and man tramples thee under foot because thou wouldst not be afraid, unless thou wert a man. . . . O man, cleave to God, by whom thou wert made a man. Cleave fast to Him, put thy trust in Him, call upon Him, let Him be thy strength. Say to Him, 'In thee, O Lord, is my strength.' And thus thou shalt sing at the threatenings of man, and what thou shalt sing hereafter is what the Lord tells thee: 'In God will I hope: I will not fear what man can do to me' (*ibid.* 11).

Serm. (*de Script. N.T.*) XCVII, iv, 4.

889

To whatsoever man attains, forthwith that to which he has attained becomes of little worth to him. Other things begin to be desired, other fond things are hoped for; and when they come, whatever they be, become of little worth. Hold fast then to God, for He can never be of little worth, since nothing is more beautiful than He. These things become of little esteem because they cannot endure, because they are not what He is. For nought, O soul, sufficeth thee, save He who created thee. Whatsoever else thou obtainest is worthless; for He alone can suffice thee Who made thee after His own image. Thus it was expressly said, 'Lord, show us the Father, and it is enough for us' (John xiv, 8). There alone can there be security, and where there can be security, there in some sort will be insatiable satiety. For thou wilt neither be so satiated as to wish to depart, nor will anything be lacking, as that thou couldest suffer want.

Serm. (de Script. N.T.) CXXV, 11.

890

In this life . . . that which was long will be nothing; for even when it was, it did not endure; when it was produced, it did not increase; nor by adding to did it grow, for in coming it was already departing.

Serm. XVI, i, 1.

891

For in that City we shall be where God is our good, God is our light, God is our bread, God is our life. In Him we shall find every good whatever good thing of ours there is, absence from which now troubles us.

In Ps. XXXVII, 28.

892

Whence the request: 'Lord, shew us the Father; and it is enough for us,' to which our Lord Himself answereth, 'I will manifest myself to him' (John xiv, 8, 21). And until this promise is fulfilled, no blessing, nothing good is enough for us, nor ought it to be, lest our desire should slacken and tarry on the way, when it ought to be increased until the goal is reached. . . . That day is a day without end. All days are together at one time, and it is thus that they satisfy us. For our day does not yield to others which succeed it, since there is nothing there which is not yet because it is still to come, nor does anything cease to be because it has passed. And this because there is one day only, which endures and does not pass away. This is eternity.

In Ps. LXXXIX, 15.

893

There is a kind of life of man, wholly of the senses and given up to the joys of the flesh, which shuns anything which is an offence to the flesh and pursues nothing but pleasure. The happiness to be found in such a life is but temporary. It is a necessity to begin with this sort of life; to persist in it is, however, an act of the will. It is into this life that a child is thrown at its birth. It avoids so far as it can whatever it dislikes, and seeks for what gives it pleasure; it is incapable of more than this. But after it has arrived at an age when the use of reason is grown in him, he can by the help of God choose another life, of which the joy is in the mind, and the happiness interior and everlasting. There has indeed been given to man a rational soul, but it depends upon the use to which reason is put in directing the will whether one turns towards the good things of exterior nature which are the inferior or to those of his interior and higher nature; that is to say, whether towards the enjoyment of material and temporal things or towards that which is divine and eternal. The human soul thus finds itself placed as it were in a medium with material creation below it and above it the Creator of soul and body.

The rational soul can therefore make a good use of even material and temporal felicity, if it does not give itself over to the creature, to the neglect of the Creator, but rather applies this felicity to the service of the Creator, of whose abounding liberality it has been bestowed. Just as all things created by God are good from the rational creature at one end of the scale to the lowest material substance at the other, so too can the rational soul make good use of all these things, provided it be faithful to true order and by distinguishing and choosing with discernment it set the greater things above the less, the spiritual above the corporal, the higher above the lower, the eternal above the temporal. By neglecting the higher things and craving the lower—and it is by the latter that it itself deteriorates—the soul casts itself and the body into a worse state; whereas by ordered charity it can raise itself and the body to a better state. . . .

It was because God wished to show that earthly and temporal felicity is also His gift to man and that it may not be looked for from any other hand than His, that He thought it necessary to assign to the earlier periods of time His Old Covenant, which pertains to the old man from whom this life necessarily takes its beginning. But Holy Scripture has always taught that the felicities the fathers enjoyed were due to God's munificence even when they pertained to this transitory life. These terrestrial gifts were openly promised and accorded, but, secretly all these things figuratively proclaimed the New Covenant which was to come, and this was revealed only to the small band of the elect whom the grace of God had by the gift of prophecy made worthy to receive it. These holy men in harmony with the times they lived in were dispensers of the Old Covenant, but really belonged to the New Covenant. When they tasted temporal felicity they knew there was one to be preferred to it which was true and eternal; and they presented the one in the form of a mystery that they might attain to the other as a reward. And whenever they had to suffer adversity they suffered it in such manner that, when delivered from it by the most manifest intervention of God, they might glorify God, the dispenser of all good things, and not only of eternal blessings, the object of their pious hopes, but also of those temporal blessings which they regarded as prophetic of the others.

'But when the fulness of the time was come' that the grace which was hidden in the Old Covenant should be revealed in the New, 'God sent his Son, made of a woman' (Gal. iv, 4). . . .

And so the Christ-Man was not blessed with any earthly felicity to the end that in Him might be revealed the grace of the New Covenant, which pertains not to this life but to life eternal. Hence the abasement to which He was subjected, His passion, the blows, the spitting upon, the outrages, the cross, the wounds, and death itself, when He seemed to have been overcome and cast down by His enemies, so that His followers might learn what reward for their piety they ought to seek and expect from Him whose children they had been made, and that in serving God they should not look to earthly happiness as their end nor should they value their faith so low as to think such a recompense worthy of it. And therefore in His most benign providence God has bestowed worldly happiness on the ungodly to prevent the godly from seeking it as a thing of great price. . . .

The Man Christ who is also the God Christ by most mercifully taking upon Himself our humanity in the form of a servant, has taught us what we must despise in this life and what we must hope for in the other. In the very hour of His passion, when His enemies seemed to be fully triumphant, He took the words of our weakness by which our old man was crucified with Him and the body of sin destroyed (cf. Rom. vi, 6), and said: 'My God, my God, why hast thou forsaken me?' (Matt. xxvii, 46; Ps. xxi, 2). . . .

It is the voice of our infirmity which, transformed by our Head, we hear in the psalm: 'O God my God, look upon me: why hast thou forsaken me?' (Ps. xxi, 2). He is forsaken whose requests are not heard. Jesus took our words to Himself, it was the words of His own body, that is to say of His Church, which He was to transform from the old man to the new; it was the language of His own infirmity as man, to whom the good things of the Old Covenant had to be denied that He might teach us to desire and look for the good things of the New Covenant. . . .

The Church suffered in Him when He suffered for the Church; so too He suffered in the Church when the Church suffered for Him. For just as we hear the voice of the suffering Church in Christ's words, 'My God, my God, etc.,' so too we hear the voice of Christ suffering in the Church in the words: 'Saul, Saul, why persecutest thou me?' (Acts ix, 4). . . .

Such is the grace of the New Covenant; for in the Old Covenant, when Thou didst enjoin that even earthly and temporal happiness should only be asked of Thee and looked for from Thy hand, then 'in Thee have our fathers hoped; they have hoped, and Thou hast delivered them that cried to Thee, and they were saved, they trusted in Thee, and were not confounded' (Ps. xxi, 5 sq.). And these our fathers, who lived surrounded by their enemies, Thou didst load with rich gifts and didst deliver them from their enemies, and didst cause them to bear away the victory over them. For him who was to be a holocaust Thou didst substitute a ram (v. Gen. xxii, 13). To another Thou didst restore health to the rottenness of his flesh and didst give him of the goods of this earth twice as much as he had before (v. Job xlii, 10). Another Thou didst preserve safe and unharmed in the midst of ravenous lions (v. Dan. xiv, 30 sqq.). And yet others, whom Thou didst keep from hurt in the midst of a furnace of burning fire praised Thee in a song of gratitude (v. Dan. iii, 23 sqq.). The Jews expected something of the kind in the case of Christ, whence they might know if He was truly the Son of God. And the Book of Wisdom speaks in their words when it says: 'Let us condemn him to a most shameful death: for there shall be respect had unto him by his words. For if he be the true Son of God, he will defend him, and will deliver him from the hands of his enemies. These things,' it goes on to say, 'they thought, and were deceived: for their own malice blinded them' (Wis. ii, 20, 18, 21). Thinking only of the Old Covenant and of the temporal happiness granted to their forefathers by which God proved to them that such good things were also His gift, they did not see that the time had come in which it should be revealed in Christ that God gives temporal good things even to the ungodly, but reserves for the just those good things that are eternal. . . .

Wherefore also James, one of the Lord's apostles, when exhorting the faithful, who after the passion and resurrection of Christ persisted in that way of life, distinguishing between the dispensation of the Old and the New Testament, said to them: 'You have heard of the patience of Job and you have seen the end of the Lord' (Jas. v, 11); for he did not wish them to support with patience the temporal ills of this life merely with a view to being recompensed, as we read was the case with Job (Job xlii, 10). For he was made whole from his sores and from the rottenness of his flesh, and everything that he had lost was restored to him twofold. . . . In order therefore that we may not look for such a reward when we suffer temporal ills, he does not say the patience and end of Job, but 'you have heard of the patience of Job and you have seen the end of the Lord'; as if he would say suffer temporal ills as Job did, but as a reward for your patience do not look for the temporal goods which were restored to Job with interest, but hope rather for the eternal goods to which the Lord has shewn the way. . . .

For there are to be found also among the fathers examples, rare it is true but yet examples, of patience even unto death, 'from the blood of Abel unto the blood of Zacharias' (Luke xi, 51), for whose blood retribution, Our Lord says, will be exacted of those who spilt it, if they persist in the iniquity of their fathers. And in the New Covenant there have been and there still are great numbers of the pious faithful remarkable for the wealth of their temporal blessings, who see in them the goodness and mercy of God's bounty and at the same time observe the precepts of the Apostle who is the dispenser of the New Covenant, when he charges them 'not to be high-minded, nor to trust in the uncertainty of riches, but in the living God (who giveth us abundantly all things to enjoy), to do good, to be rich in good works, to give easily, to communicate to others, to lay up in store for themselves a good foundation against the time to come, that they may lay hold on the true life' (1 Tim. vi, 17 *sqq.*). Such a life was manifested not only in the spirit but also in the flesh of Christ after He had risen from the dead; not such a life as the Jews destroyed in Him, when God did not rescue Him from their hands, and He seemed to be abandoned and called out 'My God, My God, why hast thou forsaken me?' That thus He might display in His person His martyrs, who would not wish to die, as He himself signified in His words to Peter: 'Another shall gird thee, and lead thee whither thou wouldest not . . . signifying by what death he should glorify God' (John xxi, 18 *sq.*). And for this reason the martyrs succeeded for a time to be forsaken by their God, when He did not will to accord them what they asked of Him, and they called out the same words which He had used, but still had in their hearts that same spirit of piety, to which, as the hour of His passion drew nigh, the Lord Himself gave utterance: 'Nevertheless not as I will, but as Thou wilt' (Matt. xxvi, 39).

Who then, if it be not our Head Himself, must first show us the life we are to lead by which we are Christians? Hence it is that He does not say 'My God, my God, thou hast forsaken me,' but admonishes us to seek the reason by adding 'why hast Thou forsaken me,' that is to say wherefore, to what end, for what reason? Assuredly He had a motive, and that no small one, when He saved Noe from the flood, Lot from the fires which came down from heaven, Isaac from the sword about to kill him, Joseph from the false accusation of the woman and from prison, Moses from the Egyptians, Rahab when Jericho was destroyed, Susanna from the false witnesses, Daniel from the lions, the three men from the fiery furnace, and others of the fathers who called out to Him and were saved, and yet did not deliver Christ from the hands of the Jews, but left Him at the mercy of their fury even to the death. Why did He do this? To what end could it be but that expressed a little later in the same psalm (xxi, 3), 'it shall not be reputed as folly in me,' that is to say to my body, to my Church, to the least of my people? For it is written in the Gospel that He said: 'As long as you did it to one of these my least brethren, you did it to me' (Matt. xxv, 40). Just as it was said: 'it shall not be reputed as folly in me,' so it was said: 'you did it to me,' and the words 'why hast Thou forsaken me' are balanced by the words; 'He that heareth you, heareth me; and he that despiseth you, despiseth me' (Luke x, 16). It is therefore not to be reputed as folly in us but that we may know that we ought to be Christians not for the sake of this life in which at times God abandons us even to the death to the hands of our enemies, but for the sake of eternal life. This is what we must learn from the example of Him, whose name is become our own.

Ep. CXL, ii, 3–iii, 6; v, 13–vi, 18; vii, 20; x, 26–xi, 28.

894

We are not Christians, except on account of a future life. Let no one hope for present blessings, let no one promise himself the happiness of the world, because he is a Christian. When this is present, let him give thanks for the consolation of God; when it is wanting, let him give thanks to the justice of God. Let him always be grateful, never ungrateful; let him be grateful to the Father when He consoles and caresses him, and let him be grateful to the Father when He chastens and scourges and disciplines him; for He always loves, whether he caress or threaten.

In Ps. XCI, 1.

895

And some, not knowing that they are Christians that they may hope for a life to come, as soon as they are alarmed by temporal ills, imagine that Christ has forsaken them, and that they are Christians to no purpose; for they do not know that the reason for their being Christians is that they may conquer the present, and hope for the future; . . . that what God has promised is not of this life or this earth; that all these trials must be endured, so that we may receive and secure what God has promised us in eternity.

In Ps. XC, *Serm.* I, 7.

896

As this visible earth nourishes and preserves the exterior man, so doth that invisible earth (i.e. God) the interior man.

In Ps. I, 4.

897

We who are Christians, are we not left to God? (cf. Ps. ix, 14). And if we are not left to Him, who does not leave us, what other hope have we?

Serm. XIV, i, 1.

898

He who on his pilgrimage groaneth not, shall not rejoice as a citizen, because there is no longing in him (for the heavenly Jerusalem).

In Ps. CXLVIII, 4.

899

For if we love Christ, surely we ought to long for His coming. For it is all wrong and I do not know whether it be possible, to fear the coming of Him whom thou lovest; to pray, 'Thy kingdom come,' and to fear lest thou be heard. . . . Who is coming to judge thee but He who came to be judged for thy sake?

In Ps. CXLVII, 1.

900

The coming of the Lord is not loved by him who declares that it is at hand or that it is far off, but rather by him who, whether it be far off or near, looks for it with sincere faith, firm hope, and ardent charity.

Ep. CXCIX, v, 15.

901

There keeps watch on this Easter night both the hostile world and the reconciled world. The latter watches, being freed, to praise the Physician, the latter, condemned, to blaspheme the Judge. The former watches ardent with pious thoughts, its light dawning; the latter gnashing its teeth, its light waning. . . . Of those, indeed, who have not been sealed in any way with the name of Christ, many on this night are not sleeping for pain, many in shame; some, too, who are nearing to belief in Christ, already are not sleeping for fear of the Lord. How then must the friend of Christ watch in rejoicing, when the enemy also is watching in lamentation? How is the Christian on fire to watch in the great glory of Christ, when the heathen blushes to sleep? How ought he, who has entered this great house, to watch on this its great feast, when one already is keeping watch who is minded to enter therein?

Serm. **CCXIX.**

902

Two seasons are signified for us, the one before the resurrection of the Lord, the other after the resurrection of the Lord; the one in which we are, the other in which we hope to be hereafter. The season of lamentation, which the forty days of Lent signify, we both signify and have; but the season of joy, and rest, and of the kingdom, which these Paschal days signify, let us signify it with Alleluias. . . . In the Church we throng to praise God after the Resurrection, since after our resurrection ours will be perpetual praise. The passion of the Lord signifies our season, in which we now are. The scourges, the chains, the insults, the spitting, the crown of thorns, the wine mixed with gall, the vinegar on the sponge, the rivallings, the taunts, lastly the cross itself, the sacred limbs hanging on the tree, what does all this signify to us but the time which we are spending, the season of lamentation, of mortality, of trial and temptation? Therefore a foul time; but let this foulness of the dung be on the field, not in the house. Let there be lamentation over sins, not over desires that have been deceived. A foul season, but if we use it rightly, a season that will be faithful to us. What is there more noisome than a manured field? The field was more beautiful before it had received the load of dung. The field was made noisome that it might attain to exuberant fertility. Therefore noisomeness is a sign of this season; but to us this noisomeness is a season of fertility.

Serm. CCLIV, iv, 5.

903

Wouldest thou rail at the seed when thou wast tilling the ground? Suppose some one were so unskilled in these matters that when the seed was brought to the field and put in the earth and buried in the furrow, if, I say, some one were so ignorant of matters to be looked for in the near future as to rail at the wheat, because he remembered the harvest, and thinking of it said to himself, What a labour it will be to harvest this grain, to gather it, thresh it, store it in the barn; we saw how beautiful it was and congratulated ourselves, but now it is withdrawn from our eyes, I see the ploughed field but I cannot perceive the grain either in the barn or here; and suppose he were to weep copiously, noting the soil and the land, but not visualizing the harvest; how he would be laughed at by unlearned people, who however were not ignorant of this particular matter, who though unskilled in other things, but skilled in that thing at which that disgracefully unskilled person railed! And what would they say to him if perchance he lamented that he knew nothing about these things? Do not be sad; this that we have buried is certainly not yet in the barn, it is not in our hands, we will come to this field later on and it will please thee to see the aspect of the cornfield, where now thou seest the bareness of the ploughed field. He who knew what was to come from the grain, would also rejoice in the tillage itself. But he who is incredulous, or rather unwise, and, more truly expressed, inexpert, would indeed at first perhaps lament, but believing the expert, would go away consoled, and with the expert would look for the harvest to come.

Serm. CCCLXI, ix, 9.

904

One who has not too carefully looked into the changes and renewings of things, merely sees leaves decay and new ones spring forth. But if he rightly considers the matter, he will see that those also which decay pass into the strength of the soil. For how would the earth be fattened otherwise than by the decaying of earthly things? Those who till the fields note these things; and those who are not tillers of the field, who always live in the town, may know from the gardens neighbouring the town how carefully the refuse, otherwise contemptible, of the city is preserved by those who even collect and deliver it at a price. Certainly this might be thought by the ignorant to be contemptible and absolutely void of any usefulness. For who stoops to look at dung? That which man loathes to look at, he makes it his care to preserve. Therefore that which seems to have been consumed and got rid of returns to the land to fatten it; the fattening matter passing into the moisture of the soil, the moisture into the root; and that which passes from the soil into the root is transferred by invisible channels to the tree, is distributed through the branches, and from the branches to the twigs, and from the twigs to the leaves and fruit. Lo, that which thou didst loathe in the putridity of the dung, thou now admirest in the fruitfulness and vigour of the tree.

Serm. CCCLXI, xi, 11.

905

As 'no man can serve two masters' (Matt. vi, 24), so no one can rejoice both in the world and in the Lord. These two joys differ much from one another, and are altogether contrary. When we rejoice in the world, we do not rejoice in God. Let joy in the Lord prevail, until our rejoicing in the world be ended. Let joy in the Lord be ever on the increase, joy in the world always on the decrease, till it come to an end. And this is not said as though when we are in the world we ought not to rejoice, but that even while we are in the world we may already rejoice in the Lord. . . . Because thou art in the world, art thou not in the Lord? . . . 'In Him we live and move and are' (Acts xvii, 28). For where is He not who is everywhere? . . . 'The Lord is nigh. Be nothing solicitous' (Phil. iv, 5 *seq.*). This is a great thing that He is ascended above all the heavens, yet is very nigh them who are on the earth. Who is this who is far off and yet very nigh save He Who of His mercy became very nigh to us?

Serm. (*de Script. N.T.*) CLXXI, i, 1.

906

What has befallen me is strange, yet true; I grieve because I do not see you, and my grief itself comforts me. . . . For do we not long for the heavenly Jerusalem? and the more impatiently we long for it, do we not the more patiently suffer all things for its sake?

Ep. XXVII, 1.

907

The wound of love is health-giving. In the Canticle of Canticles the Spouse of Christ sings, 'wounded with love am I' (Cant. v, 8). And this wound, when is it healed? When our desire is satisfied in good things. It is called wound as long as we desire and do not yet possess. For love is such that there is pain therein. When we have attained to what we desire, then the pain passes, but the love does not grow less.

Serm. CCXCVIII, ii, 2.

VI. NIGHT AND DAY

908

Any man who thinks that there is no happiness for man, save only in these temporal goods and delights, and in the affluence and abundance of this world, is a foolish and perverse man, who maketh his left hand his right. Such were they of whom the psalm (cxliii, 11, *sqq.*) speaketh; not because they had not received from God the things they possessed temporarily, but because they supposed this alone to be a happy life, and sought for nothing else. . . . Yet any just man might also enjoy the same prosperity, as did Job. But Job held it for his left hand, not for his right; for he had no right hand except his perpetual and eternal happiness with God. His left hand was therefore given up to be stricken, and his right sufficed for him. . . . He was consoled for his losses, for he had not suffered the loss of his inner riches; he had a heart full of God. 'The Lord,' he said, 'gave, and the Lord hath taken away. As it hath pleased the Lord, so is it done. Blessed be the name of the Lord' (Job i, 21). His right hand was there: the Lord himself, eternal life itself, that possession of light, the 'fountain of life' (Ps. xxxv, 10), the light of light. . . . But his left hand was as an aid of consolation, not the support of his happiness. For his true and genuine happiness was God. . . .

'His left hand is under my head, and his right hand shall embrace me' (Cant. ii, 6). But what doth it mean, that His right hand was above, and His left hand below, and that thus the Husband embraced the Spouse, supporting her with the consolation of His left hand, and laying upon her His right hand for protection? His left hand, she saith, is beneath my head. God giveth that left hand, therefore it is His; because God giveth all these temporal blessings. . . . For He Who calleth to the right hand, knoweth how to dispense the left. If therefore it be the left hand, let it so be; but let it be beneath thy head: let thy head be above it, that is, let thy faith, where Christ dwelleth, be above it. Do not set temporal things before thy faith, then the left hand will not be above thy head; but set all temporal things beneath thy faith, then the left hand will be beneath thy head, and His right hand will rightly embrace thee.

In Ps. CXX, 8, 9.

909

Is it not happiness to have living and healthy sons, beautiful daughters, full barns, abundant herds, no tumbling down even of a fence, let alone a wall, no tumult and clamour in the streets, but quiet, peace, abundance, plenty of all things in the house and in the city? . . . Is not this happiness? Ought the just to shun it? But dost thou not find the house of the just also abounding with all these things, full of this happiness? . . . What do we say? Is not this happiness? If you will; still it is the left hand. What is the left hand? Temporal, mortal, bodily happiness. I do not desire thee to shun it, but I do not wish thee to think it is the right hand. . . . For what is in the right hand? . . . God, eternity, the years of

God which fail not. . . . There is the right hand, there should be our desire. Let us use the left hand for the time, let us long for the right hand for eternity. . . . Behold the holy canticles of the lover; behold the Canticle of Canticles, of the heavenly nuptials of Christ and His Church. What saith the Spouse of the Bridegroom? 'His left hand is under my head, and his right hand shall embrace me' (Cant. ii, 6)—the left under the head, and the right above the head. . . . For He will not desert me in times of need; but yet His left hand will be under my head; it will not be put above my head, but will be beneath my head, so that His right hand may embrace me, promising eternal life. For if His right hand is above my head, His left hand will be under my head. . . . I will both support you in your weakness with the left hand, and crown you when perfected with the right.

In Ps. CXLIII, 18.

910

If thou doest what thou doest for the sake of human affairs and of this life alone, thy left hand alone worketh; but if thou dost work for life eternal, thy right hand alone worketh. But if thou hast earnest hope for eternal life, yet still the lusts of this temporal life creep upon thee, so that thou heedest this even when thou doest a good work, hoping thou mayest have some reward here, thy left hand mingleth with the works of thy right hand, and this God forbiddeth (Matt. vi, 3).

In Ps. CXX, 10.

911

Our right hand is life everlasting; our left, life in this world. Whatsoever thou doest for the sake of eternal life, thy right hand doeth. If in thy works thou mingle with the love of eternal life desire for the life of this world, or man's praise, or any worldly advantage, thy left hand knoweth what thy right hand doth (*v.* Matt. vi, 3). . . . Is it sin then to enjoy such happiness as this? No, but it is sin to make it the right hand, when it is the left. . . . Let all that earthly happiness be to you the left hand, and let your right hand be that which you will have for ever.

In Ps. CXXXVI, 15, 16.

912

As concerning the three kinds of life, contemplative, active, one made up of each, although a man may live a life of unimpaired faith and attain to the eternal reward in any of them, yet there is a difference between what is held for love of the truth and what is expended in the duty of charity. One may not be so given up to contemplation as to neglect the good of his neighbour, nor so taken up with the active life as to omit the contemplation of God. . . . Wherefore the love of truth requires a holy retiredness, and the necessity of charity a just employment. And if this burden be not imposed on us we ought not to seek it but betake ourselves wholly to the search and perception of truth. But if it is imposed on us, the law and need of charity binds us to undertake it. Yet for all this may we not abandon our striving after the truth, lest we lose the sweetness of the one and be surcharged with the weight of the other.

De civ. Dei XIX, xix.

913

God has indeed granted to some few men whom He has ordained to bear rule over churches, the capacity of not only awaiting calmly, but even desiring eagerly, that last journey, while at the same time they can meet without disquietude the toils of those other journeys. But I do not believe that either to those who are moved to seek such duties out of love of worldly honour, or to those who, while occupying a private station, covet a busy life, so great a boon is given as that, amid the bustle and agitation of their daily comings and goings, they should acquire that familiarity with death which we seek; for both of these classes had it in their power to seek sanctification in retirement. Or if this be not true, I am of all men I will not say the most foolish but certainly the most indolent, since I find it impossible without the aid of some relief from care and toil to taste and relish that only real good. Believe me, there is need of much withdrawal of oneself from the turmoil of the things which are passing away, in order that there may be formed in man the ability to say, I fear nothing; and this neither through insensibility nor through presumption, nor through vain glory, nor through superstitious credulity. By this means also is attained that enduring joy with which no ordinary delights can in any degree be compared.

Ep. X, 2.

914

In the will let him have joy in silence; if he must, let him speak to teach. When must thou needs speak and teach? When thou meetest with one ignorant, when thou meetest with one unlearned. If it delight thee to be always teaching, thou wishest at all times to have some ignorant one to teach. But if thou wishest well to others, and would have all to be learned, thou dost not want always to have those whom thou mayest teach, and therefore the exercise and approval of thy teaching will not be in the will, but in necessity. Lest thou be not 'established,' let thy joy be in hearing God, thy necessity in thine own speaking, thus shalt thou not be 'a man full of tongue' (Ps. cxxxix, 12). Why art thou willing to speak, unwilling to hear? Thou art ever going without, thou refusest to return within. For He that teacheth thee is within; but when thou teachest, thou, as it were, goest forth to those who are without. For we hear the truth from within, and we speak it to those who are without, outside our heart. We are said indeed to have in our heart those of whom we are thinking, but this is said only because we seem to have a kind of image of them stamped upon us. For, were they altogether within, surely they would know what is in our heart, and so would have no need for us to speak to them. But if it be thy delight to be busy without, take heed lest thou be puffed up without, and be unable to return by the narrow way, and thy God be unable to say to thee, 'Enter thou into the joy of thy lord' (Matt. xxv, 21), but say, because that which thou didst love was without, 'Bind his hands and feet, and cast him into the exterior darkness' (*id.* xxii, 13). For in shewing that it is an evil to be cast without, he sheweth that it is good to enter within. . . . Let us not then love most the exterior things, but the interior. Let us rejoice over the interior things; in what is exterior let us act of necessity, not of free-will.

In Ps. CXXXIX, 15.

915

'Turn, O my soul, into thy rest. . . . For He hath delivered my soul from death' (Ps. cxiv, 7 *sq.*). . . . Did it turn into its rest because it was delivered from death? Is not rest said rather to be in death? What is the action of the soul whose life is rest and death unrest? . . . Meek therefore and humble, following, as it were, Christ as its way, should be the action of the soul that tendeth towards rest; and yet not slothful and supine, in order that it may finish its course, as it is written: 'Do thy works in meekness' (Ecclus. iii, 19). For lest meekness might lead to inactivity, there is added, 'Do thy works.' For it is not as in this life, where the rest of sleep doth repair us for action, but a good habit of the soul leadeth to an ever watchful rest.

In Ps. CXIV, 6.

916

There are two perfections proposed to the human mind, the one active, the other contemplative; the former being that whereby the way is taken, the latter that by which the goal is reached; the one by which men labour that the heart may be purified to see God, the other that by which they are emptied and God is seen. The former is occupied with the precepts for the right governing of the temporal life, whereas the latter is concerned with the doctrine of that life which is eternal. In this way, also, the one operates, the other rests; for the former finds its sphere in the purging of sins, the latter moves in the light of the purged. Thus, again, in this mortal life the one is engaged in the work of a good conversation, while the other is seen only in the person of the very few, and through a glass in a dark manner, in part only, as in a kind of vision of the immutable truth (*v.* 1 Cor. xiii, 12).

De cons. Evang. I, v, 8.

917

'I will see you again and your heart shall rejoice. And your joy no man shall take from you' (John xvi, 22). Mary sitting at the Lord's feet and rapt in His words prefigured a similitude of this joy; namely, at rest from all busying, and intent on the truth, in whatever measure this life is capable of receiving it; by which nevertheless to prefigure that which shall be for eternity. For while Martha, her sister, was busied with many necessary duties, which though good and useful, yet when the time for rest comes, will pass away, she herself was resting in the word of the Lord. And therefore, on Martha's complaining that her sister was not helping her, the Lord replied, 'Mary hath chosen the best part, which shall not be taken from her' (Luke x, 39 *sqq.*). He did not say that Martha was playing a bad part, but that there was 'the best part which shall not be taken away.' For that part which is occupied with the ministering to a need shall be 'taken away' when the need itself is passed away. Indeed the reward of a good work which will pass away is rest which will not pass away. In that contemplation, therefore, God will be all in all, because nothing other than Himself will be required, but it will be sufficient to be enlightened by and to enjoy Him alone.

De Trin. I, x, 20.

918

By grace he already observes a perpetual sabbath, who works whatever good he does in the hope of future rest, and does not glory in his own good works, as if he had anything good which he had not received; for receiving and understanding the sacrament of baptism as the day of the sabbath, that is, the day of the Lord's sojourn in the sepulchre, he rests from his former labours; so that now walking in newness of life (Rom. vi, 4), he recognizes God working in him, who both works and rests, both controlling and directing His creation; and in Himself having eternal repose.

De Gen. ad. litt. IV, xiii, 221.

919

Our sabbath is in the hearts. Many indeed are idle with their members and are disturbed in conscience. If a man is wholly bad, he cannot have a sabbath, for his conscience is never at rest and he must needs live in disquietude; but he whose conscience is good is tranquil; and this tranquillity is the sabbath of the heart. For it listeneth to God who promises great things, and if it toils in the present, it expands in the hope of the future, and every cloud of sadness is made bright; as the Apostle saith, 'Rejoicing in hope' (Rom. xii, 12). And that very joy in the tranquillity of our hope is our sabbath.

In Ps. XCI, 2.

920

Peace should be the object of our desire, war looked upon but as a necessity to the end that by it God may deliver men from the necessity of war and preserve them in peace. For peace is not sought in order to rouse men to war, but war is waged that peace may be obtained. Therefore, even in waging war, be a peacemaker, so that by conquering those whom you attack, you may lead them back to the advantages of peace.

(To Boniface when on military service.)

Ep. CLXXXIX, 6.

921

In that house of the Lord (Ps. cxxi), He who built the house is praised. He is the delight of all who dwell in the house; He is their only hope here, and reality there. . . . He standeth, who enjoyeth God; but he who wishes to enjoy himself, falleth. . . . Consider what thou wilt be there; and although thou art as yet on the road, set this before thy eyes, as if thou wert already standing, as if thou wert already continually rejoicing among the Angels; as if that which is written were realized in thee: 'Blessed are they that dwell in Thy house: they shall praise Thee for ever and ever' (Ps. lxxxiii, 5).

In Ps. CXXI, 3

922

What is that good by which we are inflamed, for which we sigh, by which we are kindled, for the attainment of which we endure so many toils, as you have heard when the Apostle was read, that 'all that will live godly in Christ Jesus shall suffer persecution'? (2 Tim. iii, 12) . . . We fight outwardly against the unbelieving and disobedient, we fight inwardly with carnal suggestions and disturbances. As yet we fight everywhere, because 'the corruptible body is a load upon the soul' (Wis. ix, 15). . . . Our good, for which we sigh, will be peace. Behold, brethren, peace is called a good, a great good. You were seeking what was called a good; was it gold, or silver, or an estate, or raiment? It is peace; not such a peace as the treacherous, unstable, mutable, uncertain peace which prevails among men, nor such as the individual hath with himself. For we have said that a man contendeth also with himself, and he continues to fight until he subdues his lusts. What sort of peace then is this? One that 'eye hath not seen, nor ear heard' (1 Cor. ii, 9).

In Ps. CXXVII, 16

923

Peace there will be there, perfect peace will be there. Where thou wishest thou shalt be, but from God thou wilt not depart. Where thou wishest thou shalt be, but wherever thou goest thou shalt have thy God. With Him, from whom thou art blessed, shalt thou ever be.

Serm. CCXLII, viii, 11.

924

For that is the one true and only happy life, in which, immortal and incorruptible in body and spirit, we may contemplate the joy of the Lord for ever. All other things are desired and are without impropriety prayed for, with a view to this one thing. For whosoever has it shall have all that he wishes, nor can he possibly wish for anything with it which would be unbecoming. For in it is the fountain of life, which we must now thirst after in prayer so long as we live in hope, not yet seeing that which we hope for, trusting under the covert of His wings, before whom are all our desires, that we may be inebriated with the plenty of His house and drink of the torrent of His pleasure; for with Him is the fountain of life, and in His light we shall see light (Ps. xxxv, 8 *sqq.*), when our desire shall be satisfied with good things, and when there shall be nothing beyond to be sought with groaning, but all things shall be possessed by us with rejoicing. At the same time, because this blessing is nothing else but the 'peace which surpasseth all understanding' (Phil. iv, 7), even when we are asking for it in our prayers, we know not what to pray for as we ought. For inasmuch as we cannot present it to our minds as it really is, we do not know it, but whatever image of it may be presented to our minds we reject, disown, and condemn. We know it is not that which we are seeking, although we do not yet know enough to be able to define what we seek.

There is therefore in us a certain learned ignorance, so to speak, an ignorance which we learn from that Spirit of God who helps our infirmities. . . . For assuredly if it were utterly unknown it would not be desired; and on the other hand, if it were seen it would not have to be desired and sought for with groanings.

Ep. CXXX, xiv, 27–xv, 28.

925

O the happy Alleluias there! . . . There praise to God and here praise to God, but here by those full of anxious care, there by those free from care; here by those whose lot is to die, there by those who are to live for ever; here in hope, there in hope realized; here in the way, there in our fatherland. Now therefore, my brethren, let us sing, not for our delight as we rest, but to cheer us in our labour. As wayfarers are wont to sing, sing, but keep on marching. . . . If thou art progressing, thou art marching; but progress in good, progress in the true faith, progress in right living; sing, and march on.

Serm. CCLVI, 3.

926

Alleluia is praise of God. To us as we labour it signifies the activity of our rest. For when after those labours we come to that rest, the praise of God will be our sole occupation, our activity there is Alleluia. . . . Some sweet odour of the divine praise and of that rest reaches us, but for the greater part mortality weighs upon us. We tire of telling it, and want to refresh our limbs, and if we say Alleluia for long, the praise of

God becomes a burden to us, because of the massy weight of our flesh. For after this world and our labours here there will be a fulness without ceasing in Alleluia. . . . Let us tell it as much as we can, that we may deserve to tell it for ever. There our food will be Alleluia, our drink will be Alleluia, the activity of our rest will be Alleluia, our whole joy will be Alleluia, that is, the praise of God. For who praises anything without revolting against it, save he who enjoys it without any feeling of distaste? What a strength there will be in the mind, what immortality and endurance in the body, that neither the purpose of the mind may weaken in the contemplation of God, nor the members succumb under the perpetuity of the praise of God.

Serm. CCLII, ix, 9.

927

This will be our supreme and truly pious rest, a rest in which pride has no place, that as He rested from all his works (Gen. ii, 2), because His works were not the reason of His happiness, for He himself is the good, by which He is happy, so we too may hope to rest from all labours, and not only our own but His also, and nowhere but in Him. And this we may long for after our good works, which we acknowledge to be rather His in us than our own, that thus also He may rest after His labour, and when after our good works which we have done become justified by Him, He may give to us rest in Himself. For it is a great thing for us that we owe our being to Him; it will be a still greater thing to have found rest in Him. Just as He is not made happy for the reason that he has wrought these things, but because having no need of the kings of His creation, He rested in Himself rather than in them.

De Gen. ad. litt. IV, xvii, 28.

928

For this contemplation is promised to us as the end of all actions and the eternal consummation of all joys. . . . For that which He said to his servant Moses: ' I AM WHO AM. . . . Thus shall thou say to the children of Israel: HE WHO IS, hath sent me to you' (Exod. iii, 14). This it is which we shall contemplate when we shall be alive for evermore. . . . For contemplation is the reward of faith, for which reward our hearts are cleansed by faith.

De Trin. I, viii, 17.

929

Our whole business therefore in this life is to restore to health the eye of the heart whereby God may be seen. To this end are celebrated the Holy Mysteries; to this end the word of God is preached; to this end are the moral exhortations of the Church made, those, that is to say, which relate to the correction of morals, to the amendment of carnal concupiscences, to the renunciation of this world, not in word only but in a change of life. To this end is directed the whole aim of the Divine and Holy Scriptures, that that interior eye may be purged of anything which hinders us from the sight of God. . . . God assuredly made the sun which we desire to see with sound eyes. Much brighter certainly is He who made it, nor is the light with which the mind of the eye is concerned of this kind at all. That light is eternal Wisdom. But God made thee, O man, after His own image. Would He give thee wherewithal to see the sun which He made, and not give thee wherewithal to see Him who made thee, when He made thee after His own image? He hath given thee this also; both hath He given to thee. But thou dost love much this outward eye, and dost neglect much that interior eye; it thou dost carry about bruised and wounded. It would be a punishment to thee if thy Creator should wish to manifest Himself to thee; it would be a punishment to that eye of thine, before that it is cured and made whole. For so Adam sinned in Paradise and hid himself from the face of God. As long as he had the sound heart of a pure conscience, he rejoiced in the presence of God. After that eye had been wounded by sin, he began to dread the divine light; he fled back into the darkness and the thick covert of the trees, fleeing the truth, seeking eagerly the shade.

Serm. (de Script. N.T.) LXXXVIII, v, 5; vi, 6.

930

It is wholly credible that then we shall see the worldly bodies of the new heaven and the new earth, as we see God present everywhere and also governing all corporal things, by the bodies we shall carry, and which we shall see wheresoever we shall turn our eyes, and this with the most translucent clarity and not as now 'the invisible things of God' are seen and understood by the things that are made (Rom. i, 20) 'in part' only and as 'through a glass in a dark manner' (1 Cor. xiii, 12), where faith prevails more in us, by which we believe, than the appearance of corporal things which we perceive by corporal eyes. But even as, so soon as we behold men amongst whom we live, being alive and performing vital motions, we do not believe that they live, but see them to live, when we cannot see their life without their bodies, which notwithstanding we clearly behold by their bodies, all ambiguity being removed; so wheresoever we shall turn these spiritual eyes of our bodies we shall see incorporate God governing all things by our bodies. God therefore shall either so be seen by those eyes like unto the understanding whereby incorporal nature is seen, . . . or . . . God shall be so known and conspicuous to us, that He may be seen by the spirit of every one of us in every one of us, of another in another, and may be seen in Himself.

De civ. Dei XXII, xxix, 6.

931

'This is my rest for ever and ever' (Ps. cxxxi, 14). These are the words of God. 'My rest': I rest there. How greatly doth God love us, brethren, since, because we rest, He saith that He also resteth! For He is not at times disturbed, nor doth He rest as we do; but He saith that He resteth there, because we shall have rest in Him. 'Here will I dwell, for I have chosen it' (*ibid.*).

In Ps. CXXXI, 22.

932

I believe because of the Trinity three commandments relate to the love of God. For the unity of the Godhead has its beginning from the Father, and therefore the first commandment speaks chiefly of the one God. We are admonished by the second commandment not to consider the Son of God to be a creature by taking Him to be not equal to God. 'For every creature,' as the Apostle says, 'was made subject to vanity' (Rom. viii, 20); but there we are commanded not to take the name of the Lord our God in vain. But now the gift of God, which is the Holy Ghost, promises eternal rest, and of this the sabbath is figurative.

Serm. XXXIII, iii, 3.

VII. OLD AND A CHILD

933

New we indeed ought to be, because the old man ought not to creep upon us, but we must also grow and progress. Of this same progress the Apostle saith, 'Though our outward man is corrupted, yet the inward man is renewed day by day' (2 Cor. iv, 16). Let us not grow so as to become old after being new, but let the newness itself grow.

In Ps. CXXXI, 1.

934

Let your old age be childlike, and your childhood like old age; that is, so that neither may your wisdom be with pride, nor your humility without wisdom.

In Ps. CXII, 2.

935

Great are these two gifts, wisdom and continence: wisdom, forsooth, whereby we are form. in the knowledge of God; continence whereby we are not conformed to this world.

De bono vid. XV II, 21.